A

Peter Hernon
and Terry Ganey

Under the Influence

*The Unauthorized Story of
the Anheuser-Busch Dynasty*

SIMON & SCHUSTER

New York   London   Toronto   Sydney   Tokyo   Singapore

Simon & Schuster
Simon & Schuster Building
Rockefeller Center
1230 Avenue of the Americas
New York, New York 10020

Designed by Hedgerow Design
Manufactured in the United States of America

3   5   7   9   10   8   6   4   2

Library of Congress Cataloging-in-Publication Data
Hernon, Peter, date
Under the influence: the unauthorized story of the Anheuser-Busch dynasty/
Peter Hernon and Terry Ganey.
p.   cm.
Includes bibliographical references and index.
1. Anheuser-Busch, Inc.—History.   2. Brewing industry—United States—
History.   3. Busch family.   I. Ganey, Terry.   II. Title.
HD9397.U54A84   1991
338.7'6632'0973—dc20   91-13974
CIP
ISBN 0-671-69024-8

PICTURE CREDITS: All photographs copyrighted and reprinted with permission
from the Pulitzer Publishing Company except as noted below:

(1) Missouri Historical Society; (2) courtesy of Carola Wagner Wallenstein; (3, 5, 6)
Missouri Historical Society; (8) Terry Ganey; (9) courtesy of Johannes Westerkamp;
(10) Peter Hernon; (11) Missouri Historical Society; (13) City Archives, Bernried, Germany; (15) Missouri Historical Society; (16) AP/Wide World Photos; (18) UPI/Bett-
mann; (24) Terry Ganey; (35) UPI/Bettmann; (40) Doris Leeker; (41) St. Louis County
Police Department; (45, 47, 50) St. Louis Mercantile Library Association; (52) Andrew
Brandt; (53) Dennis Morrell

Dedicated to Our Parents:
Peter and Bertie Lee Hernon
Thomas and Thelma Ganey

Contents

Contents   7

The House of Busch

(abridged)

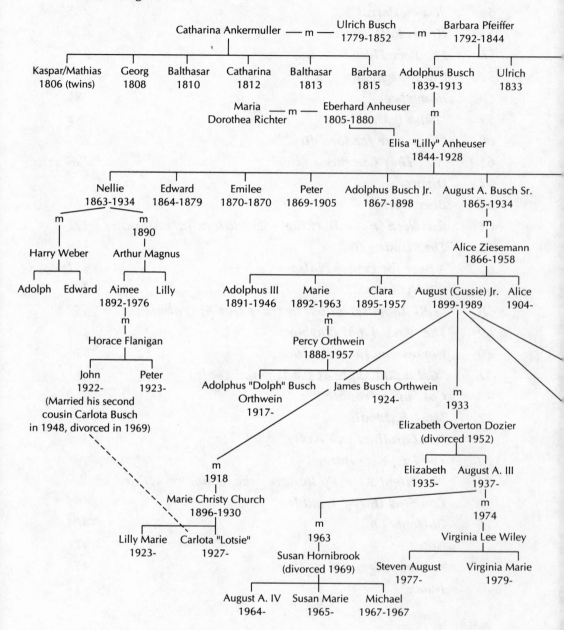

Catharina Ankermuller — m — Ulrich Busch 1779-1852 — m — Barbara Pfeiffer 1792-1844

Kaspar/Mathias 1806 (twins) · Georg 1808 · Balthasar 1810 · Catharina 1812 · Balthasar 1813 · Barbara 1815 · Adolphus Busch 1839-1913 · Ulrich 1833

Maria Dorothea Richter — m — Eberhard Anheuser 1805-1880

Elisa "Lilly" Anheuser 1844-1928

Nellie 1863-1934 · Edward 1864-1879 · Emilee 1870-1870 · Peter 1869-1905 · Adolphus Busch Jr. 1867-1898 · August A. Busch Sr. 1865-1934

m Harry Weber
m 1890 Arthur Magnus

Alice Ziesemann 1866-1958

Adolph · Edward · Aimee 1892-1976 · Lilly · Adolphus III 1891-1946 · Marie 1892-1963 · Clara 1895-1957 · August (Gussie) Jr. 1899-1989 · Alice 1904-

m Horace Flanigan

Percy Orthwein 1888-1957

John 1922- · Peter 1923-
(Married his second cousin Carlota Busch in 1948, divorced in 1969)

Adolphus "Dolph" Busch Orthwein 1917- · James Busch Orthwein 1924-

m 1933

Elizabeth Overton Dozier (divorced 1952)

Elizabeth 1935- · August A. III 1937-

m 1918

Marie Christy Church 1896-1930

m 1974

Virginia Lee Wiley

m 1963

Susan Hornibrook (divorced 1969)

Lilly Marie 1923- · Carlota "Lotsie" 1927-

Steven August 1977- · Virginia Marie 1979-

August A. IV 1964- · Susan Marie 1965- · Michael 1967-1967

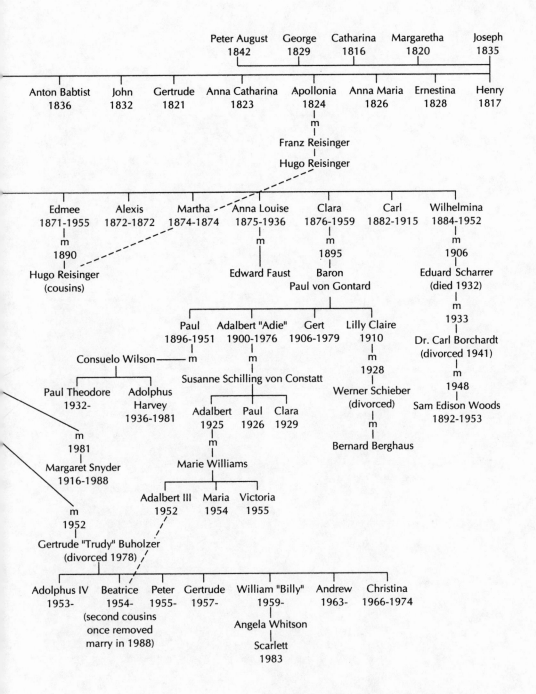

Sources: Family Tree researched by Johannes Westerkamp.
Family Tree prepared by Wilhelmina Busch Scharrer,
Stadt Archives, Bernried, Germany.
History of the Busch Family prepared by August
A. Busch, Jr., Missouri Historical Society, Jefferson
Memorial, St. Louis, Mo.
"Gussie" by Lotsie Busch Giersch
Copyright 1985 William Cooksey, Peterson Publishing Co.

Introduction

This is a true story of an American dynasty—the Busch family of Anheuser-Busch, the world's largest brewery. It is a book the Busches did not want published.

In the summer of 1989, an edict went out from their corporate headquarters at Number One Busch Place in St. Louis: Do not cooperate with authors Peter Hernon and Terry Ganey. A memorandum directed department heads, employees and 950 wholesalers across the country to notify the right people immediately if approached by either writer. Friends and relatives were asked to keep their lips sealed.

The decision to try to lower the curtain on this most colorful of families and most influential of companies was made by August A. Busch III, the fifth in a line of beer barons with the same last name. The authors met with him twice. The meetings followed a grilling by one of August's publicists, who wanted to know, among other things, our religion, whether we drank beer, and what we thought about August's major bogeyman, what he liked to call the neoprohibition movement.

During one of the sessions—each lasted less than an hour—August said his people had checked all of the family biographies recently released by the publisher of this book, Simon & Schuster. One book in particular had got his dander up for revealing an incestuous relationship within a family that once controlled a large corporation. Leaning forward in his chair, his face as red as a Budweiser label, August expressed his displeasure with a four-letter word that didn't spell beer.

We asked to interview members of his family and company. We also requested access to the corporate archives. August ultimately refused even the most limited cooperation. It was a typical response. The Busches have long tried to keep a high wall erected around their personal lives and business dealings.

Despite the obstacles, we did succeed in interviewing members of the family and their friends. Present and former employees of Anheuser-Busch—everyone from secretaries to vice presidents—also provided information for this book. Because of the fear of retribution, some agreed to talk to us only on condition that their names would not be used. More than 200 individuals were interviewed; thousands of pages of public and private documents were reviewed in the United States and in Germany, the family's ancestral home.

For nearly 130 years, the Busches have worked ceaselessly to weave beer drinking into the fabric of American life. They have made their product, it has been said, part of Americana. Few dynasties can compare with theirs for wealth and the drive to succeed. Fewer still can match the dizzying sweep of their scandals. The Busches have enough skeletons in their closets to fill a cemetery. Only the Kennedys, perhaps, can rival them for tragedy. But not even the Kennedys can compete with their influence.

The Busches have endured and prospered thanks to the emergence, in moments of crisis, of remarkable personalities, four men who have dominated one of the toughest, most ruthless businesses in the world, a business increasingly under attack for its excesses. This is the first independent, unauthorized account of the Kings of Beer.

"It is my aim to win the American people over to our side, to make them all lovers of beer. . . . It may cost us a million dollars and even more, but what of it if thereby we elevate our position? I stand ready to sacrifice my annual profits for years to come if I can gain my point and make people look upon beer in the right light."

Adolphus Busch
Paris, October 19, 1905

1

A Funeral

The bodies of Viking kings were cast adrift in fire boats. When a pharaoh expired, a sprinkling of faithful retainers and a wife or two were often sealed in the crypt to keep him company. The funeral for beer king Gussie Busch also had its fantastic moments. A gleaming red beer wagon with a uniformed driver and dalmatian perched on the seat escorted the cortege to the main gate of his baronial estate. The rig was drawn by a hitch of plodding Clydesdales, Gussie's symbol of empire. At the gravesite, other horses waited. A favorite jumper named Stocking Stuffer was there, nervously tugging at its reins when a guard of honor who looked old enough to have ridden with Custer cracked out a rifle salute. Four hackney ponies were there as well. The tiny beasts pulled a magnificent Harriman coach in a slow circle around Gussie's grave as a groomsman in scarlet coat and gray top hat blew a farewell from a long silver trumpet.

The burial of August A. "Gussie" Busch, Jr., was easily one of the most colorful partings ever beheld in this country. The perfect finale, the lingering foam in the glass. It called to mind his long and outrageous life as head of Anheuser-Busch, the world's largest brewery. Dead at age ninety, he had been the patriarch of a dynasty that rivaled any for influence, wealth and a pastureful of black sheep.

Gussie was buried on an overcast fall morning in October 1989. A line of twenty stretch limousines drove the mourners the half mile up the road from his castle at Grant's Farm to Sunset Memorial Park. But unlike his ancestors, who were buried with all the pageantry of a state funeral, Gussie was virtually put away in secret. Thirty thousand people had viewed the body and thousands more had attended the 1913 funeral of Adolphus, his grandfather and the founder of the clan. Called the Prince by a president, Adolphus looked like a baldish Buffalo Bill and lived like the other robber barons of his era. Twenty-five trucks were needed to carry flowers to his tomb. The kaiser sent his condolences. When Gussie's father, August A. Busch, committed suicide in 1934, again thousands showed up and the city mourned.

By contrast, only a scattering of spectators, no more than a couple hundred, lined the roadside and gathered behind police lines at Gussie's grave. Of course, that was just what his oldest son wanted. August A. Busch III, the reigning successor, doesn't like the media or publicity he can't control. He flies a helicopter to work and avoids the public whenever possible. He made sure there was no advance announcement of his father's burial.

The aloof, cold-filtered leader of the company had reason to be skittish. His business was drawing sharp fire from public health groups and many others for its high-powered advertising. Some even had the effrontery to suggest that his product —sixteen brands of beer—was a more dangerous drug than cocaine. Such talk was enough to drive August to red-faced, neck-burning anger. So did any suggestion that he was trying to hook teenagers on beer through ads that emphasized sex, youth and sports and came on like a runaway locomotive.

Then, too, there were all those half brothers of his who had wound up in vatsful of embarrassing trouble. Peter had shot and killed a friend. Billy's steamy custody fight for his illegitimate daughter had played both the Missouri Supreme Court and *Geraldo.* Even his own son—August IV—had twice found himself in nasty jams, the worst of them a fatal accident that bears some resemblance to Chappaquiddick. No, it was better to bury Gussie quietly and get out of the limelight.

There had been bad blood between August and his father. August had led the palace coup that forced Gussie from the throne of Anheuser-Busch—stabbed him in the back, one family member reportedly said. But that had been years earlier. Father and son had made their peace, and now August was one of the pallbearers who carried the heavy bronze casket from the hearse while friends, relatives and curious horses watched.

Keeping the names straight was often difficult. All those Augusts were particularly hard to sort out. St. Louisans frequently got them confused. Down at the brewery the workers had a way of keeping track. They had called Gussie, who was August Jr., "Doggie Daddy." His son, August III, was "Augie Doggie," and August IV, "Doggie Junior."

Their highly publicized family troubles were a bitter brew of fairly recent vintage. Less well known were the well-aged adventures of other relatives. In World War I Gussie's grandmother was suspected of being a German sympathizer. During World War II, authorities suspected some family members had ties to the Nazis. Hitler and a man who later became a ranking member of the SS paid one of them a visit.

Memorable fights and knockdown divorces had occurred over the decades. Some Busches shot themselves and one disappeared and was presumed murdered. Others like Christina, Gussie's eight-year-old daughter, were killed in car wrecks, or seriously injured. One was kidnapped at gunpoint and another carried off by a similarly armed Prussian lover who wanted to elope.

Their family tree spread over 150 riotous years, its many branches watered by the fabulous wealth amassed by Prince Adolphus, who brought bottled beer to the masses. Adolphus was buried across town from Gussie's grave in a cemetery that was Valhalla for an earlier generation's rich men. And Adolphus was among the richest of all of them. His Gothic tomb, a marvel of stained glass and gargoyles, had everything but a perpetual beer dispenser. Carved over its portals was the triumphant proclamation of another Caesar—"Veni, Vidi, Vici." His grandson's grave had none of that pretension. In a glade shaded by pine trees, it was marked by a single block of red Missouri granite bearing the word "Busch."

The tombstones of close relatives fanned out around him in a semicircle. To his right lay daughter Christina, "Our Honeybee." To his left was the grave of Margaret, his fourth wife, whom he married in extreme old age after a stormy divorce from Trudy, his beautiful third wife. He had married Trudy after an equally stormy divorce from his second wife. The first Mrs. Busch, who died of pneumonia in 1930, was also buried with the others. Even before her death, he was seeing another man's wife. He liked the ladies, Gussie did.

The burial ground had been selected by his father, August A. In failing health, he had taken his life after guiding his company through the dry decade of Prohibition. He had chosen the site because, standing there, he could look across a valley to the castle he had built at Grant's Farm shortly after the turn of the century.

An older son, Adolphus III, Gussie's brother, lay to his immediate right. Even though "Mr. Adolph" ran the company for twelve years, he was called the forgotten man—and with good reason. Gussie, his more flamboyant, more dominating younger brother, had already buried him at the brewery long before he died in 1946.

As Gussie's coffin was lowered into the ground, family members and close friends pressed near. His lawyer Louis Susman was there, the "rainmaker" who had helped him run the St. Louis Cardinals, his favorite toy. So was Frank Jackson, the black chauffeur who had faithfully listened to a generation of Gussie's raw jokes and proved that the boss really did like black folks. So was the Reverend Paul C. Reinert, the chancellor of St. Louis University and an old friend.

A few days later, at a public memorial service, Reinert sent Gussie on his way with words that could serve as an epitaph for both his ancestors and heirs, a verse from the Gospel of Matthew: "I was thirsty and you gave me drink."

2

Mud Clerk

Three men and a boy sat motionless in a horse-drawn wagon on the edge of the forest, peering intently through the thick-timbered pines at a large roebuck feeding in a glade. One of them, an old man, slowly raised his rifle with trembling hands and squinted through its telescopic sight. The forester of his 1,400 acre estate stilled the horses. Like the huntsman sitting next to him, he waited expectantly.

As the old man drew a bead on the animal, the boy seated

next to him fidgeted nervously. He was twelve years old and
fair skinned with blond hair and blue eyes.

"Gussie, be still!"

The old man spoke in German. The boy was his grandson.

The gun roared, its sound echoing among the rounded tops
of the Taunus Mountains overlooking the Rhine River. The
roebuck fell where it stood but was not cleanly killed. In its
death agony, the deer thrashed in the underbrush. The boy
took his grandfather's rifle and raced eagerly into the woods to
finish off the wounded animal with a shot to the head.

He returned as the men were passing around a flask of whiskey and smoking cigars. His grandfather offered him the silver
flask and handed him a cigar. "Don't tell your father, Gussie,"
cautioned Adolphus Busch.

Six decades later Gussie still fondly reminisced about the
1911 hunting trip with "Papa Busch." There was no one quite
like Adolphus. There has been no one like him since, although
Gussie himself came the closest. The hops, barley and malt
that flowed through his veins were supplied by his paternal
grandfather, a swaggering colossus of the Gilded Age. A friend
to American presidents and the German kaiser, Adolphus
Busch was P.T. Barnum, Buffalo Bill and Cornelius Vanderbilt
rolled into one. In a period of unbridled capitalism, he suggested fixing prices with his competitors and watched his beer
profits multiply like a fast-growing yeast. His fortune was rein-
vested in hotels, real estate, ice-making and bottling plants,
banks, utility companies, railroads and diesel engine works.
He earned an estimated $2 million a year before there was an
income tax.

With his empire floating on beer, Adolphus shuttled back and
forth among his four estates from the Pacific shore to the banks
of the Rhine. Often on the move, he cabled a steady stream of
orders to his city-sized brewery in St. Louis, the largest in the
world. He rode in a personal railroad car humbly named the
Adolphus with a retinue of family members, servants, cooks, a
physician, an engineer and financial advisers. His extravagance turned heads even in an era used to the lavish spending
of its robber baron millionaires. A president called him a
prince. His workers called him a king. He liked that.

Adolphus dripped with money. His pockets always bulged
with gold coins, which he dispensed easily to those who did
him favors. In closing business deals, he never batted an eye
no matter how large the check. He bought expensive automo-

biles like so many toys, and casually asked his children, almost as an afterthought, "Oh, would you like one, too?" He knew fine wines and beautiful architecture, drinking plenty of the former and building a good deal of the latter. The famous called him friend: Teddy Roosevelt, Enrico Caruso, Diamond Jim Brady, King Edward VII, William Taft and Sarah Bernhardt. So did the infamous: Kaiser Wilhelm. He was a vigorous, prolific man who enjoyed hunting and fathered thirteen children, one of them Gussie's father.

In the twilight of a romantic age and on the eve of the Great War, Gussie's boyhood included long summer days spent with Adolphus at Villa Lilly, the German estate he had named after his wife. Idolizing his grandfather, he witnessed his merchant prince lifestyle. It made a lasting impression. He learned what it meant to be the head of one of the richest families in America —and one of the most powerful.

"I was a big man when I was with him," Gussie said later. "And everything he touched turned to gold."

Villa Lilly is near Bad Schwalbach, a resort town fifteen miles from the Rhine River city of Kastel. There, in the heart of Germany's wine country, the Busch saga began. On a summer afternoon, Ulrich Busch walked into the office of the mayor of Kastel and proudly announced that at four o'clock on the previous day—July 10, 1839—his forty-one-year-old wife, Barbara, had given birth to a son. They had named him Adolphus. Two days after the birth, the baby was baptized in St. George's Roman Catholic church, just down the street from the rambling, three-story Busch mansion known as the Schützenhof.

Ulrich Busch was an elder lord of the German town, once a Roman bridgehead. Kastel, with its slopes of terraced vineyards, squatted on the bank of the Rhine almost in the shadows of the ancient spires of Mainz. From the upper windows of the Schützenhof, its historic skyline was clearly visible on the other side of the river: the iron tower, built in 1240 and standing like a sentinel before the medieval city; the massive St. Martin's Cathedral, whose thick, spear-shaped spires seemed to touch the floor of heaven; and St. Christopher's, the church where Gutenberg was christened.

Just downriver, Lorelei sang her mysterious, seductive song to travelers, and the castles of Teutonic knights loomed over the boats plying Europe's most important waterway—the river that had helped make Ulrich Busch rich. He was a member of Germany's powerful merchant class, and from his wooded estates logs were floated down the Rhine for ship timbers. An innkeeper, he also had extensive real estate holdings. His vineyards, some of them cultivated for 2,000 years, were especially valuable. The right mixture of soil and sunlight had made the region's wine the most famous in the Rhineland.

Ulrich's prosperity was measured not only by his financial holdings, but also by the size of his family. Indeed, he had fathered two families. Born December 12, 1779, he was approaching sixty when Adolphus came along. Many years later the Busch family and publicists of the brewery that Adolphus founded claimed inaccurately that he was the youngest of twenty-one children. In fact, there had been twenty-two—thirteen boys and nine girls. Adolphus was the next to the last to be born. With his first wife, Catharina, Ulrich had fathered five boys and two girls. Catharina died April 16, 1815, fifty days after giving birth to their last child.

Ulrich married Barbara Pfeifer, eighteen years his junior, on May 3, 1816. Twenty-six days later they had their first child. Other children came almost annually. On March 12, 1844, when Adolphus was not yet five years old, his mother died, probably from exhaustion. She had given birth to eight boys and seven girls. Three months after her death, sixty-five-year-old Ulrich Busch married for a third time, to Marie T. Fischer.

His dormitory-sized Schützenhof dominated Frankfurterstrasse and enclosed a cobblestoned courtyard. Deer antlers decorated the stucco facade, tributes to the hunting tradition of Adolphus's ancestors. By the time he was born, some of his half brothers had married and started families of their own. In a practice that would recur with later generations, Busches sometimes married their relatives. For example, a daughter of one of Adolphus's half brothers married his brother Anton. After her death Anton married her sister.

The culture into which Adolphus was born valued discipline, thrift, cleanliness, hard work and loyalty. Germans like the Busches also knew how to enjoy life, especially food and drink. They lived by an old proverb, "Eating and drinking hold body and soul together." Adolphus later put the emphasis on drinking.

Adolphus was well prepared for the future role he would play so well in international commerce. His formal education was superb. When compared with descendants like Gussie, who didn't graduate from elementary school, it was formidable. Adolphus attended schools in Mainz and Darmstadt and a high school in Brussels, where he mastered French and studied English. After leaving school, he worked briefly in his father's lumber business, rafting spars down the Rhine and Main rivers. He also worked as an apprentice in a brewery owned by an uncle. Just before his thirteenth birthday, Adolphus lost his father. Ulrich Busch died in July 1852 at age seventy-two.

In 1856, when Adolphus turned seventeen, his real education began. He went to work as a shipping clerk in a mercantile house in Cologne. Important character traits began to manifest themselves—enthusiasm, energy and sociability combined with a good dose of shrewdness. He took pleasure in work and making money. These attributes, and the ability to make important friends quickly, would pay big dividends throughout his life.

After one year in Cologne, Adolphus stepped into the river of humanity that was pouring from Germany into the United States. Poor harvests in 1844 followed by an unsuccessful social revolution of 1848 in which German democratic reforms were crushed by Prussian militarism prompted the first large wave of emigration to America.

For Adolphus, the great news of the American adventure came from members of his own family. Three brothers—George, Ulrich and John—had already made the crossing and were living in St. Louis, Missouri, which was rapidly becoming a virtual German colony. It was only logical for their younger brother to follow. German tradition dictated that the oldest son received the lion's share of his father's property, and since Adolphus was the second youngest, there wasn't much to keep him at home. Proving tradition wrong years later, he wound up with most of his father's estate.

He was probably recruited by his older brother John Baptist Busch. John had come to the United States in 1849, and after living with brother George, a dealer in hops, he established a brewery. The first brewery to brew a "Busch" beer in the United States was the John B. Busch Brewing Company, established in 1854 in Washington, Missouri, a village fifty miles west of St. Louis on the Missouri River.

In 1857, at the age of eighteen, Adolphus emigrated to St. Louis by way of New Orleans. It wasn't a final and permanent break with the Old Country; quite the contrary. He and his brothers frequently returned to Germany. Their travels kept them abreast of technological and scientific developments in Europe. Beating his American rivals to breakthroughs in the brewing industry, Adolphus would make millions with the knowledge he gathered and skillfully put to use. When he returned to his hometown, as he did more than twenty times before he died, he was greeted like royalty. He was not, however, remembered fondly by his German relatives or by their descendants. They considered him a man who had taken from them—and given nothing in return.

Many years later Adolphus liked to give the impression that he had arrived in St. Louis a poor immigrant who had to pull himself up by his bootstraps. This perception was later repeated by newspaper reporters and enhanced by brewery biographers. It wasn't true. Blessed with a substantial allowance provided by his father's estate, Adolphus's early days in his new home were leisurely. In a candid moment in his later life, he admitted that his first weeks in St. Louis were spent "hunting, loafing, getting acquainted and having a good time."

Adolphus, like many of the German immigrants who poured into the city, was in his early twenties, unmarried and in excellent shape. He was short, approximately five feet five inches tall, with a fair, boyish complexion, long and wavy hair. He quickly grew a mustache and goatee to look older. His most distinctive physical attributes were a booming voice and a pair of hooded eyes that gave a serious, thoughtful expression to his face.

For someone with Adolphus's experience in river commerce, St. Louis was the capital of the Promised Land, a bustling port on the Mississippi River where a fortune could be made quickly. He worked as what was known as a mud clerk, meeting steamboats on the city's cobbled levees to assess their cargo, study their manifests and hunt for good buys. Already an experienced trader, young Adolphus quickly made a name for himself. "He could," wrote one historian, "pick up bargains with the best of them."

After working in the wholesale supply house of a man named William Heinrichshofen, Adolphus entered into a partnership with Ernst Wattenberg. Their firm, Wattenberg, Busch & Company, sold brewing supplies, products in great demand in St. Louis. The number of breweries in the city was growing rapidly, from twenty-four in 1854 to forty in 1858, all of them

fighting for a piece of the booming beer market. The number
of potential customers had jumped from 78,000 in 1850 to
185,000 ten years later. And both the immigrants and the lo-
cals were crying for lager beer.

The lagerbier the Germans had brought with them was a
cool, light, golden brew topped with a snowy foam. Its secret
lay in the special yeasts imported from Bavaria and southern
Germany that fermented and settled to the bottom of the vat
as the beer aged. Although the aging process meant it took
additional weeks to make lager beer, the product remained
fresh longer if kept untapped and cool. Lagerbier revolutionized American beer brewing.

St. Louis had two natural resources that contributed to its
flourishing beer business. First, there was good water from the
Mississippi and Missouri rivers. Water, 97 percent of the product, was the soul of beer. The second resource was under-
ground—miles of caverns where beer could be stored and aged
at temperatures that stayed below 50 degrees year round.

The first lager brewed in America may have been served in
St. Louis. John Wagner of Philadelphia was said to have been
the first to brew the bottom-fermenting beer in 1840. By 1845
it had spread to other parts of the country. But it was possible
that Adam Lemp, a German immigrant, was selling lager in
St. Louis as early as 1838. Lemp established a grocery that
year, and as a sidelight he began brewing and selling vinegar
and beer. Whatever the exact date, the success of his brew was
so overwhelming that brewing became his main business and
the grocery was abandoned. Even before Adolphus arrived in
St. Louis, Lemp had become a wealthy man. He was rich
enough to give his son, William, a brewery of his own as a
birthday present.

While lager beer had taken St. Louis by storm, there were,
of course, a few dissenters. Mark Twain found an Irishman who
said his fellow immigrants would not touch the stuff. "They
don't drink it, sir," the man told Twain. "They *can't* drink it,
sir. Give an Irishman lager for a month, and he's a dead man.
An Irishman is lined with copper, and the beer corrodes it. But
whiskey polishes the copper and is the saving of him, sir."

But the enormous profits, based on volume and cost, were in
beer—not whiskey. In the summer before the outbreak of the
Civil War, St. Louisans guzzled 212,000 barrels of beer that
generated $1.5 million for the brewers. A barrel that cost $1 to
produce was being sold for $8. A fortune could be made by the

brewer smart enough and tough enough to carve out a major share of the market.

Eberhard Anheuser intended to be one of the money-makers. A prosperous businessman, he had acquired a clunker of a beer plant called the Bavarian Brewery, and as he struggled to make a go of it he met the brash young brewing goods supplier named Adolphus Busch. Although he couldn't have known it at the time, his fortune was guaranteed.

3

A Beer Baron and a Beer Princess

Eberhard Anheuser was already rich. A soap maker, he had acquired his fortune in the real suds business. His beginnings were similar to Adolphus Busch's. Born September 24, 1805, he was the son of John Jacob Anheuser, a shop owner in Bad Kreuznach, in the Rhine country not far from Busch's hometown. He was well educated and carefully trained in business when he emigrated to America in 1843. He settled first in Cincinnati and had his wife and children join him there.

Two years later the family moved to St. Louis, where Anheuser acquired a partner named Nicholas Schaffer. The firm of Schaffer, Anheuser and Company was prosperous enough to allow its owners to take European trips lasting as long as six months. On September 26, 1848, Anheuser renounced allegiance to the king of Prussia and became an American citizen. In 1854, his wife, Dorothea, died, leaving him to care for a family of four girls and two boys.

When a small brewery went bankrupt in 1859, Anheuser was one of its major creditors. He bought out the others and took possession of the Bavarian Brewery in 1860 under the name E. Anheuser & Company. He shared an interest in the plant, which had been struggling since 1852, with William D'Oench, who dealt in chemicals and drugs.

Anheuser used to joke about the beer business with his friend, Tony Faust, who operated a saloon famous in the German community. Anheuser was a regular customer. A rumor was started by Anheuser that Tony intended to start a brewery himself. Anheuser meant it as a joke. When curious reporters began questioning Faust, he replied with a straight face, "It is true I am going to buy a brewery, perhaps more than one." Pressed for more details, Faust added: "Just tell your readers I am buying the breweries a glass at a time."

As Anheuser gained control of the Bavarian Brewery, other beer dynasties were being found in Milwaukee. When August Krug died in 1856, bookkeeper Joseph Schlitz took over his brewery and later married his widow. Frederick Miller, fresh from Germany, got started in 1855 when he bought a brewery that had been set up seven years earlier by Charles Best. Best was a brother of Phillip Best, who was already operating another brewery that would later be captained by Frederick Pabst.

While Anheuser worked hard to make a success of his struggling brewery, Adolphus Busch, whose company supplied its brewing goods, worked equally hard courting his daughter. Only sixteen years old, she was attractive, with deep blue-gray eyes shaded by long lashes. Her blond hair fell in soft curls over a smooth white forehead. She was known among her friends as "der Lockenkopf"—the curly head. Her name was Elisa but she was known as Lilly. She was born August 13, 1844, in Braunschweig, Germany, shortly after her father had left for the United States. When she was six months old, Lilly traveled to America with the rest of her family. Her mother died when she was ten.

Adolphus probably met Lilly through his business association with Anheuser. His brewery supply business was just around the corner from Anheuser's soap company. He also had another important connection with the Anheuser family—his brother Ulrich was courting Lilly's older sister, Anna.

Three days after the inauguration of Abraham Lincoln, as war clouds darkened the nation, Adolphus and Lilly, and Ulrich and Anna, were married in a double wedding ceremony. Eberhard Anheuser gave two of his daughters away to the Busch boys on March 7, 1861, in the Holy Ghost German Evangelical Lutheran church. Adolphus was twenty minutes late for the ceremony. He explained that on his way to the church he had stopped to close an important business deal. It was a portent for the future of their marriage.

The wedding celebration contrasted sharply with the troubled events of a country moving toward a civil war. A few weeks after his marriage, Busch and his father-in-law were bearing arms to keep Missouri out of the hands of Southern sympathizers. They were part of a Federal homeguard hastily assembled after the fall of Fort Sumter on April 12, 1861.

Numbering 5,000 volunteers and about 1,200 reservists, the ranks of the homeguard were filled by manufacturers, merchants, doctors, lawyers, bankers, contractors, laborers, brewers, teachers and clerks. They even had their own band. Eighty percent of the force was German. Among those in the untried ranks of men who agreed to serve a three-month enlistment was Corporal Adolphus Busch, Company E, 3rd Regiment, U.S. Reserve Corps, Missouri Volunteers. Anheuser was a private in Charlie Company of the same regiment.

In early May, approximately 900 Missouri militiamen, bent on secession, established a camp on a hill overlooking the Federal arsenal in St. Louis. On May 10, a force of 7,000 regulars, volunteers and homeguardsmen, including Busch and Anheuser's regiment, circled the secessionists' camp and ordered its surrender.

The secessionists gave up without firing a shot. But as the Union forces, led by a marching band, escorted the vanquished back to the arsenal, thousands of onlookers gathered, many of them Southern sympathizers. There were curses. Someone threw a rock, then a shot was fired. A riot broke out and after the smoke cleared, fifteen people lay dead and there were dozens more wounded, thirteen of whom later died. One of the survivors was Eberhard Anheuser's saloon-keeping drinking buddy, Tony Faust, who was shot in the leg when a soldier accidentally dropped his gun and it discharged.

By an odd coincidence, one of those in the crowd was William Tecumseh Sherman, who was in St. Louis considering a job offer to be president of a railroad. Sherman, his son and many others hit the ground or scattered when the shooting started. Ulysses S. Grant was also in St. Louis that day. Grant had been making a meager living on a farm near the city, and when troops marched out that morning to seize the camp, the future general and president of the United States wished them luck. Both Sherman and Grant would serve the Union cause, their armies chiefly responsible for the defeat and utter devastation of the Confederacy. Adolphus Busch would acquire Grant's St. Louis property, which he called Grant's Farm. A magnificent castle was later built on it.

By August of 1861, the enlistments of the volunteers and the reservists of the homeguard had expired. Some reenlisted for three-year tours in the regular Union Army and fought the war to its conclusion. Anheuser and Busch were not among them. Anheuser was fifty-five years old by then, and Busch had become a family man. He was interested in making his fortune, not war.

Even before Adolphus and Lilly Busch had their own children, they took in Gustava von Kliehr, the orphaned daughter of one of Lilly's sisters. And then, true to German tradition, they began building a large family. On April 12, 1863, Lilly gave birth to the couple's first child, a girl they named Nellie. By the end of the war, there were two sons, Edward born in 1864 and August A., born four days after Christmas in 1865.

After participating in a footnote to the Civil War, Anheuser returned to his soap business and his foundering brewery. Busch continued dealing in hops and working in the river trade. During the war, there were huge profits to be made by people daring to take risks, and Adolphus was one of the few men willing to give the precarious business of handling cotton and Southern products his close attention. He took charge of arriving shipments, disposed of them judiciously and made money.

In 1865 Busch cemented his relationship with the Anheuser family by acquiring D'Oench's interest in Anheuser's brewery. Perhaps the funds came from the profitable sale of Southern goods during the war or from his father's estate; or perhaps they came from the sale of his interest in Wattenberg, Busch & Company. Whatever the source of his funds, he had made the best deal in beer-brewing history. Thirty-four years later, in 1899, he wrote a letter to D'Oench, who had by that time returned to Germany. Busch's letter bordered on being an I-told-you-so message. He had bought a piece of a little brewery that was producing 4,000 barrels in 1865. By the turn of the century its capacity exceeded one million barrels. "I wish we might have the pleasure," he crowed, "of seeing you here in St. Louis again, so we could have the opportunity of showing you the greatest and largest brewery in America, in which you were once half owner. . . . Now do you recollect what I paid you for your half interest?"

4

The Birth of an Empire

The beer that came from the little red brick brewery on Pestalozzi Street was not very good. In fact, it was terrible. That
would have been a fatal handicap for any other brewery, but
Eberhard Anheuser had a secret weapon. He had Adolphus
Busch.

Anheuser could not have picked a better salesman for his
second-rate beer. It didn't matter that his son-in-law didn't
really know the business and wasn't a brewer. It didn't even
matter that he preferred to drink wine instead of beer. Adolphus was, beyond any doubt, "a super-salesman" who "sold
the bad almost as facilely as he sold the good. He could have
sold anything."

There were boundless business opportunities in the United
States immediately following the Civil War, but for a brewer
the situation amounted to picking gold up off the street. Immigrants were flooding the country, doubling the population
of cities like St. Louis, and providing cheap labor and a thirsty
market. And the industrial age supplied the machinery to
make beer in greater volume to quench that growing thirst.
The new railroads enabled brewers to reach distant markets.
And as soldiers like Custer "pacified" the Indian tribes, huge
territories filled with beer-loving communities sprang up in
the West. Perhaps most importantly, there were few government laws or regulations to interfere with profits.

Adolphus saw all of these developments as if in a vision.
When he joined Anheuser's brewery in 1865, he was a robust
twenty-six years old. His business character combined Germanic thrift and the instincts of a riverboat gambler. He found
"pleasure and agreeable recreation" in work, especially "when
I see that my efforts are crowned with success."

The first problem Adolphus dealt with when he entered the
business was Anheuser's bad beer. The best and most popular
brew in St. Louis was made by William Lemp, son of old

Adam. Anheuser's beer "was so inferior" that the drinkers enjoyed conducting an unofficial taste test: "St. Louis rowdies were known to project mouthfuls of it back over the bar." Adolphus wasn't fazed in the least. He had the talent to convince people to buy his beer anyway.

Anheuser and Busch used a number of promotional schemes to sell their beer, schemes that were so abused that they later helped usher in Prohibition: free beer to customers, payments to tavern owners to stock and sell their beer, and the dispatching of their agents to various saloons to buy customers beer on the house. "All brewers had such spending agents, but Adolphus gathered a crew that was extraordinarily accomplished; he infused into its members his own masterly manner, and as a result, his beer was soon selling almost as well as Lemp's."

The fierce competition between brands led to the practice of breweries sponsoring, or even owning taverns that sold their beer exclusively. A would-be saloon owner would obtain a license and then let the breweries know that he was interested in their business. Adolphus generally made the best offer. He often paid for the license, covered the cost of fixtures and glassware and even arranged for rental of the saloon. To compete, another brewery had to open a saloon nearby, and neighborhoods were quickly inundated with more saloons than they could support. Competition was cutthroat, the abuses glaring. One hundred years later, long after the payment of incentives was made illegal, the government charged that Anheuser-Busch continued the practice under some of the descendants of Adolphus. The company paid millions of dollars in settlements when the violations were alleged by the government.

Despite Adolphus's hardnosed sales tactics, the Anheuser brewery still lagged behind the likes of the Union, Wainwright and Phoenix breweries. The biggest of all was Lemp's Western Brewery, whose plant and mansion—five blocks from Anheuser's in south St. Louis—had become the symbol of the mighty beer baron's wealth and power. Eager to share in that wealth and power, Adolphus was not afraid to gamble on the beer market's potential for growth. With confidence, he sought a loan of $50,000 to expand the capacity of Anheuser's brewery. The cautious French, who dominated the banking establishment of St. Louis, turned him down because he was considered too extravagant. The bankers' reasoning was that anybody who spent so lavishly on his office could not be a good money manager. Indeed, Adolphus's headquarters reflected a taste and elegance unknown for the times, especially considering the type of business he was in. It had easy chairs, a carpet and, instead of wooden boxes filled with sawdust, spittoons.

"After my experience with those financial geniuses I went to the old State Bank and saw the president, Robert A. Barnes," Adolphus said later. "I asked him to come down to my place; to examine my books and to see for himself how I did business. Mr. Barnes gave me the credit and I went ahead." Adolphus built a new brew house, a malt house and storage cellars, creating a capacity for 25,000 barrels. During the five-year period between 1865 and 1870, production increased 300 percent. The E. Anheuser & Company plant grew to cover seven acres and employ 600 men.

On February 19, 1867, Adolphus took another important step. He renounced allegiance to the grand duke of Hesse-Darmstadt and swore to support the Constitution of the United States. He became a citizen of his adopted country, a country that would make him wealthy beyond the dreams of any immigrant. But Adolphus would never completely sever his relationship with the fatherland. His family and business contacts and the sentimental ties that bound him to the land of his birth remained very strong and often lured him back to Germany. His business was in America, but his heart was split between the two countries.

In fact, close contacts with Europe gave Adolphus a tremendous leg up over his competitors. Developments were taking place abroad that forever changed the practice of the brewing industry. Adolphus took the lead in cashing in on them, especially on the discoveries of Louis Pasteur.

Pasteur, in a makeshift laboratory in a barroom in Arbois, France, had demonstrated how wines became diseased by bacteria. In 1866, he published a book that explained his findings, which concluded that the bacteria could be eliminated by the application of heat—pasteurization. Later, in 1877, he published a study that showed how to keep beer from spoiling, but the book did not have the same amount of detail as the one on wine because Pasteur did not like beer.

Four years before Pasteur's book came out, Adolphus had already become the first brewer in the United States to pasteurize his bottled beer. It was possible that he heard of Pasteur's discoveries during his frequent travels to Europe after 1868. Perhaps the information was brought to his attention by his older brother, Anton, who was active in the wine business where the technique was first applied. Many years later, the manager of an Anheuser-Busch brewery claimed Adolphus actually studied with Pasteur, although there is no evidence to support that. However Adolphus found out, he was quick to apply it to his own business.

It was a decisive moment. Pasteurization revolutionized the beer business because it meant that beer could be bottled and preserved for longer periods without fear of deterioration. A brewer could ship bottles of beer hundreds of miles and it would remain drinkable. Among all brewing companies, Anheuser's was the first to reach a national market. He started by shipping his bottled beer to Texas in 1872. Rail lines from St. Louis to the Lone Star State were excellent, and there were many German immigrants there but few breweries. By 1876, the year of Custer's Last Stand, thirsty men were drinking Busch's beer as far away as the Colorado mining camps.

A year later, the E. Anheuser & Company Brewing Association, with its output of 44,961 barrels, was ranked 32nd on a list of the nation's largest breweries. George Ehret of New York was first with 138,449 barrels, followed by Phillip Best, predecessor of Pabst in Milwaukee. But Adolphus was slowly, patiently, aggressively pushing his company forward. He was also building a dynasty.

5

The Birth of a Dynasty

True to his papa's tradition, Adolphus Busch believed in fathering a big family. In addition to Nellie, Edward and August, born between 1863 and the end of 1865, Lilly gave birth to eight more children between 1865 and 1876: Adolphus Jr. in 1868, Alexis in 1869, Emilie in 1870, Edmee in 1871, Peter in 1872, Martha in 1873, Anna in 1875 and Clara in 1876. Three of the girls—Emilie, Alexis and Martha—died at birth or soon after.

When sons Adolphus Jr. and Peter joined Edward and August, Busch was assured of having a male successor to carry on the family business. Like the founders of other great nineteenth-century commercial dynasties, he wanted as many children as possible to improve the odds that among the poets and playboys one would have the right combination of business acumen and personality to carry on. Girls were nice, but they didn't have a chance of running the business. Adolphus needed sons, but like his daughters, not all of them would survive. The first to go was his oldest son, Edward. At the age of fifteen, he died from peritonitis on Christmas eve in 1879 while attending the Kemper Military School in Boonville, Missouri. With Edward's death, August Anheuser Busch became Adolphus's oldest son.

Meanwhile, Eberhard Anheuser's company was fast becoming a Busch enterprise. In 1875, it had been incorporated, with Anheuser, then seventy years old, serving as president. Adolphus had the title of secretary-treasurer, but in reality he was running the firm. There were 480 shares of stock, with Adolphus receiving 238, two less than a half interest. Erwin Spraul, the brewmaster, had two shares. The other half interest of 240 shares was divided between Anheuser and his daughter Lilly, Adolphus's wife. Anheuser had 140 shares in his name, and Lilly's 100 shares were held in trust.

From the beginning, it was a closely held family corporation. The original bylaws prohibited the transfer of shares without the approval of the board of directors. The board was made up of Anheuser, Busch and Spraul. Reflecting Busch's importance, the name of the corporation was changed to the Anheuser-Busch Brewing Association in 1879.

By that time, Papa Anheuser was extremely ill. In 1877, a tumor had been discovered in his throat, and following a series of painful operations by the best surgeons in Chicago and New York, it was pronounced incurable. On Sunday evening May 2, 1880, at the age of seventy-four, the owner of the former Bavarian Brewery died at the family home at Tenth and Pestalozzi streets.

Anheuser's stock was left to his children—Lilly and Anna Busch, Cecily Schoettler, and William and Adolph Anheuser. Anheuser's sons were not positioned to take active roles in the brewery and thus become a challenge to Adolphus, who was named president. William Anheuser ran a soap company in San Francisco. Adolph Anheuser died of cirrhosis of the liver six years after the death of his father. Later, Anheuser's descendants would obtain positions in the brewery, but they always worked for the Busches.

A gulf eventually opened between the two families. According to one family member: "The story was that they even went so far as to pay a different set of dividends on stock; one for the Anheusers, another for the Busches. From then on, you saw the Anheusers being pushed out of the business." Gussie Busch, talking about his grandparents, once said, "Adolphus Busch and my grandmother, they wouldn't even allow the Anheusers in their family, and she was an Anheuser! She didn't like any of her relatives on that side of the family!"

Mabel-Ruth Anheuser, discussing the prickly family relationships, offered another view. "Well, the Busches don't want it told. You see they want to say they founded the brewery. They didn't. My husband's great-great-grandfather was Eberhard Anheuser and he was the one who owned the company. Busch was an employee."

With Anheuser's death, Adolphus had total control of the brewery. In the years that followed, he tried to buy back as much stock as possible from Anheuser's descendants, once paying a family member $60,000 for a single share. He eventually increased his stake in the company from 238 to 267 shares, and Lilly's from 100 to 116.

While Adolphus consolidated his control of the business, the Anheuser-Busch brewery grew to resemble a small city. Seven new buildings were added, among them a new brew house that looked like a storybook castle. Another technical innovation for the company was its new refrigerated ice house. A brewery no longer needed caves to cool the beer. At great financial risk, Adolphus installed a mechanical refrigeration system that eliminated the need to cut and haul ice blocks.

Adolphus also created what would later be called a vertically integrated company—a firm that owned suppliers of many of the materials necessary for its final product. In addition to the raw materials that went into the brewing of beer, the company provided its own barrels and built a bottling plant with an eventual daily capacity of 100,000 bottles, the largest in the nation. In 1876, Adolphus had launched the industry's first fleet of refrigerated rail cars; a few years later, he formed a company to build them. To keep its beer cold down the rail lines, Anheuser-Busch also built a series of icehouses and storage depots. These became branch offices from which the beer was distributed.

By 1880, the Anheuser-Busch brewery, with its stylish red brick buildings trimmed with granite, had become a major showplace in St. Louis. An early disciple of good public relations, a lesson his heirs learned well, Adolphus employed six guides to give tours. There were 3,500 employees in the main brewery, and another 1,500 worked in forty-two branches around the country. Within fifteen years of joining Eberhard Anheuser, Adolphus had become the nineteenth century's most famous son-in-law. He had built the foundation of a national empire.

6

The Monks' Recipe

The saying goes that behind every great fortune there is a great crime. In the case of Anheuser-Busch, the fortune rests on the stupendous success of its most famous brand, Budweiser. But the King of Beers was, in fact, a pretender to the throne. Long before Anheuser-Busch produced Budweiser, a European brewery was selling a beer with the same name.

The murky origin of their flagship brand was something the descendants of Adolphus Busch were reluctant to discuss. For years, its interesting past was a carefully guarded secret. Instead, legends, some spawned by Anheuser-Busch, grew up around the beginnings of the world's most popular beer. One story had it that Adolphus and his good friend, Carl Conrad, obtained the recipe for Budweiser from European monks. Another tale mentioned a special yeast brought across the ocean in an ice cream container. But in fact, the beer that helped make Adolphus rich was actually a high-quality adaptation of the Pilsener brewing process. The name Budweiser was already in use in Europe before Anheuser-Busch began using the name. A brewery in what is now Czechoslovakia had been selling Budweiser for years in central Europe and even importing small quantities into the United States.

Soon after Adolphus Busch became a brewer, he turned his attention to improving the Bavarian Brewery's inferior product. He read every technical journal he could get his hands on about advances in Europe. In 1868 and quite often afterward, he traveled to Europe to study the brewing industry. He visited Paris, where Austrian and German beers were competing head-to-head. He also focused his attention on the Pilsener beer brewed in Bohemia, then part of Austria and now part of Czechoslovakia, where beer had been skillfully brewed in the southern region for more than 600 years. The brewery in Pilsen was the largest, with cellars carved out of solid rock stretching more than five miles.

The Pilsener brewers had developed a process that used special artesian well water, drawn through sandstone rock. Their beer was painstakingly laced with carefully selected malt, and, at the right moment, spiced with a hop unlike that grown anywhere else in the world. The brewers let it age in the coolness of their rock-hewn cellars, waiting until a secondary fermentation process known as krausening boosted the beer's carbonation. The result was a frothy-headed, pale golden product that long before Busch's time was in demand in Vienna and Prague.

On trips abroad with Conrad, Adolphus meticulously noted the Pilsener process, right down to the name of a brand of beer that was being produced by a brewery in Ceské-Budějovice, sixty-five miles south of Pilsen. During the reign of the Hapsburgs, the town was known by its German name, Budweis. Its famous beer was sold in Vienna, Yugoslavia and Bavaria; some even reached New York in kegs and bottles bearing the name Budweiser.

Years later Adolphus would claim he had selected the name Budweiser because it could "be easily pronounced by English-speaking people, and in the second place the brewery bearing that name enjoyed a good reputation" in Europe. He called his American competitors "scoundrels" when they used the name Budweiser, and lawsuits were initiated to protect the label. When Anheuser-Busch was involved in a court fight over the name Budweiser in New York, Busch wrote his lawyer: "The 'Budweiser' beer is not known in Germany, and is only sold in Budweis proper and in some towns of Bohemia. Their exports to America are very limited and do not amount to anything."

Over succeeding years, Anheuser-Busch could never quite get the facts right. A story circulated by Anheuser-Busch in 1921 credited Conrad as Budweiser's creator, saying the beer "was an inspiration. Its conception . . . a mental lightning flash through an electrified brain." But decades later Anheuser-Busch claimed that Adolphus "coined" the word Budweiser. And in 1953, a company publication, *The Budcaster*, reported that Adolphus "conceived the name 'Budweiser,' and selected it as one that would appeal to the American people."

The true story followed a somewhat different course. In addition to originating with a Bohemian brewery, the brand name was first registered in the United States by Conrad, an importer of wines, champagnes and liquors. The Anheuser brewery produced the brand for him under contract. Conrad had offices in Mainz and Geisenheim in Germany and in St. Louis. To a line that included Moss Rose bourbon and Governor's Choice rye from Silver Creek, Kentucky, he added "world renowned Conrad's Budweiser Beer." Made slowly with the best ingredients available, the product was corked with a special wire fastener wrapped in foil that made it look like a champagne bottle. Conrad sold the beverage to restaurants as far away as Denver and New York.

Adolphus got the rights to Budweiser from C. Conrad and Company in October 1882 when Conrad went bankrupt. He was laden with $300,000 in debts, the largest being $94,000 owed to the Anheuser-Busch Brewing Association. An arrangement was worked out in which the brewery assumed control of Conrad's company—and the brand name Budweiser. Conrad was given a lifetime job with Anheuser-Busch. At that time, Adolphus said he saw no problem in the fact that the brewery had lost $94,000 through its unsecured loan to Conrad. He believed the reputation that Conrad had established for Budweiser would more than compensate the brewery for the loss. Once again, Adolphus had clearly foreseen the future.

The story was not yet over. Anheuser-Busch's tenuous claim to the name Budweiser was kept under wraps for many years after that. But when it filed documents in 1907 to register the name as a U.S. trademark, a German brewery stepped forward to file a complaint, arguing that the St. Louis company could not use Budweiser because it was a geographical name and because the German brewery had used it first.

In 1911, Adolphus settled the matter by paying the German brewery 82,500 kronen. That same year a similar settlement

that included a large payment was reached with a brewery in
Budweis in what is now Ceské-Budějovice, Czechoslovakia.
Under terms of the arrangement, Anheuser-Busch could use
the name Budweiser on beer sold in the United States. The
European breweries could use it on beer sold in Europe and
they could sell "Imported Budweiser" in the United States.
But Anheuser-Busch was not allowed to sell its Budweiser in
Europe.

When the Czech brewery attempted to sell its Budweiser in
the United States in 1937, Anheuser-Busch considered contest-
ing its plan. But a lawyer advised the company that it would
lose such a showdown under the terms of the 1911 agreements.
He added in strong language that the adverse publicity over
the origin of the name could cost the Anheuser-Busch brewery
millions. The evidence in the case would "seriously affect, if
not destroy" the good will of Anheuser-Busch and Budweiser
in the United States. But the Czech brewery was no match for
the Anheuser-Busch muscle. Two years later, the company obtained from the Czechs the right to use the name exclusively in
North America, the United States and all its possessions.

The cloudy origins of the Budweiser name continued to
haunt Anheuser-Busch into the 1990s. As it set its sights on
world markets, the brewery found itself legally prohibited
from selling Budweiser in most of Europe. Anheuser-Busch
had grown into a colossus, producing 200 times the amount of
beer brewed by the little brewery of Ceské-Budějovice, Czechoslovakia. But the Czechs still had exclusive marketing rights to
sell Budweiser in Western Europe; they resisted Anheuser-
Busch's offers of cash, joint-venture production and new terri-
torial division. The Budweiser beer sold in Europe is the original and is of Czech not American manufacture.

In December 1990, as Communism gave way to a free-mar-
ket economy, workers at the Czech brewery went on strike
trying to force management to merge with Anheuser-Busch.
But the suggestion of a merger created protests around Ceské-
Budějovice. The local newspaper, *South Bohemian Truth*,
reported that beer drinkers would rather die than see an
agreement with a company whose beer is "a weak imitation of
the original product." An irritated young businessman said,
"You'll never see our beer in cans, we use cans for sauerkraut
only."

7

Dealing with Pabst

"My Dear Friend Captain Pabst . . . the present way competition is running we are only hurting each other in a real foolish way." It was 1889, and fifty-year-old Adolphus Busch was writing to his nemesis, Frederick Pabst of the Pabst Brewing Company in Milwaukee. Busch, whose brewery had surged in the preceding ten years to challenge Pabst's for national dominance, observed that their saloon owners had been slyly playing one brewer off against another. They were using false statements about what each brewer was charging, attempting to extract the lowest possible price.

Adolphus had a solution. He bluntly suggested that beer prices be fixed by the four largest national brewers so that all could realize a healthy profit. "Now," Busch wrote, "a perfect understanding between your good self, Schlitz, Lemp and myself ought to be reached, matters regulated and I feel confident that each of the four concerns mentioned would then realize a profit of a half million or even a million more than they do now."

The beer trust Busch suggested to Pabst was hardly a revolutionary idea. Monopolies were one of the inventions of the business tycoons of the late nineteen century. The major scandals they created eventually led to the Sherman Anti-Trust Act of 1890 and the Clayton Act of 1914. Trusts were ultimately outlawed, but in the era of the robber baron, there was no corporate income tax, no government regulation and—if a trust could be formed—no competition. Adolphus was merely suggesting to Pabst that the brewers be as greedy as men like John D. Rockefeller, James J. Hill and Andrew Carnegie—people with whom he often rubbed shoulders on transatlantic steamers. Adolphus pointed out to Pabst that steel, sugar, oil and glass interests were all fixing prices. Only the brewers, he lamented in his letter, were "fighting each other and running the profits down."

Pabst had received a similar suggestion from Adolphus before. In 1881 he had brashly proposed that the barrel price be fixed between $10.25 and $10.75. He told Pabst he had an arrangement with Lemp, his St. Louis rival, who had slipped to second place behind Anheuser-Busch. Under Adolphus's sole control the growth of the Anheuser-Busch Brewing Association (ABBA) had exploded. Adolphus could not expand fast enough to keep up with demand. In 1877, 53,567 barrels had been sold. Four years later, output climbed to more than 186,000 barrels. In 1889, capacity was boosted to 500,000 barrels, but still Anheuser-Busch could not satisfy its thirsty customers.

As the Gay Nineties dawned, Adolphus embarked on a bold new construction plan. Adolphus and Lilly Busch were living in the Anheuser mansion next to the brewery, and the expansion could only take place after his wife reluctantly agreed to give up some of the precious space in her garden. His plan was to produce one million barrels by the turn of the century. In addition to Lilly's garden, expanding the brewery swallowed up buildings—a public school and an Episcopal church.

For more than a decade, Adolphus's beer had been sold around the world. Within two years of the introduction of pasteurization in 1872 it was being shipped to Cuba, Mexico and Haiti. By 1877, his "St. Louis Lager Beer" could be bought in saloons and restaurants from Lima to London and from Shanghai to Singapore. But the export trade was strictly for show. Adolphus made his millions selling beer in America's midsection, from humid Shreveport to Chicago.

The reason for the dramatic growth in his sales was simple. The national population swelled from 39 million in 1870 to 76 million by 1900, and most of the immigrants during those years were beer-loving Germans. Adolphus reaped a windfall. Between 1883 and 1900, the company declared nineteen consecutive dividends, ranging from $125 to $750 per share. When an English syndicate offered $12 million for his brewery in 1892, Adolphus laughingly turned it down. His profits went into asphalt mines in Utah and Arizona; hotels in Chicago, Dallas, Paris and Marienbad; oil fields in Louisiana; coal mines in West Virginia; and real estate, livestock and timber in the Northwest. All but a few of his investments paid off handsomely, and if some of them went bad, Adolphus still had his beer business: "a friend that never yet has gone back on me."

Sometimes Adolphus bought out his competition. He had a piece of the Lone Star Brewing Company in San Antonio,

Texas, and the Texas Brewing Company in Fort Worth. In 1895, he bought the Alamo Brewery in San Antonio for $70,000 with plans to close it and give its business to Lone Star. He had an interest in the Shreveport Ice & Brewing Company, and land on which an Oklahoma brewery was planned.

Adolphus also controlled companies that did business with Anheuser-Busch, among them the Manufacturers Railway Company, which transported beer from the brewery to the main rail line in St. Louis. His St. Louis Refrigerator Car Company built railroad cars to carry the beer, and the Adolphus Busch Glass Manufacturing Company made bottles for his brewery and Lemp's.

During price wars, Busch negotiated with the giants like Pabst, but in dealing with smaller, local breweries, he sometimes dictated the price, according to a story by Gussie Busch, his grandson. Many years later, Gussie told the story of a price battle in Louisiana. It captured the essential Adolphus. "It's a hell of a story. I'm almost afraid to tell it today, but . . . there were twelve breweries in New Orleans. And they got into a price war and, we ran a branch down there, and Jesus Christ, I can remember all the salesmen running up to him and saying for God's sake, you got to meet the price. They're just killing us down in New Orleans."

As Gussie remembered it, an undaunted Adolphus told them, " 'Forget it. I'm going to run New Orleans.'

"Our sales went to nothing. The guys [the New Orleans brewers] got together and they raised the price, and five minutes after they raised the price, Adolphus Busch cut the goddamn price 25 cents. They met his price and he cut it 25 cents again. They met it again, he cut it another 25 cents. And the whole goddamned works came up to him, and again I was in the office with Grandfather . . . and he turns around and says to them: 'You guys. You didn't consult me when you got together. You didn't give me a goddamn bit of consideration. Now you sons of bitches, you're going to get it. You're going to get it good! . . . The only way I'm going to compromise with you is this: I control the price of beer for the next 25 years. I can't have it in writing; whatever goddamn price I put on my beer, you go up the same goddamn price. That's the only goddamn way I'll compromise on it.'

"Every goddamn one of them shook his head, and for eighteen years we had no trouble in the state of Louisiana." Even years later, Gussie could never tell the story without laughing.

When the price competition was uncompromising and fierce,

he simply stuck it out and lost money rather than admitting defeat and abandoning a territory. His policy was one of no retreat. He once considered closing agencies in Terre Haute and Minneapolis "because they did not pay." But he said to withdraw "would create disagreeable talk. It would encourage local breweries to fight harder in the future at other stations, hoping thereby to drive the big concerns out."

The founder's dogma would still guide the brewery 100 years later.

Adolphus loved the trappings of the unrepentant capitalist. His office combined European elegance and American efficiency. The skylights, the tessellated marble floors covered by Axminster carpets, the luxurious chairs, the paintings and antique decorations gave it elegance. The ceaseless chatter of the telegraph gave it purpose. When Adolphus's elaborate new office was constructed in his expanded headquarters in St. Louis, a telegraph line was installed and a full-time operator employed to put him in immediate touch with the world.

On a typical day, Adolphus kept two stenographers and a telegrapher busy. To his secretaries, especially his favorite, Alvina Berg, who could write in English and German, he dictated messages to an ice company in Gainesville, Texas, about the stock in his Texas breweries; the Tennessee Brewing Company about whether copycat Budweiser labels had been destroyed; Fritz Sontag, the manager of his Grand Pacific Hotel in Chicago, about preparations for a beer-judging contest at the Columbian Exposition; a distributor in De Soto, Missouri, about competition from the Green Tree Brewery; a glass company in Streator, Illinois, complaining about the quality of the bottles; the Missouri Car & Foundry Company about linings for refrigerator cars for very hot weather; an agent in Baltimore, berating him for not having the money to operate an agency there.

The stream of inquiry, cajolery, criticism, encouragement, congratulations and threats was endless. Even when he traveled, Adolphus never lost touch with his office, sending back long, detailed letters and wordy telegrams that demanded answers and explanations from every nook and cranny of his enormous empire.

Under Adolphus Busch the small, struggling Bavarian Brewery that Eberhard Anheuser purchased had become a huge mechanism of the industrial age—a mixture of men, machinery and natural ingredients that produced a flood of beer and a mountain of profits. Refrigerant flowed through miles of pipes like blood through a body. Conveyers hauled tons of malt and barley through noisy machines that shredded, milled, ground and sifted. Boiling wort bubbled in huge copper kettles. The fires that once burned beneath the kettles had been replaced by jets of steam pumped into the thick mixture. Men naked to the waist shoveled coal into the boilers to generate the steam. The work could be brutal. In the hot summer of 1888, ten St. Louis brewery workers died of heat stroke. Rheumatism plagued the men who worked in the cold cellars. Hernias were frequent from lifting heavy barrels. When a worker grew old and couldn't handle the heavy chores any longer, he finished his brewing trade in the wash house. The bottle shop was a particularly dangerous place where men lost eyes when overpressurized flasks exploded.

The St. Louis brewers, Adolphus among them, drew upon the hardworking ranks of poorly paid German immigrants for their labor. Deutsch was the language of the brewery worker, and the few non-Germans who managed to get jobs survived by learning the curse words and obscenities. The men worked fourteen-hour days six days a week with six to eight hours on Sunday. They were paid $14 per week. Many of them were single men who lived in brewery-owned dormitories near the plant. Shaken from their sleep at 2 A.M., they worked until dark. It was a job that created alcoholics; as a fringe benefit, workers could have all the free beer they wanted. The beverage privilege, or "sternewirth," was encouraged by the employers partly to counteract the long hours, constant fatigue and degrading working conditions.

A new infusion of immigrants fleeing Bismarck's Germany in the 1870s found employment in the breweries and formed labor unions to better their pay and working conditions. In 1888 a four-month boycott of four national breweries, including Anheuser-Busch, brought about the recognition of Brewers and Maltsters Union Local 6 in St. Louis. Beer was supposed to be a working man's drink and the boycott was ruining the beer business among its best customers. In 1889, the union won a contract calling for a twelve-hour day, six-day week. The wage for the shortened work week remained at $14—plus free beer on the job.

To these hardworking, hard-drinking Germans, many of whom never married, the union was their life. When they marched proudly in the Labor Day parades, people on the street would say, "There go the brewery Dutch." And when

they died, they were cremated and the urns containing their
ashes were enshrined in a special room of the union's Gambri-
nus Hall.

Adolphus reluctantly gave in to labor demands and only
then to keep peace. He wrote his son August A. in June 1894
that the brewers would have to put on a united front against
the future demands of the labor unions. His fear was that "we
will cease to be the masters in our business and will have to
submit to anything that is demanded of us." In all respects,
Adolphus Busch had become a quintessential American indus-
trialist. But if he could be counted among the other industrial
aristocrats of his age, he had a singular distinction. His fortune
was based upon a rather plebeian product—beer.

8

The Blue Ribbon

Adolphus spent money as lavishly as he made it. His fortune
enabled him to buy showy estates as far flung as Pasadena, St.
Louis, Cooperstown, New York, and Bad Schwalbach in Germany. He traveled in comfort between his American mansions
in his railroad car the *Adolphus.* The lavish coach reflected its
owner's taste perfectly. Richly paneled, upholstered and car-
peted, it was a palace on wheels.

During his frequent journeys Adolphus often ordered his
train halted so he could climb down and greet an astonished
Irish switchman or some other workman. On other occasions
his engineers highballed it, setting speed records. On November 19, 1912, for example, he chartered a train that set a record
by covering the 2,055 miles between St. Louis and Los Angeles
in fifty-eight hours, clipping five hours off the old mark. A
special siding, attached to the spur that linked his brewery

with the main railroad line, brought the *Adolphus* almost to the doorstep of his St. Louis mansion.

It was called Number One Busch Place. The original Anheuser home, it was located on the brewery property. "The family residence on Pestalozzi Street is built on an elevation adjoining the brewery, and in the midst of a large and beautiful park called Busch Park, which is partly terraced and ornamented by fountains, miniature lakes, and gay parterres of flowers." Adolphus filled the place with fine paintings, expensive tapestries, antiques, statuary and nine children. His favorite part of the mansion was its fabulous wine cellar. The home was the epitome of Germanic elegance and Busch's philosophy that life should be enjoyed to its fullest.

The mansion might have been viewed as monstrously gauche, but standing next to the brewery's castle-like buildings, it almost appeared modest—at least from the outside. Inside, the permanent fixtures included massive crystal chandeliers, parqueted floors and stained glass windows. In a huge salon, a fresco depicted plump women in filmy red garments floating across the ceiling. Here Busch entertained Theodore Roosevelt, William H. Taft, Enrico Caruso and Sarah Bernhardt. When inventor Rudolph Diesel saw the place, he was overwhelmed and likened the other large homes nearby to "inhabited mausoleums."

As Busch's children grew older and established families of their own, additional houses were built—Busch Place Number Two, for his son August A., and Number Three. Near the gated entrance to this compound was a magnificent stable that housed tallyho coaches, landaus, broughams, shooting wagons and phaetons. Thirty horses were quartered there along with drivers and stablemen.

A wrought iron fence surrounded the compound and its park —the center of a fairy-tale world for the Busch children and grandchildren. There were Easter egg hunts, and at Christmas a brewery employee dressed like St. Nicholas and visited the home. A Christmas tree blazing with candles reached to the ceiling, a servant always at the ready with a bucket of sand in case the tree ignited.

When Adolphus returned from a lengthy journey, his arrival at Number One Busch Place was likened to the arrival of a king. A cannon at the brewery was fired just as it was for the birth of a Busch grandchild. Many years later, Edna Huth, whose family lived near the brewery, remembered one of Adolphus's arrivals because it was the first time she saw electric lights. "The carriage approached and made a turn into the gateway. Just as it entered the gates it seemed I was transferred into a fairyland! The whole yard of the estate lit up with electric lights and festoons of lights were draped from tree to tree. I don't think I had ever seen anything quite so beautiful!"

Although Adolphus was happy with Number One Busch Place, it had its problems. For one thing the house stood in the shadow of his pungent brewery. For another, the summers were hot and muggy, and the winters were harsh. As he got older, he fled the inhospitable St. Louis climate whenever possible.

Beginning in 1886, Adolphus, Lilly and the rest of the clan wintered in California and he often proclaimed that the state was "the grandest place in the world." He bought a mansion in Pasadena from tobacco magnate George S. Myers and named it Ivy Wall. Nearby he purchased another large home, the Blossoms, a guest house for visiting friends and family. The Blossoms alone cost $165,000, the highest price ever paid up to then for a residence in Pasadena. Adolphus predicted that all the country's rich would eventually winter there, and he was soon joined by steel manufacturer Andrew Carnegie, banker Russell Sage and financier J.P. Morgan. Their castles formed Millionaires Row along South Orange Grove Avenue.

Many years before William Randolph Hearst built San Simeon in northern California, Adolphus constructed his own paradise in sunny Pasadena. In 1892, he began development of a series of gardens surrounding Ivy Wall. Over a five-year period, he spent $500,000 transforming an arid arroyo into twelve acres of sunken gardens, fountains and terraces. In the depths of a hollow an enormous circular flower bed was cultivated in the shape of Anheuser-Busch's trademark, the A and eagle.

The garden eventually covered thirty-five acres and required fifty men to maintain. After two of his grandchildren recited fairy tales to him, Adolphus added scenes from the stories to his garden. Tiny brick castles, ceramic figures, waterwheels and thatched huts were carefully erected. Exotic birds and fish were added to his private wonderland. One visitor, tea king Sir Thomas Lipton, said, "The place is perfection."

Adolphus came to Pasadena right after Christmas. He stayed until May, and then returned to St. Louis briefly on his way to Europe for the summer, spending June through October in Germany. The less time sweating or freezing in St. Louis, the better.

For his German residence, Adolphus had attempted to buy the Kautzenburg, a castle near the Anheuser homestead of Bad Kreuznach. He offered 2 million deutsch marks and planned to rebuild it, but the Catholic Church intervened. The owner, a Catholic from the Netherlands, was told that if he sold his castle to a nonbelieving Protestant he would be excommunicated. Adolphus never visited Bad Kreuznach again. He did not take religion seriously, and the experience only deepened his resentment of the church. Baptized a Catholic and married in a Lutheran ceremony, Adolphus believed most people went to church to improve their social standing.

Denied a castle, Adolphus built his own villa. He selected a site in the Taunus Mountains ten miles from the Rhine, not far from his boyhood home in Kastel and near the resort community of Bad Schwalbach. The residence resembled a giant gingerbread house topped with a spire. He named it Villa Lilly, after his wife. When Busch arrived for his summer sojourn, villagers decorated their houses with flags and hundreds showed up to receive him like a knight returning from a Crusade.

The nearby pine forests were thick with deer, and Adolphus built a rustic lodge—Waldfriede—for hunting trips. In addition to his own 1,200 acres, he had hunting rights on an additional 15,000. Another home, named after daughter Clara, was built next to Villa Lilly for visiting family and friends, hops dealers, businessmen, American senators and European nobles. The kaiser's brother and son were among Adolphus's most famous guests; so was the Prince of Wales who later became King Edward VII. From his villa, Adolphus often took trips to Paris for elegant dining and drinking. Another favorite stop was Carlsbad in Bohemia, where he liked to take the "cure" in the resort's famous sulfur springs.

Adolphus had a fourth estate in Cooperstown, New York, which he usually visited in the early summer before going to Europe. Cooperstown was in the center of what was then the best hops-growing region in the country. His residence, called Uncas Lodge, was a sprawling frame house built on the alleged site of the wigwam of the last chief of the Mohicans. It overlooked Otsego Lake and was surrounded by places immortalized by James Fenimore Cooper, who called the dagger-shaped lake "the glimmerglass." A dormitory was later built on the estate to accommodate the Eastern college students who came every year to pick hops. Busch invited his friends to visit. "Let us meet in Cooperstown. . . . We will go fishing and sailing, we will sing; who does not love wine, women, a fine dinner, a good cigar, cheerful company and song shall not live a life long."

Wherever he went, Adolphus cut a flamboyant figure. He dressed in the most expensive European tailoring. He had a flowing mustache and thick imperial beard. His thinning hair had turned from auburn to gray; he wore it long and swept back, except for a small lock that was allowed to curl up over his forehead. By age fifty, he was thick-chested and with enough girth to suggest he drank a good deal of his own product. And, as if to emphasize the point, at the very center of his ample belly dangled a gold watch fob emblazoned with the A and eagle.

He greeted people in a loud, thick German accent. These verbal explosions were always accompanied by either a wave of the hand or his cane. He was approachable by strangers. People who knew him personally said he was assertive, even aggressive, but in a good-natured way. It was said he had the capacity for severe anger but did not hold a grudge. His posture was ramrod straight and pure Prussian.

Although his rotundness seemed to indicate he guzzled a lot of beer, the truth was that Adolphus did not particularly like what he brewed. During one interview, before the journalist could pose his first question, the beer baron asked, "Vell, vot to drink?"

The newspaperman, anxious to start off on the right foot, replied, "Budweiser."

"Ach," said Adolphus. "Dot schlop?"

He preferred wine, and he was especially fond of vintages from his home country. However, he once admitted he liked a certain French wine. "It may be said in passing that Busch himself had no exalted ideas about beer," one historian commented. "The eminent diagnosist, Dr. Meiner of Dresden, once told me how, when he explained to Busch that beer-drinking was ruining his health, the brewer blazed out with, 'I never touch beer! I drink champagne!' "

Adolphus was a connoisseur of the grape, and the cellar of Number One Busch Place contained a vast collection of expensive wines. When he ingratiated himself by sending important people alcoholic beverages, he shipped wine—not beer. Adolphus sent two cases of his favorite selection to William H. Taft, then secretary of war in the administration of Theodore Roosevelt. He reminded Taft of a conversation they once had about the best wines to serve with lunch and dinner, and how they each preferred a pure light Moselle or Rhine. No mention was made of beer.

"You will find the 'Scharzhofberger' an exquisite Moselle, and I believe it will just suite your palate," Adolphus wrote his equally rotund friend. "The other case contains Eltviller Sonnenberg, and this is the grandest and finest wine grown in the Nineteenth Century. I am the lucky owner of this vintage, and can assure you that not one bottle which has left my cellar has given me the satisfaction I feel in sending you this case. I even feel confident if you will ask our esteemed friend, the president, to join you in a glass of it, he will be delighted."

Adolphus was such an experienced imbiber that he could identify different vintages and brands by taste. It was a talent he demonstrated regularly at his unofficial club. The monied old families of St. Louis society had never extended the welcome mat to Adolphus because of his ancestry and because of how he made his fortune. But the beer baron had his own circle of friends with whom he gathered every afternoon at four o'clock.

From his mansion or the brewery, Adolphus boarded his yellow carriage for the trip up cobblestoned Broadway, waving to people on the street like a monarch on parade. The trip ended at a restaurant at the corner of Broadway and Elm, a rendezvous for prominent businessmen, actors, boxers and assorted sporting men, and those who wanted to catch a glimpse of such celebrities. It was Faust's, owned and operated by Tony Faust, the saloon keeper of long standing in St. Louis and one-time drinking companion of Eberhard Anheuser.

Regarded as the finest restaurant west of Delmonico's, Faust's menu featured oysters at 25 cents for a half dozen, lobster for 60 cents and roasted pigs with apples in their mouths. The upstairs dining room featured an orchestra and there was a roof garden. Over 100 men could belly up to a long oaken bar manned by five or six busy bartenders. A favorite beverage was Faust Pale Lager, brewed, of course, by Anheuser-Busch.

A short man with a ruddy complexion and twinkling eye, Faust always wore a bowler. He and his good friend Adolphus traveled the world together. The saloonkeeper's son and the brewer's daughter were engaged to be married. When he was in St. Louis, Adolphus went to Faust's every afternoon, playing three-handed skat or draw poker at what was called the millionaires' table. He was expert at cards and played the game as he ran his business, intent on winning.

Adolphus conducted his famous wine test at Faust's. He bet $100, sometimes more, that he could identify any vintage merely by tasting it. If someone took the bet, he had glasses filled with every kind of wine in the house and set in a row. After taking a sip from each, he announced its name. He rarely made a mistake, and whether he won or lost, he paid for all the bottles which had been opened and bought drinks for the crowd.

While Faust was his closest friend, his lawyer, Charles Nagel, was Adolphus's "conscience." But Nagel gave Busch more than just legal advice. The two men developed a mutual bond of trust that endured over thirty-five years. Nagel was loyal—a trait Busch valued above all others.

He was the son of an immigrant who had fled Germany during the social revolution of 1848. His family first settled near Houston, Texas, where he was born in 1849. His father, a physician, was antislavery and outspoken, and on the eve of the Civil War was accused by Southern sympathizers of influencing the community's overwhelming vote against slavery. The family fled to Mexico and later traveled to St. Louis, where Nagel earned his law degree in 1872. After he returned from studies in Berlin, Adolphus took an interest in the quiet young man and eventually entrusted him with all of his legal affairs.

Nagel started out drawing up real estate contracts for the brewery. He ended up advising Adolphus on matters right and wrong. His moral influence was so great that Adolphus kept a framed photograph of his lawyer on his desk as a reminder. When a devil appeared on his shoulder, he had only to glance at the picture. "I have you in view all the time," he wrote Nagel. "When I think of something bad, I look at you and you say to me: 'Don't do it!' And I don't."

Adolphus often used Nagel to carry out legal attacks on other breweries when they attempted to use the Budweiser label, but he took it upon himself to do battle with his arch rival, Pabst. He was willing to go to almost any lengths to win a fight with other brewers. This was one of the few rounds he ever lost.

In the late 1800s, beer companies competed with one another at major fairs and expositions around the world, the winners proclaiming favorable results in their advertisements. Anheuser-Busch had won medals and ribbons with its Budweiser in Paris, where Adolphus personally arranged the dis-

play, and in Amsterdam, Philadelphia, Vienna and New
Orleans. But the most prestigious award of all was given in
1893 at the Columbian Exposition in Chicago, an event which
marked the 400th anniversary of the discovery of America by
Christopher Columbus.

Adolphus's major competitor at the exposition was Milwaukee's Captain Pabst, who built a spectacular thirteen-foot-
square, gold-plated model of his Empire Brewery to attract
attention. When the judges were finished, Anheuser-Busch had
won six preliminary medals and Pabst five. The big event followed, the contest for the beer to be judged "America's best."

It was a rancorous contest. As soon as a special panel was
selected, arguments broke out over its makeup. Still more disputes erupted over how points would be awarded. At first the
judges selected Anheuser-Busch, but that was before chemical
tests were completed. When those results were announced, the
judges reversed themselves and named Pabst the winner, for
they had found impurities in Adolphus's beer.

Outraged, he appealed to the fair commission, which announced on December 21, 1893, that no first-place prize would
be awarded. Still furious, he threatened legal action and the
judges reversed themselves again, swinging back to Anheuser-
Busch. It still wasn't over. Pabst persuaded the panelists to
change their minds yet again. When the suds finally settled,
the top prize went to the brewer from Milwaukee.

Adolphus wasn't about to accept the decision. He personally
pursued one of the judges to Europe, trying to get him to
change his mind. In the summer of 1894, he tracked the poor
man to Berlin, writing back to his son August A., "You know
there is no such thing as 'fail,' when I undertake to do anything." He wanted the judge to sign a statement saying he had
found no impurities in his analysis of Budweiser. But when
Adolphus arrived in Berlin, his unsuspecting prey had already
left for Paris.

Adolphus stalked him through France like one of his stags.
"At Paris, I missed him again," he wrote his son, "as he had
left for Montreux, and from there to Baden-Baden, where I
caught up with him and by fine diplomatic talk and 1862
wines, Château Metternich, he capitulated. . . . It was a costly
battle, but I think more costly to the defeated than to us. You
have no idea what tricks were resorted to. I found out things
in Berlin which I never expected. Pabst wanted to win at all
hazards and at any cost, but to no avail."

Adolphus sent the judge's new opinion home by registered mail, anticipating a "final grand triumph." It was not to be. In September 1894, the fair's executive committee refused to reverse its decision, and the Pabst Brewing Company has reminded beer drinkers ever since on its Blue Ribbon label that the beer was "selected as America's best in 1893."

The experience soured Adolphus against similar contests and he advised August A. against entering any more of them. "Prizes," he warned, "are not given to the goods meriting same, but are secured by money and strategy."

9

Prince Adolphus

In the Gay Nineties, an era of opulence and extravagance, Adolphus Busch counted entertainers, millionaires and politicians among his many friends. He loved the grand entrance. It tickled him that every time he checked into a New York hotel he was mobbed in the lobby by well-wishers.

President Taft picked his friend out of a crowd waiting on a railroad platform to greet him on a visit to St. Louis. "The prince!" shouted Taft, whose inflated midsection matched Busch's. "There's my friend Prince Adolphus." He rushed over to shake hands.

Adolphus even believed he was more well known than the president himself. When Taft planned a visit to St. Louis, Adolphus confided to his friend Nagel: "I am disappointed that I will not be able to see the president, but he will be surrounded by hundreds of people during the whole of the day, and if I appeared on the scene, they might give me such an ovation to make Taft envious."

In St. Louis, Adolphus and his family were treated like nobility. The newspapers splashed their comings and goings, successes and failures, marriages and fights across their front pages. Adolphus reveled in it. He readily met with reporters and gave them personal tours of his ever-expanding domain. On one such visit as the brewery workers bowed and scraped before his passing carriage, Adolphus turned to a journalist and said: "See, just like der king!"

When George M. Cohan performed in St. Louis he was introduced to Busch. "Are you German, Mr. Cohan?"

"No. A harp," Cohan replied.

"Harp? What is that?" Adolphus asked.

"Irish," Cohan answered.

"Is that what Irish is? Then a German must be a bass drum," Adolphus responded.

"You're a comedian yourself, Mr. Busch."

"No, but I have a lot working for me."

When Cohan got back to his hotel room, a case of Budweiser was waiting for him with a card reading: "Compliments of Mr. Adolphus Busch—and the comedians that work for me."

Adolphus often handed out souvenirs promoting his product. A favorite was an expensive German-made pocketknife with a peephole that revealed a photograph of Adolphus Busch. To more important people he gave diamond stickpins. Simon Wolf, a Busch lawyer in Washington, received a "beautiful cane with a boar's head and a watch charm with rubies and diamonds."

In 1894, Adolphus pulled off his greatest advertising coup. He had acquired the gaudy, mural-sized painting of *Custer's Last Fight* by Cassilly Adams. The painting hung in a St. Louis saloon which had run into financial difficulties. The brewer held a $30,000 claim against the place and took the painting because he liked it. With a master's sure touch, he had it altered so that the already gory effects were heightened. More scalpings and blood were added, and lithographic copies were made with his company's name prominently displayed at the bottom. It became the most popular promotion he ever launched, exceeding even the posters of bare-breasted Lorelei "discovering" the Anheuser-Busch brewery in an early example of sex appeal advertising.

The ease with which Adolphus spent money was legendary. When James Campbell, a railroad brakeman who later became a multimillionaire, needed money for a stock transaction, he went to Adolphus.

"You look good to me, Jim. How much do you want?" Adolphus asked.

"I think $100,000 will be plenty," answered Campbell.

"That's easy," said the brewer, sitting down to write out the check.

A committee of five well-known society women once came to Adolphus seeking a subscription to establish a maternity hospital. He donated $5,000 without hesitation. The women were surprised, since they hadn't expected that much. One of the ladies, who knew him better then the others, kissed him. The other four quickly did the same. "Ladies, one thousand dollars per kiss is a little high," Adolphus said, "but I assure you I felt I have had my money's worth."

John Peckington, another Busch acquaintance, recalled sitting in Adolphus's office as he went through a large stack of mail. Tearing open one envelope with a foreign stamp, he examined the contents and handed it to Peckington. "Here, Pecky," he said, "wipe your nose with the highest priced handkerchief on earth."

It was a Bank of England note worth $50,000. "He had received it," Peckington said later, "from a customer in Australia and I wiped my nose with it."

When Adolphus became interested in Rudolph Diesel's revolutionary new engine, he arranged a meeting with the young inventor in the resort community of Baden-Baden. Diesel, whose popularity in Europe was immense, was accustomed to being wined and dined, but he was not prepared for the meeting with the American beer king. He called it "grossartig," or magnificent.

Adolphus and an entourage of about fifty family members, friends and retainers had taken over an entire floor of the best hotel in the city. Adolphus asked Diesel what he wanted for the rights to assemble the engine in America. The inventor replied one million deutsch marks, about $238,000. Without a word, Adolphus wrote out a check as if he was dispensing pocket change to a bellman.

If the Prince was willing to spend huge sums of money on his varied business ventures, he spent even more on his large family—and not always with a smile on his face.

10

Princes and Princesses

The fight was brief and ugly.

Two men fell heavily on the sawdust-covered floor of Faust's barroom. The man on the bottom was bleeding. The other, slightly larger and heavier, brushed himself off and quickly departed, leaving his opponent lying there unconscious. Several of those entering Faust's the night of November 7, 1895, got a good look at the man as he hurried out. He was one of St. Louis's best-known citizens—August Anheuser Busch, the strapping son of Prince Adolphus and the heir to a brewing fortune.

The "Fight at Faust's," as the newspapers described the incident, wouldn't be the last time the Busch family suffered embarrassing headlines. Troubling—and sometimes tragic—family events intruded on Adolphus Busch's life just as he reached the pinnacle of power and wealth. First, there was the sudden death of Edward, his oldest son, who had died at fifteen. Another son, Carl, was crippled and deaf from birth. The suspected reason was a prenatal injury caused when Lilly fell down a flight of stairs. Carl required constant medical attention and lived in a special house at Number Three Busch Place.

Among Adolphus's three surviving sons—August, Adolphus and Peter—there appeared to be plenty of princes waiting in line to succeed the beer king. But August A. was a reluctant prince. He had no interest, at least at first, in running the brewery. He attended the Lyon Public School, a building later bought by the brewery during one of its expansions, and went to the Morgan Park Military Institute in Chicago and the Kemper Military Academy in Boonville, Missouri.

August A. astounded his father with the surprise announcement that he wanted to be a cowboy. Adolphus was angry at first but was also willing to indulge the boy's whims. In 1884, when August A. was nineteen years old, he bought a Western

outfit, including an expensive .44-caliber six-shooter with
ivory grips, and, like other millionaire tenderfeet, headed
West. He traveled with his cousin, George K. Busch, the son of
Adolphus's brother John. Their adventure lasted six months,
and years later August A. always referred to it as one of the
high points of his life. When his son returned to St. Louis,
Adolphus wasted little time getting the boy down to business,
sending him to Europe to learn the brewer's art.

Back in St. Louis, August A. started as a brewer's apprentice
and then became a scale clerk. After three years at the brewery,
Adolphus put him in charge, in a very limited way, during his
prolonged absences. The elder Busch kept a tight rein over his
son, as if doubting his competency; he routinely sent him detailed instructions, often running twenty pages long, on what
to do and what not to do.

August A. married twenty-two-year-old Alice Ziesemann on
May 8, 1890. A son was born to them a year later—Adolphus
Busch III. A daughter, Marie, followed, and by the fall of 1895,
the couple were expecting their third child. Two months before
his thirtieth birthday in that same year, August A. was involved in his famous brawl at Faust's, the first of several such
encounters in the family. The Busches proved extremely willing to put up their dukes. August A. merely set the tone.

That evening at Faust's, August A. was seated at the table
where his father usually held court surrounded by cronies
when Samuel Levy and M.J. Schwald, two typewriter salesmen, asked to join them. The trouble started later as Levy and
Schwald prepared to leave. It was Levy's turn to buy, but as a
wink went around the table, instead of ordering another round
of 10 cent beer, someone suggested cigars. The waiter was told
to bring the best Havanas, which cost a dollar each. When
Levy objected, August A. tossed out a $10 bill, and called him
"a cheap screw."

A fight erupted. The witnesses agreed that August A. struck
Levy "a fearful blow in the face, and he went down as though
he had been struck with a club." August A. left Faust's hurriedly and Levy was carried unconscious to the Planter's Hotel
where a doctor bandaged his head.

The next morning, Levy filed a $10,000 lawsuit against
Busch and a friend, accusing the pair of an unprovoked assault
and serious bodily harm. Charles Nagel, Adolphus's lawyer,
represented August A. The first of several St. Louis attorneys
who, over the years, would be hired to get Busches out of sim-

ilar scrapes, he managed to have the lawsuit dropped or settled.

August A. later had a serious rival in his brother, Adolphus Jr., who was positioned to challenge him for control of the brewery. Nicknamed Bulfy, he was two years younger than August A. and appeared to have many of the attributes of his namesake. If Adolphus had a favorite son, some believed it was Bulfy. Adolphus took pains to see that the boy was privately tutored and then educated at the gymnasium of Frankfurt am Main, not far from the Busch homestead in Kastel.

Adolphus Jr. rose through the brewery ranks as rapidly as August A. He was named a director in the corporation at age twenty-one in 1889, the same year as his older brother. By 1897 he was a vice president and when both his father and August A. were traveling, Adolphus Jr. was a member of a select five-man committee that ran the day-to-day operations of the brewery.

But like his oldest brother, his life was cut short. After a four-day illness he died on April 11, 1898. An autopsy revealed he had a perforated appendix, the same medical problem that had probably killed his brother. No religious services were held. He was buried at Bellefontaine Cemetery, and the funeral was described as "the most impressive seen in St. Louis in years. Nearly 500 vehicles were in line and 5,000 persons witnessed the last scenes at the grave."

With Adolphus Jr.'s death, August A. was now heir apparent. Peter, his fun-loving younger brother, was clearly the black sheep of the family. Several months before Adolphus Jr.'s death, Peter had left for the Klondike. If it wasn't banishment, the trip was certainly meant as a last chance to make good.

Peter, unmarried and considered dashing, was twenty-six when his brother died. A free-spending playboy, he showed no interest in the brewing business. A large man with blond hair, he preferred the sportsman's life, fine clothes and baseball. When he was in St. Louis, he seldom missed a game and could recite the batting averages of the better players.

Adolphus had a hard time finding a place for Peter. The boy did not seem ready or capable of applying himself to business, and his indulgent father assigned him to the field agencies or branches, where Peter could be well provided for without doing too much damage. In later generations, the same pattern would hold true. Troublemaking children wound up with lucrative beer distributorships rather than a place in the corporate boardroom.

After stints in New York and Chicago, Peter went to California, living on an ample allowance from his father. Recounting his activities there, a St. Louis newspaper reported: "During a year or more spent on the Pacific Coast, he became famous as the greatest spender on the coast; one of the San Francisco papers devoting a page of its Sunday issue to a detailed account of his entertainments, which were almost royal." Peter also traveled through South America and Africa to see how Anheuser-Busch products were doing there. He finished the long trip with very little to show for it.

Adolphus's patience with his errant son sometimes wore so thin that he threatened to disown him. In a letter to August A., the elder Busch warned: "The boy cannot do as he pleases; he must know once and for all time that we are not to be played with, and that he must either become a useful member of society, or go into obscurity, never to be heard of again. He has so far failed to write one word to his mother, or to express a word of regret at the death of our dear Bulfy, which would prove that he is entirely devoid of all feeling."

Then suddenly Peter also died, the cause of his death unexplained. One of Adolphus's letters referred to "an accident," and another talked about "wounds" that Peter had sustained while working in Chicago.

One descendant, Lotsie Busch Giersch, wrote in a family history that Peter died after a girlfriend punctured his appendix with a hatpin. Beyond that intriguing, brief statement, no other details were offered. Peter was operated on at St. Luke's Hospital and died six days later on May 21, 1905. The death certificate listed the cause as "appendicitis, nephritis, and endocarditis."

Adolphus learned of Peter's death in Europe. He cabled back: "We are heartbroken."

Over seventy years later, another Peter Busch would be involved in an incident with similarly tragic consequences.

If death carried off so many of his sons at an early age, Adolphus was much more fortunate with his daughters. He gave them lavish weddings and great fortunes—and all outlived him. The first marriage, in 1880, however, was not a happy one. Nellie, Adolphus's oldest daughter, was seventeen years old when she married Harry Weber, a musician. After two children were born, the couple divorced and Adolphus eventually built a home for Nellie and her children at Busch Place.

When nineteen-year-old Edmee took a husband, the marriage stayed in the family. In what was to be a recurrent family practice, Edmee married her cousin, Hugo Reisinger, on February 10, 1890. Reisinger was the son of Franz and Apollonia Reisinger of Wiesbaden. Apollonia was Adolphus's sister. Hugo was in the import-export business, and after his marriage to Edmee, he sometimes bought hops and rice for his father-in-law.

In June of that same year, Nellie married for a second time. While living at Busch Place she met Arthur J. Magnus, vice president of a Chicago brewing supply company. He had been married twice before, was once widowed and once divorced. The couple moved to Chicago where they apparently lived beyond their means. Nellie sometimes overspent her allowance from Adolphus, who wrote to August A. about it. "I have written Mr. Muehlemann [brewery treasurer Eugene Muehlemann] about the two thousand dollars drawn by Sister Nellie, but wish it now understood, once and for all, that no more payments shall be made her, regardless of consequences. I am determined not to foster her nonsense in making bills; she must obey my wishes, and if she does not do this, then let her suffer. Her monthly allowance of $250 will of course, now be withheld until the amount of two thousand is made good."

Arthur Magnus committed suicide on January 23, 1906, while standing in front of a mirror in the upstairs bedroom of his spacious Chicago home. He shot himself in the heart as Nellie and dinner guests waited downstairs and his daughter, Aimee, practiced the piano in an adjoining room. The music muffled the gunshot, and the body wasn't discovered until a maid went up to tell him that his guests were waiting.

August A. speculated that perhaps heart disease had driven Magnus to take his life. "Mr. Magnus has been almost constantly under treatment and has often suffered acutely. It is possible that he may have felt another attack coming on and have ended his life rather than endure it."

It was an ironic observation. Twenty-eight years later, an almost identical explanation would be given for his own death.

During one of the Busch family's many trips to Germany, another of Adolphus's daughters attracted the attention of Baron Paul von Gontard, a member of a powerful industrial family.

Gontard was active in the Karlsruhe Industrial Works, a munitions business in Berlin. His brother, Hans, was the military tutor to the kaiser's younger sons. Paul von Gontard was smitten by Clara Busch, a small, blond, blue-eyed woman of nineteen. They were married December 16, 1895, in the St. Louis Germania Club.

The marriage marked a merger between the Busches and German nobility. Clara became a baroness, and later was a lady in waiting to the Empress August Victoria. She was one of the leaders of society and fashion in Berlin. Her mansion was a popular rendezvous for the younger court set, including the crown prince and princess. Hans von Gontard, her brother-in-law, became aide-de-camp to Emperor Kaiser Wilhelm II and was at his side through much of the Great War. After the wedding, Hans sometimes visited Adolphus in Pasadena. The connection between the Busches and the German court seemed advantageous at first. But when the Great War broke out, and anti-German sentiment rose to a fever pitch, it almost spelled disaster for the company.

As with all Busch weddings, Clara's was a dazzling affair. But it paled in comparison with that of the last of Adolphus's daughters to be married in St. Louis. On March 20, 1897, Anna Louise, the one Adolphus called Tolie, married Edward Faust, Tony Faust's son. A police guard formed a cordon around the Church of the Messiah, but hundreds of spectators crowded the steps and sidewalks. Inside the church, a great canopy, white with lilies, had been erected, and the wedding procession was led by the five-year-old nephew of the bride, Adolphus Busch III, walking stiffly in a snow-white suit with a lily for a boutonniere. Lilly Busch, Adolphus's wife, looked like "Diamond Lilly." She wore on her left shoulder an immense butterfly of diamonds, with wings of fretted gold crusted with diamonds, rubies and emeralds. Several strings of pearls with diamond clasps graced her neck. She had still more diamonds in her hair.

Newspapers reported that the bride "wore a most exquisite wedding gown, the likes of which has never before been seen in St. Louis." The wedding cost the incredible sum of $100,000, and Adolphus gave his daughter a gift suitable for a beer baron —a mansion. Tony Faust provided a five-month honeymoon in Europe, and when the couple returned, Busch gave his new son-in-law a job.

Adolphus and Lilly's youngest child, a daughter named Wil-

helmina, was born on January 10, 1884. They called her Minnie and she would lead a colorful, bizarre and hugely
extravagant life. Her strange courtship and marriage set the
tone for the rest of her days.

Wilhelmina had been educated at the Mary Institute in St.
Louis, like several of the Busch girls. Not particularly beautiful, she was a large woman, heavyset with a plain moon face,
dark brown hair and large eyes. But several young men in St.
Louis were interested, including a lawyer named Eugene An-
gert, the suitor Adolphus favored.

But across the Atlantic, a rival appeared, a man as unforgettable as Wilhelmina herself. August Eduard Scharrer cut a
dashing figure in turn-of-the century Europe, especially when
he wore his brown German army uniform with a broad hat
turned up at the side. He stood five feet nine inches tall and
had the broad shoulders and muscular arms of an athlete.
Sometimes, for effect, he wore a pistol. A pencil-thin brown
mustache added to his military bearing and made him look
older than his twenty-three years.

His father was a hops dealer from Stuttgart, and his son,
something of a playboy, was more interested in horses and
sports than in school or business. Young Scharrer was known
as an enthusiastic "automobilist" who had toured Germany
and France in his big Mercedes. When he sought Wilhelmina's
hand in marriage, the newspapers pointed out he was a mar-
tinet, who, the newspapers reported had been "reared in surroundings reeking with the spirit of war. He belongs to a
people in which the plumed knights hold high place. To him,
the methods of the warrior appeal, whether applied to affairs
of government or love."

That was one of the explanations given later for the bold
way in which Scharrer sought Wilhelmina's hand. He had met
her several times on her trips to Germany and often escorted
her to social functions. In 1902, when he and his father visited
St. Louis, he gave her a lion cub as a birthday gift. That should
have been the tip-off.

Their relationship grew stronger during another summer
trip in 1905. Scharrer was invited to Villa Lilly and that September the families took a trip to Paris in a caravan of four
motor cars. Scharrer proposed marriage, but Wilhelmina put
him off. Scharrer was not happy.

The Busches returned to St. Louis, where Scharrer joined
them in late December for Christmas, the biggest annual event

in the Busch family. Two days after Christmas, he borrowed Prince Henry, one of Adolphus's favorite horses, and took Wilhelmina for a carriage ride. When they crossed the Eads Bridge into Illinois, she suspected trouble.

In a very calm voice Scharrer explained that he was taking her to Belleville, fourteen miles away, and that they were going to be married before nightfall. He said that if she refused, he would kill himself in her presence. To emphasize the point, he pulled a huge revolver from his pocket.

"I do not believe he intended to do it," Adolphus said later. "But I think he believed that my daughter was hesitating and that a bluff of that kind would frighten her into making up her mind."

For the next hour and a half, Wilhelmina, frightened and bundled in a lap robe that bore the Anheuser-Busch insignia, tried to reason with Scharrer. They went to the Belleville House, the city's principal hotel, and Scharrer registered them as Mr. and Mrs. Scharrer. There he allowed her to telephone her parents, but as soon as Adolphus learned what was going on, he called his glass factory in Belleville. Within minutes its manager was on his way to the hotel where he told Scharrer that both he and Wilhelmina had to return to St. Louis at once.

Adolphus wasted little time in getting his daughter out of town. The family traveled to Pasadena, but undeterred, Scharrer followed and with Prussian directness forced the issue. On February 22, 1906, the county offices were closed in Los Angeles in honor of Washington's birthday. But the resolute German got a county clerk to issue a marriage license. He listed his age as twenty-eight and Wilhelmina's as twenty-two. They were married in a tiny chapel in Pasadena Hills on March 3. It was a small affair by Busch standards with only 100 guests.

Adolphus must have been furious at the way the impulsive, headstrong Scharrer had aggressively pursued his daughter. Still, he let the couple use his private railroad car for a two-week honeymoon tour of the West. Like many fathers, he learned to live with the situation but he never forgave his son-in-law. In his will, Scharrer didn't get a dime.

Eduard Scharrer took his bride to Germany, and like the Gontards, the family grew embarrassingly close to the men who were pushing their country to war.

11

"The Child We Love Most"

Lilly Busch, the matriarch of the family, lived quietly within the giant shadow cast by Adolphus. For all her servants and wealth, she remained essentially a hausfrau who prepared soup for the Prince. To those who knew her, she was lovable and magnetic, but totally uninformed about her husband's business activities.

She was far from uninformed about expensive jewelry. Lilly sparkled when she walked. Her jewels, reported one observer, "are very handsome, and some of them extremely valuable. There is a very fine ruby, set in a long marquise ring, for which it would be most difficult to find a match in this country. A necklace of the finest Oriental pearls, composed of four rows of the softly gleaming gems, are closed by a flashing aiguillette of diamonds." Like her husband, this "beautiful, accomplished and elegant woman" wasn't afraid to promote the product. "Sometimes Mrs. Busch wears on the right side of her bodice a fac-simile of the Anheuser-Busch label, composed of the eagle and the A wrought in fine enameled gold, and blazing with diamonds and other jewels."

Adolphus and his wife were considered a devoted couple. However, Adolphus had a wandering eye and Lilly was extremely jealous. One woman in particular, Alvina Clementine Berg, was a source of friction. A trusted employee, Berg first entered the brewery as a stenographer and later became Adolphus's personal stenographer and a secretary for twenty-five years. For eight of those years, she accompanied him on all his trips and looked after many of his personal affairs.

Lilly's jealousy of Berg was well known outside the company. Many years later, a New York hops dealer wrote that Lilly Busch was very jealous of Alvina Berg, even though they were all over seventy years old at the time. He thought it was pretty ridiculous. The source of the jealousy may have been a love telegram that, according to one Busch family descendant, was sent by Berg to Adolphus. The missive was intercepted by Lilly.

Adolphus had one passion in his old age—automobiles. They were often mentioned in the long-winded, detailed epistles that he sent to his son August A. from Pasadena, Villa Lilly and Cooperstown. His lengthy letters, thoughtful blends of sober business advice and fatherly affection, expounded upon politics, childhood illnesses, business philosophy, machinery, labor unions, brewing competition, railroad freight rates, marketing techniques, product improvement and almost anything else. If the elder Busch lacked confidence in August A., his many letters amounted to a how-to-succeed-in-business lecture series.

Above all, Adolphus cautioned his son not to become distracted by other business deals at the expense of the brewery. During Anheuser-Busch's attempt to secure a railroad franchise he wrote: "Our whole welfare and happiness does not depend on that Second Street Railroad, it depends solely and only upon the success of our brewery; its earnings are sufficient to make us happy for all time to come, and give us sufficient to live well, so nurse the child which we love most and which is nearest and dearest to us." In a telling afterthought, he added, "Of course, if we can get the franchise, we will make all we can out of it; we are great at taking."

He exhorted August A. to pay attention to quality. Only beer aged for two and one half months was acceptable. Three and one half months was even better. Bad beer was an invitation to suicide. "If we should permit such a thing, the entire competition of the country, and you know that the brewers of the United States are a unit against us, would fall upon our trade and do us the greatest possible harm." His comments bubbled with enthusiasm when he received reports about the unbounded growth of Anheuser-Busch. "I can plainly see the time coming when we need fear no competition."

This most extravagant of men also saw fit to caution his son about extravagance. "We must beware that we do not indulge too much in luxuries . . . which always marks the beginning of the downfall. This danger we must ward off by the good and careful training of our children and by our own simplicity. Instead of using our fortunes only for personal comfort and display, we should become more philanthropic to those in less affluent circumstances."

The incessant letters, the constant bombardment of directions and questions, eventually had an effect on August A. The man who once floored a typewriter salesman in a bar seemed to grow under his father's tutelage. Like a good coach, Adolphus did not hold back on the compliments: "You are a chip off the old block and I am proud of you!" He went on to say, "The present captain of the great ship will live to see his superior take his place, and that is what we all look forward to. You will help to perpetuate the name of Busch and to place it in the front ranks of our nation."

August A. had proven himself. He also gave Adolphus something else he greatly desired—two grandsons to join the business. In addition to Adolphus III, there was August A. "Gussie" Busch, Jr., who was born March 28, 1899. Prince Adolphus took a particular liking to this mischievous grandson, who was to one day rival his own reputation. "I would give five hundred dollars this minute," he wrote from Pasadena to his son, "to have little Gussie here to run about with him and steal chickens, oranges and all kinds of fruit from the other fellows."

Adolphus had a proven successor. He had heirs. He had defeated the competition. He was one of the richest men of his day. He had reason to be content. But a storm was coming. The worst threat he had ever faced—an army of zealots dedicated to eliminating everything he had ever worked for. Just as he was ready to relax and enjoy his remaining years, Adolphus was forced to wage the fight of his life.

12

Fighting "Fanatics"

The movement that threatened Adolphus's brewing empire and elevated his blood pressure had been percolating for more than 100 years, but it had boiled over on a summer's evening in 1890 when a tall, sturdy woman in a black dress stormed into a saloon in Medicine Lodge, Kansas. For several days she had been reading the Bible outside the saloon, praying that it would close. Kansas was a dry state, but the law was not being enforced. The woman believed she had good reason for her vigil. Her drunkard husband had died shortly after their marriage.

When prayers didn't work, she turned to violence and found it to be a more effective instrument. Nearly six feet tall, she struck a formidable figure—especially wielding an axe. Men ran and frantically stumbled out of the saloon as she smashed the place to pieces. The sharp blows struck by Carry A. Nation reverberated far beyond that small Kansas town.

By the dawn of the twentieth century, the "movement" had gained a sure footing in the United States. A whiff of reform was in the air. There was greater government regulation everywhere. Congress passed laws to protect the public from harmful foods and drugs and to conserve the nation's forests and other natural resources. The monopolies established by the Morgans, Stillmans and Rockefellers—men with whom Busch sailed back and forth to Europe—were being broken up. It was within this climate that prohibition fever began to spread.

It was not a new movement. The American landscape had felt its impact for more than fifty years by the time Adolphus reached the zenith of his power at the turn of the century. Prohibition laws were already in effect in thirteen states by the 1850s. The dry forces had their roots in religious fundamentalism and received a strong boost from the Women's Christian Temperance Union, founded in Ohio in 1874, and which was responsible to a great extent for the wave of temperance legislation passed during the 1880s. But these were still minor problems to Busch. It was true that in many states, counties had the local option to vote themselves dry. And many did in West Virginia, Maryland, Illinois, Georgia and Mississippi— even in his own state of Missouri. But neighboring counties could still supply the product—and did.

In fact, states like Kansas, Iowa, Rhode Island and North and South Dakota went totally dry. But these were rural states and the big sales were in the wet big cities. It was in the sparsely populated countryside where the antiliquor feeling ran strongest and, not coincidentally, where the Methodists and Baptists were the most powerful. Adolphus was not a religious man, but he had his own thoughts about religion and hypocrisy, and was especially critical of the way religion was practiced in America. In his savage attacks, he almost sounded like Mark Twain, a man whom he admired. To his friend,

Charles Nagel, he observed, "A great many people are religious or select a certain creed not because they believe in it but because it pays them better. . . . Many Americans put up their religious flag to promote their business and social standing. Religion proper is a secondary matter." He went on to say, "Another bad trait in the American's character is hypocrisy. He recommends and speaks for prohibition and downs the manufacturers of all liquor while, at the same time he drinks like a fish and becomes as drunk as a fool."

The temperance movement gained new vigor after 1900. Beer and whiskey sales had grown rapidly among the large numbers of immigrants from Ireland and Germany. In this regard, there was also an antiforeign ring to the cries for prohibition. And as women gained the vote for the first time, the drys gained even more influence.

The Committee of Fifty, formed in 1893 to study the "liquor problem," was at the forefront of the battle. The committee traced the nation's poverty, crime, mental disease and family decay to alcohol consumption. The drys believed that national prohibition was needed since temperance as a product of education and self-control had not worked. For that matter, state-enforced prohibition and county option laws had also failed because neighboring states and counties that were wet supplied booze for the dry areas. The ban on Sunday sales was generally ignored as well.

Busch was more than simply aware of these abuses, he was responsible for some of them. Otto Koehler, the president of the San Antonio Brewing Association in which he owned an interest, informed Adolphus in 1904 that his agent had established "clubs" in Brownwood, Texas, and that he was supplying them because the area was technically dry. They weren't in it for the profit, which was small, Koehler said, but as a matter of principle. He wanted to "show the Prohibitionists that Prohibition does not prohibit!" In other words, by breaking the law "in a nice conservative manner . . . we can soon convince the people that Prohibition is not what is claimed for it and when the time rolls around for another election, that Brownwood will be voted 'wet' again."

Congressmen and even President William McKinley had started to listen to the prohibitionists and there was talk in Washington about a nationwide law prohibiting alcohol sales. All this exasperated Adolphus, who personally took his argument to the president, a Methodist who as early as 1867 had been identified with "total abstinence."

Congressman Richard Bartholdt of St. Louis, a Republican and Busch's close friend, arranged the meeting. Adolphus had long recognized the importance of having well-connected political friends. One of the guests at his wedding in 1861 had been George Graham Vest, later a United States senator from Missouri. Busch kept in close contact with Vest about issues concerning his business. He entertained Vest at Villa Lilly and offered him the use of his railroad car, the *Adolphus*. The Busches always numbered influential politicians among their friends.

Busch told McKinley he furnished only the best beer and had helped turn a nation of hard drinkers into a "sober and temperate people." Warming up to his subject he said, "The brewers have accomplished more for the true cause of temperance than all the apostles of prohibition." Shifting gears, he claimed that brewers ungrudgingly paid their taxes, a comment that probably made McKinley smile. The president knew the U.S. Brewing Association was constantly lobbying Congress to cut the $2-per-barrel tax on beer.

Concluding his interview, Adolphus told McKinley that 85 to 90 percent of the population demanded beer. "The demand I speak of is prompted by human nature itself, and, believe me, if fanatics should ever succeed in preventing its being satisfied legitimately, the people will resort to narcotics or stimulants so injurious as eventually to undermine the health of the nation."

Beer, the drink Busch often preceded with the word "light," was, perhaps, to be preferred over whiskey, but it was caught up in the antisaloon hysteria. The brewers were targeted because they were so closely identified with saloons, which Carry Nation and her followers regarded as dens of iniquity worthy of hatchet attacks. It didn't help matters that the saloon was so often the source of local scandal.

By the early 1900s, brewers like Adolphus owned or controlled three-fourths of these watering holes. Typical of the relationship was a Chicago saloon keeper who received $1,400 in fixtures from Anheuser-Busch and was obligated to repay in eighteen monthly installments of $75 and agree to dispense only Anheuser-Busch brands.

Because breweries financed so many saloons, their managers did what they could to attract customers. Abuses flourished. In Chicago, a vice report showed that some of the worst dives in the city were owned by breweries. The California, a barroom connected with a house of prostitution, had bonds signed by brewery agents. And when a prominent Chicago gambler named Pony Moore declared bankruptcy, his largest creditor was none other than Anheuser-Busch. One writer singled out Adolphus: "This king brewer was manipulator of legislatures and promoter of villainous dives." In 1902, brewers in St. Louis were caught up in corruption prosecutions, accused of bribing public officials. A representative of the Anti-wineroom and Law Enforcement League said the brewers' political influence had filtered from banks through both political parties and into the police department. The representative said, "The brewers control St. Louis. Not in theory but in fact. They own us body and soul."

If any single brewer energized the prohibition movement it was Adolphus Busch. He had the most visible profile, and his kingly bearing and pro-German sentiments alienated many Americans. Closely identified with his company, he became the prime target of the prohibitionists. Their rising power first manifested itself on a national scale when they outmaneuvered the brewers in Congress, which passed a bill outlawing the military canteen, where alcohol was served to servicemen. Adolphus promptly blamed the reversal on "some fanatical and misinformed women."

Between 1900 and 1913, the Prince had less time for his favorite recreations. He had turned the day-to-day operations of the brewery over to his son, but because of the prohibition fight, he could not retire to leisure. During the first rounds of this battle, he was still strong. After losing eleven pounds while taking the elixirs at Marienbad in the summer of 1898, he wrote to August A. that he felt "like a morning star and a fighting cock."

The cock summoned all his strength to oppose prohibition almost singlehandedly. Of all the brewers he had the most political muscle and money and the most experience in using them. His skills as a salesman—his ability to persuade and shape opinion—were his weapons. They had always been his greatest gifts. Leading the industry as he did, he also had the most to lose. A long string of his descendants depended on beer for their livelihood. Adolphus was not about to permit the great industry he had built and planned to turn over to his children to be legislated out of existence.

The formula Adolphus used for fighting prohibition was simple but expensive: Influence politicians and buy good will. "We ought to extract a promise from every representative and senator whom we support that they in turn will watch over our interests," he said. "It is my aim to win the American people over to our side, to make them all lovers of beer and teach them to have respect for the brewing industry and the brewer. It may cost us a million dollars and even more, but what of it if thereby we elevate our position? I stand ready to sacrifice my annual profits for years to come if I can gain my point and make people look upon beer in the right light."

Adolphus carefully courted those who followed McKinley to the White House—Theodore Roosevelt and William H. Taft. A strong Republican, he was a close friend of both. The Rough Rider and the portly Taft were frequent visitors to Number One Busch Place and to the Ivy Wall in Pasadena. Adolphus had helped elect both men. "I do not know any one who has contributed more to the result in Missouri than you have," a thankful Roosevelt wrote to Busch after the 1904 election.

In fact, Busch's contributions to Roosevelt's campaign prompted an investigation. A week before the election, a group of wealthy Republicans gathered at his St. Louis mansion where Missouri Republican Chairman Thomas K. Niedringhaus told them that with another $25,000 he could carry the state for Roosevelt. Adolphus put up $10,000 of his own money in addition to $2,500 supplied by the Anheuser-Busch Brewing Association, with other brewers and Niedringhaus himself providing the balance.

When Niedringhaus filed a campaign finance affidavit after the election, the names of Busch and the brewery and others were not disclosed as contributors. The entire amount was listed under Niedringhaus's name. Committees of both the state House and Senate investigated and questioned those involved, including Busch, to determine whether a state law prohibiting corporate contributions had been violated. But Attorney General Herbert S. Hadley, a Republican, concluded that the $2,500, although contributed by the Anheuser-Busch Brewing Association, was charged to Busch and was therefore "a personal contribution from him and not from the association."

If political contributions worked wonders so did charitable donations. Adolphus viewed them as a form of advertising as well as acts of mercy. There were many small but well-publicized gifts of $1,000 to $5,000 for orphanages, hospitals and relief societies. Every Groundhog Day the papers dutifully reported that Adolphus had given $5,000 to the House of the Good Shepherd.

With the encouragement of his son-in-law Hugo Reisinger, he donated $230,000 to fund the Germanic Museum on the Harvard University campus. At about the same time, perhaps not coincidentally, several professors at Harvard made public speeches about the benefits of drinking light beers and wine. The Germanic Museum was a favorite of the increasingly militant kaiser, who also donated to the institution, which was designed to improve German-American understanding.

When Taft was secretary of war in charge of relief for victims of the San Francisco earthquake, Adolphus donated $50,000 of his own money and another $50,000 from the brewery. He was also a major contributor to Washington University's medical school in St. Louis, which was launched with $850,000 donated in the name of Robert Barnes, the banker whose crucial loan had helped launch Busch's brewery expansion many years earlier.

Adolphus also sought to mold public opinion through the newspapers with the aid of a man named Louis N. Hammerling, who in 1904 had been in charge of advertising for the Republican National Committee. Nagel, Busch's lawyer, had brought Hammerling to Adolphus's attention. Remembering their first meeting, Hammerling said later, "I never saw him before in my life, but I came, naturally, knowing what he represents. He had a good many people standing around, just as if he would be a king."

"Are you Hammerling?" Adolphus had asked.

"Yes."

"Charles Nagel told me that you can do us some service in the fight against prohibition."

"I am the boy if you have any advertising," Hammerling had replied.

Adolphus gave Percy Andreae of Chicago, the manager of the Brewers' Association Organization Committee, his authority to do business with Hammerling and guaranteed the bills.

Hammerling became the president of the American Association of Foreign Language Newspapers, which bought space in newspapers with a combined circulation of 7 million. In turn, the papers were sent stories supporting "personal liberty" on the drink question. Copies of the papers were sent to ministers, priests and rabbis. The association also had telegrams opposing prohibition sent to congressmen.

Phoebe Couzins was another of Adolphus's "press agents." She got articles favorable to brewing interests published in monthly magazines and even commanded a spot in dispatches sent by the Associated Press. At the same time, Adolphus asked the U.S. Brewing Association to pay her $250 a month for her work. "She is now engaged in a noble fight and she is certainly the most courageous woman in the country, the only one who will swing the tomahawk over the heads of the short haired fanatical women," Adolphus wrote to Henry Nicolaus, president of the St. Louis Brewing Association, in 1905. "If the New York office agrees to send her a monthly remuneration, this must be done in a private way, so no one has any knowledge of it . . . for if it ever should become known that she is in the pay of the brewers, her articles would be rejected and all her work would be in vain."

The year after Adolphus hired Phoebe Couzins, his personal life was rocked by the death of his son Peter. And while staying at Villa Lilly—on September 28, 1906—he lost the man who had been like a brother to him. Tony Faust died at seventy-one of cirrhosis of the liver at his home in nearby Wiesbaden. Shattered by the loss, Adolphus ordered the casket taken to Villa Lilly. There he lined the box which held the steel sarcophagus with leaves and branches from forests at Waldfriede where the two men had spent many happy times together.

Adolphus had significantly expanded his German properties. When his older brother Anton died in 1904, he gained control of the family estate at Kastel. Adolphus, according to Anton's granddaughter, Carola Wagner Wallenstein, talked Anton's widow into signing an agreement that gave him control of the Schützenhof and the surrounding lands until his brother's children were old enough to take care of it. But Anton's children and grandchildren never received their inheritance.

After World War I and again following World War II, when their relatives in Germany pleaded for help from the brewery, the Busches of St. Louis replied that they could not remember having any family connections in Germany, according to Carola Wagner Wallenstein. As a result, Adolphus is not remembered fondly among the Busch descendants in Kastel. (The Schützenhof had been bombed during World War II. A box with a few gold coins discovered under the floor in the ruins was turned over to a museum. A bronze bust of Adolphus was also unearthed. It now stands in Carola Wagner Wallenstein's garden.)

Adolphus had his own brush with death in December 1907, an episode that affected his health for the rest of his life. In St. Louis on Christmas eve, as he waited for the arrival of a train carrying his daughter Wilhelmina, he caught a cold that developed into pneumonia. The attack was severe and the inflammation in the lungs passed slowly and brought about dropsy. Lilly Bush later said that her husband was an invalid from then on. He constantly required a physician's attention, but liked to point out that he had outlived two of the three doctors who had treated him for the pneumonia.

In the years that followed, Adolphus searched the world for doctors who could help him. When a German doctor audaciously told him that beer was ruining his health, he shot back that he drank only champagne. To Nagel, Busch confided he was looking for "the right professor who is able to return me to my full health," and that whoever did so "I will make king." But instead of a cure, all Adolphus found was more trouble from the prohibitionists.

Between 1900 and 1910, Adolphus and his fellow brewers waged war in dry elections across the country. The stakes were high. In 1907, Anheuser-Busch paid dividends of $5,000 per share. Without those interfering prohibitionists who were driving the Prince crazy, the return would have been even greater. In Oklahoma alone the halt to the liquor traffic had cost him $1 million.

More than anything, Adolphus wanted a national figure to speak out against prohibition. He turned to the capital, hoping there was someone brave enough to make a public pronouncement and "save the nation from tyranny, oppression and fanaticism." If, in the process, Adolphus saved money, that was all right, too. But the brewer was always disappointed. Roosevelt, the tough-talking president whom he had supported, let him down by carefully avoiding taking a stand on the issue.

The campaign of 1908 to elect Roosevelt's successor was considered crucial. The brewers backed William H. Taft, whom Roosevelt had also endorsed as his successor. Among the many organizations the brewers had secretly formed to elect their candidate was the National Association of Commerce and Labor. It was financed by contributions from the U.S. Brewers'

Association to oppose Prohibition, with Adolphus as a major backer. On June 13, as Republicans gathered in Chicago for their convention, Adolphus sent a cable from Carlsbad to Jacob Schmidlapp, a rich banker from Cincinnati who was Taft's campaign financier, advising him that he had a room reserved for him in Carlsbad. He added: "Pray that our illustrious friend Taft will be nominated on the first ballot and as our president relieve the nation from its fanatical craze with which it's so badly infected."

Schmidlapp mailed the telegram to Taft the same day, writing that Busch had "prohibition legislation on his mind." Three days later, Taft was nominated on the first ballot. After the convention, one leader of the National Association of Commerce and Labor wrote to the head of a Busch-owned brewery in San Antonio: "The story of our activity at the National Republican Convention . . . marks a new epoch in the political history of the United States. I wish you could have viewed with me the power of our association as demonstrated in Chicago."

Schmidlapp dutifully sailed for Carlsbad on July 2 to meet with Busch, who had both the money and the man to help Taft get in the White House. "I want to assure you," Adolphus wrote, "that Charles Nagel of St. Louis will move heaven and earth to secure the election of our mutual friend, William H. Taft. . . . Nothing will be left undone to achieve this and no money will be spared."

The brewers had to support Taft because his opponent, the old Democratic warhorse William Jennings Bryan, was comparing saloons to slaughterhouses. "And why is a saloon a nuisance?" the fiery campaigner would ask. "Because its evil influences can not be confined to the block in which it is located or to the city which licenses it to do business. And who has a right to complain of a saloon? Everyone who lives within the radius of its evil influence—everyone who suffers from the use of the liquor which it sells." The saloons, Bryan said, were linked with gambling, prostitution, crime and political corruption, not to mention social disease.

Among all the campaign matters Taft had to deal with, the prohibition question was more of an annoyance than an issue. On September 17, Carry Nation called on him with a list of questions. He refused to respond and she left proclaiming that Taft was a foe of temperance. Actually he was a personally temperate man who took a drink only now and then. He accepted the cases of wine Adolphus had sent him, however, and wrote Busch a Fourth of July toast from a Canadian vacation in 1907 saying he had to use Scotch whiskey that contained "alcohol enough to make the ceremony binding." But to others, Taft confided that intoxicating drink "does not agree with me and I know that I am better off without it." And like Roosevelt, he believed in the local option.

Taft defeated Bryan in the general election. Adolphus was delighted and cabled the new president from Bad Schwalbach. "Didn't I tell you so? All Germany rejoices with me at your glorious victory and all are now in good cheer." Taft's victory was also Busch's, since, as one of the rewards for his hard work in the campaign, Charles Nagel was given a cabinet post. Busch's lawyer, the man he called his "conscience," was appointed secretary of commerce and labor. With the appointment, Adolphus had a clear conduit for influencing the White House.

And he certainly attempted to influence. After Taft took office, there were letters from St. Louis, cables from Carlsbad and Villa Lilly and telegrams from Pasadena. Adolphus peppered the president with suggestions about appointments and recommendations on public policy. The inquiries touched on everything from the personal to the obscure. Adolphus asked Nagel to arrange a good military assignment for Carl Conrad's son and to help another friend's son win an appointment to the Supreme Court of the Philippines. He often pestered the White House for restoration of the military canteen. "You cannot imagine what it would mean to us if Congress did the right and fair thing by giving its soldiers a happy home and letting them partake in light happy drinks."

Nagel's prickly sense of right and wrong was evident when, shortly after assuming federal office, he sent Adolphus a frank fifteen-page analysis of the temperance issue. "The brewer," he bluntly told his patron, "has resisted rational control of the retail liquor business: that is, the saloon. In that respect, his position has in my judgment been unwise, short sighted and often reprehensible. He has kept his eye upon the quantity of the output, and has refused to see that in his business the safety of society is necessarily a primary condition."

Nagel also had the courage to warn Adolphus about his efforts to help a rich friend, Herman Sielcken, a coffee importer from New York City and Germany who was under federal investigation for monopolistic practices. Undeterred, Adolphus turned his attention to international relations, which in this case were also family relations. In October 1909, the same year he turned seventy, he sent Nagel a letter for the president, asking that his son-in-law Eduard Scharrer be appointed to the German Embassy in Washington. After his marriage to Adolphus's youngest daughter, Wilhelmina, the couple had returned to Stuttgart, where Scharrer made an unsuccessful attempt at being a businessman. Adolphus asked the president to petition Kaiser Wilhelm II to appoint Scharrer to Washington.

"Lieutenant Scharrer," he wrote, "is well acquainted with many of the most influential and prominent officers of the German army, who will certainly make every effort to aid his appointment. . . . I feel confident that the German Emperor will respond to your wishes. I also beg to mention that my name is well known to His Majesty. His Majesty highly appreciated my donation towards the building fund of the Germanic Museum at Harvard and prior to that he honored me by bestowing the Kronen Orden second class upon me." Scharrer never got the Washington appointment.

In addition to receiving other awards, Adolphus had also been decorated by the kaiser for the courtesies he extended his brother, Prince Henry of Prussia, during the St. Louis World's Fair of 1904. But to his frustration, even the kaiser was saying things that upset him. In what Adolphus would have considered treason, in a speech in 1910 the German ruler had exhorted his naval officers to join the Temperance League. It was a strange message since heavy drinking was considered a manly virtue in German military circles.

That same year, Adolphus was dealt another blow, one which made him angry, boiling mad. He felt betrayed. The president of the United States, his friend, William Taft—the man he had helped elect and thought he could count on for loyalty—had made a public statement supporting *total abstinence* from alcohol! How could he say such a thing? Busch had been sending him cases of wine for years. "I never thought a man like him could use those words 'total abstinence'!" he said in outrage.

It was true that Adolphus had wanted a public statement from someone of authority in Washington to counter the "fanatics" pushing prohibition. But not this kind of a statement. Moderation meant temperance, but abstinence was the buzz word for prohibition.

Adolphus glanced down again at the newspaper clippings in

his trembling hand. "Taft Preaches Temperance in 3000 Sunday Schools," read the headline. "Columbus, Ohio, Feb. 12—President Taft, in a letter dated December 29, 1910, and read in 3000 Sunday schools in the United States today sounded the keynote of a total abstainer's movement." Alcohol, Taft said, was the cause of poverty, degradation and crime. Those who abstained from liquor avoided a dangerous temptation. The president pointed out that Abraham Lincoln himself had taken the pledge.

Adolphus could not believe it.

Wintering in Pasadena, he took time out from his guests, including Hans von Gontard, aide-de-camp to the kaiser, to dictate a foaming letter of complaint to Nagel. "You will undoubtedly say when you read this that I am rather excited. I can forget and forgive, but I must mention that my heart was terribly hurt to learn that such a great and illustrious and learned commander whom I dearly love and admire . . . could step down to talk such nonsense to stupid Sunday school boys."

Adolphus went on to say that if Taft made the remark about Lincoln he was misinformed, because Busch was convinced Lincoln drank alcohol. He had seen—or so he liked to say—Lincoln and Stephen Douglas drinking whiskey together in St. Louis after their historic debates on the eve of the Civil War. "Let every man do as he pleases," Adolphus said. "No one on earth has the right to mix up with the personal freedom of another." He concluded by saying that anyone who tampered with that freedom belonged in hell. The average American politician, in his opinion, had "the privilege of being a coward and of concealing his honest convictions especially on questions of religion and prohibition." But he did not believe that privilege extended to the president.

As he dictated his letter, a familiar old thought entered Adolphus's mind, if only he weren't seventy-one and plagued by poor health aggravated by these infernal prohibitionists and their movement. "I often think about it," he mused. "I often . . . wish I was again forty years old and could rule this country with absolute despotism. How pure the air would be after my term was over."

13

The Original Party Animal

In the spring of 1911, Adolphus and Lilly celebrated their fiftieth wedding anniversary with a party so grand, gaudy and expensive that it would have made even the Astors and the Vanderbilts envious. "No golden wedding in the history of the world is believed to have been celebrated so elaborately," proclaimed *The New York World*.

At the brewery headquarters in St. Louis, in dozens of major cities where branches were located, and at the Busch mansion in Pasadena, where Adolphus and Lilly were residing, thousands gathered for the occasion. Thirteen thousand people assembled in the St. Louis Coliseum for free food and all the beer they could drink—40,000 bottles worth. As they danced to a fifty-piece band, photographs of Eberhard Anheuser, the Busches and their homes, the sunken gardens in Pasadena and the brewery were flashed on a large screen. His employees sent Adolphus a gold plate the size of a telegram engraved with anniversary wishes.

Out in Pasadena, the Busch family watched as Lilly, seated on a miniature throne, was crowned with a diadem of gold studded with diamonds and pearls. Adolphus had purchased the crown in Frankfurt for $200,000. The children gave their parents a set of twelve full-sized dinner plates made of solid gold and valued at $25,000. The grandchildren presented a solid-gold flower basket that cost $15,000 and a gold calendar embossed in rubies. Anheuser-Busch branch managers and executives chipped in for a gold vase worth $200,000. The kaiser, Teddy Roosevelt and neighbors in Pasadena sent gold loving cups. Herman Sielcken, the coffee king Adolphus tried to help, gave a basket woven with fine strands of gold. And President Taft sent a freshly minted, uncirculated $20 gold piece in an ivory frame.

In turn, Adolphus and Lilly gave each of their children a

mansion. Edmee and Hugo Reisinger received a home on Fifth Avenue, reportedly one of the most costly residences in New York City. Clara and Baron von Gontard got a splendid mansion within a few blocks of the Reichstag in Berlin. Busch's daughter Nellie, married for a third time, to Jacob Loeb, received a fine house near Lincoln Park in Chicago. Eduard and Wilhelmina Scharrer were given a mansion in Stuttgart. Ed and Anna Faust built a mansion at Number One Portland Place, a fashionable part of St. Louis. One room was finished entirely in gold fixtures.

Adolphus had wanted to give August A. Number One Busch Place, which the Prince considered the best house in St. Louis. But August A., in rare defiance of his father's wishes, insisted on building what came to be called a castle on property that had once been worked by a struggling farmer named Ulysses S. Grant. Adolphus, quite a judge of such things, derisively pronounced the proposed home palatial, but eventually he went along and funded construction of the huge French style château. He wrote off his son's debt saying: "To our dearest boy his home! To our treasury department in St. Louis, pay to the order of August A. Busch the cost of his new mansion on Grant's Farm in sums as he may make demand for it. Eternal happiness in the new home and long life!"

All of this splendor was not lost upon the public. A newspaper commented, "The ways of beer have been pleasant ways for them. It pays to succeed and to get rich. In the meantime, every man who drank a glass of the Busch beer contributed his mite to the happiness in California."

Later in that same year of 1911, the lavish scope of Adolphus's ability to throw a party was put on display in Pasadena. His estate's name had been changed from Ivy Wall to Busch Gardens, and in addition to becoming a Pasadena tourist attraction, the gardens were a not so subtle promotion for Anheuser-Busch. With prohibition brewing, it was a good year to get the doctors on the side of beer. Adolphus invited 7,000 participants of the American Medical Association convention in Los Angeles to spend a day at the gardens they would never forget. As one doctor entered the grounds he said, "This is the Garden of Eden." The gardens were indeed a botanical paradise of roses, carnations, daisies, pansies and pink geraniums. For hours, guests strolled across rustic bridges over shaded ponds, gazing at splashing fountains and paddling ducks. Wandering troubadours entertained while sweating Hispanic workers wearing white outfits with red sashes and sombreros served platters of sliced meat, mounds of beans, piles of potatoes, tamales, gallons of olives and mountains of freshly baked rolls. And, of course, there was plenty of free beer.

The gala anniversary party and the AMA reception were the only bright spots in 1911 for Adolphus Busch. Despite his ceaseless efforts and money, prohibition forces were gaining ground in Congress. Not satisfied with the elimination of the military canteen, they wanted to outlaw the interstate shipment of alcoholic beverages. There were political problems, too. Teddy Roosevelt, unhappy with Taft's performance, was talking about coming out of retirement to run for president.

Adolphus did what he could to deal with these troubles but his strength was fading, and in ill health he became reclusive. "You will never see Adolphus Busch," a hotel manager told a St. Louis visitor. "No one has seen him for a year or more. He is surrounded by doctors, nurses and guardians and is never permitted to be seen at close range." The visitor went to Faust's restaurant and was told: "Adolphus Busch is a dead man. He is kept alive by the doctors and nurses and is never seen."

Adolphus did receive a few important visitors. Later in 1911 he hosted Roosevelt, who discussed Taft's administration. After the meeting, Busch told Nagel he believed the former president "will stand firmly and bravely by the present administration." But Adolphus was soon proven wrong as Roosevelt launched a third-party bid to challenge Taft's reelection.

In June 1912, the Democrats nominated a reformer for president, New Jersey Governor Woodrow Wilson. Adolphus promised that all his people in the forty-six states would work for Taft. "They could not have done anything more stupid than to nominate the weakest candidate of the bunch," he wrote Nagel on Wilson's nomination. "I have a kind of feeling that the fellow is a prohibitionist and that he is leaning that way and therefore all the German orators, all the liberal men ought to accuse him of an enemy to personal freedom and on that account already kill him with a big stick. Whether he is a narrow minded church fellow I don't know, but I should not wonder at all if he is and for that he ought to get another knock with the stick."

But Taft was doomed. The feisty Roosevelt had not lost any of his political punch, and his Progressive Party took enough votes away from Taft to put Wilson in the White House. On November 5, the voters overwhelmingly elected a man

Adolphus had described just four months earlier as a "know-nothing and temperance crank" who had "no chance at all."

From then until Wilson's inauguration on March 4, 1913, Adolphus worked feverishly to wring a few final drops out of the lame-duck Taft administration. On December 29, he wrote to Bartholdt, his man in Congress, that he wanted the Congress to restore his beloved military canteen, and that he was certain Taft would support the idea before leaving office. "My standing with him at the present time is such that I can do it," he wrote. "Confidentially, I will tell you that I offered him the position of president of the Bank of Commerce in St. Louis at a salary of $50,000 per annum and he declined, preferring to take a professorship at Yale."

When Adolphus failed to get Taft to support the canteen despite repeated desperate pleas, he pulled out all the stops. He wrote his old friend Nagel: "There never was a demand, Charles that I made on you that is more valuable and that is nearer to my heart than this. And therefore I count on your devotion and friendship you hold for me to take the leading and positive position to gratify this, my sincerest wish."

It didn't work. Not even Nagel could win back the canteen. But Taft did perform one last duty to Adolphus's liking. Congress had passed the Webb-Kenyon bill to prohibit interstate shipment of alcoholic beverages into dry states. On February 12, 1913, Adolphus wired Taft "to beg of you to veto" the bill because he thought it was unconstitutional. Just before leaving office, Taft did just that. It was Adolphus's last great victory.

14

Veni, Vidi, Vici

In the spring of 1913, Adolphus made his annual homecoming to St. Louis. But unlike the grand arrivals of the past, the one on May 13 was somber. His fragile health could no longer be concealed. He could not stand or walk without assistance, and he was lifted, almost fainting, from the train into a wheelchair. An elevator had been installed just off the dining room at Number One Busch Place because he could no longer climb the stairs.

On sunny days in late May and early June, Adolphus was driven about the brewery in a carriage. Although he was deteriorating physically, his mind remained sharp and he greeted many of the workers by name. Family matters still troubled him. In one of his frequent letters to August A., he referred to the "castle" his son had built at Grant's Farm against his advice and which he and Lilly had paid for. He anticipated complaints from his daughters who had received less-imposing mansions. "I consider all such differences squared," he told August A. "What I have done, I have done of my own free will, and I want it so understood and treated by all of you."

When the family went to Chicago on June 4 for the wedding of his granddaughter Lilly Magnus, Adolphus stayed behind because of illness. But a newspaper reported he gave his "favorite granddaughter" a $1 million check for a wedding present. Adolphus and the rest of the Busch family left June 9 for New York and sailed to Europe. It was to be his last trip to his beloved fatherland. At Villa Lilly, Adolphus continued to dictate telegrams and letters to his son, to political friends and business associates. He was in frequent communication with his attorney, Nagel, who was back in private practice and was defending Busch in a New York lawsuit that accused him of misrepresenting the value of telephone company stock that he sold for $750,000. The case, Adolphus told Nagel, was a "very ugly thing" and a "most just, unfair and cruel mean attack on the part of some shyster lawyers."

He still went hunting, shooting deer from a cart driven through his private forest preserve by his personal huntsman. Sometimes his grandson Gussie went along. Adolphus also continued to entertain guests like Congressman Bartholdt; he made it clear he had not given up his fight with the prohibitionists in Congress.

Although Taft had left office and Nagel returned to St. Louis, Adolphus was filled with new ideas for staving off prohibition. He discussed the formation of the Liberalists party, which "should entitle me to the right to carry equal name and fame as those who signed the Constitution, if I say so." He also had the ingenious idea that liquor sales could be protected if Congress passed a law forbidding states to interfere with the collection of federal revenues. Since beer and liquor were taxed by the federal government, he reasoned a law protecting those taxes would also protect the product. "It is not necessary that the words 'liquor' and 'beer' are named," he cunningly suggested. "On the contrary, leave it out. Certainly, the law must be cleverly and smartly and intelligently worded dwelling only on the revenues of the general government collected in all states for their maintenance and administration. I suppose a nice diplomatic trick would catch the sleepy heads to vote in favor of it, or such a law could be attached to some appropriate bill where the 'solons' would not discover it at all."

In September, Adolphus was decorated yet again in Germany, this time by Phillip, Duke of Hesse, for his philanthropy to the German people. Later that same month, he learned that his friend and business associate Rudolph Diesel had drowned in the English Channel during an overnight crossing from Antwerp. It was later determined that Diesel, plagued by ill health and mounting debts, had committed suicide by jumping overboard.

Seriously ill himself, Adolphus insisted on hunting, even if it meant he had to be carried. On October 4, he was hoisted into a hunting box to shoot stags, but he returned home the next day feeling ill. Summoned to Germany, August A. arrived at Villa Lilly on October 8. Doctors had removed fluid from around his father's lungs and he seemed improved. "He rallied splendidly and we thought the doctors were again mistaken," August A. said. "He even spoke of returning to the shoot which had been interrupted and I was to have joined him." But Adolphus had shot his last stag.

On Friday, October 10, the Prince joked with his family and seemed cheerful. He dealt with the fifteen letters that had piled up on his desk. "He smoked a cigar and chatted freely," his son later recalled. "Just after noon he became weak but was in no pain whatever. He spoke to all of us and was quite clear of mind on all subjects. I don't think father thought he was dying."

Adolphus Busch died peacefully in his sleep at 8:15 P.M., October 10, 1913, not far from the village where he had been born seventy-four years earlier. Although he had suffered from dropsy, death was attributed to heart disease. The records of the cemetery in which he was buried also indicated heart disease was the cause of death. But there was another possibility. Many years later, a biography checked by Busch's grandson Adolphus III said the company patriarch had died of cirrhosis of the liver.

In addition to Lilly and August A., those with Adolphus in his final moments were daughters Wilhelmina Scharrer, Clara von Gontard and his adopted daughter Gustava Kluhn, née von Kliehr. Also present was Carl Conrad, the man who was the first to sell Adolphus's famous Budweiser so many years before.

The passing of Adolphus Busch marked the beginning of one of the most elaborate funerals of the twentieth century. The obsequies began when the population of the village of Bad Schwalbach and surrounding towns—places where Adolphus had been treated like a king—turned out to mourn as his double-lined casket was placed in a private railroad car for the trip to Bremen. His favorite steamer, the *Kronprinz Wilhelm*, brought his body back to America. When the ship arrived in New York harbor on October 21, Ed Faust and Charles Nagel went out to meet it in the *Calumet*, a customs service revenue cutter. As soon as the ship docked, the casket was unloaded and taken by hearse to a special five-car train that included his private car, the *Adolphus*. Within an hour of the ship's arrival, thirty members of the Busch family and fifteen servants were on their way to St. Louis.

In St. Louis several hundred people gathered outside the fence surrounding the brewery yard for the return of the *Adolphus*. It was raining heavily by the time the train, pulled by three locomotives, arrived at 9:20 P.M. Ten brewery employees carried the casket to the Busch mansion. Lilly seemed to bear up well, but when August A. met his wife, Alice, he was on the verge of collapse. She led him to an automobile and they went straight to Grant's Farm. Because of illness, he was unable to participate in funeral preparations the following day.

One hundred rooms at the Planters and Jefferson hotels had been reserved for out-of-town guests. There were 180 honorary pallbearers. The secretary of agriculture, the presidents of Harvard, the University of California and the University of Missouri attended, as did the president of the Bank of Commerce of New York, and an old rival, Colonel Gustave Pabst of Milwaukee.

On the morning before the funeral, the family opened the doors of the mansion to give 5,000 brewery workers a last look at their prince. It was estimated that as many as 30,000 viewed the body when the house was opened to the public. Detectives were posted in all the rooms to keep people from walking off with expensive vases and statuary. The casket rested in the main drawing room blanketed with orchids. Petals covered the floor and the immense room was filled from floor to ceiling with orchids, violets and chrysanthemums. A myrtle wreath was sent by Prince Adelbert, the German emperor's son who had visited Villa Lilly. Employees sent a huge wreath of roses that said "Our Beloved President." Twenty-five trucks were needed to haul the floral arrangements to the cemetery.

At the house the day of the funeral, musicians from the St. Louis Symphony Orchestra played Rubinstein's "Kammenoi-Ostrow," Tchaikovsky's "Andante Cantabile" and other selections. Adolphus had asked that a piece from a Wagner opera be played at his funeral but it would have required a seventy-five-piece orchestra. Three men presided over the funeral service at the mansion—Charles Nagel, Baron Friedherr von Lesner, attaché of the German Embassy in Washington, and the Reverend John W. Day. Adolphus, who cared nothing for religion, had been baptized a Catholic, married in the German Evangelical Lutheran Church and was buried with the help of Rev. J. W. Day of the Unitarian Church of the Messiah.

At 2 P.M., when the funeral began, St. Louis halted business for five minutes. Power to the street cars was shut off. Factories stilled. Hotels went dark. The city council had called for the moment of silence over the objections of some members who argued that a private citizen did not deserve such a tribute.

Services were also held in thirty-five cities served by Anheuser-Busch branch offices. The largest was the Adolphus Hotel in Dallas, where three hundred people in the Palm Room heard music identical to that played in St. Louis. The hotel was a monument to the elegance and style of its namesake. The beer baron had poured $2.5 million into the building in 1912, an unheard of amount in the raw East Texas town. The fixtures included Louis XIV wrought iron grillwork, chandeliers displayed at the St. Louis World's Fair of 1904 and paintings by Old Masters. It was hailed as the most beautiful building west of Venice by the American Institute of Architects.

Nagel, tall, silver-haired and distinguished, gave the funeral oration in St. Louis as he had at the burials of Adolphus's sons Peter and Adolphus Jr. The voice of Adolphus's conscience seemed constantly on the verge of breaking. In the overblown oratory of the day, he called Busch "a giant among men. Like a descendant of one of the great and vigorous and ancient gods, he rested among us and with his optimism, his far seeing vision, his undaunted courage and his energy shaped the affairs of men."

The Reverend Mr. Day quoted Scripture. "Know ye not that there is a prince and a great man fallen this day?" Baron von Lesner, the kaiser's personal representative, then placed a wreath decorated with the German coat of arms onto the casket.

To the strains of "Aase's Death" from Grieg's *Peer Gynt* suite, the casket was carried from the mansion escorted by seven grandsons, and was placed on a truck for a final tour of the brewery. The procession was led by a 250 piece band as 25,000 people stood watching outside the wrought iron fence. Then the cortege wound its way to Bellefontaine Cemetery, the burial place of the city's rich and famous. The route was thickly lined with people, as many as 100,000.

At the grave, Congressman Bartholdt spoke in German, but used an English term to declare that Adolphus was "the high priest of the square deal." A trombone quartet, assembled on a nearby hill, played "Es ist Bestimmt in Gottes Rat" (It is decided in God's counsel). The reverend said another prayer as the casket was lowered into a vault lined with Italian marble. It was almost dark when Adolphus Busch reached his final resting place. It took nearly an hour for the crowd to depart.

For days after the funeral, there was tremendous speculation over what would happen to the Busch estate. People wanted to know who would get his shares of the Anheuser-Busch Brewing Association, the Manufacturers' Railroad, the Busch-Sulzer Brothers Diesel Engine Company, the St. Louis and O'Fallon Railroad and Coal Mine, the Hotel Adolphus, the corner saloon lots all over the city of St. Louis, and his interests in the breweries in Houston, Fort Worth and San Antonio. They were curious about the fate of the real estate in Texas, New York and California; the Grand Hotel in Paris; the villa in Germany; the palace in Pasadena; the estate in Cooperstown; the Grand Pacific Hotel in Chicago; the stocks in utilities, four St. Louis banks, the bottling companies, railroads, mines and asphalt companies. In all, Busch held stock in fifty companies, including a German ammunition and weapons factory in Berlin of which his son-in-law, Baron von Gontard, was managing director. At an estimated value of $50 million, it was the largest estate ever probated in Missouri. Adjusted for inflation, Busch's fortune would equal $570 million in 1988 dollars.

Adolphus's will established a trust to maintain his riches and keep them intact. Adolphus named his son, August A., Lilly and Nagel as trustees with broad powers. The estate was divided into eight shares, with August getting two, Lilly one, and each of the five daughters one each. However, Busch willed that the trust would always control the funds going to two of his daughters—his "little girl" Wilhelmina and his spendthrift Nellie. Adolphus also fired a parting shot at son-in-law Eduard Scharrer, whom he had never forgiven for trying to elope with Wilhelmina. Scharrer was to receive nothing from the estate if he outlived his wife.

August A., whom Adolphus had once bombarded with critical letters, received control of the brewery, the railroad, the diesel company and the bottling companies. Because he also was given voting control of the trust, it was virtually impossible for any of his five sisters to contest his decisions. He was also ordered to take care of Adolphus's invalid brother, Carl.

Ed Faust, who had expected to be a member of the trust, was given a consolation prize. He was named an executor of the will along with Lilly and Nagel. The job entitled them to receive 5 percent of the estate and made Nagel a millionaire. The real power, however, rested with the trustees. But as Nagel pointed out, "There will be no one in a position to do things on the large scale that Mr. Adolphus Busch used to adopt."

As if anticipating that his will would create family dissension, Adolphus's last testament asked his children to "be happy and contented with the assurances" that he had tried to be fair with everyone. It proved a false hope. In the years that followed, a distance grew between the Fausts and the Busches to the point that they stopped speaking to one another.

Adolphus also gave $210,000 to charity and $10,000 to Alvina Clementine Berg, his longtime private secretary who had aroused Lilly's jealousy. Berg's bequest was equal to twice her annual salary. She was also made secretary to the trustees because of "her intimate acquaintance with Busch's private affairs." Lilly was willed the villa in Germany that bore her name.

Adolphus's estate was so large that a separate corporation was established to handle it. While some assets were quickly sold off (the railroad car the *Adolphus* went to the president of Mexico), others were kept. In 1967, fifty-four years after his death, what was left of the corporation was finally liquidated. The beneficiaries sold the railroad and the refrigerator car company to Anheuser-Busch Incorporated for 230,505 shares of stock, the equivalent of $12.5 million.

Adolphus's old demon, prohibition, followed him even to the grave. When Dr. Hugo M. Starkloff, a leader among German-Americans in St. Louis, proposed a memorial to the Prince and launched a fund-raising drive, the plan ran into immediate opposition. A church group protested, saying a monument to Busch would be "a monument to the liquor traffic with which his whole life was identified." When Nagel's funeral eulogy was printed in the Congressional Record, there was a storm of protest from the Women's Christian Temperance Union. The WCTU also killed a plan to name an elementary school after Adolphus, saying it would "tend to glorify the liquor business in the minds of public school children."

The monument idea was discarded. But the Busch family eventually built a memorial of its own—a $250,000 mausoleum so solidly constructed that the U.S. Testing Bureau estimated it would last until the year 9922. There were no references to a deity in this Gothic chapel built of pink granite. It was the tomb of a beer king and its trefoils and facade were carved with hop flowers, hop vines and barley. The same motifs also decorated the marble floor and wrought iron doors. Gargoyles loomed out from below the slate roof. "Busch 1838–1913" was emblazoned on a granite shield over the gated doors. It was in error. Adolphus had been born in 1839.

The shield was also inscribed with the words of another Caesar: "Veni, Vidi, Vici." It now remained for Adolphus's son August A. to live up to that motto.

15

"Here's to the Kaiser!"

In December 1913, two months after the death of Adolphus Busch, 4,000 men and women marched in Washington, D.C., demanding passage of a constitutional amendment that would prohibit liquor in the United States. The drys were feeling their power. They had elected more representatives to Congress and to the state legislatures than ever before. Fourteen states had voted to outlaw alcohol, and the pressure was on for a national ban.

But the real boost the drys needed to outlaw liquor occurred half a world away. On June 28, 1914, the Archduke Francis Ferdinand, heir to the Austrian and Hungarian thrones, was driving through the sun-warmed, flag-bedecked streets of Sarajevo when a college student stepped from the crowd and emptied a pistol into his open touring car. The nobleman from the House of Hapsburg and his wife, Sophie, were killed. Within six weeks of the assassination, the Great War began.

August Anheuser Busch, the once reluctant captain of America's largest beer empire, was caught between those two cataclysmic events. Of German descent *and* a brewer, he was the target of both prejudice and prohibition, forces that could destroy his family and his fortune. Unlike his father, August A. was a shy, retiring man whose only wish for the future was to live the quiet life of a gentleman farmer at the fantasy kingdom he had created for himself at Grant's Farm.

In early August of 1914 as fighting broke out, August A. and his family were summering at Villa Lilly. One hundred seventy-five miles from the French frontier, they were well out of the war zone. But the excitement attracted August A. to Frankfurt, where he watched troop trains depart for the front every fifteen minutes. He also witnessed the return of captured French prisoners of war as the German armies approached Paris.

Like many Germans, August A. believed that the kaiser was not responsible for the war but had been forced into it. Yet for all his pro-German sentiment, he wasted little time leaving the country. He had $25,000 wired to him to bring his family home. In addition to his mother, Lilly, and his wife, Alice, there were daughters Marie, Clara and Alice, and son August A. "Gussie" Busch, Jr. Also at the Villa Lilly was his sister Edmee, Mrs. Hugo Reisinger of New York. All prepared hastily to return to the United States.

There was one exception. Lilly, Adolphus's widow and matriarch of the family, was torn. She wanted to go home, but she also wanted to remain in Germany, where two of her daughters faced the prospect of widowhood. Clara's husband, Adjutant Paul von Gontard, was an executive of a Berlin munitions factory and a member of the kaiser's guards. Wilhelmina's husband, Lieutenant Eduard Scharrer, had obtained an assignment in the army and was dispatched east. Several other relatives—Anheusers and Busches alike—were also involved in the fighting. Lilly finally elected to remain in Germany, a decision that she and her family would deeply regret.

With thousands of other war refugees, August A.'s family fled Europe in late September, traveling down the Rhine and boarding a steamer for America in Amsterdam. It was so crowded that the captain gave up his quarters to the Busches and slept on the floor of the chart room. When they arrived in New York, the Busches were quoted like authorities on the effects of the war in Holland and Germany. They verified rumors about English and French prisoners. August A. declared the war would be over in three weeks or by Christmas at the latest.

"Are you alarmed about the safety of your mother?" he was asked.

"Why no, not at all," August A. replied. "My mother is safe at Villa Lilly and will remain there all winter."

From the very early days of the war, the Busches, their friends and many other German-Americans openly sided with the kaiser. Two of the late Adolphus Busch's best friends publicly proclaimed support for the Germans: Charles Nagel and Congressman Richard Bartholdt. August A. himself threw a political dinner at Grant's Farm in honor of the kaiser's birthday. He began the Democratic Party function with a toast: "Here's to the kaiser!" But the war did not progress as he and others predicted. The Allies halted the German advance in the west at the Marne and at Ypres, and a long stalemate followed, during which American public opinion gradually turned against "the Huns." The Busches' early support for Germany was not forgotten.

Despite America's neutrality and the large number of German immigrants in the American population, there was an outcry when Germany became the first to use poison gas in April 1915. When a U-boat sank the liner *Lusitania* the following May killing 128 Americans, anti-German sentiment reached a fever pitch. It was against this backdrop of growing hostility toward the Germans that the Busches' Teutonic connections were scrutinized.

In one case, at least, it seemed the family was actively aiding the Germans. Lilly moved in with her daughter Wilhelmina, who had turned her estate in Bernried, Germany, into a care center for wounded German soldiers. Letters received by friends of the family in Pasadena, parts of which were later published by newspapers, indicated that Lilly was helping Wilhelmina administer to sixty-five to seventy-five wounded men.

"My place is in Germany for as long as the European war lasts," Lilly wrote. "When peace comes I shall think about returning to Pasadena." In the meantime, the brewery continued to send her money. Between September 15, 1914, and March 23, 1917, Anheuser-Busch cabled $293,883.77 to the widow of the founder.

Anti-German sentiment and the growing prohibition movement severely hurt Anheuser-Busch. In 1914, five more states —Arizona, Colorado, Oregon, Virginia and Washington—went dry. At the same time, Canadians and Australians began a boycott of Budweiser because of its German name and German-language label. Anheuser-Busch sales fell to $14.8 million in 1914 compared with $17.4 million the year before. The brewery quickly put English-language labels on Budweiser bound for Australia and Canada. Sensing the changing mood, August A. also began to wear a little American flag button on his lapel.

In 1915, his reputation was further damaged when the Texas attorney general filed charges against seven Texas breweries for violating antitrust laws. The breweries were accused of interfering in Texas politics by funding the Texas Brewers' Association fight against statewide prohibition. The charge in the Texas court was that the brewers had used funds to influence legislation in favor of the brewery interests of the state.

August A. was called as a witness. It was pointed out that he received a salary as president of the American Brewing Association of Houston, served as an officer of the Lone Star Brewing Company of San Antonio, and was an investor in the Texas Brewing Company of Fort Worth. But after having his name removed from corporate documents that linked him to the suspected breweries, he refused to appear. There was embarrassing testimony, however, to the effect that Busch interests influenced what went on in Texas.

Further embarrassment followed when letters from Adolphus Busch emerged in the Texas investigation. One letter, written February 1, 1911, from Pasadena to the president of the Galveston Brewing Company, concerned a lug to be placed on each brewing company in Texas. The money was to fund the fight against the drys. "Now whatever money is necessary for the campaign has to come forth," Adolphus had written. "Everybody must do his full duty, and be forced to do it." Adolphus offered $100,000 more to keep Texas wet. "Everyone interested in the business should be willing to sacrifice all and everything he possesses to save our business from being wrecked by a fanatical part of the people."

The Texas brewers eventually pleaded guilty to the charges and paid a $280,000 fine. In the court of public opinion, the payment of the fine appeared to be an admission of guilt.

If all that wasn't bad enough, the public got a revealing look at the fabulous wealth that beer could generate with the disposition of the estate of Adolphus Busch. In July 1917, it was reported that during the period between July 1, 1914, and November 1916, the brewery paid $11,450 in dividends on each of the 480 shares of Anheuser-Busch stock. The inventory of the estate also showed that Adolphus had left $35 million in real property and $17 million worth of personal property. Lilly Busch's personal property tax disclosure for 1914 showed assets of $1,608,688, the largest in St. Louis.

August A. tried to counter these damaging reports by saying Anheuser-Busch only made 6 percent on the invested capital of the brewery. He denied published reports that Clara and Wilhemina, his two sisters in Germany, earned $1,000 a day from the estate. Their income, he said, was "considerably less" than one third of that amount, and none of the money had left the United States since the war began.

August A. gave $100,000 to the Red Cross and donated to other charities, hoping to show both his loyalty and generosity. He made a contribution to the German War Relief Bazaar and then followed it up with a $100 donation to a similar fund drive for the French. "I am," he said, "an American first in all things, notwithstanding I have many blood relations now fighting in the German ranks and regardless of the fact that many sentimental ties bind me to the Fatherland."

But even his bequests could turn sour. After $100,000 had been contributed in the names of August and Lilly Busch to the YMCA, New York's Dr. J. Wilber Chapman, titular head of the Presbyterian Church, said he was happy to see that more than $1 million had been raised in St. Louis. But in a reference to Anheuser-Busch, he added: "I wish you had refused to accept $100,000 of that fund gotten by the breaking of mothers' hearts and the blighting of thousands of homes."

During the Allies' desperate year of 1917, August A. had to break all his "sentimental ties" with Germany. That January, a German communiqué was made public revealing that Germany sought an alliance with Mexico in the event of war with the United States. And on February 1, 1917, U-boats began unrestricted warfare in the Atlantic, doubling the number of American merchant ships sunk. The entry of the United States into the war was imminent.

On March 28, shortly before the United States declared war on Germany, Busch, as president of the Busch-Sulzer Brothers Diesel Engine Company, had offered to produce submarine engines "so that Uncle Sam will be able to lick 'em all." He even made a point of mentioning that he had gone down in an American submarine in 1915 off the Atlantic Coast.

On the evening of April 6, the day the U.S. declared war on Germany, August A. attended a dinner meeting of the St. Louis Club and proposed a resolution pledging loyalty to the United States. He had it sent to President Wilson. But the temperament of the times had changed dramatically and would have devastating consequences for August A. and his brewery. President Wilson described it best to a reporter when he said that once the United States was in a war, citizens will "forget there ever was such a thing as tolerance." He said a spirit of "ruthless brutality" would enter every fiber of national life, including the Congress, the courts and law enforcement.

Conformity became the only virtue, and August A. and Anheuser-Busch quickly conformed. Within days of the declaration of war, German no longer was the language of the brewery workers. Busts and paintings of Bismarck were removed. The minutes of the unions' meetings were no longer recorded in German.

Anthony Busch, a cousin once removed of August A.'s, recalled many years later that the day after the declaration of war he was beaten up by classmates because he could not speak English very well. Federal agents put his home under surveillance because his father, Ernst, was a foreign-born German. The family's house was even searched by agents looking for a suspicious radio that turned out to be a crystal radio set.

A month after the declaration of war, Joseph Magnus, a grandson of Adolphus's, enlisted in the army. But the patriotic gesture was overlooked in the glaring publicity over August A.'s son, Adolphus III. Twenty-seven years old, Adolphus III was known as a onetime playboy and lover of horses. He sought a draft deferment on the grounds that he was the vice president of a coal company and the sole support of a wife and child.

Lilly, meanwhile, was still in Germany. For nearly three years she had remained either at Villa Lilly or with her two daughters, who were nursing wounded German soldiers. The belief that it was better for her to remain in Germany rather than risk the danger of leaving changed abruptly on October 12, 1917, when President Wilson established the office of alien property custodian.

A man named A. Mitchell Palmer was empowered to enforce laws against trading with the enemy and to confiscate all American assets owned by enemy aliens or people living in the country of the enemy. Palmer was a former congressman from Pennsylvania who had helped Wilson win the presidential nomination. He later became famous for the "Palmer Raids" of January 1920, in which as attorney general he jailed thousands of so-called anarchists and Communists with little regard for their constitutional rights.

Within one month of his appointment, Palmer was in control of trusts worth more than $506 million. Among the vast properties under his administration was the estate of Lilly Busch, which he ordered inventoried and collected for safekeeping at the St. Louis Union Trust Company. Title to all the property was placed in the control of the federal government. Palmer's job was to see to it that the assets of enemy aliens could not be used against the United States, but he eventually won the power from Congress to sell the assets.

By early November the anteroom of Palmer's office was crowded with lawyers seeking to protect the assets of clients with German roots. Among them were two St. Louis lawyers, Charles Nagel and Harry B. Hawes, who represented Lilly

Busch. Palmer told the pair that Lilly should travel to neutral territory or to the United States to prevent her property from being confiscated. Faced with the sudden prospect of losing millions of dollars in Lilly's estate and their own inheritance, the Busch children hurriedly made plans to extract their mother from the warring fatherland. Her escape would be the greatest adventure of her life—and the most humiliating.

16

Behind the Lines

The mission to get Lilly Busch out of war-ravaged Europe went to Harry Hawes, who had the same trusted relationship with August A. that Nagel had enjoyed with Adolphus. Hawes, then forty-eight years old, had also been a good friend of Peter Busch's, August A.'s late, fun-loving brother. Like August A., Hawes was an active Democrat and a Missouri state legislator with a reputation for political chicanery. And like others who associated with Anheuser-Busch early in their careers, he eventually moved up in the political world. Before Hawes's career was finished, he would become a U.S. senator from Missouri.

Nagel had a low opinion of Hawes because of his many conflicts of interest, which Nagel characterized as Hawes's attempts to "take the short cut to happiness in politics." Nagel once bluntly told August A. that St. Louis had suffered because of Hawes's "political trickery, corruption or oppression." Hawes was skilled at using political power for financial gain, helping to nominate and elect St. Louis city officials and then collecting legal fees from them. While fighting an attempt by Hawes to get his law partner appointed United States attorney in eastern Missouri, Nagel told August A. that Hawes was "squarely responsible for the most outrageous political misconduct that has ever prevailed in our community."

Despite such warnings from his father's most trusted adviser, August A. stuck with Hawes. In rejecting Nagel's advice, he might have been trying to free himself from Adolphus's pervading influence. He wanted to be his own man with his own inner circle and his own coterie of advisers. He admired Nagel, but he wasn't about to let Nagel dictate to him. He had had enough of that from Adolphus.

In late November, in preparation for his mission to rescue Lilly, Hawes cabled the Spanish ambassador in Berlin, who represented American interests there. Addressed to Lilly, it stated that her four children in the United States wanted her to come home. She was asked to meet Hawes in Zurich, Switzerland, on December 15. When he left for England, Hawes told his friends that he expected to be gone six weeks. His mission would take a good deal longer than that.

Arriving in Switzerland, a country he considered "a nest of spies," Hawes found that Lilly was not sure she wanted to leave Germany. Daughters Wilhelmina and Clara had encouraged her to remain with them. "The consternation of her two children in Germany can be imagined," Hawes said later. "She was asked to leave Germany in the middle of winter, cross the mountains of Switzerland, pass through neutral Spain on the way home. A journey of 6500 miles was one which few women at seventy-four years of age would have had even the temerity to consider."

Hawes eventually had to dispatch a Swiss lawyer across the German border to meet with Lilly and talk her into returning to the United States. The lawyer finally convinced her to make the trip. The first leg of the journey began on January 14, 1918, when she left southern Germany by way of Lake Constance. "I shall never forget my first impression of Mrs. Busch as she stepped out of the little steamer which crossed the lake from Germany, landing at the frontier town of Romanshorn," Hawes said later. "She had the springy step and stride of a girl of 20."

But Lilly Busch was far from healthy. Frail and ailing, she became sick in Switzerland and was bedridden there under the care of a doctor for more than six weeks. Meanwhile, her villa and surrounding property in Bad Schwalbach were seized by the German government. "Good heavens, who now will look after my chickens?" she said after hearing the news. Her two daughters in Germany, thinking she should return to reclaim Villa Lilly, sent a German lawyer to Switzerland to urge her to do so. The two daughters brought to bear "every pressure possible" in an effort to induce her to remain, and "they almost succeeded," Hawes said. After wrestling with her dilemma, Lilly made her decision.

"My place is with my boy, Gussie [August A.], and I am going home."

Bringing his mother home was only one of the problems confronting August A. during those early months of 1918. His family's loyalty to the United States was now being questioned openly. Equally menacing, the prohibitionists were using wartime rationing arguments to encourage Congress to outlaw the consumption of alcohol completely. In September 1917, food control bills had been approved that prohibited the production of distilled liquor. Railroad cars and coal shipments were diverted from the breweries. Beer production was cut by 30 percent and eliminated entirely by the fall of the following year when wartime prohibition was instituted. Even before Congress passed the act, August A. was pouring all of his energy into a new nonalcoholic beverage called Bevo that he hoped would save the fortunes of his company.

At the same time, he constantly had to defend his family and brewery against loud and constant anti-German and anti-brewer sentiment. He did everything he could to look patriotic and everything he could to publicize those gestures. He announced that he was buying $1.5 million worth of Liberty Bonds in his name and that of his mother. He also said that when his new $10 million Bevo plant was finished he would turn it over to the government for war munitions work. He issued public appeals to support the Red Cross. He changed the label of all Budweiser products, eliminating the double eagle that some people believed represented the Austrian coat of arms. He offered a $500 prize in the name of his mother for the best recruiting poster.

But no matter what he did, there was always another fire to put out. He was forced to deny that income from Anheuser-Busch had been sent to his sisters in Germany since the United States had entered the war. His announcement was precipitated by reports that a nonintoxicating drink manufactured by his brewery was being boycotted at U.S. army camps because of stories that 75 percent of the profits of the brewery were going to the German army officers who had married the daughters of Adolphus Busch. August A. insisted that his sisters' income was being invested in Liberty Bonds. But his denial wasn't enough to prevent a minister in New York from proclaiming from the pulpit that Anheuser-Busch annually sent $400,000 to the kaiser—comments that were printed in a newspaper. "The U.S. government knows better," Busch countered, blaming the rumors on "gossip mongers," "fanatic zealots" and "jealous competitors."

His public relations gestures continued to backfire. When he provided three portable cottages to the Liberty Loan Committee in St. Louis to be used as sales booths for war bonds, there were complaints about the wooden storks in nests on their rooftops, a German symbol as traditional as the American weathervane. "Why are German houses with German storks on the chimneys up on 12th Street?" one letter writer asked. "Are these typical American homes?" The storks and nests were promptly removed and replaced with American flags.

There were even complaints about Lilly. When several St. Louis newspapers reported she was on her way home to reclaim her fortune from the federal government, a clipping of one of these stories was sent to the Justice Department with the observation: "I would suggest that these parties be searched the same as other persons from Germany. It's best to be sure than sorry and see that they don't slip one over on us by sending some secret code or other information to agents here. The Busches were great friends of the kaiser, and she has been over in Germany since before the war."

There were other veiled warnings about Lilly. It remained to be seen whether the Justice Department would take them seriously.

On March 3, 1918, as Russia signed a peace treaty with Germany but before Germany launched its last-ditch offensive on the Western Front, Lilly was well enough to begin her trip home from Zurich. With Hawes, a Swiss maid and a woman companion, she set out for France and passage to America. Along the way, Hawes was financed by money sent through the State Department to safe homes he had designated. They found the French frontier town of Belgarde crowded with wounded soldiers and internees on the way to Switzerland. Reaching Paris, Lilly witnessed "from the doorway of her hotel a German air raid made by 64 machines lasting some three hours." Bombs fell within a block of the hotel. "It was a sad introduc-

tion to the gay Paris which she and her husband knew so well
and loved so much in their earlier days."

From Paris, they went to the small Spanish border village of
Hendaye, where Mrs. Busch again became ill and remained for
ten days. Resuming their journey, they went to Santander. But
Germany had threatened Spanish shipping because of that
country's continued trade with America, so no vessels sailed
for weeks. Finally, on May 24, Lilly and forty-four other first-
class passengers boarded the Spanish steamer *Alphonse XIII*
for a trip to Havana. At the start of the journey, the ship
sighted a German submarine, U-65. To avoid any further encounters, they steamed into the Bay of Biscay and south down
the coast of Africa to the Canary Islands.

As the *Alphonse XIII* crossed the Atlantic, August A. prepared
for a trip to Key West, where Hawes and Lilly were expected
to arrive on June 15. Unknown to him, the United States government, which had been monitoring the progress of her journey, also prepared a reception. The director of Naval
Intelligence in Washington, D.C., had sent a telegram to the
7th Naval District at Key West: "Question, search and report
destination."

Lilly arrived in Havana on June 15. To inquiring newspaper
reporters who met them, Hawes denied reports that Mrs.
Busch had donated $1 million to war relief in Germany and
that the kaiser and the crown prince had visited her at Villa
Lilly. The U.S. naval attaché in Havana examined and
searched the party and their baggage. Lilly, her maid and her
companion were searched by a woman agent appointed for
that purpose.

At 7:40 P.M., June 16, aboard the little steamer *Mascotte*,
Lilly finally arrived in the United States after a journey that
had taken months. August A. was waiting there to greet her,
behind a fence on the dock. He had been there five days, and
had a car and train reservations for St. Louis. But the government had other plans. Two men, an investigator from the Justice Department and an officer from Naval Intelligence, were
eager to question Lilly.

Hours passed. When August A. finally saw his mother, she
was crying. "There's my boy Gussie," she shouted, stepping
down the gangplank supported by Hawes.

"Mother, dear!" August A. cried out in a voice choked with
sobs.

The aged woman stretched out her arms toward her son as
he rushed to the fence.

"Gussie [August A.], they won't let me see you tonight!"

Two sailors and a marine guard started to separate the two, but a U.S. marshal permitted Busch and his mother to embrace. Then she was taken away. Lilly had been interrogated for more than two hours on the ship, but now the real grilling was to begin. For the next day and a half, she was in the custody of U.S. government agents at Key West. Their questioning was brutally thorough. "After the interrogations," Hawes later recounted, "Mrs. Busch was taken into a room accompanied by the marshal's wife and there subjected to an examination of her person, this examination being conducted by a man doctor, who laid the old lady on a bed and examined her private parts, making a very thorough examination of her vagina and womb."

Lilly's traveling companion and Swiss maid received the same treatment.

After forty hours of detention, Lilly was finally released and the Busches departed immediately for St. Louis. She was greeted at Union Station by six carloads of family members, including grandchildren and great-grandchildren. She seemed cheery and vigorous and even paused to have her photograph taken. Lilly Busch was home at last.

One possible reason for her rough treatment in Key West became apparent shortly afterward. "We established the fact that at least $1 million worth of German war bonds were bought in the country by the Busch family." The charge was made by Alfred Becker, the deputy New York State attorney general, who said the bonds financed the purchase of *The New York Evening Mail* and other newspapers to print German propaganda. "One of the strangest points in this whole business," Becker commented, "is that American citizens could be gulled into financing their own seduction." The Adolphus Busch estate, August A. and Lilly were among the subscribers to the German war bonds. It was possible, Becker said, that the Busches may not have known that their money was being used to purchase a newspaper for propaganda purposes.

August A. at first denied buying the bonds. "This whole damn business has become sickening. The whole damn thing is absurd. I deny the whole thing. None of the family has bought them." But a day later, he admitted his error. "The purchase of the German securities occurred more than two years ago, long before our country went to war with Germany and the sale of this paper in the United States was sanctioned by the United States Government." Busch said he thought the money was going to be used to take care of the many interned German ocean liners in American ports. "Had I the least suspicion that any of the money was to have been used in any way contrary to the interests of the United States I would have told them to go to hell." Later, August A. said the information on the war bonds had been stirred up by "overenthusiastic agitators and envious competitors who had attempted to prejudice the public against Anheuser-Busch."

The owner of *The New York Evening Mail*, Dr. Edward Rumely, was arrested because he had financed his newspaper with $1,350,000 obtained from Dr. Heinrich Albert of Berlin and had concealed the fact from Palmer, the alien property custodian. A U.S. government investigator said that Rumely had told him he got the money to buy the newspaper from Lilly Busch and Herman Sielcken, the millionaire coffee merchant who had been a close friend of Adolphus Busch's. The name of Kurt Reisinger, Lilly's grandson, was reported as the person who had represented Sielcken's interests in the United States, which Reisinger denied. Rumely was later convicted of violating the trading-with-the-enemy act. He served a thirty-day sentence and was later pardoned by President Coolidge.

The government had developed the case about the newspaper's financial support while Lilly Busch was in Germany, and after Sielcken had died at a resort there. It possibly was one of the reasons why she was questioned so closely at Key West. Hawes complained about the "cruel and unusual treatment" in the strip search of Lilly Busch. Attorney General Thomas W. Gregory, Navy Secretary Josephus Daniels and Treasury Secretary W. G. McAdoo all investigated. A naval officer was dismissed from the service, a Justice Department investigator was suspended for one week without pay, and the deputy collector in charge at Key West was severely reprimanded. But McAdoo pointed out that "the Office of Naval Intelligence had given information that Mrs. Busch was suspected of carrying communications and that that office and also a representative had received instructions that she should be subjected to search and examination."

Although Lilly had returned to America, her assets remained under the control of the alien property custodian. For the rest of 1918, Palmer was under increasing pressure to release her property, but he stubbornly resisted efforts by Nagel and Hawes, and even those of President Wilson. "Her property,"

Palmer said, "consists largely of an undivided interest in great brewery properties in this country, and there are many facts and circumstances tending to cast doubt upon the loyal Americanism of some of those associated with her in business. The Judiciary Committee of the Senate is now investigating the activities of the so-called German brewers in America, which investigation may lead into fields not yet fully explored and may result in disclosures which would embarrass us if in the meantime the Busches had been given the clean bill of health which the restoration of Mrs. Busch's property would imply."

The U.S. Senate investigation was a severe embarrassment to the brewing industry of America and to the Busches. The efforts of Adolphus and Charles Nagel to sway public opinion by buying space in foreign-language newspapers came to light during the committee's hearings. One of Adolphus's letters, introduced as an exhibit in the hearings, was particularly revealing. It demanded that the president of the Texas Brewing Company, in which Busch had an interest, help finance the anti-prohibition campaign, not merely at the state level, which had already been revealed in the Texas investigation, but in the halls of Congress.

"We must pay over to the U.S. Brewers Association whatever it may require to represent us properly before Congress, where we have most important bills to defend," Adolphus had written. "Then we want to defeat any bill which may be brought up to increase the revenue tax on beer, with which we are now threatened. We want further to see that no Prohibition is enforced in the District of Columbia or embodied in the Constitution of Oklahoma, when the latter is admitted to statehood."

But the disclosures carried little weight with the attorney general's office, which continued to bombard Palmer with recommendations to release Lilly's property. "Mr. Busch until his death was a highly regarded citizen of St. Louis," said LaRue Brown, a deputy attorney general. "He was, of course, a brewer, but brewers were not formerly regarded with the degree of reproach which latterly has become to be attached to their names. He was a very public spirited citizen."

When the armistice was signed November 11, Palmer was still resisting. He pointed out that Mrs. Busch had remained in Germany for nine months after the United States declared war on Germany, that one of her daughters was the wife of a munitions manufacturer and the other was the wife of a captain in the German Army. "Moreover she came out not in the performance of any duty to the United States, but upon the very urgent insistence of her son and counsel that she must do so in order to avoid the seizure of her property as enemy property, or if seized, in order to enable her to recover it."

President Wilson finally told Palmer that the federal government had no legal right to retain the property and he advised him to "release it as soon as possible." This was done on December 6, 1918.

The return of Lilly's vast fortune should have been a cause of tremendous rejoicing among members of the Busch family. It was, however, overshadowed by an unmitigated disaster. A few days earlier, Anheuser-Busch had shut down its beer-brewing facilities. Although the armistice had ended the war, wartime prohibition still remained in effect and the prospects for the future were bleak. As for Lilly, her ordeal in Key West wouldn't be her last run-in with federal agents.

17

"What Would Father Have Done?"

In January 1920, barely two years after the guns had gone silent on the Western Front, August A. Busch faced the greatest crisis of his life. An ugly stepchild of the Great War, national prohibition had made his business a crime. The great American Dry Out had begun, ushering in one of the most fantastic, radical experiments in social planning ever seen in this country. The Twenties were about to Roar. It would be the era of bathtub gin, speakeasies and powerful speedboats running in illegal hootch from Bimini; of flappers, hip flasks, Thompson submachine guns and a short, bullet-headed killer from the Five Points of New York City who set up shop in South Chicago with the family Bible and cards printed, "Alphonse Capone, Second Hand Furniture Dealer."

August A. had always had to measure himself against the colossal shadow of Adolphus and in moments of difficulty was fond of wondering aloud, "What would father have done?" On midnight, January 16, 1920, when the Eighteenth Amendment took effect, he stood alone. There were none of those densely written, hectoring letters offering advice that Adolphus had liked to pop off from Villa Lilly or the Ivy Wall. There had been suggestions on what brewing method to use, where to buy coal and why a troublesome daughter couldn't limit her spending. There was even one exhorting him to use porcupines for rat control instead of cats, which were considered more expensive because they ate grain.

If his father's letters had occasionally irritated, August A. might have welcomed his advice on the eve of what promised to be a disaster. At age fifty-five, he was in his prime, a heavy-chested man with thinning hair parted down the middle, a florid face and muttonchop sideburns. He was finally his own master, and if his experiences in the next decade ruined his health and drained his fortune, they also proved his mettle.

Prohibition, in varying forms, was nothing new to the United States. From 1623, when the Plymouth Colony outlawed drunkenness in one's home, to prohibition during the Great War, regulating the consumption of alcohol had been a favorite pastime. But the ease with which national prohibition was written into law was surprising. When the Eighteenth Amendment was finally voted on by Congress in 1917, the country accepted the results "not only willingly, but almost absent-mindedly." The Senate passed the measure by a one-sided margin after only thirteen hours of debate; the House polished it off in a single day. By January 1919, only two months after Armistice, the Eighteenth Amendment had been ratified by the required number of states and was part of the Constitution.

Problems were foreseen. When President Wilson momentarily astounded the country by vetoing the Volstead Act, which gave the amendment its enforcement teeth, he predicted it would be a miserable failure. His veto was quickly overridden. Wilson, once labeled an incorrigible dry by Adolphus Busch, couldn't help lashing out. "These miserable hypocrites in the House and Senate . . . many with their cellars stocked with liquors and not believing in prohibition at all—jumping at the whip of the lobbyists. . . . The country would be better off with light wines and beers."

August A. couldn't have agreed more. He had preached that

gospel for years. He had never hesitated during the decade that preceded Prohibition to spend money to get the message out that beer was a temperance drink. As more and more saloons were closed by dry laws, he fought back by setting up a special division called the Mail Order Department. Quart and pint bottles of beer were shipped through the mails direct to the consumer. The technique had made millions for Sears, Roebuck with girdles and farm tools, so Busch was more than willing to give it a try with beer. He also adopted a strategy that was to become a recurrent Anheuser-Busch theme down to the present—the best way to quiet opposition wasn't necessarily by correcting perceived abuses but, rather, by trying to reform the consumer. To this end the company eventually spent more than $650,000 to set up a Brewing Industry Protective Fund "to educate misinformed people concerning the beer business in relation to the public welfare."

August A. had held press conferences; he had run full-page advertisements; he had joined the Schlitz Brewing Company in buying $36,000 worth of bonds in a publicity company that helped place favorable stories on the front pages of 11,000 newspapers. His biggest hedge for the future, however, was his multimillion dollar investment in a nonalcoholic beverage called Bevo.

On January 9, 1916, during an interview while seated at his father's old rolltop desk, August A. had discussed the rising tide of prohibition. No, he didn't think the nation would go dry. But even if it did, he was already hard at work launching Bevo, a name derived from "pivo," the Bohemian word for beer. The beverage would contain less than one half of one percent alcohol. Drinkers, August A. claimed, had yearned for years for something nonintoxicating that would "touch the spot."

People began touching the spot so profusely that Busch invested $10 million in the largest bottling plant ever constructed and still one of the largest structures of its kind anywhere. The Bevo plant dwarfed the 110 other buildings that comprised Busch's red-brick fiefdom. The cornices were graced with man-sized granite figures of the "Bevo Fox" clutching a tankard and dressed in a Tyrolean cap and breeches. The construction came at a price: eight men were electrocuted when a cable touched a power line.

By 1918 Bevo was selling 5 million cases a year and at a dime or 15 cents a bottle was reaping $6 million in profits.

With sales so healthy, the future looked promising even when the brewery was forced to close in December of that year due to wartime prohibition. August A. considered Bevo his ace in the hole, and when production resumed in 1919, sales continued to bear him out. Bevo took fire and was soon selling throughout the world. No one could have predicted that the beverage was about to take a monumental nosedive.

The problem was that after Prohibition started, the public quickly developed a liking for the illegal hard liquor and bathtub gin that began pouring into the cities. If much of it tasted like rotgut, it only had to be mixed with a sweetener. Drinkers preferred cocktails or near beer that could be spiked with alcohol. In a matter of six months, the American public had learned how to get a kick out of breaking the law, and the malty-tasting Bevo was in serious trouble.

Bevo's flop stunned August A. He began talking seriously of converting his plants to pork production. He had always had a fondness for hogs and had imported wild boar from Germany in hopes of cross-breeding them with American stock on his estate at Grant's Farm. He had even spoken of developing cholera-proof pigs. The year before Prohibition, he had incorporated the Bevo Packing Company for $1 million. A sign placed on one of his buildings showed him in overalls driving a herd of pigs. The inscription to this curious poster read: "I am a piker now, but quality is my motto. Watch me grow."

It was, he claimed, a joke meant for his wife. But as Prohibition hit home, the jokes dried up with the flagging Bevo sales. By mid 1920, August A. had changed tactics and was calling for strict enforcement of the law on the theory that if the public had to face total abstinence, it would beg for repeal. It was tricky terrain for a brewer who had an uneven track record in correcting the abuses that had brought on Prohibition in the first place. The memory of the Texas trials, which had implicated his father in questionable acts, remained vivid, as did the similar indictments in Philadelphia in 1916 of seventy-two breweries, whose representatives had succeeded in delaying the proceedings by simply announcing that they didn't have any records. Asked why, they admitted they burned them every month.

August A.'s problems with the saloon, that bane of the prohibitionists, hadn't been forgotten. The corruption-plagued saloon was bad news for the brewers, and Busch had often pledged himself to reform. But the slipperiness of his stance had been made all too obvious in 1918 with revelations that the saloons in East St. Louis—many of them owned by Anheuser-Busch—were staying open on Sunday in blatant violation of the state's blue laws.

Located across the Mississippi River in Illinois, the East Side was notorious for its honky-tonks and red-light district. A flood of thirsty St. Louis residents poured across the bridges every Sunday. The mayor admitted his saloons were breaking the law, but so what: they pumped $175,000 a year into the city's treasury. The local police had a venerable tradition of being on the take, including the police chief, who stood guard in full uniform while hoodlums rifled the City Hall safe to remove incriminating documents. It was no secret the cops didn't go out of their way to enforce the law.

The scandal had been investigated by U.S. District Judge Kenesaw Mountain Landis, who later cleaned up the Chicago Black Sox scandal and became the first commissioner of baseball. The results of his inquiry were highly embarrassing for August A. An agent of Anheuser-Busch, called to testify, calmly announced that the brewery controlled thirty-two saloons in the community and that all of them stayed open on Sunday and had done so for the past ten years.

Only a day earlier, Busch had told reporters that lawless saloons were responsible for the spread of prohibition sentiment. Commenting on this remark from the bench, Landis sent a copy of the agent's testimony to the brewery by special delivery. August A. was forced into some fast and unconvincing damage control. "Personally I know nothing about law violations in East St. Louis. If the officials there will permit me, I will aid them in preventing law violations." It was still his view, however, that the brewery was "not responsible" for lawbreaking. "The enforcement . . . depends entirely on whether or not the officials of the city want the law enforced."

The East St. Louis debacle was cited by critics who questioned August A.'s sincerity about reform. Under fire, he had tried another approach aimed at muting criticism. He suggested that Americans adopt the German saloon system, which, he claimed, served only beer and light wines. The Deutsche Wirtschaft, as it was called, was aimed at the family trade—momma, poppa and der kinder. August A. wanted good music, good food and, of course, good beer—but no hard liquor. The Germans, he insisted, also prohibited "treating," or what today would be called buying rounds. Treating, Busch said, was bad news. "A man goes into a saloon to get a glass of beer. He meets a friend, or a group of friends, and sometimes twenty or thirty drinks are consumed. The treating system ought to be prohibited."

The result of August A.'s crusade was the construction in 1917 of possibly the most whimsical building ever built in St. Louis—the Bevo Mill. Located on Gravois Road, five miles from Grant's Farm, it was a replica of a Dutch windmill of the picture postcard variety. It was to be, Busch announced, a "high class" café. There was no bar, no sawdust, no nudes. Bevo was served in abundance.

The Bevo Mill soon ran into problems. It was pointed out that, contrary to Busch's claims, German saloons did indeed sell hard liquor and that diehard saloon patrons wouldn't go for the lighter stuff. More serious, the idea ran afoul of wartime hysteria. There were cries that the mill, with its slowly revolving blades and Teutonic menu featuring such heavy delicacies as bratwurst glockein, was an insidious attempt to force German ways upon patriotic St. Louis.

Neither the Bevo Mill nor Bevo turned the tide for August A. after Prohibition became the widely violated law of the land. People, as Will Rogers said, had decided to "vote dry as long as they can stagger to the polls." Busch admitted it was becoming a "man's job" to keep his labor force busy "in vast plants made idle by radical changes in public opinion."

What would Father have done? Like the departed prince, August A. was willing to experiment. He announced plans for a new soft drink called "Kicko—the drink with the Right Kick." What that meant was never fully explained, but the label showed a man riding a kicking mule. Two other soft drinks were introduced—Buschtee in a lime-green bottle aimed at the ladies; and Caffo, a coffee-flavored beverage. Both proved total failures and were withdrawn within a year. Bevo sales fell off the charts, but the beverage hung on in a lingering death until 1929 in the forlorn hope it would make a comeback. The product ultimately represented a $15 million investment and a $4 million loss.

Under the terms of the Prohibition amendment, the brewery was able to keep the Budweiser name before the public by brewing a de-alcoholized near beer. Lavish claims were made about the product, the most lavish by August A.'s son Gussie, who became increasingly active in the brewery after the "dark era" began. Gussie said that the new Budweiser was "such a perfect imitation of our Budweiser beer that our experts could not determine, from taste, which was the beverage and which was the beer." But was Budweiser near beer, with an alcohol content of less than one-half of one percent, as good as the real thing? Adolphus would have roared; a fifty-page letter would have been fired off with the threat of banishment. Regardless, Budweiser near beer was never embraced by a public that increasingly preferred to brew the real stuff or buy it from a bootlegger fresh from Canada. The situation became so bleak that the company briefly considered selling the famous Budweiser trademark to a foreign brewing company.

If August A. had been told in 1920 that Prohibition would last thirteen years, he wouldn't have believed it. Even as the Eighteenth Amendment took effect on that cold January night in 1920, he had reason to be hopeful for the future. His company was no longer turning a profit, but he wasn't beaten. He would keep fighting and perhaps someday the public, with his help, would come to its senses. In 1920 only 583 breweries remained open compared with 1,771 twenty years earlier. It would have been easy to liquidate his holdings and raise his beloved pigs, but he and his sons, Adolphus III and Gussie, were determined to keep the company going.

The Prince had shown the way by his relentless diversification. If August A. had to make ice cream instead of real beer, or truck bodies and refrigeration cabinets or yeast in the decade to come, so be it. He never wanted to be caught again with "all his eggs in one basket." His great fortune remained intact. There were still cruises to take to his estates in Germany and summer trips to Cooperstown. There was no need, so far, to cut back on one of the most regal lifestyles ever beheld in a country long accustomed to the excesses of its millionaires. He was still master of the roaming deer and pig herds at Grant's Farm.

18

A Jumping Frog Named Budweiser

August A. liked to get to work early. He was usually hunkered down behind his father's old desk at the brewery by eight in the morning. But by noon he was often seen waiting impatiently outside his office for the eleven-mile drive back to Grant's Farm in his black Rolls-Royce or the yellow Pierce Arrow. As Prohibition darkened his business days, he took greater pleasure in his role as country squire. His lifestyle was often described as "baronial," and for sheer extravagance it rivaled the standards even of his father.

During the boom years of the 1920s, there were plenty of nouveaux riches to go around, but no one had anything on August A. or on his increasingly colorful family. There were race horses and carriages to buy, expensive automobiles, mansions to build and enough animals to stock a zoo. August A. bought animals the way other millionaires laid down hard cash for Old Masters. Grant's Farm with its 215 acres, lakes and Deer Park was his feudal domain, and if the cottages nestled around the castle didn't have thatched roofs, it was mere oversight.

Grant's Farm must have given its owner unvarnished pleasure if only because he knew his father had been dead set against his building it. Adolphus thought the country setting south of St. Louis was too remote, the cost too exorbitant. The Prince told his headstrong son not to make any improvements on the estate. He made it clear he did not want the place built. August A. went ahead anyway.

If the French Renaissance château wasn't as opulent as the Vanderbilts' 240 room Biltmore it wasn't far behind. The Big House dominated a hill on what was once part of the "hard-scrabble" homestead of a failed farmer named Ulysses S. Grant before he went off to war. August A.'s brother-in-law, Edward Faust, snippily called it "a very pretentious home" shortly after work began on the place in 1910. Tiffany art glass bejeweled the reception hall, hunt room and other parts of the mansion. The Tiffany contract alone cost $150,000.

August A.'s most original touch, however, was the $250,000 "Bauernhof" built behind the château. Modeled after a German farm manor, its arched stone gate opened into a cobbled quadrangle. There was room for twenty of Busch's blooded horses and thoroughbred hunters, a cow barn, harness and tack rooms, and a timbered hall to accommodate his growing collection of rare coaches. The second story included five large apartments, rooms that would serve as battlegrounds in stormy divorces to come. The spacious quadrangle was dominated by a clock tower, and at every angle on the roof black and white storks, a Teutonic good luck sign, craned their plaster of paris necks from nests of straw.

From the start, Grant's Farm was meant as a millionaire's private menagerie. Even before it was finished, a herd of Jersey cattle was installed along with an angry bull that one day set off on a rambling chase after August A., who had to run for his life. The Jerseys were joined by Shetland ponies, rare white Jerusalem donkeys, goats, lambs, German shepherds, at least eighty deer, including spotted axis deer from India, European red deer, roe deer and Japanese deer, Japanese chickens, flocks of pink-legged flamingoes and a white ox. There were also two elephants named Peggy and Tessie that Busch rode wearing a sports coat and gray fedora, wild boars from France, a jumping frog named Budweiser and possibly the most incredible pigs ever beheld.

Three blue pigs were presented to August A. by a fellow pig fancier from Lynn, Massachusetts. "They bear a delicate azure tint during the early days of their life, but as the grip of age fastens upon them, their color deepens to a rich ultramarine blue. Their snouts also are tastefully touched with blue. Their hair, also blue, is long and rich with an inclination to curl. Their blue whiskers present a more pleasing aspect . . . and their eyes are of an appealing hazel brown." A joy to behold and a pleasure to slaughter. When properly cooked, "their flesh formed a most delicate tidbit."

Of a late afternoon, August A. made the rounds of his estate, often in a buckboard. He wore a straw hat and the knee-high leather boots he favored and carried a walking stick and huntsman's horn. When he blew on this silver trumpet, his deer timidly stepped out of the woods to receive a handful of grain.

If he went riding, a monkey named Joko sat behind him dressed in a suit of green velvet.

For the elephants, August A. hired a trainer in Hollywood. He also had a special saddle made for them so that he could give his grandchildren rides, four at a time. He himself often climbed up on one of the beasts, shotgun in hand, and set out on a plodding tour of his property. With so many animals, he hosted full-blown circuses complete with a big top. "The children," he once said, "have to be amused."

When his animal collection became too large, August A. gave some of them to the St. Louis Zoo, donating a pair of lions he had bought in Germany before the outbreak of the war, as well as chimps, parrots and exotic birds. A frequent visitor at the zoo, he was so well known to the animals that they bellowed their greetings as soon as he set foot on the grounds.

Like his father, August A. was a keen hunter and wing shot. He had become handy with firearms during his trip out West as a young man and used his specially engraved .44-caliber revolver to pot jackrabbits. To satisfy his craving for game birds, he bought 437 acres of marshy ground near the Missouri River at St. Peters, Missouri, about thirty miles west of St. Louis. The place came to be called the Shooting Grounds, and Busches have dispatched ducks by the thousands there since 1916. It was called "shooting de luxe."

He carved out eight to ten lakes of ten to fifteen acres each, seeding them with grass and setting up zinc-floored blinds equipped with telephones so that a hungry or thirsty hunter need only ring up a steward for "a nip of a little something warm and stimulating." Horse-drawn wagons were outfitted as portable buffets. For an added treat, the place was stocked with "peccary, a South American wild hog, one of the most vicious mammals in the world to afford sport for Busch and his guests," namely "visiting celebrities who are accustomed to good hunting on their native heaths."

Even more than hunting, August A. loved good horseflesh. His formidable stable of harness horses was considered the best west of New York City. There were also blue-ribbon hunters, jumpers and four-in-hand teams. For a while, he owned a race horse named Chief Uncas who turned in what was probably one of the most dismal performances ever recorded at the Kentucky Derby. Busch paid $9,600 for the horse in 1923, beating out oil magnate Harry Sinclair in a bidding war in Saratoga Springs. August A. took a party with him to the Derby Day festivities in Louisville in May 1925. He had high hopes, and when the gates clanged open Chief Uncas got off to a strong start. But the horse quickly faded, finishing dead last in a field of twenty, a quarter mile behind the pack. The joke around town was that many of August A.'s friends who were present for the start of the Derby on Saturday stuck around over the weekend to watch Chief Uncas finish.

It was for the tallyho, the Rolls-Royce of horse-drawn vehicles, that Busch reserved his greatest affection. The sport had started in England, an outgrowth of the mail coach routes of the early nineteenth century. It wasn't long before the nobility were racing them—often with disastrous result. So many fatal wrecks occurred that in 1820 Parliament declared the racing of coaches a criminal offense. The law was sneezed at, and by the 1880s the lords and earls were making up to twenty miles an hour pounding down the macadam outside London. In the United States, Edward Harriman, a railroad builder, took up the sport, as did Alfred Vanderbilt, who liked to burn up the roads between New York and Newport driving a magnificent yellow coach.

When Vanderbilt went down with the *Lusitania,* his famous coach was purchased by August A., who also acquired Vanderbilt's team of four hackneys. Sitting high in the box, Busch was often seen driving up the St. Charles Rock Road on his way to the Shooting Grounds. Other coaches in Busch's collection included an opera bus owned by his father; a postilion-driven Victoria that had made a hit during the 1904 World's Fair when it was loaned to Prince Pu Lun, a cousin of the emperor of China; assorted phaetons, surreys, traps, sleighs, a bobsled and a rare pony coach that had belonged to Harriman.

Some of these curiosities went with Busch on his yearly excursions to the family estate at Three-Mile Point near Cooperstown. The family's arrival near the end of June at the pitch-roofed Delaware & Hudson train depot had all the gaudy excitement of a circus coming to town. That is exactly what it was—August A.'s private circus. The boxcars coupled to his Pullman unloaded horses, goats, Shetland ponies, Jerusalem donkeys, fox hounds and Tessie the elephant. Townsfolk started to gather as soon as the train pulled in to behold the procession of beasts and Busches out to Three-Mile Point.

On a typical day, August A. was up by five in the morning to put in some time at his desk. His work finished, he strolled down to his private trout pool to feed scraps of liver to his fish.

His role as paterfamilias—he was called Papanunu—was never more evident than during his summers in Cooperstown. Most of his ever-increasing brood of grandchildren went with him, and he delighted in amusing them just as he did back in St. Louis.

August A. said that he cared nothing for "society." He much preferred the pleasures of the family. He doted on his often troublesome children, lavished them with gifts, mansions, limousines, thoroughbred horses, magnificent balls and good jobs. He endured their excesses, usually, but not always, in silence. There were five children: Adolphus III, the playboy, horse-riding older son; Gussie, the playboy, horse-riding younger son; the daughters, Marie, Clara and Alice. They were more than a bundle for any father. But his sons rarely spent much time in Cooperstown, which perhaps added to the attraction the place held for August A.

19

The "Completely Forgotten Man"

When Adolphus Busch III was born on February 10, 1891, at his father's home, Number Two Busch Place, a gun salute was fired at the brewery to mark the occasion. A crown prince had been born and there were loud cheers on all the humming bottling lines. Although he was later president of the company for twelve years, his reign was eclipsed and, to some family members, deliberately overlooked during his brother, Gussie's, long, colorful tenure. The "completely forgotten man," he was called. It wasn't always such.

As a child Adolphus III was shy and reserved, traits that followed him into adulthood. He attended private schools, but like the other Busches of his day, his formal education was sketchy. He did not finish college, preferring his father's stables to the classroom. Horses were his great love as a boy. It would appear that he led a quiet life into early manhood.

All that changed in 1912, the year before Adolphus's death, when his grandson and namesake was the subject of romantic rumors about his engagement to a showgirl. The young man was considered "one of the most conspicuous catches in the country," and for months the story was headline news in New York and St. Louis. Adolphus III, after all, was regarded as the "Beau Brummel of St. Louis's younger society set . . . of dapper, slender build, unusually good looking and always groomed to the minute." Dark-haired and with a taste for exquisite tailoring, he was said to be a "conspicuous patron of the theaters and has a wide acquaintance among theatrical people."

One of those theatrical people was Ethel Amorita Kelly, an actress he met while she was performing in St. Louis. Adolphus III admitted they had had several dinners together, but said that was about as far as their relationship went. He denied rumors that he was about to marry Ethel. The work of her press agent, he claimed. Besides, he couldn't marry her. A lowly clerical worker at the brewery, he was too poor. "I am working only on a nominal salary and haven't enough money of my own to support a wife." Moreover, August A., sharply opposed to any marriage, had hired a private detective to investigate Ethel.

Back in New York, the actress stood by her guns. Yes, they were engaged and had been for months. She displayed a bracelet that Adolphus III had given her. "I understand Mr. Busch's family is very much against our marriage, but I do not think that will prevent our union." Ethel hated "gossip." "Affairs of the heart belong to the owner of that organ and their privacy should be unassailed. I refuse to say any more."

In St. Louis, August A. had a great deal more to say. "This is all tommyrot. How many more times must we be asked to deny this ridiculous story? My son never was engaged to Miss Kelly, and will not marry her. . . . The whole story is a falsehood."

Adolphus III didn't marry Ethel. Instead, a year later, he married Florence Parker Lambert, the divorcée of a multimillionaire and nearly ten years his senior. Adolphus III had known Florence through their mutual love of horses since the age of fourteen. The marriage of the blond thirty-one-year-old mother of three to the twenty-one-year-old brewery heir was considered a scandal. And once again August A. had branded as false stories of the engagement. He and other family members made it clear that they thought Florence, a belle from a wealthy Richmond, Virginia, family, was too old for their boy. The newspapers delighted in playing up the age difference. It was noted that when she married her first husband, Marion L.J. Lambert, in 1899, Adolphus III was only seven years old. Another report stated that when Florence applied for a marriage license her "age was definitely stated for the first time."

In seeking a divorce from Lambert, whose family had made millions by producing Listerine mouthwash, Florence had charged that her husband "humiliated and insulted her publicly and privately, and unjustly nagged, criticized and found fault with her." She likewise claimed that he "went long distances from home for the sole purpose of leaving her." The charges would have a familiar ring seventeen years later when she divorced Adolphus III.

Florence was a lovely woman. In addition to her skills as a horsewoman, she was reported to be "of athletic trend and an enthusiastic roller skater and automobilist." Her wedding to Adolphus III took place after he was finally able to win over his entire family to the match. August A. took it in good grace. Florence, he now said, was an admirable woman. The couple was married at Grant's Farm in a private ceremony on June 21, 1913. It was, by Busch standards, a low-key affair with only family present and none of the extravagance of past weddings or the even greater opulence of weddings to come. August A. announced that he was going to build a home for the couple at Grandview Farm, not far from his estate.

Four months later, Adolphus, who had not attended the wedding, died in Germany. There was a question about what his gift to the couple would be; the papers recalled that he had given sizable checks to other grandchildren when they married. The answer came barely two months after his death when Adolphus III presented a claim that would prove successful against his grandfather's estate. Adolphus, he said, had promised him a $10,000 wedding present but hadn't paid him. A year later, in 1914, he made another successful claim. His story now was that shortly before his wedding he had been promised $40,000.

A girl, Marie Eleanor, was born in May 1914 to Adolphus III and Florence on Grant's Farm, roughly the same place, the papers observed, where the first child of Ulysses S. Grant and Julia Dent was born. But while Grant's child was "the poor son of a poor farmer" the Busch daughter was "heralded as heiress to one of the largest fortunes in America." Marie, or

Lammie as she was known, lived into a healthy old age and in her seventies thought nothing of jetting off to Hong Kong or Tokyo on a shopping spree. While she was still a girl, however, Lammie's mother, according to one family member, made it clear she didn't want her daughter to think of herself as a Busch. This was after Florence's marriage to Adolphus III had begun to exhibit cracks.

Adolphus III made the news again in 1918 when he had sought a military deferment during the war on the grounds he had a dependent wife. The request was denied, but the war ended before he was called for duty. A few months earlier, he had offered his services to the government as a horse buyer, saying his knowledge of horseflesh was a valuable asset. This, too, was denied. Marking the occasion, a newspaper carried the headline, "Busch a better horse buyer than soldier, he says."

The fact was that Adolphus III was a superb horseman. Gussie recalled years later that his brother was a fine four-in-hand driver. "Adolphus . . . made a sensational drive at the Old Coliseum that had everybody go crazy. The Vanderbilt coach and others were against him. It didn't look like he had a chance, and August A. turned to him and said, 'For Christ's sake, let me see what guts you've got!' Jesus, Adolphus Busch got wild, and he pulled out the whip and Big Ed was the horn blower and he was so scared that he got down from the top of the box of the coach and got down where he could jump off. . . . That goddamned coach was on two wheels half the time. My brother won it. . . . They threw hats and coats and every other goddamn thing into the ring for him."

August A.'s comment about "guts" and his son's stiffening reaction was significant. No doubt there was tension between a father trying to run a brewery in the looming shadow of prohibition and an oldest son who had a reputation as a horse-loving playboy.

There was no question that Adolphus III enjoyed living well. When his home was robbed in January of 1915, it was a major event. Diamonds, pearls and other jewelry valued at $12,800 were taken from a bedroom while he and Florence were dining with August A. at Grant's Farm. Adolphus III posted a $500 reward, hired private detectives, and ran boldfaced ads in the newspapers describing the jewelry. The stolen pieces included a $3,000 stick pin encrusted with diamonds and a pear-shaped pearl, a $3,000 woman's ring set with a large pink pearl, and a ring set with three large-carat diamonds surrounded by forty-six smaller diamonds. It was one of the biggest heists in the city's history, and the newspapers saw fit to editorialize. "Burgling a Busch . . . is a more dangerous business than the burglars themselves seem to realize."

Two years later, in 1917, there was more trouble for Adolphus III and his family. They had a narrow escape when their Grandview Farm mansion caught fire and burned to the ground. A short circuit was blamed. The home, located on a ridge overlooking a sweeping valley, was rebuilt. An unlucky place, it was to become the scene of increasing friction between Adolphus III and his wife.

Florence Busch, according to a family member, was a "very opinionated, loud woman." During social gatherings, the children of other Busch family members sometimes played a game by trying to guess how long she would talk at dinner. Florence was given to pounding on the table to make a point and on one occasion banged away so vigorously that she broke her wrist. A longtime Busch employee recalled that Florence drank a lot and had a "deep roaring voice." The employee worked for Gussie during much of the Prohibition period and had an intimate look at the family. The worker saw Florence at a bank one day; displeased by the service, she "just roared."

Helen Busch Conway recalled that her father, Ernst Busch, August A.'s cousin, was often summoned to the home of Adolphus III to ease the tension when the couple were fighting. Ernst, a witty, jovial man, tried to smooth things over by making small jokes during the periodic blowups. It wasn't easy. Both Adolphus III and his wife appeared to have a drinking problem. "They all drank too much," Helen said.

There was another problem which was revealed in 1919 when Adolphus III was stopped for speeding with a passenger in his car. "The deputy agreed with Busch not to disclose the identity of the woman who was with him." Some ten years later, the last straw occurred when Florence invited a female friend of hers from Texas to spend some time at Grandview Farm. Florence threw Adolphus III out of the house, Helen Busch Conway said, when she caught the woman sitting on her husband's lap. "It was very painful," recalled a friend of the family's.

Adolphus III's divorce took place in 1930 at a secret court session arranged by a friendly state legislator in the chambers of an equally compliant judge. But that wasn't enough to keep the papers from having a field day. The headlines said it all: "Adolphus Busch Divorced by Wife in Secret Hearing." Adolphus III, Florence charged, had deserted her nearly a year earlier, saying he never wanted to live with her again. The divorce papers were filed for Mrs. Busch by State Senator Richard Ralph, who also represented Adolphus III, and by Ethan A.H. Shapley, a member of the law firm of Adolphus's old friend, Charles Nagel. Senator Ralph was "a close personal and political friend" of Judge Mulloy's, who heard the case after hours in closed chamber and admitted he was going to be criticized for the special treatment. The hearing lasted twenty minutes. Granted custody of her daughter, Florence received Grandview Farm and nearly thirty acres of land.

The divorce occurred in late July 1930. Two months later, Adolphus III married a "Dallas Woman." His marriage to another divorcee, Catherine Milliken Bowen, took place, appropriately, at the Adolphus Hotel in Dallas. Busch was thirty-nine, his new wife thirty. A graduate of the University of Texas and St. Mary's College, Catherine came from a wealthy, politically prominent Texas family. After the ceremony, the couple left for Cooperstown, where Adolphus III's father greeted them at Three-Mile Point. By then, August A. was well acquainted with marital smashups in the family. And there would be many more to come.

20

"A Simple Coming Out Ball"

If the stormy marital problems of Adolphus III made headlines during the era of Prohibition, so did the debutante balls and marriages of the three Busch girls, Marie, Clara and Alice. August A. doted on his daughters. Following the footsteps of his father, he threw some of the largest, most garishly expensive balls the city had ever seen in their honor, and his magnificent gifts when they wed always made the papers. When two of

them had their appendixes removed, each medical bulletin
was dutifully reported. When another was pursued by a German aristocrat in search of a rich bride, the headlines chortled,
"The Baron? No, a Plain American Jones Wins the Great Heiress."

August A. lived long enough to see all three of his daughters
married, but not necessarily happily. He did not survive to
read about their divorces, which would come later, often in
dizzying succession. Only one marriage, Clara's, would last.
The other girls, at varying times, would marry up—investment
bankers and doctors—or down—the huntsman at the stables
or, in graying middle age, the gardener.

The Busches' taste for the extravagant as exhibited at their
coming-out balls helped coin a phrase used in St. Louis society, which in the days of Adolphus and August A. never warmly
embraced the family. Gaudy displays of wealth and privilege
were labeled "Buschy." Among members of the social elite it
had been rumored that the Busches were excluded from the St.
Louis Country Club, the city's most prestigious. Jealousy
might have had something to do with it, and also their line of
work. The making of beer was considered unsuitable for proper
gentlemen. Another reason, recalled Mabel-Ruth Anheuser, an
in-law, was the family's "Buschy" behavior. "They [some
Busch family members] were always overbearing. I think
they're very crude. I have always found it difficult having that
name because there was always that feeling, well, they get the
best of everything."

If they were excluded, that presented no problem. August A.
simply established his own country club. And if his girls
wanted some of the biggest balls and weddings St. Louis or,
for that matter, New York had ever seen, they would get their
wish down to the last bottle of champagne. When Marie, August A.'s oldest daughter, dewy-eyed in pink satin and French
maline, made her entrance into society in 1912, her mother
announced the party would be "a simple coming out ball." The
ball was held at the Sunset Inn, later to become the Sunset
Country Club, which her father helped establish a few miles
from his estate. The decorations required twenty-five florists
working for ten days and included 7,000 roses. The band
played for 400 guests until 4:30 in the morning. The champagne alone cost $3,000. It was August A.'s first big party for
one of his girls and if it didn't quite measure up to the balls
hosted by his father, he was learning.

In 1915, Marie married Drummond "Drummie" Jones, a local tennis champion, horseman and bridge player. The two had met on the tennis courts, and when August A. realized the couple were getting serious, he decided that the young man needed a job. A place was found for him in the Busch-Sulzer Brothers Diesel Company, and if Drummie didn't know anything about machines that was hardly an obstacle. In Horatio Alger fashion, he was expected to start at the bottom of the ladder—but not dwell there. Drummie won his first big promotion shortly before his engagement.

Clara, August A.'s second daughter, made the headlines in 1913 when she was operated on for appendicitis. The illness was a serious matter for the Busches, as two of August A.'s brothers had died from it. The papers reported Clara's first attacks in Cooperstown and mentioned the hurried trip her father made from St. Louis. Her unassisted walk to the operating table was described in detail.

The following year, fully recovered, Clara had a ball that outshone her sister's. It opened to "a symphony from the throats of hundreds of canaries hidden in a canopy of flowers and ferns." August A. spent $20,000. Again, there were acres of roses and orchids shipped in from the East Coast. The 500 guests made their way into the country on a dark night by following lanterns set out to mark the road. They danced the fox-trot, castle walk and hesitation. "There was no tangoing, showing that society has eschewed that dance." Breakfast was served at 6:30 in the morning, and the guests were warned that the bar would close at 4 A.M.

Clara's ball helped fashion another well-established St. Louis tradition—the close, some would say cozy rapport that existed between the family and local police. So much jewelry glittered from the throats and wrists of debutantes and matrons that St. Louis detectives were on duty and plainclothes patrolmen were posted at all the entrances. Everyone agreed that Clara's coming-out party was a bang-up affair even if it had to share news space with reports of fighting along the Somme during the Great War's first months.

A year later Clara married Percy Orthwein, the son of a wealthy St. Louis grain broker. A skilled illustrator, Orthwein was a Yale graduate and had studied art in Munich and Heidelberg. He later became chairman of the board of the D'Arcy Advertising Company after having served as account executive for Anheuser-Busch, one of the firm's largest accounts. He would also find a place on the beer company's board of directors. August A.'s wedding gift to his daughter was a mansion on Lindell Boulevard, one of the city's most exclusive streets.

Although Clara's ball was an improvement on Marie's, it wasn't until Alice's debut that all the stops were let out. Alice, or Pummie as she was known to the family, was named Queen of Love and Beauty at the Veiled Prophet Ball in 1922. The masqued affair owed its inspiration to the New Orleans Mardi Gras, and the queen was supposed to be an unmarried virgin. Then eighteen years old, Alice was "somewhat slender" with chestnut hair. An excellent dancer and tennis player, she was also a fine rider. "The love of good horseflesh being an attribute of the Busch family . . . she not only is an expert in the saddle, but also drives her choice thoroughbreds in the shafts of a French cart. . . . Just to bring her proficiency up to the mode, she is adept at the wheel of her own motor."

Alice had attended Mary Institute in St. Louis but received much of her education at home from tutors. Years later, she observed that her sister Clara had struggled to graduate. "Believe me, I was proud of her, and still am. I went to school only on Fridays."

When Alice married Louis Hager, Jr., in 1923 at Grant's Farm, bride and bridegroom walked beneath a canopy of roses and passed down an aisle framed by mounted baskets of lilies. Her gown had a five-foot train of lace and silk, and she was married in a flower-bedecked arbor. As usual, August A. gave the couple a mansion. Alice eventually divorced Hager to marry the huntsman at the Busch riding club. Divorcing again, she married twice more, outliving both husbands. But none of those wedding ceremonies matched the first for splendor.

Prominent among those in attendance was August A. "Gussie" Busch, Jr., August A.'s younger son. Gussie had made frequent appearances in the society pages as a horseman and in the regular news pages when he was arrested for careless driving in 1919. A groomsman at Alice's wedding, he gave his sister a dozen after-dinner coffee cups of china and silver. If still relatively unknown in 1923, Gussie's day was rapidly coming. Once he strode onto the scene, the dynasty would never be the same.

21

Peck's Bad Boy

None of August A.'s children compared with his younger son, Gussie. Short, thick-chested, his thighs iron-hard from squeezing the flanks of horses, his fists toughened in early manhood by bareknuckle fights in his private boxing ring, August A. Busch, Jr., was his father's most striking piece of work. Gussie, Gus, Junior, and later, Daddy, Colonel, the Boss, the Big Eagle, was a man whose daughter once toasted as "the greatest stud of them all." He was also tyrannical, profane, a relentless womanizer, prolific, shrewd, a vindictive bully, a brawler, a hard drinker, a superb rider, a teller of tall tales, one of the giants of his profession. He changed the history of brewing.

When he reached early manhood on the eve of the 1920s, Gussie Busch was primarily known as a dashing ladies' man and award-winning rider. As a child, he was an award-winning hellion. His younger sister Alice recalled how Gussie induced her to play "fire" with her playhouse, which was decorated with costly Brussels carpets. The boy merely wanted to try out his toy fire engine pulled by a goat named Giannini. He shot sparrows and made Alice cook them in the playhouse and offer them to their playmates. Like his more handsome brother, Adolphus III, he also wore the playboy's badge when he got older. One of his earliest memories was of climbing out a bathroom window as a boy and visiting a brothel madam who had taken a liking to him. Society matrons with eligible daughters reportedly bolted their doors when he appeared. Family legend has it that while still a teenager Gussie amused himself with the female servants at Grant's Farm. "Let's just say," he said long afterward, "I was the original Peck's Bad Boy."

His formal education was typical of August A.'s children: he had very little of it. "Without doubt I was the world's lousiest student," he said. "I never graduated from anything." Accounts of his schooling varied. He reportedly dropped out shortly after entering high school. However, when he divorced his third wife, he said that his education stopped at the fourth grade. Young Gussie attended Smith Academy, an exclusive boys' prep school, but left long before graduation. A classmate recalled that there was little evidence then of an emerging intellect. A poor student, Gussie was a dim bulb who was teased by his classmates because of what was thought to be a German accent.

Private tutors were hired to fill in the yawning gaps in his education. They had their hands full. Helen Busch Conway's earliest recollection of her second cousin Gussie was of him playing with the horses at Grant's Farm while his frazzled tutors hurried behind, trying to get him to buckle down to his spelling lessons. "The tutors would chase him from stall to stall and he would be cursing and trying to saddle a horse. He was a spoiled child." His father, kindly and forgiving with his offspring, was indulgent, even negligent with their schooling. "He was," said an acquaintance, "the kind of guy who would pat them on the head and say, 'Well, if you don't want to go to that bad old school today, you just don't have to.' "

In ripe old age, Gussie displayed a bandaged finger broken against the jaw of someone who had offended him. His punching skills were acquired early. After he married his first wife, he erected a boxing ring at his mansion. One of his favorite partners was Ernst Busch, his father's cousin who worked at the brewery. Ernst and Gussie had regular sparring sessions. Gussie knew how to throw a Sunday punch. One evening Ernst returned home "with a tremendous shiner and the brewery sent over slabs of meat to put on it," recalled his daughter, Helen Busch Conway. Gussie's preferred recreation was to go with a few friends to neighborhood saloons and pick fights over women. Crowd in tow, his excursions continued until one night a professional fighter decked Peck's Bad Boy, leaving him stone cold on the floor.

After a brief stint in the home guard during the Great War, Gussie went to work for a bank in South St. Louis. "I worked my way up from cleaning windows to cashier." He was that rarest of window washers, often arriving at work in a red, chauffeur-driven roadster. Gussie later joined his father's small railroad, the Manufacturers Railway Company. The president of the line was William Cotter, with whom Gussie had problems. "I went with Cotter for a while . . . and couldn't get along with him at all. Then I started with the brewery."

Following a night on the town, he was often late to work. Some mornings when he didn't wake up at all, his cousin Ernst was dispatched to Grant's Farm to roust him out of bed. After one particularly long night of carousing, he couldn't be budged, so Ernst resorted to an unusual wake-up call. He pulled back the covers and poured alcohol on Gussie's behind.

Describing his early experiences at his father's brewery, Gussie said he worked almost everywhere. "I became a union guy and went through the whole goddamn plant from A to Z. Worked in the malt house. Worked in the brew house. Worked in the cellars. Worked in the bottle shop. Did everything." It apparently didn't take him long to learn A through Z. Gussie joined Anheuser-Busch on January 1, 1924. Four months later as the company struggled for survival making near beer and other products during Prohibition, he was appointed general superintendent. "I was made superintendent pretty goddamn quickly."

In a business where most of the important executive jobs were held by family members, one of the more irony-freighted jokes was that you could tell that talent, like cream, rose to the top by the fact that all of the key positions were held by Busches or their relatives. But events showed that August A. had chosen wisely in advancing Gussie with a speed remarkable even for family-owned companies. The father knew a beer man when he saw one; and by any standard, Gussie was to prove that he had hops and barley in his veins.

He had already proven himself a true son of August A. by his skill with horses. Fearless and gutsy were words commonly used in describing his talent in the saddle. He could also be hard on his mounts. "Friends," *Time* later wrote in a profile, "remember young Gussie as difficult for other children to get along with . . . that he was hot-tempered and impatient with dogs and horses." "He was," said Helen Busch Conway, "such a marvelous horseman. . . . He had the strongest legs. He could squeeze the insides out of a horse." He could also handle a team with the skill of a professional. By fourteen he was driving coaches in competitions. He had style and a sense of humor, once putting on a blond wig and dress to compete in a ladies' event.

Most of Gussie's friends were horse people; his brother and sisters rode beautifully, as did their father. Their love of the sport, as well as their exclusion from the city's crusty, old-money society, prompted August A. and his sons to establish the Bridlespur Hunt Club in the mid-1920s. The Busches and their friends rode to the hounds as often as they pleased, and if the bluebloods shook their heads, so much the better. Gussie was a particularly hard case for the country club crowd. "He was very pushy and had a very bad temper," said a family friend. "He was also a bad loser. When he lost a tennis game, you could hear it all over, the cursing."

The first hunt at Bridlespur was held in May 1928. The men wore smart pink coats with collars of robin's egg blue, white breeches, boots and velvet hunting caps. The ladies were decked out in high silk hats with mesh veils. As master of fox hounds, Gussie put in a lot of saddle time. The rides could be rough and tumble. "I remember once the hounds found a fox . . . and they ran for an hour without check. One by one, the quitters dropped out, and finally there was no one left but Julius Van Ralde and myself. Van Ralde's horse hit the top rail of a fence and went down, and Van Ralde landed face first in a cow pie. He sat up and put his hand to his cheek and yelled, 'I'm bleeding!' I could see the son-of-a-bitch wasn't hurt. So I tossed him my handkerchief and let him to figure out his problem for himself!"

Huntleigh Village, with its grazing horses, ducks and wandering peacocks, was the focal point of Bridlespur's horsey set. The riding trails meandered through the village, around the mansions, swimming pools and tennis courts. Clara and her husband Percy Orthwein lived there in a château on forty-eight acres; so did Alice and members of the Gontard clan. Adalbert "Adie" von Gontard, the son of Adolphus's daughter Clara and Baron von Gontard, was a longtime resident. "We bought," Adie remembered, "a pack of foxhounds from Percy Rockefeller in 1929 and life really started."

Gussie, for his part, lived in a gray-stone mansion on Lindell Boulevard, a home provided by August A. when he married Marie Christy Church in April 1918. A polished, attractive woman who traced her ancestry to William Clark of the Lewis and Clark expedition, Marie had attended Miss Wright's School at Bryn Mawr, Pennsylvania. An acquaintance recalled that Marie was beautiful and refined, and not at all like Gussie.

His bride was twenty-two, Gussie nineteen. Marie was Catholic and they were married by a priest at the home of her widowed mother. More than 300 guests attended and spectators waited outside in the rain hoping for a glimpse of the couple. Lilly Busch, Gussie's grandmother, gave them a

$10,000 check and the choice between a silver set and an automobile. The bride chose the silver. Gussie gave her a platinum bracelet studded with diamonds. Throughout his life, he liked giving women—even married women—expensive jewelry.

While the newlyweds were on their honeymoon, their mansion was refurbished by a small army of craftsmen. The fittings included costly stone, hand-carved mahogany woodwork and art glass from France and the Far East. The yard was large enough for Gussie's mare, Untried. By the mid-1920s, he was earning $20,000 a year and employing a butler, chauffeur, upstairs maid, cook, laundress and yardman. He drove to the office in his grandmother's Rolls-Royce. Parrots and other exotic birds—and there were more birds to come—fluttered in the home's breakfast room. Gussie brought his pet schnauzer —he loved these small, shrill terriers—to the office and had it sent home in a chauffeur-driven car. He was heartbroken the day the dog ran into the street and was killed by a motorist. Like his father, Gussie was assembling a menagerie of his own.

A trusted employee during this period suspected that Gussie's marriage had been arranged by his father. Gussie once told this employee that he had given up another woman to marry Marie. The marriage, which produced two children, Lilly and Carlota, ended tragically in 1930. Marie caught a cold while Gussie was recovering from a two-week bout with the flu. Against the advice of friends who feared her cold would get worse, she put on a stunning, bare-backed dress for a party. She developed pneumonia and died in the mansion four days later.

At the time of the funeral, a visitor to the home went upstairs to view the body. Gussie had covered his wife with an ermine coat. "She was so beautiful," the visitor recalled. "Her skin looked just like alabaster." Shortly before the funeral, Gussie carried Marie's body down the staircase and laid her in the coffin, still wrapped in ermine. He was outraged when the Catholic church refused to let a priest preside over his wife's burial in Sunset Park because the cemetery wasn't consecrated ground.

Shattered by his wife's death, Gussie went to Florida. The sun, water and polo fields revived his spirits. Within a few months, he was back to work at the brewery.

22

Tom Mix and the Kaiser's Grandson

With such an exuberant collection of sons and daughters, in-laws and other worrisome relatives, August A., no matter how pressing the demands of Prohibition, also had to wrestle with some prickly family disturbances. The extent of his domestic difficulties was revealed in a letter he wrote his mother in 1919 shortly before Christmas. He had just learned that, only re-cently recovered from her strip-search ordeal, she wasn't plan-ning to return to St. Louis for the holidays, preferring to remain in her California mansion, Ivy Wall.

Her son accepted her decision. "I understand that the family friction existing makes it easier for you to be away." In a tell-ing line, he added, "This seems the fate of all families when money is left." August A. predicted more problems ahead. "I already feel that my little family, although they are good to one another now, will have friction over one thing or another when Alice and I are no more. I intend to leave the shooting grounds to the two boys, but I know in advance that some day this will brew trouble." He was right. The day would come when bitter arguments erupted over the property.

One of August A.'s more troublesome family problems in-volved a feud with his sister Anna Louise, who had married Edward Faust, the son of Adolphus's old friend, Tony. The dis-pute lasted for years, brother and sister refusing to speak to each other. The cause of the break probably involved Adol-phus's will. Anna had put in a whopping claim of $26,908 to cover repairs to the mansion that Adolphus had given her when she married Faust. The amount wasn't contested. Ed-ward Faust, after all, was one of the executors of Adolphus's estate. Whether August A. objected to the payment isn't known, but Faust shortly resigned as a brewery vice president.

The tension between the families spilled into the open when Faust made some cutting remarks about his brother-in-law.

The occasion was a party the Fausts hosted at their home. Faust took pains to compare his "simple little entertainment" with the lavish ball August A. had thrown for his daughter Clara. "Mr. Busch must have felt pretty bad about the publicity the newspapers gave him on that occasion. Do you know what the California newspapers said the ball cost? One million dollars." Neither of the Fausts had attended the ball. And August A. had made it clear that he would not attend their party.

It was domestic squabbling of the sort he was loath to see. He much preferred living the good life as squire of Grant's Farm. If he didn't entertain as regularly as his father, he still received a steady stream of visitors, among them Prince Friedrich Wilhelm von Hohenzollern, the grandson of the kaiser. The youthful prince was making a grand tour of the country in a Lincoln town car loaned by Henry Ford. If the Busches were still sensitive about the anti-German attacks that had scarred them during the Great War, they didn't show it. The nobleman was invited to ride at Bridlespur. The memory of the war still fresh, though, one of his St. Louis sponsors took pains to point out that the prince was "thoroughly democratic."

Another visitor, a favorite of August A.'s, was the cowboy star Tom Mix. Mix surpassed even W.C. Fields in his professed dislike of children. No matter that he was adored by millions of youngsters as the white-hatted knight of the silver screen. The Busch children were told to say only hello and make a quick exit. Mix, a former sheriff, swapped stories about the Old West with August A., who still cherished his sojourn in New Mexico as a greenhorn cowboy. The movie star even agreed to be photographed in his ten-gallon hat astride one of Busch's white donkeys.

Will Rogers dropped by for a visit. He was given a country-cured ham and two Berkshire pigs. August A. also sent a German shepherd to Rogers's ranch in California. "The dog," the humorist wrote, "did wonderful until some one here by mistake gave him a drink of half of one-percent beer. He would have been six years old next month."

August A. continued his father's tradition of donating to various charities. He routinely arranged elaborate Christmas parties for thousands of orphans, making sure each child got a warm sweater, coat and a bag of candy. Like another famous millionaire, John D. Rockefeller, he carried a bag of dimes with him and tossed the coins to children from the window of his limousine.

As Prohibition continued, the crisis deepened by the Depression, August A. was forced to cut back on his charitable donations. He later apologized for it and encouraged his children to do the right thing when the company, which provided their fortunes, was back on its feet. That moment proved years in coming. And in the meantime, August A. and his sons, Adolphus III and Gussie, had to wage the fight of their lives to keep Anheuser-Busch afloat.

It was during this period that a longtime caretaker at Grant's Farm died. Jacob Sonnen, who was also August A.'s masseur, was seventy-one years old. In ill health for years, he left half of his estate, nearly $19,000, to his former employer. His lingering health problems and the manner of his death proved heavy with portent. Jacob Sonnen committed suicide by shooting himself.

23

Scarface Al and the Golden Gates

During Prohibition, August A.'s problems were staggering. His de-alcoholized Budweiser wasn't doing well. Bevo, the soft drink in the squat ten-ounce bottle, had flopped badly after a promising start. His board of directors—most of them family members—opposed some of his major diversification plans. Things were so bad that in 1922 he declined his $40,000 salary as president until the company's slumping financial condition improved. A man in his predicament hardly needed additional trouble from an Italian immigrant doing a lucrative business in illegal liquor—Al Capone.

By the mid-1920s, Scarface Al was an American phenomenon, as renowned as Gene Tunney and Charles Lindbergh. The young Neapolitan roughneck, still in his twenties, had 700 men at his beck and call, many of them skilled practitioners of the art of killing with the sawed-off shotgun and the Thompson submachine gun. After perfecting the practice of the "rubout," usually in a hail of machine gun bullets fired from a speeding car, Capone developed more finesse. He became a skilled handler of politicians. He controlled judges and police captains and elected his own mayor in Cicero, Illinois, the Chicago suburb he ruled from his headquarters at the Hawthorne Hotel.

Capone made some of the most vivid newspaper copy of the day, traveling the city in an armored limousine equipped with bulletproof windows and flanked by cars of heavily armed men. When he went to the opera, he was accompanied by eighteen bodyguards wearing tuxedos that bulged under the left armpit. He controlled 10,000 Chicago speakeasies and the sources of supply as far as the Florida coast. Federal agents estimated his gang's annual take at $60 million.

In his later years, Gussie told friends that he once had met the mobster. It was an old story with him. Capone had directed his thugs to steal some of the brewery's "golden gates," the device used to tap beer kegs. With Capone in control of a half dozen Chicago breweries that were turning out the real thing in the midst of Prohibition, he could put them to good use. Learning of Capone's intentions, August A. dispatched Gussie to talk to him. The meeting took place in Miami, where the gangster lived in a hacienda-style mansion on the waterfront at Palm Island.

When young Gussie asked why Capone wanted the golden gates, the mob boss offered a deal: Don't ask questions and I'll guarantee plenty of sales for your yeast and sugar products. Naively, Gussie asked Capone to seal the deal in writing. The gangster answered to the effect, You've got my word, take it or leave it. "Daddy took it," wrote Gussie's daughter Lotsie, "and Capone was true to his word. Daddy made the brewery a fortune."

Gussie, in old age, returned to the subject of the golden gates. But this time he made no mention of Capone. During the bootleg era, the company lost 250,000 of the devices, which sold for two dollars apiece. August A. wanted to report their disappearance to police. "I said, no, no," Gussie recalled. "Let's not do it a damn bit. We knew that the underworld had taken them. And what the hell, we were selling them."

Capone reportedly had another connection to the Busch family. "Pleased with Miami's free and easy ways," wrote Polly

Redford in her book on the city, *Billion-Dollar Sandbar*, "Capone decided to make it his winter home, and bought a Spanish castello on Palm Island from Clarence M. Busch, of Anheuser-Busch (Budweiser) Brewing Company. The white-stucco home was set back from Biscayne Bay and included a huge swimming pool, gardens and cabanas." The house was sold to Capone for $40,000 through intermediaries so that residents of upscale Palm Island wouldn't launch a protest. The improvements, which cost $200,000, included a very high wall. Capone later claimed that he was at the home at the time of the St. Valentine's Day Massacre, the mass execution of a rival Chicago mob. He died there in 1947.

August A.'s difficulties weren't limited to Capone and his associates. Two products that helped keep his company going directly contributed to the national mania for breaking the Prohibition laws. In 1921, Anheuser-Busch introduced Budweiser Barley Malt Syrup and six years later brought out Budweiser Yeast. Both ingredients were crucial to the flourishing home brew trade. "The extent to which brewing has been revived in the home in the United States is almost incredible," wrote H.L. Mencken. "In some States every second housewife has become a brewer.... In one American city of 750,000 inhabitants there are now 100 shops devoted exclusively to the sale of beer-making supplies, and lately the proprietor of one of them, by no means the largest, told me that he sold 2000 pounds of malt-syrup a day."

Busch's malt syrup had a ready audience for the reason that it made a superior home brew. "August A. Busch realized that most people who purchased his malt syrup had no intention of using it to make bread or cookies," observed one historian. "While he frowned upon such perverse application of his product, he was powerless to stop it." Gussie, typically, was more to the point in his analysis. "If you really want to know, we ended up as the biggest bootlegging supply house in the United States. Every goddamn thing you could think of. Oh, the malt syrup cookies! You could no more eat the malt syrup cookies. They were so bitter.... It damn near broke Daddy's heart."

The same thing occurred with the company's yeast. Stopped by a plant foreman, Gussie was told that a local baker wanted to buy 500 pounds. Unable to believe the baker needed that much yeast, he called him only to be told point-blank to either deliver it or he would go somewhere else. "You knew perfectly well where the hell it was going," Gussie said. "It was going to the bootlegger to make hootch."

Gussie's personal dealings with bootleggers were circumspect. One employee recalled that Gussie's regular supplier was a short, pleasant man with red hair and a ruddy face who fit the part perfectly. "I think Mr. Busch paid him with cash out of his own pocket," the employee said. "He must have made the deliveries to his home. I never saw him deliver his merchandise there in the office." Occasionally he brought along a few samples, small bottles of apricot brandy. It was all very friendly. Gussie, this employee insisted, also took beer out of the plant for his personal use before it was dealcoholized. The worker particularly remembered the jugs of Michelob that he drove out to the Shooting Grounds.

The illegal sampling of beer must have been a major problem at the brewery during Prohibition. Locks were changed regularly. "Jesus, we spent thousands of dollars on locks damn near every month," Gussie said. As the man in charge of brewing operations, it would appear his own attitude was one of benign neglect when it came to employees drinking on the job. The consumption of real beer on the premises was so methodical, he recalled, that he was tipped off in advance whenever a group of workers got together to toss back a few so that he wouldn't risk seeing them. August A., by contrast, insisted on strict compliance with the law. "Daddy," his son said, "wouldn't let us take one bottle out of the place."

The yeast business was one of August A.'s finest moments. He not only had to go up against a virtual monopoly of the product by Fleischmann & Co. of Cincinnati with its superb distribution network, but he also had to tackle a recalcitrant board of directors. It was part of his plan to develop products that were logical spin-offs of the brewing business. Stung by the poor sales of Budweiser near beer, Bevo and soft drinks like the chocolate-flavored Carcho, the board balked. August A. persevered, and six weeks later the board reversed itself and gave him the go-ahead. The first samples were produced in 1926. When they fell short of Busch's high standards, they were scrapped. Starting over, the company made its first commercially sold yeast in 1927. August A.'s commitment paid off; the business eventually accounted for more than a third of the company's sales.

Adolphus III was put in charge of the yeast operation. Gussie stayed with the brewery. Relations between the brothers were sometimes strained. Long after Adolphus III's death, Gussie still bristled when it was suggested that the yeast department had saved the company. They survived, he said, by selling real estate, not yeast.

To get badly needed capital, August A. had set up a special liquidation committee to sell off such unneeded holdings as obsolete ice houses and warehouses. By 1924, the company had sold 50 percent of its property. "We used to own the corner saloon. . . . The gasoline stations paid us a fortune [for them] for we had the best goddamn locations," Gussie said. "That was the thing that saved Anheuser-Busch. It wasn't the yeast department, because I could remember when . . . [they] fixed the books to show the goddamn yeast department in the blue, and it was in the red so bad it was awful. The beer was in the red on account of the yeast department." Gussie, it must be remembered, ran the beer department.

The array of products August A. brought out during Prohibition was dizzying. He made glucose, corn sugar, corn oil and gluten livestock feed. He made truck bodies and ice cream cabinets as well as the ice cream that went into them. He made a chocolate-coated ice cream bar called Smack. He made a product called Malt-Nutrine for nursing mothers. He tried to get into the pharmaceutical field by offering industrial alcohol as well as a gargle. An eau de cologne and a bay rum were planned.

Like Adolphus, August A. heavily advertised the new products. The hype often reached the sublime. During the publicity frenzy that surrounded the discovery of King Tutankhamen's tomb, the company couldn't restrain from commenting, "So far it has not been reported that any Budweiser was found in the tomb . . . although Budweiser made before the adoption of the 18th amendment is still on sale at Cairo. Undoubtedly the reason that Budweiser was not found in the tomb was because it was not made 3,000 years ago—for Budweiser always was a drink for kings and everybody else."

Nor could the company refrain, deep in the dry abyss, from restating that Budweiser "never was intoxicating." Rather it was "a healthful and invigorating stimulant." Every case of the original Budweiser had contained a statement signed by several doctors, who concluded that "While it exhilarates, the beer does not intoxicate and may be used with advantage by young and old. We consider this beer a healthful and invigorating stimulant."

August A. expected his salesmen to reach for the last drop of zeal to meet the challenge of selling nonalcoholic beverages in a country that was drinking the hard stuff in record quantities. His drummers were exhorted to put Budweiser and Bevo in every ballpark in the land. One salesman in particular was praised for his unusual enterprise. He had drawn up a mailing list that included the name of every taxpayer in his county. "Being a friend of the county clerk . . . this dealer was able to buy it on very reasonable terms. The list contained several thousand names. The dealer took pride in keeping it correct." The salesman wrote a series of letters to these people "in a friendly, chatty vein," and boosted his sales 500 percent.

It was the kind of initiative to gladden August A.'s heart. As a result of his own efforts, his stature in his beleaguered industry was probably never higher than when he was struggling to keep his head above water. Even in St. Louis, where the beer wars had been fierce, old competitors sought his advice. In a moment of panic, the Lemp brothers, who had long operated the city's most popular brewery, visited August A.'s office. A batch of their Prohibition beer had turned out bad. They didn't know what to do. "You'll think that I'm nuts," August A. told them, "but the only way you're going to get out of this is open up the goddamn vats and let all the goddamn stuff go down the goddamn sewer and clean it up and start again."

One of the gravest crises August A. had to face during Prohibition occurred when a banker arrived at his office one morning and demanded the immediate repayment of a loan. Busch had long found it personally painful to take out loans when he needed capital to expand or update his plant. But during the 1920s, he had had to borrow $6.5 million to do just that. There had been a few smaller loans in the past, but never anything so large. "For decades," he said, "we had been in a position of being able to loan to the banks, rather than to borrow from them." Times had changed. "Borrowing was essential." So millions had been borrowed, and now a nervous banker was on his doorstep. The impetus for his visit was the recent closing of the Lemp Brewery five blocks south of the Anheuser-Busch plant. It had been sold to the International Shoe Co. for ten cents on the dollar. With that in mind, the banker wanted his money.

"He comes to my daddy and I'm in his office," Gussie said, "and I thought Daddy would have a heart stroke, he was so goddamned mad. And he turned and said, 'So you're calling the loan, isn't that right?' The banker said, 'Yes, I'm forced to do it.' . . . Daddy turned to him and said, 'Okay, I'd like to have you give me fifteen or twenty minutes and if you just wait in my office, I will be back to you.' "

August A. went to see his mother. In one of her rare stops in St. Louis, Lilly was staying half a block away at Number One Busch Place. Her son told her the story and suggested she put her money with his and offer it to the bank to cover the loan, a proposition to which Lilly readily agreed.

"August A. came back to the banker and said, 'You will have enough collateral within the next hour and a half that will be four times the value of the loan. . . . And I want to tell you, you son of a bitch, as soon as this loan is paid off—you bastard, what a great banker you are—I'm going to live to see the day that Anheuser-Busch is never going to do any goddamn business with you again as long as you live. I'm going to spread this goddamn thing all over the goddamn country to hurt your goddamn bank because you're such a nonsensical, dirty son of a bitch.' And he lived to see it and he did it too!"

24

A Case of Smuggling

Lilly Busch's willingness to back her son in his moment of crisis was one of her last great gestures. She lived her life peacefully, but her remaining years, clouded by scandal, were far from uneventful.

Since her dramatic return from Germany during the Great War, Lilly had spent most of her time at her Pasadena estate or among the pine forests of the Rhineland. She opened the Busch Gardens to visitors, and, as if still trying to prove her patriotism, donated the admission fees to disabled veterans.

Undeterred by her experiences during the war, she continued to travel to her villa in Germany.

Her trips home were infrequent, and Number One Busch Place was seldom occupied. When she was in St. Louis, she made daily visits to her husband's grave and, while away, reminded August A. to have flowers placed there on the anniversaries of Adolphus's birth and death. Lilly also attempted to honor her husband's memory by offering to donate a fountain to Forest Park. Cast in Berlin, the $14,000 bronze and marble fountain contained a medallion bearing her husband's likeness. Its most striking feature, however, was a life-sized nude of a young woman. Officials took one look and pronounced it "unsuitable for public display."

The dowager beer queen was largely removed from public controversy, except for periodic court actions—often over money. She was a plaintiff in a lawsuit filed by the trustees of Adolphus's estate against the Internal Revenue Service, protesting income taxes totaling $220,638. She was also a petitioner to the U.S. Justice Department for $400,000 lost by investing in bonds sold by the Imperial German government.

For the most part, however, Lilly kept out of the spotlight. Very late in her life all that changed dramatically, and once again her name appeared in headlines. Despite attempts to keep it secret, the event called to mind her detention as a suspected German sympathizer. On its front page of November 18, 1927, *The New York Times* described the incident this way: "Mrs. Busch and Daughters fined $56,363 for Trying to Smuggle Clothes and Bracelet."

Lilly was eighty-three years old in the fall of 1927 when she returned with two daughters, Nellie and Edmee, to New York City after a summer at Villa Lilly. As their ship, the *George Washington*, approached New York harbor, the Busches wired ahead for permission to be "expedited" through customs. The request was granted because Lilly was said to be in poor health. But when the big steamer docked on November 4, thirty-four trunks were seized by customs agents and taken to a warehouse to be examined. Lilly, seated in a wheelchair on the dock, was questioned and then allowed to travel by ambulance to the Waldorf-Astoria. This time she wasn't strip searched. Nellie and Edmee weren't as fortunate. Both were questioned and physically searched by matrons of the U.S. Customs Service.

Authorities had been tipped off that the Busches were bringing in goods that had not been declared. After the luggage was searched, customs officials determined that property worth $28,500—mostly jewelry—had been purchased on the continent. A $57,000 fine was assessed "as settlement in lieu of prosecution for smuggling."

With his mother too ill to answer questions, August A. tried to explain what had happened. Years earlier Adolphus had given Lilly a rope of diamonds that hung to her knees. She decided to break up the strand for bracelets in Germany. "The rope originally was made by Tiffany and hence, was of American origin," August A. claimed. "Mother, however, neglected to take out a certificate of American origin upon her departure with the jewels. Upon her return the customs officials chose to ignore her story of their origin."

They also ignored his version. The veracity of August A.'s account was never considered by a court. The Busches paid the fine and considered the case closed. They tried to keep the incident secret, but the story broke two weeks after the trunks were seized.

The smuggling affair darkened Lilly's last days. The following February she suffered a heart attack. Pneumonia developed. Her four children who lived in the United States were summoned to her bedside in Pasadena on February 17, 1928. A week later the devoted widow of Adolphus Busch died.

A train brought the body to St. Louis for the funeral. After lying in state at Number One Busch Place, where she and her husband had entertained Teddy Roosevelt, William Howard Taft, Sarah Bernhardt and Enrico Caruso, Elisa "Lilly" Anheuser Busch was buried in the mausoleum that contained the remains of Adolphus. Once suspected of being a German sympathizer, she was honored by the American Legion and by a member of the staff of the German ambassador.

Lilly left an estate of $8.5 million, including 52,820 shares of Anheuser-Busch stock, most going to her children. She gave $100,000 to a hospital in the name of her deceased invalid son Carl. She also bequeathed money to German relatives; a perpetual income was set up for General August Anheuser of Karlsruhe and his daughter, Fraulein Anna Bella Anheuser. Lilly's estate was large enough to become a private corporation, just like her late husband's. Lawsuits were filed for years to come over claims to the inheritance. Ten years after her death, a judge was still trying to determine whether one of her descendants deserved a share.

The Pasadena mansion, Ivy Wall, was sold and its gardens subdivided. All that remains of Adolphus's famous tourist attraction are handsome residential streets with names like Busch Garden Court, Busch Garden Drive and Busch Garden Place. The backyards of the tidy, tile-roofed bungalows contain a few of the stone fairyland statues that Adolphus had erected for his grandchildren.

Villa Lilly, remote and majestic, still stands outside Bad Schwalbach in Germany. With Villa Clair it is part of a drug-abuse treatment center for teenagers run by the government of Hesse. In a room at Villa Clair, where politicians and other dignitaries once visited, a white marble bust of Adolphus stares down from its mounted perch. The Prince now gazes at a Foosball game.

25

A Kidnapping

On a bitterly cold night on the last day of 1930, August A.'s thirteen-year-old grandson, Adolphus "Dolph" Orthwein, was kidnapped by a man armed with a revolver. It was one of a wave of kidnappings that reached its highpoint in 1932 with the abduction and murder of the twenty-month-old son of Charles Lindbergh. During the three years before that, it was estimated 2,500 people were kidnapped in the United States.

Dolph, nicknamed Buppie, was a fifth-grader at Country Day School, an exclusive boys' academy in St. Louis, where he was a good student and a substitute on the football team. Slender with "delicate features and intelligent eyes, set far apart," he had just been allowed to wear long trousers. August A.'s favorite grandson, the boy had been a frequent visitor to the big estate in Cooperstown.

The son of Clara Busch and her husband Percy Orthwein, Dolph lived in his parents' hilltop mansion in Huntleigh Village. On the night of the kidnapping, he had received permission from his mother and father, who were preparing for a New Year's Eve party, to have dinner with his grandparents. He got into his father's Lincoln sedan for the short trip to Grant's Farm, but as the chauffeur slowed to climb the steep drive that opened onto the main highway, a man wearing a mask ran from behind a tree and pointed a pistol at the rear window. The startled chauffeur stopped the car and was ordered out. The gunman slid behind the wheel. After driving a short distance and turning off the lights, he handcuffed Dolph and told him to lie in the back seat. The boy was taken to a secluded house in nearby Webster Groves and placed in a chair with a blanket over his head.

The chauffeur gave the alarm. "The parents rushed outside," recalled Walter Orthwein, Dolph's older cousin. "Mrs. Orthwein had been dressing for dinner and was just wrapped in a sheet. The chauffeur blurted out that the boy had been kidnapped." Becoming hysterical, Clara Orthwein was put to bed. The father and the driver notified the police. The abandoned Lincoln was soon found less than half a mile from the Orthwein home. Police began arriving along with the first contingent of newspapermen and family members, many of them dressed in evening clothes.

August A. was among the early arrivals. Nervous and restless, he was in a grim mood. He was armed with a heavy automatic. Gussie arrived with two bloodhounds, who were given some of Dolph's clothes to smell. It was midnight by then and the hounds took off on a rambling chase across fields and forest, leading a winded pack of reporters, police and friends of the family in a fruitless one-hour tour of the countryside.

The announcement of a reward—"no questions asked"— was broadcast over the radio. August A. considered offering $10,000 to see whether an informer might be tempted to step forward. He called every relative he could think of who might have cash on hand. With the banks closed for the holiday, it wasn't easy raising that much money—even for a millionaire.

By morning, however, a major break occurred when an elderly black man, Pearl Abernathy, told police that he believed his son, Charles, had kidnapped the boy. The elder Abernathy indicated where he thought Dolph could be found. Percy Orthwein and a few friends raced to the house in Webster Groves and found the boy standing by the side of the road. Unharmed but tired, Dolph was driven straight to Grant's Farm, where there were loud rejoicings. Visitors were met by butlers and maids "who forgot their stations as servants to shout, 'He's safe! He's safe!' " In tears, August A. led the family in a thanks-giving prayer.

Within hours Dolph was calmly recounting his adventures for a mob of reporters. No, he didn't get a good look at the kidnapper. No, he couldn't tell whether he was a Negro. Yes, he got something to eat—scrambled eggs and an orange while the kidnapper ate pigs feet. "He didn't talk to me except when I asked him something, but he treated me pretty well." What kind of weapon did the kidnapper have? "A .38-caliber." How did he know that? "I asked him and he told me."

Charles Abernathy, meanwhile, had fled to Kansas City. Three days after the kidnapping he was tracked down by Harry Brundidge, a reporter for *The St. Louis Star*. It was Brundidge's biggest scoop and his newspaper played it to the hilt. Aberna-thy, who was twenty-eight years old, readily agreed to surren-der, but not before he was encouraged to tell his story in detail. He had seven children; his real estate business had gone bad and he was broke; he couldn't feed his family; he only meant to commit robbery, not kidnap anyone. The account was ban-nered by the *Star*. Brundidge, who had traveled to Kansas City with a St. Louis County sheriff, hired a Packard limousine for the return trip to St. Louis. During the long drive, Abernathy continued chattering away and the headlines kept coming.

"Throughout the drive back, Abernathy was in high spirits, like a happy child. Occasionally he burst into song. His favor-ite tune was 'Don't Hurry and Don't Worry.' " At one point it was suggested that Abernathy drive. The sheriff reasoned that it might arouse suspicions if anyone noticed a car in which a Negro was a passenger and not the driver. Abernathy thought it was a wonderful idea. " 'This Packard is some automobile,' he observed, patting the steering wheel. 'I'm going to enjoy this ride.' "

Later, when Brundidge took over, Abernathy turned to the sheriff and said, "You'd better get a couple of hours sleep. You ought to be fresh in the morning so you can grill me."

"You ought to get some sleep yourself," the sheriff replied.

"No, sir," said Abernathy. "You don't want me to go to sleep. The best time to grill a man is when he's worn out."

It went on like that for hours, every detail dutifully de-scribed for the *Star*'s breakfast readers.

August A. later met the kidnapper. The confrontation, which

occurred in the prosecuting attorney's office, wasn't a pleasant one. Abernathy was still in an expansive mood.

Busch stopped in the doorway and glared at the prisoner. Abernathy smiled. "You're Mr. August A. Busch, aren't you?" he asked.

His face flushing, Busch snapped, "I am."

"I have seen your pictures in the newspapers," Abernathy said, waving his hand toward a chair. "Sit down, sit down."

That was too much for August A., who hurried out of the building to his waiting limousine.

Abernathy served eight years of a fifteen-year sentence.

As a result of the incident, August A. began to give serious consideration to his personal security. He was determined not to be taken alive by a kidnapper. He added a sawed-off shotgun to his arsenal and often carried a double-barreled derringer in his hat. When he himself was later targeted by kidnappers, he purchased even more weapons, one of which he would later pick up in a moment of desperation.

26

The Floating Rum Palace

Still early in the Dry Decade, August A. had one of his regular trips to Villa Lilly in Germany. It turned out to be a significant voyage. He traveled aboard his favorite steamship, the luxury liner *George Washington*. He had made many crossings aboard the fondly nicknamed *Big George*. Formerly a German steamer, the ship had fallen into American hands during the outbreak of the Great War and had carried President Wilson to the Paris Peace Conference. By the time August A. took his trip in late May 1922, the four-stacker was owned by the United States Shipping Board.

Shortly after putting out of New York, the bars opened for business, selling everything from fine Scotch whiskey and choice wines to English and German beers. It was a revelation for August A. He couldn't believe his eyes. He was aboard a floating rum palace—and one owned by the United States government, which was flagrantly violating its own national regulations. Prohibition might be the law of the land, but it was clearly not the law of the sea.

The occasion gave August A. a choice opportunity to fire a widely publicized broadside against the hypocrisy and sham of Prohibition. It was later regarded as a turning point in a fight against the Eighteenth Amendment. The brewer drew blood and enjoyed every minute of it. No sooner had the seagoing bar reached port in Cherbourg than August A. sent a telegram that was forwarded to President Warren G. Harding. He included one of the *George Washington*'s wine lists. "This makes the United States," the brewer declared, "incomparably the biggest bootlegger in the world."

Harding, who recognized a time bomb when he saw it, said he was "unacquainted with the subject" and handed the matter to Albert Lasker, chairman of the Shipping Board. Other salvos followed, and for weeks the public exchange was fierce, with August A. getting the better of the argument and winning support in the national press.

Lasker didn't waste any time before slugging below the belt. He accused Busch of selfish motives. "It is, of course, notorious that the Adolphus Busch who founded your brewery was possibly the kaiser's closest friend in America, and that your family for many years has maintained a castle in Germany." Busch was only trying to assist the German merchant marine at the expense of American shipping in a blatant attempt to help his brewery, Lasker declared.

With Lasker's neck thus exposed, Adolphus III, who handled the initial skirmish while his father was abroad, neatly chopped it off with the help of papers like *The New York Times*. "Respecting your entirely irrelevant intimations that we are German sympathizers," Adolphus III declared, "we remind you that all the facts and most of the falsehoods on that point were thoroughly dealt with and disposed of finally by the government during the war. See the files." Warming to the subject, he continued, "The temperature in my office is well above 90, and the law prohibits me from making here in America a glass of beer. . . . Yet, as I write, I contemplate . . . the disbursement of American Government money from the Treasury in payment for German and British beers and wines to be sold by our Government at a profit. The prospect does not, I assure you, tend to lower the temperature."

The New York Times editorialized: "A brewer is a person freely to be insulted by the virtuous, as chairman Lasker has just shown, but even a brewer has the right to report a violation of the Volstead Act."

The argument still smoldered when August A. returned to the country aboard the *Big George*. Again the bars were running "wide open." Busch noted that all of the liquor was consumed before the ship docked in New York harbor and that an enjoyable time was had by all. The government, in its wet department, he declared, was buying Scotch and other liquors in England, while its dry department was trying to stamp out the liquor trade. "Mr. Busch," commented the *Times*, "just back on an American steam saloon, tells us that a number of passengers resolved to carry ashore some of the whisky the Government had sold them and see if the Government would prosecute its own wrong. This ingenious idea wasn't carried out, because the supply of strong drink gave out."

It was explosive stuff. Pandemonium reigned at the White House. Harding, a befuddled if amiable man whose administration would go down as one of the most reekingly corrupt in American history, didn't know what to do. The president was completely unequipped to deal with prickly issues like Prohibition. He was, after all, "almost unbelievably ill-informed," commented William Allen White.

When it came to Prohibition, Harding straddled the issue. In his State of the Union message, he obscurely referred to the Eighteenth Amendment and "conditions . . . which savor of nation-wide scandal. It is the most demoralizing factor in the public life." But he did nothing to stop abuses and let his attorney general handle the Shipping Board mess.

August A. was vindicated in his attack. Liquor on board American ships was banned and the United States extended the three-mile limit for contraband liquor to twelve miles. If a foreign ship approached the American coast it had to padlock its liquor supply or dump it overboard.

It was one of the first occasions the Anti-Saloon League was caught off balance. Put on the defensive, its shrewd, vocal leader, Wayne Wheeler, couldn't resist a potshot at August A. "I am of the opinion that roses will begin to grow on cranberry bushes when the wets and Mr. Busch announce themselves for law enforcement."

The exchanges became more acerbic as the nation's Prohibition record became more abysmal, the corruption and abuses more appalling. By 1923, when Harding fortuitously died just as Tea Pot Dome and other scandals were about to break over his administration, it was clear that Prohibition was more than a scandal. Violating the law had become a national sport. As far as the public was concerned, the Prohibition agent, not the bootlegger, was the criminal. Lost federal and state revenue was estimated at one-half billion dollars, while enforcement had cost $50 million to create "a great army of Prohibition detectives, spies and agents provocateurs, four-fifths of whom are already corrupt." Liquor was available in copious amounts to anyone who wanted to buy it, but at prices up to 500 percent higher than before Prohibition.

No one was better at marshaling these facts than August A. and his minions. Not long after Calvin Coolidge succeeded Harding, he delivered a densely packed, thirty-page letter to the president. The document ignited another firestorm. The occasion was Coolidge's decision to call a governors' conference to discuss Prohibition enforcement. August A. saw his opening and crashed through with his facts and figures blazing. Prohibition, he wrote, "has corrupted the Federal service to an extent never before known in the history of the Republic." Thus launched, he referred to national voting records to show that Prohibition represented the will of less than 3 percent of the American voting public.

The letter was widely excerpted, running to two columns on the front page of *The New York Times*. Safe and dry in the Oval Office, Coolidge was silent. He made no comment. He knew that Prohibition was like handling liquid nitro and so he kept a safe distance. Unfortunately for Busch and the rising movement to change the law, Coolidge was in office for over five long, narcoleptic years.

When Coolidge declared in August 1927 that "I do not choose to run" for reelection, his slumbers on the Prohibition issue were carried on by Herbert Hoover. August A. knew better than to expect a receptive ear from Dr. Hoover. He didn't trust him —and for good reason. In an incident that was forever chiseled in August A.'s memory, Hoover, who favored continuing the "Noble Experiment," had once asked him for a drink. Hoover had visited him in Cooperstown one summer. They went for a leisurely cruise of Lake Otsego aboard Busch's yacht, the *Chief Uncas*. James Orthwein, the brewer's grandson, recalled how angry August A. was when they got ashore. "Grandfather was absolutely livid. He told me later that Hoover had asked him for a drink when they were out in the middle of the lake."

It was precisely the kind of hypocrisy August A. had decried for years. He was damned if he was going to support Hoover for president in 1928, not when there was a wet alternative in Al Smith, the Happy Warrior from New York City's Lower East Side. Busch declared early for Smith, who was nominated by the Democrats on a wet plank that would have let the states vote for themselves on whether they wanted Prohibition within their borders. August A., as usual, didn't mince words. "After eight years of miserable prohibition failure, with its paralyzing corruption, its demoralization of youth, its rum-running, moonshining, bootlegging and consequent terrible crimes" it was time for a change.

August A.'s efforts notwithstanding, Hoover was elected in a landslide, but the defeat was seen more as a reaction to Smith's Roman Catholicism than to his wetness. Straw polls and various state referenda showed that support for Prohibition was on the decline.

When Hoover threw out a ball to open the baseball season, he was greeted by cries of "Beer! Beer! We want Beer!" Reading the signals, the president wasted little time in setting up a special commission to examine Prohibition and its failed enforcement. After laboring for nineteen months, a hopelessly divided eleven-member panel chaired by George Wickersham landed in dark paradox. Although everyone agreed Prohibition was next to impossible, the commission recommended continuing the experiment. *The New York World* couldn't resist commenting in a column:

> "Prohibition is an awful flop.
> We like it.
> It can't stop what it's meant to stop.
> We like it.
> It's left a trail of graft and slime,
> It's filled our land with vice and crime,
> It don't prohibition worth a dime,
> Nevertheless, we're for it."

The hopeless failure of Prohibition was underscored yet again when Senator James Reed of Missouri, who had close ties to August A., chaired a congressional investigation that detailed graft in the Anti-Saloon League. The league, Reed's committee discovered, was basically a band of fund-raisers who exploited gullible church people. The fact that August A. and other brewers were pouring dollars into the fight to end Prohibition was not examined. Representative Richmond Hobson of Alabama was shown to have received $170,000 to deliver lectures supporting the dry position. William Jennings Bryan, the perennial presidential candidate, had landed a whopping $700,000 contract for a four-month lecture tour booming the blessings of Prohibition. The league's director, Wayne Wheeler, admitted that his organization had collected $67.5 million through 1925. These were not the best of times for professional drys. August A. reported that one noted temperance leader had offered to make a public profession of a change of heart—as long as the brewery coughed up $50,000 to make him see the light.

Following the well-established path trod by Adolphus, August A. had always maintained close ties with well-placed, sympathetic politicians like Reed. Senator Harry Hawes, who had rescued August A.'s mother from Germany, was also a politician squarely seated atop a Busch beer keg. Hawes consistently tried to get the Volstead Act modified to help his friend back in St. Louis. But August A.'s strongest backing was reserved for Reed. Missouri's "Fighting Senator," Reed was once knocked out by the mayor of Kansas City during a disagreement in a stockyard. Awakening, he uttered his most memorable line: "What hit me?" Reed fought long and hard in the wet trenches. No matter that he also had close ties to the corrupt political machine of Tom Pendergast, the Boss Tweed of Kansas City. A quarrelsome fellow, Reed had great influence in the Senate and was considered a dark-horse presidential candidate in 1928 and 1932.

August A. boosted the election of "our esteemed and good personal friend Senator Reed." He also encouraged Otto Mathi, one of his key executives, to talk to Boss Pendergast to promote another wet candidate for governor, Lloyd Stark. In a telegram to Mathi, Busch urged him to get Reed "to assist you with Pendergast" on Stark's behalf.

Pendergast, whom Busch took pains to cultivate, lived to regret the support he gave Stark. Once elected, the governor repudiated the Boss's help and instigated the federal investigation that sent him to prison in 1939 on charges of income tax evasion. When Pendergast, who once operated a string of five saloons, died in 1945, Anthony Buford, August A.'s and later Gussie's chief lobbyist, sent white gladiolus and acacias. The brewery sent an elaborate arrangement of lilies and more white gladiolus. The vice president attended the service, another man Pendergast had put in the Senate—Harry S Truman.

27

August A. Proposes a Beer Cure for the Depression

With sympathetic politicians working on his behalf and with the national mood lurching toward repeal like a drunken sailor, August A. had to deal with another crisis, one as nearly mortal as Prohibition. The stock market crash of October 1929 saw stocks plunge off the charts and stockbrokers plunge out of windows, a splattering of fortunes and brains that ushered in the Great Depression.

At first Anheuser-Busch appeared able to weather the storm, which rapidly turned from dark clouds to nightmare for millions of Americans. August A.'s diversification program had actually improved his company's fortunes to the point that by 1927 Anheuser-Busch was able to increase the salaries of its executives for the first time since 1920.

From its founding, the company had never failed to earn a profit, but all that had changed in 1919 when substantial losses were posted. Still more losses followed from 1920 through 1922, but by the following year Anheuser-Busch seemed to have turned the corner, reaching the break-even point in income. A reorganization occurred in 1925, the year the company's fifty-year charter from Missouri expired. The original 480 shares Adolphus and his father-in-law Eberhard Anheuser had offered, each with a par value of $500, were increased to 180,000 shares at a par value of $100. Each stockholder received 375 new shares for every one of the old 1875 issue. The company remained very much of a family concern with almost all of the stock securely in the hands of Anheusers and Busches.

Anheuser-Busch began to record losses again as the Depression scoured the economy more deeply, and by 1932 the board ordered a 10 percent pay cut for all executives and salesmen. August A. resisted suggestions that he cut his work force, but he canceled his display advertising, which, for a Busch, could be likened to cutting off his oxygen supply.

The irony was that as grim as the Depression was to Anheuser-Busch's prospects and to his personal fortune, which was taking a substantial hit as stocks fell in value, it also offered August A. another chance to bash the evils of Prohibition. His masterpiece was a pamphlet called *An Open Letter to the American People* issued in May 1931. He sent a copy to every senator and congressman and ballyhooed it in full-page ads in national magazines; he welcomed interviews by reporters, who dutifully trekked out to Cooperstown and to the brewery in St. Louis. His unsurprising proposal was that the surest way to ease the Depression was to bring back beer—salvation through suds.

The legalization of beer, August A. claimed, would put 1.2 million Americans back to work in the brewing and related industries. There would be a large new market for grain, helping the farmers. Railroads would prosper by the immediate need for 180,000 boxcars to transport grain—and beer. Coal operators and miners would benefit by the demand for coal to fire the breweries' boilers. Finally, the government would save the $50 million it wasted every year trying to enforce Prohibition and would recoup the nearly $500 million in taxes it had lost since beer was outlawed.

The drys answered with grapeshot. Leading academics were polled, among them George Cutten, the president of Colgate University. "Mr. Busch's open letter is so foolish that it seems to be unnecessary to make any answer to it." The American Businessmen's Prohibition Foundation challenged August A. to prove his assertions. The group's president, Richard H. Scott, head of the Reo Motor Car Company, charged that beer would only worsen the misery "due to the fact that large numbers of men now employed would, no doubt, spend their earnings for liquor, leaving their families to suffer." Dr. Eugene Crawford of the Methodist Episcopal Church, South, agreed that beer would put people to work, especially among "the undertakers, the grave diggers, the insane asylum guards, the poor farm employees, the hangmen, the penitentiary wardens, employees and directors of soup kitchens . . ."

But by 1932, Prohibition was in its death throes. An election year, Franklin D. Roosevelt, the Democratic candidate, had declared for repeal after some adroit fence-sitting. Hoover didn't have a prayer, saddled as he was by the worsening Depression, his pledge to continue the Noble Experiment and his deadly dull campaign style. In the November election he lost decisively. Roosevelt, who had promised a "New Deal" and good old beer, logged 472 electoral votes to Hoover's 59, and carried all but six states. With Prohibition the decisive issue of the campaign, Roosevelt had ridden into office on a beer wagon.

Less than a month after his landslide victory, the House Ways and Means Committee began the long debate on how best to modify the Volstead Act. August A. wasn't caught napping. A long statement of his was included in the Congressional Record. Above all, he wanted to beat back any proposal to legalize beer with an alcohol content of 2.75 percent instead of 3.2 percent, which he favored. The "masses" wouldn't go for it, he declared. People "want and are demanding a beer in all respects satisfying, and that will, so to say, furnish that warmth, satisfaction, and contentment that a mild stimulant like a good, wholesome beer supplies."

Busch also wanted to head off any attempt to require brewers to use only domestic materials, and, lastly, he didn't want his product taxed too heavily. "In conclusion permit me to say that beer having always been recognized as the drink of the wage earner, the importance of keeping it at a price within his means should be borne in mind." Translation: go lightly on the excise taxes. As taxes go up, beer consumption—and profits —go down.

Convinced the end of darkness was finally at hand, August A. allowed himself to rejoice publicly. "Happy days will be here again—and soon," he exulted early in December, 1932. "It won't be long now and after beer we'll have the rest—wine, schnapps, everything! The pendulum is swinging the other way. This is going to be a free country."

28

A Case of Budweiser for FDR

Save in the backwashes of the Bible Belt, Prohibition started beating a retreat in the predawn hours of April 7, 1933, with a raucous, national street party—a coast-to-coast blowout unlike anything seen in this country. Not even the whooping that followed the armistice ending the Great War or Lindbergh's solo flight across the Atlantic compared. Beer was back and Anheuser-Busch proclaimed the fact in full-page advertisements.

At the big Bevo plant down on Broadway in South St. Louis, the freshly painted scarlet trucks started to assemble hours before midnight, the official witching hour for the return of what August A. liked to call "non-intoxicating" beer. Three hundred trucks squeezed up to the loading docks; another 1,200 lined up bumper to bumper waited their turn. When the illuminated clock atop the Gothic brewhouse struck midnight, a crowd of 25,000 cheered, brass bands played, car horns and steam whistles blasted, bells tolled. Within twenty-four hours, the revelers had drunk the town dry.

The stage for this stupendous binge had been set barely a month earlier when, nine days after his inauguration, Roosevelt recommended that Congress officially sanction the return of beer. "I deem action at this time," he said, "to be of the highest importance." Congress, as thirsty as everyone else, quickly responded by approving a law authorizing the sale of beer with a 3.2 percent alcohol content. Moments after Roosevelt signed the beer bill, August A. had fired off a telegram to the new president, praising him for his "wisdom and foresight" and for restoring to the "American people an old and time-honored industry." Prohibition had endured for just over thirteen years.

August A. was now ready to give the people what they wanted—at least until the barrels and cases were emptied.

Months earlier, he and his sons, Adolphus III and Gussie, had started preparing the plant for repeal, pumping $7 million into renovations and new equipment. Most of the burden of this effort fell on Gussie's shoulders. He handled the brewing operation while his brother headed the yeast business and other ventures. Their father was sixty-seven and in failing health. August A. had heart problems that soon became ominously more severe. He had been troubled for years by gout and claustrophobia. Increasingly, he left work early in the day, turning the brewery over to his younger son, who was more than willing to take charge. Gussie was rapidly coming into his own as general manager. He was thirty-four as Prohibition ended and was determined that Anheuser-Busch would be ready to hit the streets with plenty of Budweiser.

Throughout the dry years, the company had regularly dispatched its chief brewmaster, Rudolph Gull, to Germany to stay abreast of the latest brewing techniques. With repeal definitely on the horizon, Gussie sent three of his top brewmasters to Europe for a refresher. In a move that had great repercussions, he also hired a young German brewmaster named Frank Schwaiger. Joining Anheuser-Busch one week before Prohibition ended, Schwaiger came to be regarded as a divinity, a god at creating beer, the only man Gussie Busch dared not fire.

True to form, the company tried to hit upon a good advertising gimmick to celebrate beer's return. They picked a masterpiece, choosing what became one of the most famous corporate symbols in the world—a hitch of high-stepping Clydesdales pulling a beautifully appointed red and yellow beer wagon. Years later, the legend was promoted that it was Gussie's inspiration. Actually, it was Charles Nagel, Adolphus's wily old lawyer, who suggested the idea to the board of directors. On December 28, 1932, the board approved Nagel's motion to buy a team of six Clydesdales "for advertising purposes" and agreed to spend $15,000 for the team. Gussie was dispatched to find the animals; he purchased sixteen of the huge horses in the Kansas City stockyards, got another $10,000 from his board and had an old-time beer wagon built. Two days before the beer flowed, he sprung a surprise on his unsuspecting father. "I asked him to come down and look at a new car with me. And then we had 2 six-horse hitches drive up." An emotional man, August A.'s eyes must have filled when he beheld the sight of those solemnly majestic animals waiting in the street with their bright red wagons.

On the great night itself, August A. was at home at Grant's Farm suffering from one of the frequent gout attacks that put him on crutches. Letting Gussie run the show at the brewery, he stayed by the radio and heard one of the most unusual transmissions ever broadcast in America. The fledgling CBS radio network had arranged a nationwide hookup to broadcast the merriment occurring in St. Louis and its two rival beer cities, Milwaukee and Chicago. At the Anheuser-Busch brewery, Gussie spoke a few words into the microphone. In the raspy, growling voice that became his trademark, he announced, "April 7th is here. And it is a real occasion for thankfulness . . . made possible by the wisdom, foresight and courage of a great president. . . . There is a song in our hearts; it's 'Happy Days are Here Again.' " His moment in history over, he strode to a VIP table where assorted politicos and socialites had bellied up. "Beer," he grandly announced, "is now being served."

The city and country went wild that night. In New York, 32,000 speakeasies were able to offer the real McCoy legally. In St. Louis, crowds in a carnival mood gathered in every hotel, restaurant and beer joint they could find, dancing on the tables and knocking back ten-cent glasses until the supply ran out around dawn. Only five people were arrested for drunkenness, but in the spirit of the hour they were not jailed. Four gangsters who tried to hijack two Anheuser-Busch trucks were not as fortunate. Anticipating such pranks, police were patrolling the streets in force, and the four were caught after a car chase. The beer was saved—and consumed.

The first truck out of the Busch plant had headed for the airport, carrying cases of the new Budweiser for President Roosevelt and for that special hero of August A.'s, the former governor of New York and wet presidential candidate, Al Smith. The truck sped to the airport under police escort. When the beer arrived in New York City and in Washington, D.C., it' was loaded onto wagons drawn by teams of Clydesdales. In New York the horses caused a sensation as they plodded down Fifth Avenue and stopped at the Empire State Building, where Smith, all smiles, was waiting at a microphone. In Washington, the team pulled up to a White House already deluged with similar shipments from other brewers.

Legal beer, "Democratic beer," beer with the right jolt of alcohol, an avalanche of orders. It was all a dream come true. Best of all, within nine months, the required thirty-six states had ratified the Twenty-first Amendment, repealing the notorious Eighteenth. But Prohibition had taken a heavy toll on the nation's breweries. of the 1,392 in operation in 1914, only 164 remained. August A. had reason to be proud. With courage and doggedness, he had waged a seemingly hopeless battle to keep his brewery going. The cost had been staggering—$34 million, of which a good part was a total loss. But Anheuser-Busch had survived.

29

An Elephant Named Tessie

Despite the silver lining of repeal, August A. was a troubled man. It was more than the rapid decline of his health. The huge expenditures that had kept his company limping along through the worst days of Prohibition were a burden. There was no guarantee that Budweiser would regain its preeminence as the nation's best-selling beer. In fact, the famous brand took an alarming nosedive. His personal fortune had been reduced by stocks gone bad during the worsening Depression. He was worried about money and he was worried about his family, which, as usual, taxed his patience to the maximum. Perhaps worst of all, he worried that he was out of touch with the business of making beer.

Shortly before repeal, August A., disturbed by the taste of Bevo, his disappointing nonalcoholic cereal beverage, had offered some suggestions to one of his plant supervisors. Years later Gussie's voice still quivered in anger as he described how the supervisor curtly informed August A. that his suggestions weren't worthy of consideration. Gussie tore into the man, an assistant to Rudolph Gull, the brewmaster.

"I turned to him and said, 'You son of a bitch. You're talking to the president, my father. You get the hell out of the office. You're fired!' "

After the man left, August A. was stunned.

"When the door closed," Gussie recounted, "tears started to come down his eyes and he said, 'My God, you realize what you've done? I don't know anything any more about brewing. . . . I'm not up to date on all the processes. And Gull will go with him.' "

"Look," Gussie answered, "nobody can talk to my daddy this way in front of me. You don't have to worry about a goddamn thing. I know the brewery from A to Z. Gull won't leave. . . . Nothing will happen."

Nothing did. Gull's assistant stayed fired but the famous brewmaster remained.

August A. may have worried that he was out of touch with the latest brewing techniques, but no one doubted his commitment to his product. Soon after beer returned, alarming reports of Budweiser's slumping sales began to arrive. Customers were complaining about the taste. It wasn't sweet enough. When the company's branch and district managers assembled to discuss the problem, most favored changing the taste. August A. addressed them. He had a few words to say. "Nobody," he roared, "will tinker with the Budweiser taste or the Budweiser process as long as I am president of Anheuser-Busch."

The American public, he said, had grown accustomed to sweet drinks after thirteen years of mixing their bootleg liquor with soda and ginger ale. He promised they would change their minds and return to Budweiser. Weak and sick by then, August A. wasn't finished. Convinced that the sweeter taste of his competitors' beer would send people flocking back to his product—he was soon proven right—he warned that the day would come when demand for Budweiser exceeded supply. "Somebody is going to suggest that we can sell more Budweiser and make more money if we produce it faster. This we will never do!"

Gussie never forgot his father's words, which amounted to his last will and testament as a brewer.

During this period, Gussie was seeing a lot of Elizabeth Dozier, the wife of one of his friends. The relationship had started to simmer even before his first wife's death. Their affair was a badly kept secret, and August A. wasn't pleased with the prospect of his son marrying her. One of Gussie's assistants recalled a conversation with Dora Schofield, August A.'s personal secretary and, since the era of Adolphus, the family's confidante. Schoey said that August A. "was depressed" at the likelihood that Gussie would marry "the Dozier woman."

It was even rumored that August A. himself had had several secret affairs. A longtime acquaintance of the family's, who as a teenager worked in the law firm of Charles Nagel, remembered hearing stories that August A. had had some unfortunate encounters with women. "Listen, he chased anything . . . from what I knew about the old boy."

August A., so the rumor went, was hopelessly smitten by one Nellie Muench, a vivacious redhead considered the most striking woman in St. Louis and certainly one of its most entertaining citizens. After a series of sensational trials during the mid-1930s—she was accused of kidnapping and other crimes—Nellie was convicted of using the mails to defraud and sentenced to ten years in prison. She had run Mitzi's Shop, a chic dress boutique. With floor-to-ceiling mirrors, gilt furniture and beautiful models, it was among the city's preeminent conversation pieces. Wealthy businessmen were frequent visitors, perhaps lured by stories that Nellie enjoyed walking around her dressing rooms in the nude, smoking a Cuban cigar.

One prominent St. Louisan, who was related to a seamstress at Mitzi's Shop, recalled nearly fifty years later the rumors about August A. and Nellie. "Busch, the story went, loved her madly, but couldn't have her." There was no evidence, however, that August A. and Nellie even knew each other.

In addition to his concern about Gussie's affair, August A. was taxed by mounting financial worries in the months immediately before and after repeal. One was especially disturbing. For years the Busch family had been involved with the Lafayette-South Side Bank. It had been founded by Adolphus, and in 1932 August A. was chairman of the board. Like many financial institutions during the Depression, it was in trouble, and August A. invested a considerable amount of his fortune to keep it afloat. "He felt he was personally responsible for people having put their money in the bank," said his grandson Adolphus "Dolph" Orthwein. "He took almost every last penny he had to keep it open. It was something he didn't have to do, but he felt he was honor bound. He felt people were losing money because of his name and reputation. . . . The bank was a hemorrhage that nearly drained the family fortune."

The national bank holiday President Roosevelt declared shortly after taking office provided breathing room. The bank was reorganized and August A.'s son Adolphus III was named chairman of the board. The family helped pump more than $600,000 into the bank, which allowed it to reopen.

A bitter lawsuit with one of his cousins, Lily Anheuser Suhre, added to August A.'s financial burden. The Anheusers and Busches had feuded for years, but needing money to cover stock losses during the 1920s, Lily went to see "Cousin August." She asked him to buy over 800 shares of Anheuser-Busch stock. Against the advice of his lawyer and with mounting debts, August A. agreed out of sheer generosity. One of his vice presidents, R. A. Huber, bluntly warned him to forget the request. "In the first place you are a heavy borrower at the bank, and I would take upon myself no more bank obligations. Secondly, if you once go into this transaction, you will find that it will never be completed."

Events proved the warning prophetic. August A. paid Lily $56 for each share, although they were worth no more than $45 to $50 during Prohibition, when stocks in a struggling beer company were hardly a hot item. The situation changed drastically; with beer legal again, the value of the stock shot up, reaching as much as $200 a share. That's when Lily sued, alleging that her cousin had prevented her from repurchasing the stock as he had promised. The dispute ground its way through the courts for years before the Missouri Supreme Court ruled in August A.'s favor.

Testimony revealed that August A. controlled 166,573 of the company's 180,000 shares of common stock. It also disclosed that his physical problems were serious and that he had a jaundiced view of doctors. "As to who my personal physician is . . . I change about," he declared during a deposition taken early in 1934. "I generally doctor myself with gout medicine. They know less about my health than I do."

Another family problem that beset August A. involved Ernst Busch, a cousin who worked for the company as a brewmaster. Years earlier Adolphus had encouraged Ernst to leave Germany, where he had attended brewing school, and come to the United States. He was largely responsible for hands-on brewing at the plant, recalled his children, Helen Busch Conway and Dr. Anthony Busch, a psychiatrist. Ernst and August A.'s family got along splendidly until Ernst died suddenly in 1927. That's when the difficulties started. August A. and other family members were convinced, Ernst's son and daughter said, that

Ernst had kept a secret formula for brewing beer and somehow gained access to their father's safe-deposit box to look for it. Their mother was summoned to the brewery and directed to open her husband's safe. No formula was found. The Busch family, Dr. Busch said, believed that his father had somehow expropriated the formula and weren't pleased. "They got nasty."

Dr. Busch and his sister speculated that whatever stock their father may have owned in Anheuser-Busch was probably removed from his safe-deposit box or office safe. Their relations with the family deteriorated. Dr. Busch said August A. had promised he would pay for his education, but later reneged. Before he went to medical school, he asked Gussie, his father's old sparring partner, for a job at the brewery only to be told, "There's no place in this plant for you."

Family disturbances, trouble with the banks, dwindling resources, failing health. August A. had already suffered several mild heart attacks and his circulation problems had worsened. By the early 1930s he was a beleaguered man. As his financial difficulties mounted, he was forced to do something he dreaded —sell his beloved animals. His extensive menagerie had become a costly drain as the Depression worsened. "It was very painful for him," recalled Dolph Orthwein. "He couldn't face me. At one point my pony had to go."

So did Tessie, the little elephant August A. had purchased during the 1920s and taken to Cooperstown on his summer vacations. He sold the beast to the Ringling Brothers Circus. Later the circus came to St. Louis and Dolph accompanied his grandfather to see the show. As the elephants paraded into the ring, they were startled to see them led by Tessie. It was more than August A. could bear. "Tessie!" he cried out. "Tessie!" The elephant's head came up. Breaking ranks, she trotted around the ring, searching for her former master. "He was sitting three rows back, but she came right up to him," Dolph said. "There were tears in his eyes." August A. offered to buy Tessie, but the circus wouldn't sell.

Finally only a few deer remained at Grant's Farm. Most of August A.'s horses, dogs and pigs were sold. Their removal was a wrenching blow. Animals never made demands on him—not like his family. They "never deceive you."

30

The Dutch Act

In early December 1932, August A. revealed murky reports that he had been targeted for kidnapping. The brewer informed reporters that he kept two loaded revolvers constantly at hand. He did not tell them about the double-barreled derringer hidden in his hat or that he had added a sawed-off shotgun to his well-equipped arsenal. The details of the kidnap plot, reported to August A. by St. Louis police, were not disclosed, but news stories describing the threats recalled that barely two years earlier, August A.'s grandson Dolph Orthwein had been kidnapped.

August A. wasn't the only brewer to be targeted. In June 1933, the Ma Barker gang kidnapped William Hamm, an executive of the Hamm Brewing Company, as he left his office in St. Paul, Minnesota. He was held for four days and released unharmed after a $100,000 ransom was paid. Ma and one of her sons were later killed during a shootout with federal agents in Florida.

In that same year, Gussie Busch was involved in an extortion plot. He received two threatening letters, demanding $15,000. Police arranged an ambush on a dark city street, but made no arrests. In the fall of 1933, Louis Hager, Jr., and his wife, Alice, August A.'s daughter, were told that if they paid $5,000 they would be given the names of several persons who planned to kidnap their son for a $100,000 ransom. Three Filipinos were later arrested and convicted, including a twenty-five-year-old chauffeur fired by the family for wrecking several automobiles.

Under the circumstances, August A. had good reason to develop a certain paranoia about kidnappers. After arming himself to the teeth, he convinced his grandson Dolph Orthwein that he would never be taken alive. The prospect of entrusting his business—or his life—to someone else wasn't appealing. His method of protecting himself was more direct. Whenever he climbed into his Cadillac limousine, a holstered revolver was within easy reach of his chauffeur. Another pistol was hidden near the passenger seat; a third was tucked in August A.'s suit pocket. A weapon was with him wherever he went. It was around this time that August A. did something else that startled close friends and family members. He purchased sixty blue-steel, .32-caliber Police Special revolvers with pearl grips and gave them to wealthy friends and associates he thought might be potential kidnap victims.

The Busch infatuation with firearms was already well established during the days of Adolphus. In failing health and shortly before he died, Adolphus was still being wheeled out onto the grounds of his German estate in a hunting cart so that he could blast roebucks with a telescopic rifle. With August A. the family inherited a healthy fear that there might be people in the world who would do them harm. They began to take precautions. The children of August A. and his children's children all learned how to handle weapons. Guns were part of their birthright. Young Busches slept in rooms that bristled with rifles, pistols and shotguns. Grant's Farm was a virtual arsenal.

August A. was so attached to his weapons that he offered a "liberal reward with no questions asked" for the return of his favorite pistol, a cherished souvenir—the .44-caliber Colt revolver he had used to shoot antelope and rabbits during his brief stint as a cowboy some forty-five years earlier. The revolver, which had an American eagle engraved on the grips, had been taken from a desk drawer in his office, where it was kept well oiled and loaded.

Worn out by worries, August A.'s time finally began to run out in September 1933 shortly after he returned from a vacation at Cooperstown. It was to be his last trip to his favorite retreat, and he had a happy time, riding his carriages, feeding his trout, enjoying the company of old friends. If Tessie was gone and there were fewer animals roaming about than in years past, he still had plenty of grandchildren to play with in the bracing weather of a Cooperstown summer.

Back in St. Louis, August A. was staggered by another of his breath-robbing chest pains. The gout attacks worsened and he developed dropsy, his legs swelling with fluid. He canceled plans for a January trip to Florida. On a Saturday morning early in February he made one of his rare visits to the brewery. He appeared to be exceptionally nervous, telling a few people that he had almost given up hope of recovering his health. He mentioned a picture of himself made several years earlier. The sketch showed a smiling Busch wearing a hat, his hands thrust into the pockets of a double-breasted, cashmere overcoat. It was, he said ominously, the one he wanted the newspapers to use "if anything should happen to me."

On the Sunday following his brief trip to the office, August A. felt good enough to host the regular family dinner at Grant's Farm. He went for a ride in a tallyho, taking the grandchildren on a tour of the estate. On Monday morning, feeling much worse, he didn't go to work. His nervousness had increased.

At nine o'clock that evening, August A. retired to his second-floor bedroom, which offered a sweeping view of the grounds from its turreted windows. A cousin, John Busch, who for several weeks had served as a part-time nurse, slept in a twin bed next to his. August A. kept getting up, his face contorted in agony as he paced the floor. He was having trouble breathing. "Can't you do something to relieve me?" he begged his cousin.

The request became a repeated refrain. He paced a while longer before he collapsed onto his bed.

Shortly after midnight, Dr. Paul Rutledge, his most recent physician, was called. August A., in a bad way, was wearing a bathrobe and slippers. Dr. Rutledge tried to talk to him, to "soothe him," but his words didn't help. His patient begged for a painkiller. Around one in the morning the doctor gave him a quarter grain shot of morphine, two sedative tablets, and a glass of warm milk. By four o'clock August A. was sleeping peacefully and the doctor crept out of the room. Orders were given not to disturb his wife, Alice, who was sleeping in another room.

August A. rested for less than an hour. By five o'clock he was up again, doubled over and clutching his chest. Frantic now, he kept walking to the window, staring into the gray dimness as the sky lightened. "I can't stand this any longer!" he cried out. "Please, do something!"

John Busch, recalling later that August A. was "almost like an insane person," noticed the strange look in his elderly cousin's eyes. August A. finally dozed off and at seven o'clock was strong enough to sip tea. His maid, twenty-one-year-old Margaret Henry, was summoned. Wearing her gray and white uniform and a starched white cap, she gave August A. a massage.

It seemed to help and he dozed off again. Sunlight was streaming now through the curtained windows. Buckets rattled as stablemen headed to the Bauernhof, the gabled replica of a German farmhouse were some of August A.'s prized horses, the few that remained, were quartered in neat, straw-banked stalls. A wagon rolled up the cobbled driveway.

Oblivious to everything but his ceaseless pain, August A. lay in bed with his hands over his face. He finally turned to his cousin. "John, get your breakfast and come back this evening."

"All right, boss," his cousin replied. He went downstairs to the kitchen pantry after promising to call the doctor again later in the morning.

Sometime during the next hour, or possibly earlier, August A. picked up a pamphlet. It was entitled *An Open Letter to Rev. Charles E. Coughlin*, the "Radio Priest" whose nightly broadcasts from Detroit had generated a national following. August A. had long been an avid listener of Coughlin's. A flaming, persuasive orator, the priest was a shrill critic of Roosevelt's New Deal and would later be muzzled by the Catholic church. A week earlier, August A. had sent Coughlin a check for a substantial donation.

The pamphlet was written by James Warburg, a New York banker who sharply disagreed with Coughlin's more radical monetary theories. On the back, August A. scrawled six words in pencil: "Goodbye precious mama and adorable children."

He underlined precious and adorable.

Tony Feichtinger, August A.'s longtime chauffeur, knocked on the bedroom door at eight o'clock, as was his habit. August A. told him to come in and close the door.

"You want me to get some music on the radio, boss?" Feichtinger asked, thinking it might cheer him up.

When he nodded, Feichtinger walked to the large RCA console across from the bed. His back was to August A. He had switched on the radio and was waiting for it to warm up when he heard a shot. Turning around, he saw August A. half raised in bed, his right arm extended, fingers twitching. He had taken a Police Special from the nightstand and shot himself in the left side. The bullet had just missed his heart, but its tearing, upward path accomplished what August A. had intended. The pistol fell on the adjoining bed.

Family members hurried to the bedroom. Alice Busch threw herself screaming on her husband's bed. August A.'s grandson, Dolph Orthwein, then nearly seventeen years old, was one of the first to reach the bedroom. "He lived for maybe fifteen minutes after he shot himself. I could see his face. You could see the terrible pain. . . . It was horrible to see him lying there."

August A. had committed what St. Louis police grimly called "the Dutch Act." The graphic phrase had been coined because so many of the city's most prominent German brewers had committed suicide by shooting themselves. August A. was the fourth of his caste to take his own life. Thirty years earlier, the president of Anheuser-Busch's most serious competitor, William Lemp, Sr., had fired a bullet into his head in his mansion located on a bluff overlooking the Mississippi River a few blocks south of August A.'s office. In 1922, Lemp's son shot himself twice in the heart, again in the family home. And in 1920, Otto Stifel, the president of the Union Brewery, had killed himself at his country estate after losing most of the $2.5 million he had inherited from his father.

August A.'s suicide, with its Prussian overtones, was a courageous act, insisted his German-born nephew, Paul von Gontard, who was visiting San Francisco. "When my uncle found out how sick he was, he knew he was not the man to be an invalid. I am shocked, but I understand. It was a man's death, and a man's way out with the least sorrow for everyone."

31

"This Is Where I Want to Be Buried"

A coroner's inquest was held on Valentine's Day in the timbered hunt and trophy room on the main floor of the Big House at Grant's Farm. Heavy with oaken beams and nostalgia, it was August A.'s favorite room in his mansion. Glass-covered gun cases lined the walls; and mounted heads of moose, deer, buffalo and wild German boar—many of them shot by August A.—gazed down upon the proceedings. John Busch was briefly questioned, as were Tony, the chauffeur; Margaret, the maid, still wearing her white linen cap; and Dr. Rutledge, who had administered morphine and warm milk during the dying man's final hours.

The verdict: "Suicide due to long illness, causing him distress and agony, which caused him to shoot himself."

Reporters converged on Grant's Farm the morning of the shooting. They were met by George Eads, August A.'s public relations man, who described the circumstances of the suicide. There was no question at all about why August A. had shot himself. Dora "Schoey" Schofield, his secretary, summed it up as well as anyone. "I guess he just thought it wasn't worth it anymore." An examination of the body revealed that the bullet had entered the left side just below the heart and veered upward and slightly to the right. The work of the undertakers didn't completely efface the effects of the wracking pain that had driven August A. to reach for his pistol. It still showed on his ashen face.

If no one doubted why he took his life, a great deal of speculation focused on how much money he had left and on who would succeed him. Even before the funeral, the newspapers commented at length on the question of succession, often using the metaphor of a ruling dynasty. "The scepter of power" was expected to pass to Adolphus Busch III. In a family where tradition was as important as bloodlines and good beer, "Mr. Adolph" was next in line to the throne by virtue of the Old World tradition of primogeniture.

Adolphus III was forty-two, appeared regularly on lists of the ten best-dressed men in America and was still a fine coachman. Dark-haired with dark eyes and bushy eyebrows, he bore a strong resemblance to his father. He now finally had a chance to get out from under his shadow—and that of his better-known younger brother, Gussie. Adolphus III, it was reported, was "less solidly built" than his brother, who was expected to become second in command.

August A. got his wish about having his favorite picture used in the newspapers. The drawing received prominent display. He was less fortunate in his desire for a simple funeral. No doubt remembering the regal burial of his father, he stated in the last paragraph of his will in language that could not be misunderstood that he did not believe in elaborate funerals or monuments. "I therefore hope and request that my family will avoid all possible extravagance . . . and that my funeral services and burial will be conducted with the utmost simplicity."

Although less grand than the funeral for Adolphus, who was borne to the tomb with all the pageantry of an expired pharaoh, the obsequies for August A. were anything but simple. The body, dressed in a dark blue suit, white shirt and a blue tie tinged with red, was displayed in an open casket in the spacious living room of his mansion. Over 10,000 people paid their respects. When the service began at eleven in the morning on Friday, February 15, 2,000 spectators had gathered outside the mansion. Musicians from the St. Louis Symphony Orchestra played selections from Tannhäuser, Schubert's "Ave Maria," and Tchaikovsky's "Andante Cantabile," the same song that had been played at Adolphus's funeral. Although August A.'s suicide would have been condemned by the Catholic church, nuns knelt in prayer by the casket, which was banked with lilies. There was even a five-foot-high replica fashioned from red and white roses of August A.'s fanciful solution to the wicked saloon—the Bevo Mill.

Blanketed by violets and lilies, the heavy casket was carried by twelve pallbearers down the main steps of the mansion and loaded into a hearse for the short, half-mile journey to Sunset Cemetery. August A. had carefully chosen the site himself; it was a few feet from the grave of his daughter-in-law, Gussie's first wife, Marie Church Busch. "I can see my home from here," he had announced, standing on the grassy hilltop. "This is where I want to be buried."

His grave, shaded by pine trees, was cut diagonally so that it faced Grant's Farm. The place had none of the Gothic splendor of Adolphus's gargoyle-studded, slate-roofed mausoleum. The grave was marked by a block of red Missouri granite that bore a single word, "Busch."

August A.'s lawyer, Daniel Kirby, delivered the eulogy. Kirby spoke of the hardships Busch had faced—the long battle with Prohibition. The struggle had killed him, Kirby suggested. August A.'s love of children was mentioned, how he had "sought to give them a place where they could enjoy a little part of the dream life, surrounded by the fancies of Fairyland." Kirby also underscored an attribute that was to carry heavy repercussions for the future. "Owning but a minority interest, August Busch had the greater responsibility of acting as trustee for many families whose welfare depended on the success of his leadership."

The words took on particular significance when the content of August A.'s will was revealed one month after his death. He had taken pains to explain why he had made no charitable bequests. "During my life I have given generously to charitable, religious and benevolent organizations, as well as to civic and other public causes. My duty is now to my family." He also left a note for his wife and children. Filed with his will, it was a message he didn't want them to forget. In it, he mentioned that Prohibition and the Depression had taken a toll on his fortune. But when business conditions improved, he wanted them to do "What I would like to have done and what I know your hearts will prompt you to do in behalf of the needy and deserving." He signed it, "Lovingly, Dad."

Some thought the stated value of his probated estate—$3,417,364—was shockingly low. The explanation offered by his sons was that August A., like his father and mother, had made substantial gifts to his family at Christmas and on other occasions, amounts that were not publicly disclosed. There were also the business losses. Most of August A.'s wealth was in the 23,889 shares of Anheuser-Busch stock he owned; he had controlled far more through voting rights—nearly 167,000 of the company's 180,000 shares of common stock. The bulk of his estate was left to his wife, Alice, with the curious recommendation that she try to limit her yearly expenses to $60,000.

The will, to use his words to his mother years earlier, would "brew trouble" when some family explosions occurred over its property divisions. There were battles fought with blows over a huge alimony payment and there were disputes over the ownership of Grant's Farm and other properties. To his younger son, Gussie, who would be in the thick of many of these arguments, August A. left all of his "sporting pictures." All of his guns "and other hunting equipment and supplies of every kind . . . also all my mounted birds and animals" were to be divided equally between Gussie and Adolphus III.

With August A. buried, attention focused on "Mr. Adolph," his older son, who would preside over the company's fortunes for the next twelve years. But all the while, Gussie stood in the wings, waiting impatiently and conspicuously for his time in the spotlight.

32

Monkey Business

It wasn't difficult for Gussie to upstage Adolphus. Shy and quiet, Mr. Adolph, or "The Third" as he was sometimes called, spent hours brooding alone in his office. Adolphus III was more dignified than his younger brother, more compassionate. A nervous man like his father, he drank too much, some relatives thought. As his company faced the Depression and the return of beer, he was content to worry about its yeast business and let Gussie push the brewery through the early days of repeal.

There was no question about who was in charge of Anheuser-Busch. August A. may have left the bulk of his wealth to his widow. But under the terms of a trust established the year before he shot himself, the voting power of the stock rested solely with Adolphus III and Gussie. The idea was to make sure his sons controlled the brewery. The two brothers, however, used their power in very different ways. "Under Adolphus the company was run with a considerable degree of deference to the family," said one relative. "When Gussie got in power, he used it as a club. He used it as a weapon." As for the other family members, according to this relative, Gussie "deliberately tried to chop them out and get them to sell their stock."

But Gussie's opportunity to ride roughshod over his relatives lay twelve years into the future. In the early 1930s, family members still controlled nearly all of the company's stock. The 480 original shares had been increased to 180,000 to facilitate estate settlements. The descendants of Eberhard Anheuser and Adolphus owned all but 4,000 shares. Anheuser-Busch was still very much a family operation. In the beginning at least, Gussie had to be diplomatic.

In addition to himself and Adolphus III, six descendants of Anheuser worked for the company when beer returned. Prominent among them were Leicester Faust, the head of the grain department; Ed Magnus, who ran the diesel company; and

Adalbert "Adie" von Gontard, the engineering supervisor. Like Adolphus III and Gussie, all three were grandsons of Prince Adolphus.

Although Gussie feuded loudly with each of them, his favorite foil was Adie, whose career ran parallel to his own. The son of Adolphus's daughter, Clara, Adie von Gontard had emigrated from Germany in 1923 to work for Anheuser-Busch. A year younger than Gussie, he became chief engineer in 1926. Adie lived in Huntleigh and when he brought two chimpanzees to his mansion he trained them properly. The chimps were dressed in dinner jackets and taught to sit at table like gentlemen and drink beer. During Adie's frequent outdoor cocktail parties, the chimps liked to swing down from trees, gripping bottles of Budweiser.

"It was so Dutchy I couldn't believe it," said a woman who attended parties at the Gontards' Melody Farm estate. "But I loved it, especially the monkeys." At first, Gussie and Adie appeared to be soulmates; both liked to joke about women, and Gussie could break into red-faced laughter doing an imitation of Adie's thick German accent. They rode horses together and partied. But the moment would come when Gussie forced Adie out of the brewery.

Throughout his life Gussie was acutely suspicious of relatives who worked for Anheuser-Busch. It was as if he viewed them as competitors for his job. He quarreled with them and often undermined or plotted to block their advancement. In the years immediately after repeal, however, he needed all the help he could get running the brewery. He had a difficult time meeting demand as the country went into a beer-drinking frenzy. Under August A.'s decree, the company refused to tamper with its recipe for Budweiser. And as he had predicted, customers were soon drinking his beer in record numbers. The brewery had soon sold over 2 million barrels of beer, twice the amount sold at the turn of the century.

During this busy period, Gussie relied most heavily on Frank Schwaiger, the young brewmaster he had lured from Germany shortly before the end of Prohibition. Only twenty-six, Schwaiger was the top graduate of a prestigious brewing school in Germany. Hiring him was one of the shrewdest decisions Gussie ever made. In those crucial days immediately after repeal, other breweries had to rely on the technical skill of men who were out of touch with modern brewing practices or who had forgotten how real beer was brewed. Not Anheuser-

Busch. Schwaiger was an expert at the brewer's art. And in the decades that followed his arrival, much of the credit for the quality of Anheuser-Busch's products and the company's tremendous growth belong to this quiet, granite-faced Bavarian.

Schwaiger, who started out as a $150-a-month brewmaster, died a millionaire. He was the sultan of suds, the protector of Budweiser's purity. No one, not even Gussie himself, dared question him. "Schwaiger was supreme," said Robert Weinberg, a former Anheuser-Busch executive. "He was accountable only to God. Schwaiger was one of the few who I saw tell the old man off and the old man took it."

No one had a better taste for beer than Frank Schwaiger. The story was told of the day a bartender bet him $100 that he couldn't pick out the difference among beers. Schwaiger accepted the bet and the bartender set three glasses—each with a different beer—in front of him, and he promptly identified each brand. The bartender bet him double or nothing he couldn't do it again. This time the brewmaster paused over the third glass.

"See," the bartender said gleefully. "You don't know what it is."

"No," said Schwaiger, shaking his head. "It's Pabst. But from the Peoria plant?"

Schwaiger eventually became chief brewmaster, succeeding the aging Rudolph Gull, the grand old man who had come to St. Louis at the invitation of Prince Adolphus. Of Gull, Gussie said, "He was fantastic. One of the greatest men who ever worked for Anheuser-Busch. It had nothing to do with his wife, who was the biggest bitch that ever happened."

With Schwaiger tending to Budweiser, it was truly "Happy Days Are Here Again" for everyone connected with making beer—the brewers themselves, the farmers, hops dealers and bottling companies. And among the happiest of perks were the gifts that suppliers often gave to brewery executives to assure their continued business. As the man in charge of buying hops and controlling beer sales, Gussie was a regular recipient of these favors. An employee recalled that he received clocks, linen, tablecloths, and that a hops seller once paid for the construction of a fence around the property at the Shooting Grounds in St. Peters.

The employee also recalled that Robert Baskowitz, the brewery's principal bottle supplier, gave presents to Gussie. Baskowitz became one of his closest friends and business associates. One family observer said, "not a shard of glass" was sold to the brewer without Baskowitz's involvement. Later Gussie and his friend entered the horse business together. Baskowitz's tradition of gift-giving continued into the next generation when his son gave a pistol to Gussie's son, a gift that would have tragic repercussions.

One employee joined Gussie in the 1920s. Entrusted with his business affairs as well as his personal and household finances, this highly regarded worker had an intimate look at Gussie, and both admired and was frightened by the man.

In the beginning, this assistant liked Gussie. He put in long days and had a sense of humor. Sometimes he brought his schnauzers to work. The lair of a beer baron, his office was paneled in pine with hunting prints on the walls. The ceilings were high, the rooms big. Nearby was the boardroom with nearly life-size, gilt-framed portraits of his father and grandfather and Eberhard Anheuser, his great-grandfather. Periodically, his workday was interrupted by tailors from New York City who measured him for his formal, business and riding attire. Before he left for home in the evening, he and Adolphus III were shaved by an elderly black barber.

Unfortunately, the employee was placed in the middle of many of Gussie's personal activities, which often was like being at the epicenter of an earthquake. The employee sometimes was caught up in his frequent domestic disturbances with his second wife, Elizabeth Overton Dozier. "It was a stormy marriage," the worker recalled. Elizabeth was an attractive, slender woman with dark eyes, dark brown hair and a "queenly disposition." In 1916 she had married Lewis Dozier, Jr., president of the United Wooden Heel Co. She and her husband often went to the theater and parties with Gussie and his first wife, Marie. "They were," said a friend of the family, "two young gay couples."

While Gussie was still married to Marie, his assistant unwittingly participated in arranging for Gussie to purchase a piece of jewelry from Cartier's in New York as a gift for Mrs. Dozier. It was paid for through a New York hops dealer. Gussie's wife found out about it because Cartier's sent a letter concerning the jewelry to the Busch home and "Mrs. Busch opened the letter." The assistant said Gussie discussed the incident with his confidant and assistant, Dick Upshaw. Gussie told Upshaw that while his wife might understand his having an affair with the office help, she was upset over his involvement with someone in her own social circle.

"That hurt her," the employee said. "I think it broke her spirit."

Since his teenage years, Gussie had been a ladies' man. His second cousin, Helen Busch Conway, recalled an incident that occurred shortly after Gussie had returned from visiting the woman whom he later married. Helen said she was at Grant's Farm and had to go to an upstairs bathroom. On the way, she passed by a room where she saw Gussie kissing the wife of one of his cousins. "It scared me, because I didn't know what to make of it."

Gussie and the men who came to his office often talked openly about sex. He and Adie von Gontard would talk about cute girls and tell jokes with sexual overtones. "They were far advanced about sex," recalled Gussie's assistant. "The things that are discussed openly now, they were discussing back then." Once Gussie said, "It's better to keep a woman than it is to marry one."

Sometimes women dropped in on Gussie at his office. After the visit of one attractive female, he told his assistant that the woman had said she would be available for him if he needed her. "He said to me once, 'As long as I can look at myself in the mirror in the morning, I feel all right.' "

33

Scandals

In the three years following the death of his first wife, Gussie busied himself with the brewery, horses and Elizabeth Dozier. He threw himself into the riding events hosted by the Bridle-spur Hunt Club, the fox-chasing organization founded by August A. because his family could not get into the St. Louis Country Club. The Busches and their friends galloped after foxes all over St. Louis County.

As master of the foxhounds, Gussie was responsible for appeasing farmers whose pastures were trampled, nurturing fox cubs and erecting split rail fences for the horses to jump. Wearing their pink jackets and bowler hats, the club members tested their courage by kicking their horses over every obstacle in their path. Gussie was known to boot an exhausted horse into solid timber. After these romps, he and his fellow riders warmed to bootleg whiskey. "He rode with elan," said his niece Sally Busch Wheeler. "It was thrilling."

It was also expensive. One hunt club member recalled one fund-raiser. Gussie put $1,000 of his own money into a hat and passed it around. Others added to the hat and a club member kept track of the total. He was shocked to find out after the money was added up that they were $1,000 short. "It turns out that Gussie withdrew money to make up for what he put in the hat. He said that with all the money that everyone else put in, we wouldn't need his. He took his $1,000 back!"

One of Gussie's assistants, who took notes for the hunt club, said his Bridlespur activities did not detract from his work at the brewery. His biggest distraction, the employee said, was Elizabeth Dozier. "They would have a tryst every two weeks." Gussie would take along "a small keg of Michelob. He told me to tell whoever was calling for him that he was over in the coal mines." In case of an emergency, Gussie said he could be reached at the Shooting Grounds in St. Peters.

Elizabeth often called Gussie on his private phone pretending she was a secretary, calling Gussie at the request of a businessman. Gussie's assistant recognized the voice and thought the charade ridiculous.

By the summer of 1933, the marriage between Lewis and Elizabeth Dozier had disintegrated. Lewis left on June 10 and divorce papers were quietly filed. Even before the divorce was granted, the rumors that Gussie would marry Elizabeth Dozier were already common. Her marriage was dissolved on September 8 and she obtained custody of her three children. Two weeks later, on September 22, 1933, Gussie married Elizabeth at the Savoy Plaza Hotel in New York City. Unlike his wedding with Marie Church, the ceremony was quiet with no attendants. In obtaining the license, Gussie said he was thirty-four; his fiancée thirty-eight.

After a brief honeymoon, the couple returned to live in Gussie's mansion on Lindell Boulevard. It was not a happy marriage, and there was trouble almost from the start. Elsa Doll, the woman who cared for Gussie's two daughters, left abruptly, saying Gussie's new wife could arrange for the care of the children. At first the girls did not warm to their new stepmother. One of them, Carlota, briefly ran away from home to try to live with Elsa.

Gussie's new wife had picked the right moment for the marriage. Dick Upshaw, Gussie's sidekick, remarked to a fellow employee that Elizabeth only married Gussie when she knew that beer was coming back.

The scandal of Gussie's marriage to Elizabeth Dozier was not the only one involving the Busch family. In the 1930s and the 1940s, two of August A.'s daughters, Alice and Marie, grabbed more than their share of space in the society pages.

Alice, Gussie's younger sister, was an Auntie Mame kind of character, quick-witted and nearly as colorful as Gussie. Pummie was a tall, slender, attractive woman who eventually married four times. She had the singular distinction of marrying a man who had already married into the Busch family, and then taking another husband who was distantly related to the family.

On June 17, 1936, Alice divorced her first husband, Louis Hager. Ten days later, there was another divorce in the Busch clan. Arthur D. B. Preece, the huntsman at the Bridlespur Club, divorced his wife, Lilly. Preece had married Lilly Busch Magnus, Alice Busch's cousin once removed. Lilly's father, Edward, was the son of the former Nellie Busch, August A.'s sister.

The marriage between Preece and Lilly Magnus proved ill-fated. On January 29, 1933, a prewedding luncheon for the couple at the home of George Tiffany, an Anheuser-Busch executive, was broken up by more than a dozen armed bandits who had planned to rob wealthy guests as they arrived for the party. Tiffany was beaten, and he and six members of his household were bound and gagged. After waiting for almost three hours for the arrival of the guests—they had gotten the time wrong—the gang left, taking several rifles, shotguns and silver pieces.

Preece was a strapping horseman with an English accent, whose skin was as tanned as his riding boots. Six months after he and Lilly divorced, he married Alice. Although this union complicated the family tree considerably, it did not last long.

Before 1937 ended, Alice filed for divorce, alleging mental cruelty. Trying a third time, her next marriage was in 1939 to Webster Tilton, a New York broker. It was the second marriage for Tilton. The couple lived in Cooperstown on the property purchased decades earlier by Prince Adolphus. In 1959 Tilton died of cancer.

Alice married for the fourth time in 1961 to Carl-Werner Gronewaldt, who traced his lineage back to the Anheusers. Gronewaldt was the grandson of Gustava Kluhn, the adopted daughter reared by Adolphus and Lilly Busch. For fifteen years, Carl and Alice divided their time between Cooperstown and Palm Beach, Florida. Gronewaldt died of a heart attack in 1977 while visiting his mother in Berlin.

Following in the footsteps of her sister, Marie Busch married three times—once to a tennis player, then to her gardener and, finally, to her chauffeur. Her first husband, C. Drummond Jones, a bridge expert and tennis champion, died on New Year's Day 1946. Four months later, Marie married her gardener, Constantin Dantes. Dantes had a stocky build and curly brown hair and looked younger than the forty-five years he claimed as his age. The marriage was one of the shortest on record with the Busch family. Less than two months later, Dantes sought a divorce, saying Marie had berated him and accused him of being unfaithful.

Later that summer, on August 30, 1946, Marie married her chauffeur, Andrew P. Szombati, in a secret ceremony in Toledo. She did better with the chauffeur than she had with the gardener. Their marriage lasted six months. They were divorced on February 7, 1947. A year later, Szombati was arrested trying to crash an ice skating party at Grant's Farm for Gussie's daughter Carlota. The thirty-five-year old Szombati was charged with disturbing the peace. When sheriff's deputies arrived, they found him pinned down by a chauffeur who had him in a half nelson. With only two cents in his pocket, Szombati said he was employed as a dancer. He claimed he only wanted to visit his brother-in-law Gussie.

Marie did not marry again. She died December 22, 1963, of a heart attack. She was seventy-one.

By the late 1930s, the marriage between Gussie and Elizabeth was showing signs of severe strain. Elizabeth drank heavily at times, and there were arguments. One of his assistants recalled that Gussie came into an office alcove, put his foot on the radiator and said, "I don't know what's going to happen to me but I'm not going to stay married to that woman." He began spending more and more time away from home, often in his eleven-ton "land yacht," one of his favorite toys in those years.

Like his grandfather, Gussie traveled in style. His thirty-three-foot-long motor coach slept eight. The interior was fashioned after a Pullman car with plush gray upholstery. The seats could be made into berths. It also had a stove, refrigerator, writing table, closet, baggage room, shower, bath and kitchen. The rear of the bus, which was painted brewster green, resembled a railroad observation car with a lighted sign stuck to the tail that said: THE ADOLPHUS.

Gussie traveled often in' this bizarre vehicle, taking it on business trips or to horse shows. It was usually crowded with beer salesmen, politicians, family members, brewery executives, friends, horse people and hops salesmen. Gussie held on-board gin rummy games that lasted for days. When asked for a beer, he growled, "You want a what?" Anyone who said "beer" instead of "Budweiser" owed $2 to the kitty. It was one of Gussie's rules of the road. He had many of them.

Once, there was a bus trip that wandered from Los Angeles, to San Francisco, then to Las Vegas. It was a long, grueling journey. Gussie wanted to stop in Kansas City for a horse show. Some on board didn't want to. They were tired and had to get back to business. Angered, Gussie said, "All right, now how many want to stay and how many want to leave?"

After everyone gave their reasons for leaving, he announced his decision. "Well, I'm democratic. We're staying." A friend recalled that if anyone had gotten up and left Gussie would have remembered it. "That's the way he was."

One day an employee had to tell Gussie's wife, Elizabeth, that he was getting his bus readied for a trip. Elizabeth didn't like what she heard. She told the employee that Gussie's son was "more grown up" than his father and that "being married to Busch is like sitting on a bomb."

The brewery chauffeur, Carl Rohlfing, sometimes took a staff member to Gussie's mansion so that he could catch up on paperwork. The employee would have dinner with Gussie and Elizabeth and work afterward. One evening, Elizabeth joined them as they worked at a table in the foyer. When they finished, Gussie left his assistant with his wife, who promptly ordered a bottle of wine. The assistant drank one glass. When a second glass was declined, Elizabeth said, "You're a teetotaler, aren't you?" On the way home, the chauffeur told the employee, "She will drink that whole bottle before she goes to bed."

In the spring of 1939, this same assistant was caught in a quarrel between Gussie and Elizabeth that underscored the deterioration of their marriage. Gussie and fellow executive Albert Nierdieck were scheduled to attend a meeting together in Chicago. Nierdieck ended up going alone. The next morning, he telephoned Gussie's assistant and explained the change in plans. Gussie had gone to the Shooting Grounds. If anyone called, the assistant was to say that Gussie was in Chicago. The trouble started a few hours later when Elizabeth called the office asking for Gussie. The assistant told his wife that Gussie was in Chicago, and stuck to the story when Elizabeth continued calling. The employee later was told that Gussie and Elizabeth had quarreled. "Nierdieck told me they had had a terrible battle. They were throwing china at each other." Gussie and Elizabeth eventually reconciled.

About a year later, in February 1940, Gussie did take a trip to Chicago for the U.S. Brewers' Association convention. When he disembarked from the Wabash *Blue Bird*, he was attracted to the pretty hostess who thanked everyone for riding the train and wished them a pleasant stay in the Windy City. "Honey," Gussie asked her, "what's your name?"

The young woman told him, and Gussie asked if she was staying in town. When she said she was, he invited her to a party he said he was having at his hotel room. Later that night, the woman came to the room, which was filled with a half dozen of Gussie's cronies—hops dealers, publicists and beer salesmen. After a few drinks all around, Gussie came over to the woman. "Honey, let's you and I go fuck."

The woman did not bat an eyelash. "Mr. Busch," she said, heading for the door, "I thank you for your hospitality, but I believe this is where I get off."

34

The Man in the Mask

While Gussie struggled to get his brewery humming after repeal and fought with his wife, political events in Germany disrupted the lives of his aunt Clara and her husband, Baron Paul von Gontard. After the Great War, the baron continued to manage a munitions factory and served as president of Mercedes-Benz & Manser Corporation of Stuttgart. On November 25, 1930, his daughter, Lilly Claire, married Werner Schieber, a successful German manufacturer. Lilly Claire was said to be the wealthiest heiress in Berlin, and society turned out in force for the dazzling affair. The church of St. Matthias was filled with men and women in formal attire. Outside, lines of shiny black limousines and uniformed chauffeurs waited at the curb.

All went well until the bridal party emerged from the church. That's when an elderly woman suddenly approached and grabbed the father of the bride by the arm. "Give me back my son, Baron von Gontard!" she cried out. "You have had him put in prison for fifteen years although he is innocent. You have taken away my son. Give honor to God and speak the truth at last."

People in the church stumbled over one another to see the commotion. Gontard hustled his daughter into a waiting limousine. Police whisked away the woman. She was identified as the mother of Walter Bullerjahn, who was known as the "German Dreyfus," because many people believed Bullerjahn was innocent and had been railroaded.

Convicted of treason by a German court in 1925, Bullerjahn had been accused of informing a French armistice commission of a hidden cache of arms. At the time, the Allies were conducting a search for weapons that exceeded limits established by the Treaty of Versailles. The French discovered the arms in the Karlsruhe Industrial Works plant in Berlin, where Gontard was the general manager and board chairman.

The case against Bullerjahn was a circumstantial one until a most unusual witness appeared. His identity was kept secret and he testified behind closed doors, which prompted German newspapers to call him "The Man in the Mask." The magistrate allowed the unusual procedure because the witness was of high social standing. Based on the testimony of this secret witness, Bullerjahn was convicted. Many were upset over the use of a secret witness's testimony. The German Supreme Court reversed the verdict in 1932, acquitting Bullerjahn after he had served six years in prison.

Baron Paul von Gontard, it was revealed later, was the secret witness, the Man in the Mask.

In addition to Adie von Gontard, who worked for the brewery, and Lilly Claire, the Gontards had two other children— Paul, a big-game hunter, who wrote two books and produced movies on his travels, and Gert, who edited an anti-Nazi literary magazine in Berlin. Gert narrowly avoided arrest in Germany because of his anti-Nazi views and made his escape by pretending to be his brother, Paul, who was already a resident of the United States. Gert was divorced in 1940 from the former German movie actress, Lucia Toelle, whom he charged with infidelity. She countered with a statement that he was a "philanderer by instinct."

Shortly after Adolf Hitler came to power, on March 16, 1933, Baron Paul von Gontard was arrested in Berlin on charges of illegally and secretly removing funds from Germany. He was accused of attempting to evade taxation by transferring 6 million marks to Holland and Switzerland. His wife, Clara, said the money was her property, part of a trust fund established by her father, Adolphus Busch.

The baron, sixty-eight years old and suffering from diabetes, was confined to the Moabit prison hospital. His home in the fashionable Bendlerstrasse, the meeting place for the kaiser's court thirty years earlier, was searched by Nazi police and his bank accounts and property near Berlin were seized. Because of his health, he was later freed on a bond of one-half million marks but was warned not to leave the city.

Lilly Claire, meanwhile, divorced Schieber and in 1937 married Bernard Berghaus, who, a U.S. State Department official said in November 1942, was a high Nazi official. In February 1939, with the German invasion of Poland just seven months away, Clara returned briefly to St. Louis. As war clouds gathered, and possibly remembering her mother's troubles during the Great War, she had her U.S. citizenship restored in federal court.

The Gontard estate west of Berlin was used by the Nazis soon after war began. Their stables and outhouses stored military equipment and grain, and forty-two refugees were quartered in their mansion. Clara and the baron were allowed only two rooms for their private use. Their cars and horses were pressed into military service and they were obliged to suffer the indignity of using buses and trams.

The couple moved to Zurich, Switzerland, where the baron, now seventy-five, died on October 3, 1941. Clara lived in the Bauraulac Hotel in Zurich with her daughter Lilly Berghaus and Lilly's two children. They were regularly visited by Lilly's husband, Bernard, whose travels between Switzerland and Germany attracted the attention of Sam Edison Woods, the American consul general.

Woods, who later became closely involved with the Busch family, was more of an intelligence officer than a diplomat. He monitored Berghaus's movements and sent secret cables back to Secretary of State Cordell Hull. "Rumored here Mrs. Berghaus is the Gestapo agent at Zurich's best hotel," Woods reported on November 18, 1942. "Also reliably reported Berghaus closely associated with Karlsruhe Waffenfabrik and has recently bought interest in the Oerlikon Waffenfabrik in Switzerland but which is producing armaments for Germany."

Woods learned that Clara von Gontard was receiving 15,000 francs a month from Anheuser-Busch and the St. Louis Union Trust Co., which controlled the Busch trusts. "Legation opinion that because of German currency restrictions, Gontard is using part of the money she receives from the United States for at least partial support of the Berghauses," Woods cabled. He recommended that some action be taken against Clara von Gontard and Lilly and Bernard Berghaus. The State Department passed along Woods's recommendation in the form of a "frozen credit" letter to the Treasury Department for "such action as may be deemed appropriate." Like her mother in the preceding war, Clara's loyalty was under suspicion.

Meanwhile, a member of the Gontard family was having his troubles in the United States. In 1944, Clara's son Gert was accused of conspiring with others to avoid the military draft. One of the codefendants in the case committed suicide. Gert was acquitted after an eight-day trial in federal court in New York City.

Clara Busch von Gontard married again after the war. She

was seventy-one when she took her second husband on February 16, 1948—Adrian Liengme of Switzerland, an executive in the International Red Cross and a retired watch manufacturer from Zurich. The couple lived alternately between Switzerland and New York. Liengme died in 1952, and Clara passed away June 26, 1959, of a heart attack at her summer home in Biel, Switzerland. She was the last surviving beneficiary of the trust established in 1913 on the death of her father, Prince Adolphus. At the time of her death, she was worth about $6 million.

Clara lived the longest of the Prince's daughters. Within a month after August A.'s suicide in 1934, the spendthrift Nellie Busch Magnus Loeb, who had been involved in the diamond smuggling incident, died in Chicago. It took several years of court litigation to determine the settlement of her sizable estate. Her grandsons later occupied key positions at the brewery and in the administration of President Richard M. Nixon.

On April 16, 1936, Anna Louise Busch Faust died of pneumonia in the beautiful St. Louis mansion her father had given her. She was sixty-one. Three months later, her sixty-seven-year-old husband, Edward A. Faust, died of heart disease. Their son, Leicester Busch Faust, worked at the brewery.

Edmee Busch Reisinger married Charles Greenough after her husband's death in 1914. They were divorced in 1923. Among her later boyfriends, it was said, were an admiral, a marine captain and an army general. She lived to be eighty-four, dying in 1955 after giving large sums of money to the Germanic Museum her father and her first husband started on the campus of Harvard University.

The Prince's daughters led colorful, and extremely comfortable lives. But none could compare to Wilhelmina, who had the most fabulous life of all.

35

Budweiser Goes to War

Immediately after the attack on Pearl Harbor, the brewers, remembering the disastrous effects of the last war on their German-rooted industry, scrambled to show their patriotism. They didn't want another round of "Rats in the Vats" and similar slurs. On December 19, 1941, Gussie chaired the first meeting of the Greater St. Louis Brewers Victory Committee. George Eads, an Anheuser-Busch vice president, said prohibitionists could again be expected to use the war for "propaganda purposes."

The brewers resolved to prove their loyalty to everyone. They decided to check their employees for enemy aliens and report them to the government; they sponsored blackout drills, defense bonds sales and Red Cross war relief drives. But the news releases describing these activities never appeared in the papers, whose pages were crowded with genuine war news. The brewers were chagrined at not getting favorable publicity.

Gussie finally grabbed some headlines when he joined the U.S. Army. He received a commission in the ordnance department. At forty-three, he looked resplendent in his tailor-made uniform, which James Kirkpatrick described as "the fanciest major's uniform of anybody in the army." Kirkpatrick, a brewing industry spokesman who later became Missouri secretary of state, attended Gussie's large going-away luncheon sponsored by the brewers. "He and his brother stood up at the head table, embraced and kissed each other on the cheek. It was quite a sight."

There needn't have been any worry. Gussie wasn't going to war; he was going to Washington. The war not only helped him flee from Elizabeth; it also helped beer sales. Many new army camps were built in dry counties in the South. The introduction of army posts and the beer that went with them amounted to an invasion that greatly increased beer's geographic coverage. The Anti-Saloon League, no doubt remembering the happy days of World War I prohibition, unsuccessfully fought for restrictive zones around military bases. Bills presented to Congress during 1941 that sought to prohibit the sale of beer to servicemen were killed in committee or defeated.

Like Gussie, Budweiser put on a new uniform. Budweiser Lager Beer went to war in olive drab cans. During 1944, Anheuser-Busch shipped the equivalent of 607,083 barrels of beer to domestic and overseas military camps, 16.4 percent of its output for the year.

When Gussie entered the army on June 22, 1942, most of his brewery duties were assumed by Richard Upshaw. Gussie was assigned to a desk job on the second floor of the Pentagon. The suspected connections of his German relatives to the Nazis did not keep him from being promoted, and he made lieutenant colonel by January of 1943 and full colonel in November 1944. His duties dealt with ammunition production. He was awarded the Legion of Merit medal for his service and years later proudly wore the ribbon on his lapel.

To all appearances, a number of women shared Gussie's military life. In later years, recalling his days in the army, Gussie referred to a buddy named Jack Pickens of Little Rock, Arkansas. Pickens, Gussie said, was "in the service with me. We used to smell powder together—that is women's face powder." Edward Vogel, Jr., a brewer who later went to work for Anheuser-Busch, smiled broadly when he recalled Gussie's war record. "I met him once up in Chicago when he was in the army," he said. "He was with a lot of Wacs. He had a pretty soft job."

With so many temptations, Gussie's marriage to Elizabeth disintegrated even further. One of Gussie's assistants was told by Upshaw that Gussie had several dinner dates with other women. During the war, the marriage between Gussie and his wife became intolerable. She constantly found fault with him and nagged and criticized members of his family. She made accusations regarding his moral behavior—charges he said were false and unfounded—which led to violent quarrels. Elizabeth, Gussie said, drank excessively and used drugs in front of their children and other members of the household, setting a poor example. They had two children by then, a girl and a boy.

The couple's actual separation may have come as early as May 1943. That was when Gussie and one of his daughters from his first marriage, Carlota, moved from the mansion on Lindell Boulevard to Grant's Farm. The castle had been closed since shortly after August A.'s suicide. Alice, his widow, lived in a smaller mansion that had been built near the Big House. Gussie and Carlota took up residence in the Bauernhof, the two-story carriage house that contained an eighteen-room apartment.

Gussie later dated his separation from April 1945. By that time, his oldest daughter, Lilly, was married to Robert Hermann of the United States Navy Reserve. The wartime wedding occurred in Washington and was attended by Missouri Senator Harry Truman, who within a year would become the president of the United States.

In Europe at about the same time, another wedding took place. Gussie's colorful aunt, the incredible Wilhelmina, finally married the man of her dreams.

36

The Last Queen of Bavaria

•

Of all the Busch girls, none compared with Wilhelmina, or Minnie as she was known to her friends and family. Swept off her feet by an armed, love-crazed Prussian army officer, the youngest daughter of Prince Adolphus moved to Germany. Six months after the death in 1913 of her father, Minnie and her husband, Eduard Scharrer, bought a city-sized estate near Bernried, a small village on the Starnberger See just south of Munich. Minnie had seen the area while on a hunting trip and fell in love with the alpine lake nestled in the rolling green hills of farmland, pasture and timber, framed by the snow-capped Bavarian Alps to the south.

They called their villa the House of the White Peacock. In all they owned about one-third of the village and surrounding countryside. More than 100 workers, descendants of indentured servants, were employed by squire Scharrer to tend his herd of horses, milk 300 cows and maintain the sprawling estate. In that sharply divided class society, the populace retained some of its subservience and considered the Scharrers with measured amounts of fear, respect and admiration. Minnie and her husband were benevolent landholders, who were glimpsed only rarely when their chauffeur-driven Cadillac, the first car in the area, carefully negotiated the narrow streets of the village. During the financially troubled years of 1915 to 1923, they gave 4 million marks to Bernried to help its poor. Even in those highly inflationary times, these contributions were sizable. In April 1922, Scharrer spent 10,000 deutsch marks for the erection of a war memorial in Bernried.

The years did not take the military edge off the former cavalry officer. Scharrer, who received the Iron Cross for his service in World War I, was a strong nationalist, and like many other veterans, he probably bitterly resented the German surrender. Such feelings were especially sharp in that region of Bavaria and the neighborhood of Munich, which spawned Hitler and the Nazi party. Scharrer occasionally donned his army uniform for public events. In 1928, when the kaiser's son, Friedrich Wilhelm, the crown prince of Prussia, paid an official visit to Bernried, Scharrer marched beside him wearing a gleaming spiked helmet, his chest bedecked with medals.

Wilhelmina's husband was like many of the industrialists and businessmen who helped finance Hitler's rise to power. But there was some question whether Scharrer actually contributed to Hitler's campaign. Ernst Hanfstaengl, Hitler's companion in the early years, recalled that he accompanied the future führer to the Bernried estate to solicit money. "They had a colossal nouveau-riche establishment full of white peacocks, borzois and tame swans, but we got no change out of them, at least not on that occasion," Hanfstaengl said. Authors who later interviewed Hanfstaengl have interpreted his remark to imply that Hitler "was more successful at some other time" with Scharrer.

A copy of the house guestbook of Eduard and Wilhelmina contains the signature of "Adolf Hitler" dated September 22, 1930, when the Nazis were seeking support to win control of the Reichstag. The visit made a lasting impression. Hitler recalled it twelve years later as his conquering armies occupied Europe and were rolling through parts of Africa and Soviet Russia. Some believed Hitler's criticism of Wilhelmina, whom he described as "the sort of Jewess one sees in caricatures," was a sign that he did not get the contribution he sought. But it also might have been a reflection of his disgust with boundless extravagance or the fact that America had entered the war against him.

"She, the wife, was a daughter of the big brewer, Busch, who had made his fortune in the United States," Hitler said. "She looked like a ball. Nobody ever checked up whether she was wider or taller. She had hands laden with rings which were so big that she couldn't move her fingers."

An admirer of fine automobiles, Hitler was attracted to Scharrer's car. "Its radiator was plated, not in nickel, but in gold," he said. "It furthermore contained a thousand little articles of everyday use, starting with a lavatory, all in gold."

In his ramblings, Hitler talked about the "Prussian princes" Eduard and Wilhelmina received at their mansion. It was a reference to August Wilhelm, the fourth son of the kaiser and a fanatical supporter of Hitler's. Known as Auwi to his friends, the prince's signature in the Scharrers' guestbook was accompanied by a hand-drawn swastika and the notation: "Thanks for four days of recreation in the lovely Bernried. What a joy it was to find the woman in charge better and on the road to recovery. The struggle goes on against all difficulties. Heil Hitler." It was dated August 17, 1931. August Wilhelm, who helped legitimize Hitler with a connection to royalty, later became a Gruppenführer in the S.S.

Walter Eberl, the burgermeister of Bernried whose father was the game warden in Scharrer's forests, said that while Scharrer was possibly involved in politics, Wilhelmina was not. "She was against practically anything that was connected with war or political affairs. She liked nature and animals and things of beauty, art, antiques, gardening, garden architecture and religion."

To those who worked for her, Minnie was considered a fine but demanding lady. Her eccentricities were the stuff of legend. Several times a year she took trips to Vienna, Paris and Switzerland for the baths. When she traveled, it was in the fashion of a Busch—like a small circus on the move, with servants, half a dozen dogs and several dozen trunks of luggage. Her enormous wardrobe included dozens of wagon-wheel-sized floppy hats with spear-length feathers that she wore indoors, a hazard for servants waiting on her. Minnie had eight servants with a hand bell designated to call each one.

She also had a collection of wigs—red, blond and black—

that she wore beneath her huge hats. Even though she had a car, she often traveled in a horse-drawn coach in the style of a Prussian princess with two footmen wearing black top hats clinging to the back. When she entered a village, one of them blasted a warning on a long brass trumpet so that the residents would clear a path.

When Minnie left on a long trip, she always sent word on the exact date and hour of her return. Her homecomings were pure theater. A servant was expected to dress like a shepherd and greet her with a herd of sheep. This scene was repeated every time she pulled up in her carriage after an extended absence. The pastoral image, she said, put her at peace.

Minnie loved children. Her husband, however, didn't share her warm feelings and often scolded youngsters in the village and the offspring of his workers. Minnie probably wanted a child of her own, but had been denied one by Scharrer. Some thought that was why she had decorated her home with so many dolls and cradles.

On March 3, 1931, Eduard and Minnie celebrated their silver wedding anniversary. The entire village turned out, with many of the men wearing traditional lederhosen. It was their last anniversary. Within a year, Eduard Scharrer, the man who once tried to elope with the daughter of the American beer king, died at the age of fifty-eight. "He liked food and drink and perhaps that helped him to his death," said Walter Eberl, the burgermeister.

But Hitler, in 1942, had a different recollection of how Wilhelmina and her first husband parted. "Unfortunately for him, Scharrer had a flame," Hitler said. "His wife was furious, and threw him out of the house. He died in poverty. She finally offered herself to a young lover. It's a painful situation for a husband to be so dependent on a wife as rich as Croesus."

Like her sisters Edmee, Clara and Nellie, Wilhelmina did not remain a widow. On Christmas Eve 1933, she married Carl Borchardt, a physician with a practice in Seeblick, a small village on the Starnberger See. Borchardt was a hulk of a man and some people thought he was Irish with his red hair and ruddy complexion. With age he grew very fat.

In May of 1934, three months after the suicide of her brother August A., Minnie returned to the United States. It was more than just a social visit; she used the opportunity to regain her United States citizenship lost when she married Scharrer in 1906. With the end of Prohibition, the dividends from her American investments had swelled dramatically. The American government filed a deficiency claim against her for under-payment of 1933 income taxes, and Minnie paid the $8,523 more on income from two trusts created by her parents.

In 1938, at the age of fifty-four, she decided to use some of this wealth to create a fantasy life—an idea she had been dreaming about for some time. With St. Louis beer money and other income, she built the last great castle ever constructed in Germany. All of the Busch mansions paled in comparison. Hohenried, one of the most beautiful places in Bavaria, commanded a panoramic view of the Starnberger See. The Bavarian Alps provided the majestic backdrop.

A convert to Catholicism, Wilhelmina made sure her castle, constructed between 1937 and 1939, reflected her spiritual beliefs. The chapel and courtyard were decorated with religious scenes. The castle was built symmetrically, with a four-story main stone building measuring more than 175 feet across. Four massive towers were attached to the main structure, and at the top of each was an onion-shaped dome. There were fountain-filled gardens and courtyards. The main drawing room offered a sweeping view of a lake and, beyond, the Alps. Ten gardeners and an architect were employed full-time. The castle's palatial interior had marble floors, and its walls were covered with expensive tapestries, paintings and polished oak panels. The fireplaces were big enough for a tall person to stand in.

Dr. Peter Mathes, a director of the medical clinic that now occupies the grounds of Hohenried, believed Wilhelmina had excellent connections with the Nazi government. She would have needed them, he thought, to build such a lavish structure when the rest of Germany was on a war footing. Burgermeister Eberl also speculated that Minnie was allowed to proceed with her building plans because the government wanted good relations with America.

With a fortune to spend, Minnie put antique dealers all over Europe on notice that they were to call her first when they discovered any treasures. Her castle was filled with Louis XVI furniture, Ming vases, porcelain and precious clocks. One of the rooms was furnished with articles once owned by Napoleon Bonaparte. Minnie's 1,000-year-old chapel had been removed stone by stone complete and intact from the Greek island of Corfu in the Mediterranean and reassembled in her castle. She loved white and her estate was populated by a strain of white stags, which she would watch from a parapet of her castle. There were dozens of servants and a nearby village whose inhabitants regarded her as resident royalty and thus dubbed her the Last Queen of Bavaria.

At Hohenried, Minnie created her own vision of heaven on earth, a place where anyone could find pleasure. But her marriage to Dr. Borchardt, her rotund husband, was not a happy one. They were divorced in 1941. A month later the United States and Germany went to war.

Minnie fled to Zurich, Switzerland, and the Nazi government seized most of her property. Later, the Swiss government used the castle as an embassy. Like her mother, Lilly, during World War I, and sister Clara during World War II, Minnie's loyalty came under question and she was suspected of having connections with the Nazi government.

In April of 1942, Minnie attracted the interest of Sam Woods, the American consul in Zurich who had alerted the State Department about the activities of her sister Clara. Wilhelmina, who was an American citizen, had traveled to Germany under a German passport and returned to Switzerland. Questioned by Woods, Minnie admitted making the trip, saying she had gone back to Germany to fight lawsuits that had been filed against her property there by her ex-husband.

Minnie also acknowledged during Wood's inquiry that she received 10,000 francs a month from Anheuser-Busch and the St. Louis Union Trust Company. Under the arrangement, the brewery and bank bought Swiss francs in New York which were paid to her through the Schweizerische Bodenkredit Bank in Zurich. Woods said the financial arrangement showed "she claims exemption from restrictions affecting Americans but from which Germans are exempt."

There was another indication of a connection between Minnie and the Nazis. A man claimed in 1947 that property he used to own in Munich had been taken by the Nazi government without compensation and sold to Wilhelmina. Woods thought Minnie "evidently" had violated the law and recommended the brewery and the bank "be carefully questioned and all necessary actions taken including nondelivery of telegrams between her and parties in the United States."

Wilhelmina was placed on the American black list. Commercial and financial transactions were prohibited between persons on the list and American citizens or firms. Her life became more difficult without the dividends from Anheuser-Busch. It was certainly a bleak time for Minnie. With her loyalty to America under suspicion, she was disliked and distrusted by many of the Swiss. A tall Texan, however, came to the rescue of the Last Queen of Bavaria. Minnie was befriended by the man who helped bring on her troubles in the first place—the American foreign service officer, Sam Woods.

At fifty-two, Sam Edison Woods was something of a legend in the U.S. State Department. His genial manner masked a cloak-and-dagger career. Early in January 1941, as the U.S. commercial attaché in Berlin, he had sent a confidential report to Secretary of State Cordell Hull warning that Hitler planned to attack Russia. Woods received the information from a monk and a member of the German general staff. The intelligence, after being checked out by the State Department, was turned over to the Soviet government, which ignored it.

Woods identified his German source as "Ralph," a high-ranking official in the German government before the Nazis came to power. "Ralph" got his information from a Roman Catholic monk, who had obtained the intelligence from a member of the German general staff. After the United States and Germany went to war, Woods was assigned to Zurich, where he reestablished contact with "Ralph." He got a big assist from Wilhelmina.

"I knew Ralph kept in touch regularly with an assistant to the head of a monastery near Munich," Woods said. "Then the question was how to get word to the monastery. I remembered that Miss Busch, who was living in Zurich, had lived near Munich. I invited her to lunch. I asked her if she knew anyone who was going to Munich from Switzerland and who could be trusted. She told me a man was leaving for Munich the next day. She introduced me to him and I decided he could be trusted. For the first time, I mentioned Ralph's full name. I sent word through the traveler to the monastery that I wanted Ralph to get in touch with me. Three days later, a priest stopped me on the street and asked what I wanted from Ralph."

Woods used his contact to learn the status of Germany's development of an atomic bomb. With the aid of cooperative Swiss, he also succeeded in slipping 224 interned American airmen out of Switzerland. Ralph survived the war, but the monk apparently was discovered as an informant and executed. His body was found in a lake.

After Minnie helped Woods get in touch with Ralph, she was removed from the black list. In January, 1944 a State Department spokesman, discussing the decision, said the government

was confident Wilhelmina was "a loyal American." Her removal from the list would have been quickly forgotten if it
hadn't been for Drew Pearson, a columnist with a nationwide
radio broadcast. Pearson reported that "quiet moves were
made by very high people to take her off. The Treasury Department was opposed and some of our allies were shocked. However, the secretary of state himself, Cordell Hull, went over
their heads and took Mrs. Busch Borchardt off the black list."

Toward the end of the war, American troops occupied Minnie's castle. The property of a woman who had nursed
wounded German soldiers during World War I now served as
a hospital for wounded GIs. Meanwhile, Sam Woods and his
first wife had been divorced. At war's end, Woods was appointed the U.S. consul at Munich and Minnie returned to her
castle. By then they had already fallen in love.

On February 22, 1948, fifty-six-year-old Sam Woods, the
strapping son of a poor Texas farmer, married an equally
strapping Wilhelmina Busch in a ceremony in the castle
chapel. Minnie, who was sixty-four, wore a red wig. The guests
included Admiral Nicholas Horthy, former regent of Hungary,
and Prince Albrecht, heir pretender to the Bavarian throne.
Horthy's presence at the ceremony was criticized by German
newspapers, who compared him with Hitler. Back in St. Louis,
"the family was a little apprehensive about the marriage between Sam Woods and Wilhelmina Busch," said a close friend
of the Busches. "They were afraid of what might happen and
it did happen."

Members of the Busch family from St. Louis traveled to Hohenried. Gussie, Wilhelmina's nephew, brought his family over
for a visit, and his son, August III, killed two deer hunting on
the estate. Gussie longed for one of Wilhelmina's desks once
owned by Napoleon. With his help, Sam Woods was named to
the board of directors of Anheuser-Busch in 1951, a decision
Gussie lived to regret.

Sam and Minnie spent their last years restoring and maintaining their properties. They donated a sizable chunk of the
estate to Bavaria, and it became a national park. Woods retired from diplomatic service in 1952 and spent his time turning a stream that ran through their estate into a series of
cascading ponds, calling the terraced creek the Mississippi.

In 1951, when she was sixty-seven, Wilhelmina Busch Woods
developed a heart condition. Late the next year, she was operated on. She died the following day, November 23, 1952, with-

out having regained consciousness. Sam Woods wept deeply at her bedside. Within six months, he was also dead, felled by a cerebral hemorrhage one week after his sixty-first birthday.

Minnie and Sam were buried on the Hohenried estate. The grave, in a glade by the shore of the Starnberger See, offered a marvelous view of the St. Benedict Mountains that she loved. Inscribed at the base of the Italian marble sarcophagus was the sentence "Love Never Ends." Near their graves were the marble busts of Adolphus and Lilly Busch. Another tombstone marked the grave of a dog. The inscription read, "Peggy, we miss you."

Minnie's estate was left to Sam Woods, who made his own will less than a month after her death. In it, he bequeathed the castle and the estate, worth between $3 million and $5 million, to his first wife and their children. The fear the Busches had when Sam married Wilhelmina was realized. Gussie never got Napoleon's desk. When Minnie's estate went to Sam's relatives, a friend said, "Gussie went through the ceiling. He was really mad."

Although all of Minnie's property wound up outside the family, the original principal left in trust by Adolphus Busch—valued at approximately $10 million by the time her 209,500 Anheuser-Busch shares were distributed—went to fifteen of his descendants, Gussie among them.

Hohenried castle is now a rehabilitation clinic for heart attack victims, with 540 patients and 405 employees, and was photographed by the Milton Bradley Company for one of its 500-piece puzzles. Its medical director, Dr. Peter Mathes, said no one today—not Donald Trump when he was in the chips, not the late Malcolm Forbes, not Sam Walton—could live in the style of Wilhelmina Busch.

"She wanted to live like the queen of Bavaria. When she died, the dream came to a close."

37

Pigs With Painted Toes

After the war, Gussie returned to St. Louis a bundle of restless, nervous energy. At forty-six, he seemed to have reached a mid-life crisis. He considered entering politics and was courted by the Missouri Democratic party to run for mayor. He toyed with the idea of leaving the brewery and joining U.S. Steel. But his future was decided on August 29, 1946, when his older brother, Adolphus III, died at Barnes hospital. Mr. Adolph was fifty-five and had been hospitalized for eight days. His death was attributed to cardiac failure and cancer of the stomach.

Adolphus III had been ill for some time. Helen Busch Conway recalled seeing him not long before his death; she noticed how badly his hands shook as he held a glass. Removed from the public spotlight, his illness was not well known and his death came as a surprise. He was buried next to August A., his father, in Sunset Cemetery.

A week after his brother died, Gussie was elected president of Anheuser-Busch. The grandson of Prince Adolphus proudly took over the office on Pestalozzi Street that had been used by his father. It was later said that Gussie was considered a light-weight when he took command of the brewery. The truth was otherwise. Gussie, as he liked to say, knew the business from A to Z. He had had enough self-assurance to countermand a decision by his older brother. In the summer of 1944 when a brewing problem had tainted the taste of Budweiser, Adolphus III had the beer shipped anyway. Informed of the problem, Gussie overruled his brother and ordered the beer dumped into the sewers. Adolphus III, it was said, never forgot it.

Adolphus III left his estate to his wife, Catherine Milliken Busch, and his two daughters, Sallie Marie and Marie Eleanor Condie. His mother, eighty-year-old Alice, survived him and retained an interest in two important trusts—one created by her in December 1937, and the other by August A. in May 1932.

Gussie, with the power to vote the trust's stock, had virtual control of the company, especially when he was able to persuade his aunts—Edmee, Clara and Wilhelmina—to support him. A year after the death of Adolphus III, Anheuser-Busch stock was split five for one. Eighty percent of it was in the hands of family members who had no intention of putting any up for public sale.

Gussie Busch became the highest-paid executive in St. Louis. In 1947 his annual salary was $132,222. He reopened Grant's Farm, and began restoring the animal herds that had been sold off by his father many years before. Although his brother's will provided for the distribution of his property to his wife and daughters, Gussie managed to obtain sole control of the Shooting Grounds, which August A. had willed to both his sons many years before. "Somehow Gussie bought that from the estate," said a member of the family. Herbert and Marie Eleanor Condie, the son-in-law and daughter of Adolphus III, and their son Parker "were expecting it to come to them. Parker and his dad loved to shoot. To this day, Parker doesn't know what happened."

The Shooting Grounds and hunting lodge provided an endless source of pleasure for Gussie. It was his secluded getaway of 1,500 acres of fields, woods and swamp, the place where he met Elizabeth Dozier before they were married and, afterward, the place where he went to get away from her. The property was also a meeting place for close friends and powerful politicians, like Sam Rayburn and Lyndon Johnson.

Gussie had an elaborate corral built where he practiced calf roping. Although over forty, he loved to play cowboy. On cold September dawns, when the mallards flew south and the big gray geese came honking down from Canada, he crouched in a richly appointed duck blind and blasted away with his shotgun. On see-your-breath mornings when golden leaves fluttered to the ground, women in tweeds and men in hunting boots gathered for shooting parties.

The engraved invitations to such affairs began "Mr. August A. Busch Jr. requests the pleasure of your company at a live bird and target shoot." Mrs. Busch was not mentioned on the invitation. It was as if Elizabeth had dropped out of sight. But Gussie lied when he was confronted by reports that he was separated. During an interview at the Shooting Grounds he explained Elizabeth's absence by saying she didn't like the country.

The biggest event Gussie held at the Shooting Grounds was the annual schlachfest, an old Bavarian-style feast. Guests shot ducks or rode horses while the servants butchered pigs. Returning ravenous, they found wagonloads of pork decorated with ribbons and red geraniums. The toenails of the pigs' feet were daubed with red nail polish. As a special favor, ladies received small live pigs wearing scarfs of red and green. When everyone was mellow from beer, sausage and kirsch, Busch led the singing. He usually wore a Tyrolean costume or lederhosen.

No one threw a party like Gussie. In fact, one of his blowouts —the wedding and reception for his daughter Carlota—received a national award, the International Stewards' and Caterers' Association rating it as one of the ten best parties of the year in the United States. On June 21, 1948, she married her second cousin, John Flanigan. Like Carlota, Flanigan was a great-grandchild of Adolphus Busch. He was the son of Horace Flanigan of Purchase, New York, and Aimee Magnus, the daughter of Nellie Busch, August A.'s sister. Because of the couple's close blood relationship, permission for the Catholic marriage had to be granted by the church. Approval was granted by Francis Cardinal Spellman of New York.

The noon wedding was held at the St. Louis Cathedral followed by a reception at Grant's Farm that began at 1:30 P.M. and continued into the early-morning hours. The castle accommodated over 800 guests who were entertained by two orchestras. Swans and white Pekin ducks, the latter sent by plane from New York, swam on the lake. There was also imported champagne and a six-tiered wedding cake. Hundreds of wedding gifts were displayed in the gun room.

Gussie drove his daughter and new son-in-law to the gate of Grant's Farm in a coach and four where a limousine was waiting to take them to the airport for the first stage of a three-month honeymoon in Europe. It was like a prince and princess leaving the castle. But the couple did not live happily ever after. The marriage of John Flanigan and Carlota Busch—like so many others in the family—ended in divorce. But on her wedding day, before Carlota left Grant's Farm, she threw her bridal bouquet. Standing at the foot of the grand staircase, Gussie caught it.

Adolphus Busch, in his prime, millionaire brewer and bon vivant, friend of American presidents and the German kaiser. He preferred wine to his own beer, which, according to one published account, he called "dot schlop."

The Schützenhof, the Busch family homestead in Kastel, Germany, where Adolphus was born in 1839. One of twenty-two children, he emigrated to St. Louis in 1857 to seek his fortune.

Eberhard Anheuser, wealthy St. Louis soap manufacturer and owner of a brewery that made bad beer. When young Adolphus married his daughter and joined the business, the product, and the brewery's fortunes, vastly improved.

3.

Lilly Busch, the daughter of Eberhard Anheuser, the wife of Adolphus and the mother of their thirteen children.

4.

At the turn of the century, the Anheuser-Busch brewery included some of St. Louis's most imposing structures.

August A., Adolphus's son, in a snappy carriage in front of the portico of One Busch Place, Eberhard Anheuser's palatial residence next door to the brewery. Inherited by Adolphus and Lilly, it was a monument to Victorian taste—with heavy Germanic overtones.

7.

Ivy Wall, the Busches' estate on Millionaires' Row in Pasadena, California. Its elaborately landscaped grounds were later opened to the public as the first Busch Gardens.

The Villa Lilly, the Busches' estate in Germany near the Rhine. Adolphus had a strong sentimental attachment to his homeland.

In the year before his death, Adolphus still pursued his favorite sport, hunting and killing the roebucks that roamed his German estate.

A mausoleum befitting the wealth and grandeur of "Prince" Adolphus at Bellefontaine Cemetery in St. Louis. The plaque over the door bears the inscription "Veni, Vidi, Vici."

10.

11.

August A., Adolphus's successor at the brewery. With the outbreak of World War I, the family business was threatened by ugly anti-German sentiment and the looming threat of Prohibition.

The Bevo Mill, built in South St. Louis by August A. shortly before Prohibition. A restaurant which served only beer and wine, it was meant to be a socially acceptable alternative to the notorious saloon.

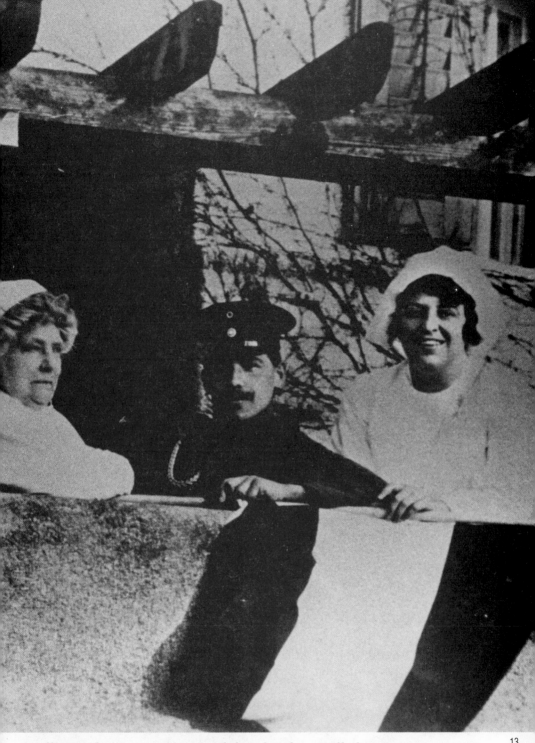

Lilly Busch, now a widow, with her daughter Wilhelmina in
Germany in the early days of the war. On her return to America,
Lilly was detained on suspicion of being a German sympathizer.
Wilhelmina found herself in the same unhappy predicament during
World War II.

August A. "Gussie" Busch, Jr., married Marie Christy Church in an elaborate ceremony in April 1918. His father's wedding gift was a mansion on St. Louis's fashionable Lindell Boulevard.

15.

Alice, August A.'s daughter, as Queen of St. Louis's Veiled
Prophet Ball in 1922. The Busches' extravagant displays of
their wealth, and its rather plebeian source, did not always sit
well with St. Louis high society.

August A. took time off from the brewery in 1922 to travel to Europe aboard the *George Washington* with his daughters Clara Orthwein (far left), Marie Jones (third from left) and Alice (right). He is proudly holding his grandchildren Jacqueline Busch Jones (left) and Adolphus Busch Orthwein.

Struggling to keep the brewery afloat during Prohibition, August A., a quiet family-loving man, much preferred the company of his oldest son, Adolphus III, and his collection of exotic animals on his estate at Grant's Farm.

Adolphus "Dolph" Orthwein, August A.'s grandson, was reunited with his mother shortly after his release by a kidnapper in 1931.

18.

19.

Gussie Busch and Elizabeth Overton Dozier, a divorcée four years his senior, at a horse show before their marriage. After the death of his first wife, Marie, Gussie would start his second family with Elizabeth.

20. The famous Anheuser-Busch Clydesdales, champing at the bit, ready to deliver the first shipment of beer at the end of Prohibition. The brewery was saved.

21. In excruciating pain from a terminal illness, August A. shot himself in February 1934. Crowds gathered for his funeral outside the "Castle," the palatial home at Grant's Farm he built against his father's wishes.

Adolphus III (right) and his younger brother, Gussie, escorted their mother at their father's funeral. Adolphus III would head up operations at the brewery, while Gussie waited impatiently in the wings.

Wilhelmina, Adolphus's most flamboyant daughter, lived in great luxury in Germany. She entertained German nobility in the 1920s, and in the early 1930s Adolph Hitler paid a visit to her estate to solicit funds for the Nazi Party.

23.

Hohenried, Wilhelmina's storybook castle south of Munich. Her neighbors dubbed her "the last queen of Bavaria."

24.

25.

Gussie at the reins of a vintage fire engine, his daughter Carlota at his side. With the death of his brother Adolphus III in 1946, Gussie took control of the brewery and ran it with the same dash and bluster.

Gussie, at age forty-three, went to war in 1942 at the army's ordnance department in Washington. His absence and his amorous escapades strained his marriage to Elizabeth.

26.

27.

28.

Gussie, a fearless horseman, taking a fence on one of his favorite jumpers, Yankee Doodle.

Gussie, his mother and another guest arriving for the wedding of his daughter Carlota "Lotsie" Busch in 1948.

Lotsie feeds a piece of cake to her new husband, John Flanigan, at the wedding reception at Grant's Farm. Lavish debutante balls and weddings were a Busch family trademark.

Gussie was tagged out at first base by his young son August III at a softball game in 1948. In 1975 August tagged his father out again when he forced him from the presidency of the brewery.

President Harry Truman
with Gussie at Grant's
Farm in 1950. Then a
Democrat, Gussie would
change his political
allegiance when winds
began to blow from the
Republican side.

A disenchanted Elizabeth
left the courtroom after the
hearing in 1952 that
granted her a divorce and a
reported million-dollar
settlement from Gussie.

Gussie with a friend at the
Bauernhof, the elaborate
stables at Grant's Farm. A
lover of all animals, he re-
stocked his father's
menagerie.

33.

34.

Gertrude "Trudy" Buholzer
Busch, Gussie's third wife
and twenty-eight years his
junior. They met in
Switzerland at her father's
restaurant, married in Hot
Springs, Arkansas, on
March 22, 1952, and
started Gussie's third
family at Grant's Farm.

35.

Anheuser-Busch acquired the St. Louis Cardinals in 1953, and Gussie had a new toy. Here Cardinal star Stan "the Man" Musial (left) shows Gussie (second from right) how to hold a bat.

36.

Trudy and her mount at Grant's Farm in 1968. In moments of tension and crisis in her marriage to Gussie, she would ride for hours.

Gussie played gin rummy by his own rules, even when his hand was held by his chauffeur, Frank Jackson. Among his cronies were sportscasters Harry Caray (seated right) and Jack Buck (standing right).

37.

Christina, Trudy and Gussie's youngest child, with her parents and Liz Carpenter, the former secretary to Lady Bird Johnson, in 1970. Four years later, when she was eight, Christina was killed in an automobile accident.

39.

An indulgent and fun-loving father to all of his eleven children, Gussie wrapped his arms around his sons Adolphus IV (left) and Peter at Grant's Farm.

40.

David Leeker at a family Christmas celebration not long before he was shot to death by Gussie's son Peter at Grant's Farm. A fascination with firearms ran deep in the Busch family.

41.

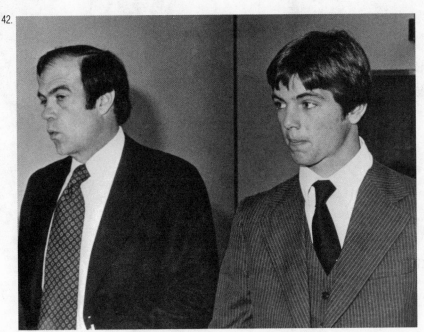

Mug shots of Peter taken after his arrest.

42.

Peter and one of his lawyers at a court appearance after the shooting. Peter pleaded guilty to manslaughter.

43.   Gussie and Trudy arrive in court for their son Peter's sentencing. Given a suspended sentence and placed on five years' probation, he was also ordered not to handle firearms during that period.

44.

Trudy and a visibly failing Gussie at St. Louis's Veiled Prophet Ball in 1977. The couple divorced in February 1978.

45

Gussie with his fourth wife, Margaret Snyder, a former secretary at the brewery, attending the National League playoffs in 1982. Their brief marriage ended in 1988 with Margaret's death.

Gussie, a demanding, sometimes tight-fisted owner, was the Cardinals' number-one fan, even when his team wasn't number one.

47.

A standing-room-only crowd roared its approval when the aging king of beer took a turn around Busch Stadium aboard a Clydesdale-drawn beer wagon in 1982. He died at the age of ninety in 1989.

The reigning king of beer, Gussie's son August III. After a fun-loving youth, he settled down to serious business, eventually ousting his father in 1975 to take over the brewery in a moment of crisis.

48.

49.

Susan Hornibrook Busch, August III's first wife. Their marriage came apart in 1969 as rumors swirled that Susan was involved with sportscaster Harry Caray.

August III and his second wife, Virginia, on the tennis court.

50.

August III and his former wife, Susan, talking to their son August IV outside the St. Louis courthouse where he was acquitted of assault charges. Prosecutors alleged he had tried to run over two undercover detectives. It was August IV's second serious brush with the law.

Preferring his helicopter to horses, August III was a relentless worker, a demanding boss, and an aggressive and unforgiving competitor.

53. Gussie's son William "Billy" Busch, as unstoppable on a polo pony as he was in the barroom brawl when he bit off his opponent's ear.

54. Angela Whitson and her daughter, Scarlett, leaving Grant's Farm during the stormy custody battle with the little girl's father, Billy Busch.

Adolphus IV, with his daughter Katie. Gussie's oldest son by Trudy, Adolphus IV watched from the sidelines as his half-brother, August III, ran the company.

The feasting fox that graces Anheuser-Busch's world headquarters in St. Louis is the German symbol of hospitality. Some also see it as the symbol of the wily tactics of four generations of the Busch family that have made their brewery the largest in the world.

38

Give the Baby Some Budweiser

Under the Germanic, almost feudal Busch tradition, girls had as much a chance of entering the business as Gussie did of getting through the day without a drink or a swear word. He needed a son, but he kept getting daughters—three of them by two wives. When Carlota was born, the doctor brought him the news with words to the effect, sorry, pal, it's happened again —another girl. Finally, after four years of stormy marriage, the moment he had been waiting for arrived. On June 16, 1937, an heir was born and the whistles blew joyfully at the brewery on Pestalozzi Street. With the birth of August A. Busch III, Gussie got everything he could have hoped for—a future ruler, who would push Anheuser-Busch to heights that even Adolphus might have found improbable.

The bells rang at Grant's Farm. Elizabeth, the woman he had regretted marrying, had finally come through. Gussie made sure the boy was properly christened, marking the birth with a bizarre ceremony—a taste of things to come. His son's first nourishment was not mother's milk, but the family's lifeblood. "Five drops of Budweiser from an eyedropper were the first things in my mouth when I was a few hours old," August related. "Father had arranged it with the doctor."

As a small boy, August was slender with blue eyes and light brown hair. He remained short of stature, reaching about five feet nine inches as an adult and favoring cowboy boots with lifts, some said, to boost his height. The slender frame would give way to an amply muscled, stocky body with square shoulders and a thick neck supporting an oversized head. As an adult the eyes—penetrating, suspicious and ice-blue—dominated the broad, oval face.

August spent his early years in Gussie's mansion on Lindell Boulevard across from Forest Park. With his mother and father frequently on the warpath, it couldn't have been a happy home. Gussie made extended business trips and his mother, who drank, was often irritable. After his parents divorced, Gussie became even more remote. August's broken home life was blamed for his glacial coldness, "his apparent lack of warmth in dealing with other people." But it also may have contributed to the boy's sense of rugged independence. "I expect that during his childhood they did things to him that were irreparable, that scarred him forever," said a former Anheuser-Busch executive. There was about him the sense of "a lost childhood, one he never allowed himself."

August often seemed lonely growing up, recalled one acquaintance. The boy, she was told, didn't get along well with his mother. For all its traumas, however, it must have been a remarkable boyhood. There were frequent weekend trips to Grant's Farm and its servants, liveried footmen, bizarre animals and carriage rides. Gussie often took his son to the brewery. To a boy like August, these trips must have been more fascinating than a journey to Disneyland. He learned the feel of the huge plant before he understood its workings. On those rare evenings when the family was together, he absorbed the traditions of the dynasty and the nuts and bolts of the business. "You sit around the dinner table since you're 12 and listen to that damn stuff," August said later. "You have to get something out of it."

Gussie also taught his son how to shoot. Proficiency in firearms, after all, was part of the Busch heritage. Many of the animal heads the boy saw mounted in the gun room at Grant's Farm, their necks festively decorated with wreaths at Christmas, had been bagged by Gussie's father, August A., whose father before him, Prince Adolphus, taught him how to handle a rifle not long after the Civil War. August started hunting with Gussie "probably before I was ten years old." He became expert at shooting skeet, duck, quail, deer, antelope, bear, moose and other animals.

As a youngster with a pellet gun, he also bagged cats, pigeons and crows, and on one occasion it was suspected he might even have potted a human, which precipitated an encounter with a policeman and an early appearance in a newspaper story. The experience might have sounded the first warning bell in his mind about the press and contributed to his intense mistrust of the media.

On November 1, 1949, the day after Halloween, St. Louisans read this headline: "August A. Busch III Questioned by Police

in Halloween Fracas." Two twelve-year-old girls were treated
for air rifle pellet wounds of the legs and stomach after paying
a trick or treat visit to the Busch mansion on Lindell Boulevard. August and his mother, then estranged from Gussie, were
questioned by police. August, twelve at the time, admitted he
had stood at a second-floor window with a gun, but denied
shooting anyone. His gun, he claimed, was "partly dismantled" and couldn't be fired. He produced the rifle, which, indeed, was missing several parts. His story "was verified by a
servant and the mother." The gun, everyone insisted, hadn't
been fired. "Police turned young August over to his mother."

On another occasion, August and his friend and former
grade-school classmate John Krey were disciplined for shooting cats. Pigeons were another favorite target. A senior brewery worker recalled how the boy shot the birds with a BB gun
at the Anheuser-Busch plant. Of the Busches, he said, "The
average worker thinks they are in a different world. Which
they are."

Another view of August's skill with firearms was offered by
Martin Quigley, a former executive with Fleishman-Hillard,
the brewery's public relations firm. Quigley, now a novelist,
was at Grant's Farm one morning in the late 1950s, helping
arrange an NBC television broadcast. "Young August came
through with a small tractor with a little trailer behind it. He
had, as I recall it, an over and under .410-gauge shotgun. He
was permitted on the farm to shoot crows and blue jays. And I
looked back in that wagon and . . . here he's got about eight
dead crows and six dead blue jays that were shot. . . . That is
part of the . . . way all those people were brought up."

August also shot animals in the estate's Deer Park with a
lever-action Winchester. When the herds of bison, antelope, elk
and deer became too large, August and his father culled them
with rifles, a practice that later had to be abandoned when the
estate was ringed by suburbs. "We don't hunt Grant's Farm
anymore. Downtown St. Louis is just across the fence."

As a teenager August had a few mishaps with automobiles.
This, too, was part of the family legacy, one littered with auto
accidents, some of them fatal. In 1954, when he was seventeen,
he lost control of his car and sheared off a telephone pole while
taking guests home from a party at Grant's Farm. One passenger suffered a broken ankle in the wreck. Another was treated
for head lacerations.

August attended several grade schools, including a presti-

gious private boys' academy in St. Louis, Country Day. He was
there for the fifth and part of the sixth grade before he left. His
departure wasn't for any disciplinary reasons. A mirror reflection of Gussie, he simply didn't attend school all that much.
David Millstone, a fellow student, remembered August as "a
bit moody and a bit unto himself. He was the kind of guy that
nobody thought would be anything but a spoiled playboy all
of his life because he didn't seem to take anything seriously.
How wrong we were."

Quiet was a common descriptive word, shy another. "He
wasn't one of the guys," said a classmate. "They came and
picked him up in a big car and took him out quite a bit." Even
when he tried to belong, it wasn't easy for a boy who came
from a family whose members often demanded special treatment. A former Country Day student recalled waiting for a bus
after school. When the limousine arrived to fetch August back
to the mansion, he wanted to leave with the others on the bus.
"He stood there and threw rocks at the car."

August entered Ladue High School in St. Louis as a freshman in 1953. Teachers and classmates recall, again, that he
was a quiet boy who was often absent. An average student, he
showed no particular promise for the future, and yet a spark
was beginning to glimmer. Before he graduated in 1956, he
was voted the class member most likely to succeed.

Auggie, a name he was called in high school and which he
disliked, was no one's fool. When thieves rifled his gym locker
and stole money from his wallet on several occasions, he arranged a trap to catch them. Robert Bassman, a chemistry
teacher, helped him. Bassman's solution was to dust a pair of
August's trousers, his wallet and a few dollar bills with a powder dye that turned a bright purple when moistened. "The next
day, Auggie coated these things and hung them in his locker,
and after the gym class he went in the showers. . . . He was
taking his shower and another kid came in just happy and
smiling and he turned on the water and the kid's hands turned
purple. We had him."

Bassman liked young Busch. A former air force pilot who
flew C-46s over the Hump, between China and India, during
World War II, he often spoke to August about flying. The boy
had just started taking flying lessons and was an eager listener.
Sometime later, after August got his pilot's license, he invited
friends like Eugene Mackey to go flying with him. "I think we
probably went up in a Piper Cub. I remember that he was a

very cautious, good pilot." Mackey, an architect, also recalled August's fascination with guns and his frequent absences from class. He never attended school functions. A reason might have been the boy's sensitivity to his parents' divorce, which set him apart from most of his classmates. "I don't think there was anyone in my class whose parents were divorced," Mackey said. "He never talked much about his family."

The two worked together on the *Rambler*, the school year-book, August serving as business manager in his senior year. It was his one major extracurricular activity. His ambition, as he recorded in the yearbook, was "to be a baby brewer." Under the caption, "pet peeve," he entered, "Falstaff."

When August graduated, the faculty wondered whether Gussie would attend the commencement. The story was that he hadn't attended the ceremony when his daughter Elizabeth graduated from high school. "The betting among the teachers was that he wouldn't attend," said principal Richard Stauffer. "I said, 'Oh yes he will. He's German and the son is the important one in a German family, the one to carry on the name.'"

Gussie was in the front row.

39

The Swiss Miss

As he approached his fiftieth birthday, Gussie faced a void in his life. He finally had a son, but he seemed to be a man looking for love. Separated from his wife, he stayed in the Bauernhof at Grant's Farm. He and Elizabeth continued to feud and their battles spilled into the newspapers. In December of 1948, he published notices in the St. Louis papers, announcing he would no longer be liable for his wife's bills or for those of

their children, August and Elizabeth. At the time he was paying $2,000 a month to his estranged wife.

Gussie busied himself with his animals at Grant's Farm,
buying buffaloes to begin a breeding program. He still rode,
but age was beginning to take its toll. During the St. Louis
National Horse Show, Gussie entered the ring astride Yankee
Doodle, his prize white gelding jumper. More than 8,000 fans
cheered as he circled for a series of jumps, but the horse stumbled as it tried to clear a three-foot hurdle. Gussie went crash-
ing to the ground. He stood up slowly and walked out of the
ring. Once out of the sight of the crowd, he collapsed. His left
shoulder was broken.

Along with his domestic problems, Gussie also had beer
trouble. In the wake of his brother's death, Anheuser-Busch's
performance had slipped. In 1946, Pabst narrowly nosed out
his brewery for the national lead in beer sales. For the first
time since repeal, Anheuser-Busch was no longer the number-
one brewery in America. In 1947, Schlitz became the biggest
beer seller and Anheuser-Busch dropped to fourth place. These
years were the low point for Gussie. But in the summer of 1949
his life changed dramatically. He met the girl of his dreams.

While on an extended European vacation, he had visited
Paris and his aunt Wilhelmina in Bernried before traveling to
Lucerne, a beautiful old city with picturesque towers and
quaint shops straddling a crystal lake. One afternoon Gussie
stopped for lunch at a locally famous restaurant, the Old Swiss
House. The large timbered building, resembling a rural chalet,
was on the Löwenplatz, a fifty-yard walk from the famous lion
carved into a cliff in memory of the Swiss Guards killed during the French Revolution. One of the quotations from Goethe
that decorated the wall seemed particularly apt for Gussie:
"That which you inherited from your fathers, you have to earn
to keep it."

A sixteenth-century atmosphere prevailed inside the Old
Swiss House. The menu featured beluga caviar. But what Gussie wanted was not on the menu; she was passing out menus.
He stared at the hostess, a tall, slender young woman with
dark blond hair and eyes as blue as Lake Lucerne. She was
twenty-two-year-old Gertrude Josephine "Trudy" Buholzer.

Those who knew her said Trudy had an electric personality
that lit up every room she entered. She was much more educated and sophisticated than Gussie. Born February 17, 1927,
Trudy had twelve years of elementary and high school and
three years of college. Her education included a finishing

school in Lugano, Italy, and she spoke French, Italian, English and German.

Gussie approached the innkeeper. "Who in the hell is that beautiful girl?"

"That's my daughter. Why are you interested?" answered Willy Buholzer.

Gussie quickly changed the subject and began talking about how he was in Lucerne looking for schnauzers. But for the rest of the meal, his attention was riveted on Trudy. He ran up a big tab and left a hefty tip. And before leaving, he asked her for a date. "He . . . proposed to me that first night," Trudy said later. "That's the way he is. When he says he's going to do something, he does it."

There was only one little problem with Gussie's marriage proposal: he was already married. But that hardly seemed to matter. A few days later, he traveled to London, where he met his niece, Sallie Marie Busch, and his sister Marie Busch Jones. The ladies telephoned Trudy and invited her to join their party in London. She accepted and stayed with the Busches, returning to Switzerland at about the same time Gussie departed for the United States.

Badly smitten and still very much a married man, Gussie invited her to Grant's Farm in December. Trudy got her first glimpse of the glittering life of a Busch. She was showered with gifts: a $2,500 diamond ring, a Mercury automobile, an $1,800 fur stole, evening gowns worth about $700 and a $2,000 bank account. Gussie called her Troodles, and gave her the ring "because of my extreme admiration and love for her." Trudy shared Gussie's zest for life. She loved chasing foxes and travel.

For the next two years, Trudy Buholzer was a regular guest at Grant's Farm. She spent extended vacations with Gussie, traveling with him all over the country—New York, San Francisco, Miami, Chicago, Hot Springs. She was treated to an eye-opening view of society's rich upper crust. When President Harry Truman visited Grant's Farm in June 1950, Trudy was one of the hostesses who greeted him. News of these exploits reached Lucerne, where the Buholzers displayed to their restaurant customers photographs of Gussie with the president.

Still, Trudy's parents wanted to know where their daughter's relationship with Gussie was headed. Gussie could only hedge. "If and when I get a divorce," he told them, "my hope is that I can marry your daughter."

The first step in that direction finally occurred on August 7,

1951, when Gussie's lawyer, Mark Eagleton, whose son Tom was destined for great things in Missouri politics, filed a suit for divorce against Elizabeth. It alleged general indignities— that she disregarded her duties as a wife, nagged, provoked quarrels, possessed a violent temper and mismanaged the household. More explosively, it accused her of drinking excessively, using drugs and being a poor example to their children. At the time the suit was filed, their daughter Elizabeth, sixteen, was living with her mother, while August, then thirteen, stayed with his father.

Elizabeth's lawyer, Daniel Bartlett, filed a request for Gussie's income tax returns, his expense account records and dozens of financial records from the brewery relating to his compensation. Elizabeth said Gussie had an estate of $2 million and an annual income "greatly in excess of $200,000." Bartlett was blunt about why they wanted the financial records. "How else," he asked, "could we find out how much money Mr. Busch has been spending on other women?"

Eagleton filed a seventy-five-question interrogatory to Elizabeth. Among the questions he asked were: "How much was paid the yard man in 1940?" and "How much was spent for whisky, wine and gin?" Elizabeth filed countercharges that led to a series of depositions taken in closed session from twenty-seven people, including Gussie and people close to him. Other than Gussie himself, the witness who testified the longest was Trudy Buholzer.

A divorce trial was avoided, but only at great expense to Gussie. A $1 million settlement—the largest ever arranged in Missouri—was granted February 20, 1952, to Elizabeth. Under the terms, she received a $450,000 gross alimony payment, a property settlement of $480,000 paid in cash over a ten-year period, and the Busch home and furnishings, valued at $100,000, for a total of $1,030,000. She also obtained custody of the two children and $1,000 per month for their schooling. Gussie retained visitation rights.

Such a colossal settlement would have broken an ordinary man, but Gussie was able to manage nicely. He borrowed some of the money he needed from his mother—a loan that later precipitated a brawl with one of his relatives.

At last Gussie was a free man. A month later, at the age of fifty-three, he married twenty-five-year-old Trudy Buholzer in Hot Springs. The marriage was performed on March 22, 1952, by Associate Justice Sam Robinson of the Arkansas Supreme

Court in Busch's cottage on the grounds of the Majestic Hotel. Gussie's fourteen-year-old son, August, was the best man. Trudy and Gussie left for their honeymoon aboard the *Adolphus*, his lumbering land yacht. Back in Switzerland, the bride's mother breathed a sigh of relief. "We are very glad that the wedding has come to pass."

Martina Buholzer needn't have worried. One year later, on March 9, 1953, Gussie and Trudy were married a second time in a Roman Catholic ceremony in the living room of the Bauernhof. Having their marriage recognized by the church was especially important to Trudy's father, Willy, as one of Trudy's relatives was a bishop in Wisconsin.

Before the Catholic wedding could occur, an investigation had to be conducted to determine whether Gussie was free to marry under the laws of the church, which disapproved of divorce. A young, newly ordained priest, Jerome F. Wilkerson, got the delicate assignment. Father Wilkerson's research into Gussie's marital situation took him to various places, especially since his former wife, Elizabeth, would not cooperate by supplying records.

Wilkerson happily discovered that in the eyes of the church, Gussie's marriage to Elizabeth Dozier wasn't valid because at the time she married him, she was still considered married to her first husband. As far as the Catholic Church was concerned, Gussie's marriage to Elizabeth wasn't binding. The bottom line was that he could marry Trudy in a Catholic service.

Before the church wedding took place, Gussie had to receive instructions in the faith. The lessons were required of any non-Catholic who married a Catholic. Around this time, Wilkerson attended the wake of the father of one of the beer-brewing Griesediecks of St. Louis. Bob Griesedieck told him he understood he was giving religious instructions to Gussie. When the priest confirmed that fact, Griesedieck smiled and said, "Why? Gussie already thinks he's God."

40

Making Friends

In 1950, Robert Lewis, the head of the Brewers and Maltsters Union in St. Louis, was called to a New York hotel to meet with Gussie Busch. He never forgot the encounter. "That's when good old Gussie tried to buy me off."

Described by Robert F. Kennedy in *The Enemy Within* as the "tough, honest, outspoken" opponent of Jimmy Hoffa, Lewis was an anomaly in the brewers' union. He was of Irish descent in a union populated by "krauts," as he grinningly referred to his union brothers. He went to work at Anheuser-Busch as an apprentice brewer in 1936, and was elected to represent St. Louis brewery workers shortly after he returned from serving in the army during World War II.

Lewis sometimes had to prove his leadership with his fists. And he was rugged, not only physically, but in his resistance to the breweries' efforts to compromise him. He had succeeded Joseph Hauser, who had headed the brewers' union for many years and who had a friendly working relationship with Gussie and other executives at Anheuser-Busch. It was common for Hauser to buy tickets to Busch-sponsored horse shows and handle requests from Anheuser-Busch executives to find jobs for the sons of politicians. Lewis, who believed Hauser had "been on the take for years," made it a point of keeping his distance from the Busches and maintaining an adversarial relationship with all the other St. Louis brewers.

The day he met Gussie in New York, contract negotiations were pending. Trudy was there along with another brewery executive and his wife. Trudy kissed Lewis on cheek when he entered the hotel room. Gussie offered the union leader a sample of his raw sense of humor. "He told me he had just taken a piss in front of St. Patrick's Cathedral. I figured he had taken a leak in the lavatory compartment of the *Adolphus*, his land yacht." Gussie ordered everyone out of the room and then began a discussion with Lewis.

Gussie told Lewis he "had to take care of himself." He said it over and over again. "You got to take care of yourself." A package wrapped in paper was next to Gussie. Lewis realized it "could have contained horseshit, for all I know," but he got the very clear impression that it was stuffed with money. He was convinced Gussie was trying to buy him so he would use his influence to soften the union's position. Lewis blew up in anger. After a stream of obscenities, he stormed out of the room.

A few days later, back in St. Louis, he got a telephone call from the head of another St. Louis brewery. He was asked if he took "it." Lewis played dumb, but he understood perfectly.

This was not the only attempt by Gussie Busch to try to pacify Bob Lewis. James Carroll, vice president of sales for Anheuser-Busch, offered the union chief a share in a Florida distributorship if he left the union. Carroll matter-of-factly admitted that other union people had received money from the brewery. Lewis believed Carroll's offer could not have been made without Gussie's knowledge. "He [Carroll] had this ring on his finger. . . . He took it off and threw it across the conference table and said, 'This seals it, Robert.' And I said, 'What do you mean?' And he said, 'I promise you I'll have everything drawn up legally. You'll never ever be wanting for anything at all.' I pushed the ring back. It was a big goddamn diamond ring. I told them to forget it. What he did was absolutely wrong."

Carroll, like Lewis, was an Irish Catholic and he confided in the union man that there was an ethnic rivalry in the brewery's upper echelons. "People like Carroll were bitter about the fact that members of the Busch family were pulling down exorbitant salaries for doing nothing. Carroll felt underpaid compared to the Busch family members working in the brewery. 'This company, Bob,' he said to me, 'is so polluted with relations.' " Carroll offered some parting advice: "Don't stay in this business. It's too corrupt."

"Making Friends Is Our Business." It was one of Gussie's favorite sayings. Typically, he claimed credit for it, although it was crafted by someone else. The statement perfectly summed up the business of selling beer. Like his grandfather Prince Adolphus, Gussie cultivated all kinds of friends to help him. Lewis had turned him down, but he had other friends in the labor movement and they were highly placed. He also had friends in the White House, in the Senate, in the governor's office, in the mayor's office and in the police department. If making friends was Gussie's business, making the right kind of friends was even better business.

The beer industry, perhaps more than any other, needed friends not just to thrive but to survive. Despite repeal, there was always a vocal segment of the population that wanted to outlaw the sale and distribution of alcoholic beverages. The size of this group varied with the times, but opponents of the brewing industry were always there. As Carroll put it: "The battle will never be won, but if we keep fighting, we won't lose it."

Carroll had made the statement in 1945 when he warned about efforts in Congress to curb the transportation of alcoholic beverages and malt supplies for beer. "Our industry has friends in the Senate and the House. They need articulate support from us in the way of anti-prohibition petitions, which they can insert in the Congressional Record as visual evidence that the folks back home are not all Drys."

Political friends were extremely important to Carroll's boss, Gussie Busch, who long before had learned the necessity of being close to influential people in government. Like his father and grandfather, he fretted over a host of problems that fell within governmental jurisdiction: advertising restrictions, local option, Sunday bans on the sale of liquor, legal drinking ages, closing hours for taverns. Above all, the brewery worried about taxes; if taxes went up, beer sales went down. Import duties on hops and the availability of brewer's rice were other worries. Finally, there were those periodic scrapes with the law—alleged violations of antitrust laws for example. A well-placed friend in government often came in handy.

Gussie was a friend of almost every American president to hold office after repeal. Like Prince Adolphus, who courted Teddy Roosevelt and William Taft, Gussie was close to Franklin Roosevelt, Harry Truman, John Kennedy, Lyndon Johnson and Richard Nixon. He wasn't exactly a friend of Republican Dwight Eisenhower, but he made sure Anheuser-Busch was. For while Gussie swore eternal allegiance to the party of Franklin Roosevelt for ending Prohibition, he privately saw to it that both sides of the political street were greased. Under his direction Anheuser-Busch made sure it had the ear of whoever was calling the shots in Washington, Republicans or Democrats. When it came to currying influence, Gussie wore whichever political hat was required.

Prince Adolphus had his Charles Nagel and August A. His Harry Hawes. Gussie had his own connection to the world of power and influence. His name was Anthony Buford. A short, horse-faced man with a thick build, Buford was the son of a state senator from southeastern Missouri where the Buford roots sank so deep that a mountain—the second highest peak in the state—was named after his family. A lawyer, he joined Anheuser-Busch as a lobbyist in 1931. He became the general counsel of the Missouri Brewers Association in 1933, but quit in 1945, devoting himself full-time to Anheuser-Busch. For nearly thirty years, Buford was the fixit man in the Busch empire, arranging one-on-one meetings with President Truman and hosting Lyndon Johnson at his 825-acre cattle farm in rural Missouri. In the state capital in Jefferson City, Buford was known as a practitioner of old-fashioned press-the-flesh lobbying. With Tony around, a legislator never wanted for food or drink.

Buford's feats of legerdemain were legendary. Phil Donnelly, a state senator who was personally a dry, handled the beer industry's legislation as a personal favor to Buford. When Donnelly later became governor, Buford stayed overnight in the governor's mansion during visits to the capital. He recommended to the governor appointments to agencies like the Department of Liquor Control. Buford's contacts in government enabled him to get advance copies of state beer sales statistics, which he sent to Anheuser-Busch prior to their publication.

Buford was present at a secret meeting in November 1940 when Missouri Democratic leaders schemed to take the governor's election away from the Republican candidate who had won by a very narrow margin. The plan called for an official "investigation" that would disclose "election fraud," throwing the contest into the Democrat-controlled state House of Representatives where the Democratic candidate would be elected. The scheme fell apart, but the Anti-Saloon League and the Women's Christian Temperance Union claimed that Anheuser-Busch was behind Buford's efforts. He denied the accusation. When the state constitution was rewritten in 1944, the Anti-Saloon League tried to get county option written into it. Buford was there to help beat it.

Buford was Gussie's special sidekick. He got the beer baron close to House Speaker Sam Rayburn, Senate Majority Leader Lyndon Johnson and Supreme Court Justice Tom C. Clark. Buford and his wife, Ann, entertained Gussie and his wives, who in turn threw parties for them. Buford was Gussie's traveling companion on his memorable trip to Europe in 1949 when he met Trudy Buholzer.

He was frequently enlisted to exact political favors for the family. He wrote Tom Clark, then an assistant attorney general, seeking a navy promotion for Adie von Gontard, Gussie's cousin. "Personally, I do think that Adie is entitled to a promotion but I wonder if it can be done since he is out of service." Adie did not get his promotion.

Buford also wrote Clark, who later was named attorney general, in behalf of other members of the Busch family. He asked whether Alice Busch's husband, Lou Hager, could be transferred to the Navy Department in Washington. He probed into a loyalty check of a Japanese man whose son wanted to marry into the Busch family. Clark also got letters from Gussie's daughter Lilly who wanted a favorable military transfer for her husband, Robert Hermann.

At Buford's request, Clark wrote the U.S. ambassador to Mexico, asking that Gussie's visit there in February 1948 be made a pleasant one. At Buford's request, Clark wrote the U.S. ambassador in England in 1949 asking that invitations to royal affairs be secured for Sallie Marie Busch, Gussie's niece. At Buford's request, quick approval was obtained for Gussie's plan to bring exotic birds into the country. And when Gussie's land yacht was ticketed by the Highway Patrol for being overweight, it was Buford who tried to get it fixed.

A St. Louis lawyer once encountered Gussie Busch walking down Park Avenue in New York City accompanied by Buford and John Wilson, a brewery vice president. "Gussie would say something and Tony and Wilson would burst into gales of laughter; they would double up and they'd be laughing so hard, and then Gussie would say something else that was supposed to be funny and they'd double up again. I wondered what it must be like to spend your life laughing at Gussie Busch's jokes."

Gussie began making his own high-level political contacts early in his career. He was among the largest contributors to FDR, giving $5,000 to his campaign the year after repeal and another $2,500 in 1936. That gave him an entree to the Roosevelt White House, and when the president's oldest son, James, came to St. Louis in 1935, he met with Gussie to discuss the yeast business.

Gussie was closer to Harry Truman. That was only natural, since Truman was from Missouri. But Gussie and Anheuser-Busch had even stronger connections to the man from Independence. Truman's biggest supporter in Kansas city was Tom Pendergast, the corrupt boss of a powerful political machine. Pendergast, in turn, was an old ally of August A. His son Jim had an Anheuser-Busch distributorship in Kansas City.

Even before he became president, Truman occupied a key position as far as the brewery was concerned. In 1939, he was a member of the Senate Interstate Commerce Committee, which held hearings on a bill that would have prohibited the advertising of alcoholic beverages on radio. Many of those testifying in favor said radio advertising was responsible for increased liquor and beer consumption. They were especially worried about the use of beer money to broadcast sports, with its close connection to college-aged young people. They pointed out the appalling loss of life from accidents attributed to driving while intoxicated. The bill failed to become law.

As vice president–elect, Truman attended a party arranged by Tony Buford in Gussie's honor in Washington. The party took place in January 1945 in the Shoreham Hotel suite formerly occupied by the president of the Philippines. After Truman succeeded Roosevelt, the relationship between Anheuser-Busch and the new president was not lost on the Women's Christian Temperance Union. "It may be—and let us hope it is the case—that the awful responsibilities attached to the office of the President of the United States, and of which he has shown such a keen appreciation, have changed his thinking now that he has to think for the whole people of this country and not only for the state of Missouri with its Anheuser-Busch breweries."

When Truman staged his famous come-from-behind victory over Republican Thomas E. Dewey in the 1948 election, some of the credit went to Gussie Busch. Attorney General Clark wrote Gussie immediately after the votes were counted, saying his help "meant so much at the right time."

While Truman was president, Buford sent him cases of Budweiser, metal trays, ducks and, after a 1949 fishing trip to Florida, six kingfish. Buford also helped pay for an expensive portrait for Truman. Meanwhile, Gussie did his share to cement the relationship. The president was his guest at his private shooting lodge at St. Peters and at Grant's Farm, where Gussie took him on a carriage tour. They galloped off so quickly the Secret Service agents lost them. "Gussie and Truman went through the Deer Park on the tallyho and eventually they came back," said Walter Orthwein, a friend of the family and distant relative. "They were gone maybe half an hour. . . . They were both just delighted with themselves."

Gussie's friendship with Truman lasted long after he left the White House. After Anheuser-Busch acquired the St. Louis Cardinals, Gussie sent Truman free passes to the games. When Gussie and Trudy were in Kansas City for horse shows or baseball games, Harry and Bess were invited to dinner aboard the new *Adolphus*, the railroad car the brewery bought so Gussie could travel with the team.

Vowing his support for the Democratic party, Gussie once boomed, "I'll be damned if I bite the hand that fed me." The Democrats, after all, had repealed Prohibition and made his business profitable again. Gussie's pledge, however, did not stop Anheuser-Busch from covering its bets with the man who succeeded Truman: Republican Dwight Eisenhower. While Gussie was an out-front Democrat, the brewery's vice president and financial officer, John Wilson, served as the chairman of the Eisenhower Victory Dinner held in St. Louis on June 24, 1953. "You will be pleased to know that we are sending to the National Committee a minimum of $50,000," Wilson wrote to Eisenhower. He pointed out that expenses for the dinner were being taken care of "through other sources," and, "We also hope to raise somewhere between $20,000 and $30,000 at a similar dinner to be held in Kansas City next week." To make sure Eisenhower got the complete message the letter was sent on Anheuser-Busch stationery.

While Eisenhower was president, the company's Denver branch manager, C. Sid Salveson, sent cases of Budweiser to Eisenhower's home in Abilene. Wilson even supplied swans for Eisenhower's farm in Gettysburg. The campaign contributions and gifts did not prevent the Eisenhower administration from going after Anheuser-Busch for buying the old Regal brewery in Miami in 1958. Attorney General William P. Rogers complained that by buying the brewery, Anheuser-Busch had created a beer monopoly in Florida; eventually it agreed to sell the plant. Putting on a good face, Gussie later claimed that it was the best thing that could have happened: Anheuser-Busch was forced to build an entirely new brewery in Tampa, which was more efficient and in the long run more profitable.

These were the good old days for Gussie. He had pals in

Washington, a brand-new wife, a brand-new brewery and—
best of all—a brand-new toy.

41

"A Personable and Able Huckster"

In 1953, Gussie Busch acquired control of the St. Louis Cardinals. It proved to be one of the shrewdest moves of his career.
His life was never the same—and neither was professional
baseball. The Cardinals were quickly transformed into a traveling billboard for the brewery. And Gussie, almost overnight,
was transformed from a brewer of modest national reputation
into a celebrity, whose elfish face graced the cover of *Time*. He
became one of baseball's most colorful curmudgeons, rolling
into spring training in his private railroad car, kicking holes
in the wall when his team performed poorly, and raging Lear-
like against the rise of player militancy. Gone were the days
when his public relations flacks practically had to beg for coverage. Reporters now scampered after him by the dozens. The
beer baron had become a baseball baron and the copy was
good, very good.

The twining of beer and baseball dates back almost to the
beginning of the sport as the national pastime. Gussie even
had a precursor of sorts, a hard-drinking St. Louis tavern
owner with a bulbous red nose named Chris Von der Ahe, who,
in 1881, introduced beer to the ballpark. It was a turning point
in the history of sport. Thereafter, beer would provide bucket-
fuls of money for virtually every professional team in the land
and for hundreds of colleges as well.

The St. Louis Brown Stockings had played their first game
as members of the National League in 1876, and Dutchman
Von der Ahe observed that his tavern near the ballpark did a

brisk business in lager when the team was in town. Reasoning that he would do even better if he could sell beer inside the stadium, he bought a piece of the Browns. When Von der Ahe died in 1913 of cirrhosis of the liver, a newspaper headline referred to him as the "Man Who Put St. Louis on the Map."

Gussie forever redrew the map in 1953 when he convinced the brewery to buy the Cardinals and make him president. The team was then owned by a diminutive, five-foot-five-inch real estate tycoon named Fred Saigh. Saigh had run afoul of the Internal Revenue Service, pleading no contest to charges that he owed the government $19,099 in taxes for the years 1947 and 1949. Before the sentencing—he got fifteen months— Saigh did something which by today's sagging standards of sports ethics seems extraordinary. He announced that he was selling the team for the good of baseball. The sport "is bigger than any individual or group. . . . I feel that in no way, directly or indirectly, should it be embarrassed."

Tradition has it that Gussie Busch stepped forward to keep the team in St. Louis. Although partly true, there was never any doubt that the brewery bought the Cardinals to help sell beer even if a cleverly directed public relations campaign emphasized the purchase as a civic gesture. Gussie, in fact, had never been a baseball fan. He admitted he could probably count on the fingers of both hands the times he had gone to the ballpark. "Baseball without some of the glamour around the players can be pretty dull," he said. "There's lots of standing around."

Saigh agreed to sell the Cardinals to Anheuser-Busch for $3,750,000, about half a million less than he had been offered by a group of investors in Milwaukee. It later rankled him when it was suggested that the brewery had saved the team for St. Louis. His intention all along, Saigh insisted, was to assure that the Cardinals remain in town, even if meant taking less money. The sale hit him hard. Gussie told friends years later than when he returned to the room where the papers had been signed to retrieve a fountain pen, Saigh was sitting alone at the table, hands over his face, sobbing.

During an elaborately staged press conference to announce the purchase, Gussie told reporters with a straight face, "I am going at this from the sports angle and not as a sales weapon for Budweiser Beer." It didn't bother him at all, he said blithely, that broadcasts of the Cardinal games were being sponsored by a rival brewery, Griesedieck Brothers. "I don't think that makes a great deal of difference." He had given his board of directors an entirely different vision, however. "Development of the Cardinals will have untold value for . . . our company. This is one of the finest moves in the history of Anheuser-Busch."

Gussie was roughly handled by critics who wondered about the brewery's real reason for buying the team. Willing to give him the benefit of the doubt, but sensing a double-edged motive, the *Post-Dispatch* editorialized that "Mr. Busch gives every evidence that he thinks of the Cardinals as a baseball club and not as a device for selling beer. . . . It would be a mistake to forget that the record of his new property will be written not in bottles but in the box score."

Far less tolerance was displayed by Edwin Johnson, an acid-tongued United States senator from Colorado. Early in 1954, Johnson introduced a bill that would have made baseball clubs owned by beer or liquor interests subject to antitrust laws, an idea that was anathema to Gussie. Johnson fired bullets at Gussie himself, calling him "a personable and able huckster" who regarded baseball as "a cold-blooded, beer-peddling business and not the great American game which good sportsmen revere." He blasted the "lavish and vulgar display of beer wealth and beer opulence."

With his public relations specialist Al Fleishman in tow, Gussie testified before the Senate Judiciary subcommittee against Johnson's proposed legislation. He managed to smile through the proceedings even though associates knew he was boiling mad.

Johnson, who admitted his bill was doomed, kept lobbing grenades. If a ball club could be owned by a major corporation such as a brewery, the sport, he declared emphatically, "goes out the window. It just becomes a contest between big business. Not only will there be a monopoly in beer, but there will also be a monopoly in baseball." Johnson disputed objections that he was "picking" on Busch and that no one had complained when the brewer Jacob Ruppert owned the New York Yankees. "Yankee Stadium has always been known as the House that Ruth Built. The business of brewing and baseball always were kept completely separate by Ruppert. Not one cent of Ruppert's beer money went into baseball and Colonel Ruppert did not use beer to publicize or advertise his baseball club, nor his baseball club to publicize or advertise beer. These evils followed Ruppert and were not initiated by him."

Was Gussie using the Cardinals to peddle his product? Johnson might have wondered whether bears live in the woods. The senator gleefully held up an issue of *Business Week* that said that "buying the Cardinals is the kind of verve" that helped Anheuser-Busch beat out rival Schlitz in sales in 1953.

Shortly after he steamrolled his company into acquiring the baseball team, Gussie left no doubt where his true interests lay. The aging stadium where the Cardinals played—Sportsman's Park—was a disgrace. After making an inspection that included a visit to the rest rooms, always the first stop on one of his impromptu tours, Gussie was incensed. The place was filthy. He would rather have his team play in Forest Park. Bill Veeck, the owner of the rival St. Louis Browns, also owned the stadium. Gussie offered him $1.1 million for it. Veeck accepted and announced he was moving the Browns to greener pastures in Baltimore.

The deal concluded, Gussie decided the park needed a new name. He had just the right one in mind. Budweiser Stadium. "What the hell," Gussie said later, "Budweiser . . . was the means by which we were able to buy the Cardinals and fix up the ballpark and even make a living. It seemed only natural" to name the park after his beer. Unfortunately, "All hell broke lose." Some of the fire and brimstone came from Ford Frick, the commissioner of baseball. A protest was also lodged by a Protestant church group that opposed naming a baseball park after an alcoholic beverage.

Fleishman and others convinced Gussie to change his mind, something he found almost congenitally difficult. They suggested another name—Busch Stadium. Gussie reluctantly bought the idea. "What caused me to change my mind was when it was pointed out . . . that it was the Wrigley family which owned the club and the park, and if they changed the name of the park to Juicy Fruit Stadium, or Doublemint Stadium . . . that wouldn't make any more sense than if another company had bought a baseball park and called it Grapenut Stadium or Shredded Wheat Stadium . . . I knew at once that when this came up, that I had made a mistake."

Over the years, Fleishman saved Gussie from similar gaffes. Many agreed that Fleishman, a burly, soft-spoken man who rarely touched beer, was the creator of the Busch image, the keeper of the sacred flame. "Fleishman orchestrated the idea that they were saving the team for St. Louis," said Bob Broeg, the dean of St. Louis sportswriters. Another longtime St. Louis newsman, Ted Schafers, put it more succinctly. Gussie "was known as a hellion who chased women right and left. He was a heavy, two-fisted drinker and was disliked by more polite society. . . . People just put up with him. He had no reputation at all as a civic leader. . . . Al Fleishman created his image as a community leader and do-gooder." A lawyer familiar with Gussie agreed. People "used to tell Gussie Busch stories the same way they tell Polish stories. . . . The tremendous esteem in which many in the community hold him today came fairly late in his life," largely due to the crafty work done by Fleishman.

After Anheuser-Busch bought the Cardinals, Gussie-watching became a favorite St. Louis diversion. He enjoyed his new celebrity status. Fleishman recalled that Busch visited New York shortly after buying the team and decided to meet some sportswriters. "He arranged a little get-together at Toots Shor's—and 350 people showed up. He never got over that." He not only never got over such attention, he learned to love it. The publicity benefits that accrued from owning the Cardinals were obvious, and as a preeminent showman to begin with, Gussie made the most of them. "Suddenly . . . I became a 'national sports figure.' Not many people wrote to me when I was just a brewery president, but as owner of the Cardinals . . . I began to receive thousands of letters."

After taking his first road tour with the Cardinals, Gussie decided he didn't want his stadium cluttered with tawdry advertising signs on the model of Brooklyn's Ebbets Field. He much preferred the "clean, green dignity" of New York's Polo Grounds, which had one large sign hawking Chesterfield cigarettes. "Get that crap off the walls at home," Gussie directed. He would go with a single sign—a huge Anheuser-Busch eagle glowing in red and blue neon fluttering over the scoreboard. Other signs popped up later, along with the incessant playing of the Budweiser theme song, the prancing Clydesdales and the relentless product hawking that transformed every Cardinals game into one long beer commercial. But in the beginning at least, Gussie showed restraint.

With typical flair, he also showed that he was going to have fun. There was a "squeal of brakes" when he arrived at his first spring training in St. Petersburg, driving his motor bus. His large entourage followed in a fleet of Cadillacs. Gussie quickly slipped into a Cardinals uniform and worked out with two of his favorite players, Stan "the Man" Musial and Red Schoendienst, both old duck-hunting buddies. In following years, Gussie arrived in St. Peterburg aboard his private railroad car, the *Adolphus*. In the era before teams traveled by air, the palatial Pullman was attached to the train that carried the Cardinals on their road trips. Gin playing and "heavy drinking" were the rule when Gussie toured with the team.

At first Gussie and his party resided at the Vinoy Park, a citadel for unreconstructed millionaires in St. Petersburg. He later acquired property in Pass-a-Grille, a spit of expensive sand that jutted into Tampa Bay. His compound there included a residence, two guest cottages and a flat-roofed boat house. While other baseball owners had to be content to arrive at the ballpark in limousines, Gussie often came by boat, boarding a yacht for the short commute across the bay to the Cardinals practice field.

He also picked up a band of Gussie groupies—a gang of well-heeled, party-hardy Florida businessmen collectively dubbed the Bat Boys. During one of their periodic visits to St. Louis, the Bat Boys—twenty-one strong—started their evening with Scotch and water at Grant's Farm and followed with Budweiser and highballs in Gussie's private suite at the ballpark, the Redbird Roost. When the game ended, "there was a cheerful thud," a reporter commented. "A Bat Boy had fallen from his bat rack" at the bar. "Friends found his feet for him." Knowing when to say when, Gussie decided to let his chauffeur drive him home.

Gussie soon discovered that his skill at running a brewery counted for little in the arcane world of baseball. Although he learned quickly, he would face an eleven-year drought before the Cardinals made it to the World Series. The team finished in third place in 1953, Gussie's inaugural year, and then dropped to sixth in 1954. They finished in the second division six times during that sorry first decade. The problem was that Gussie wanted a pennant in a hurry and started hiring and firing managers as well as players. The cost of big-league talent staggered him. He was shocked to learn that the Giants wouldn't part with Willie Mays for $1 million.

Bing Devine, twice the Cardinals general manager, recalled that Gussie once offered a $25,000 bonus to sign Fred Walker, a questionable pitching prospect, because he knew the boy's father, Dixie Walker, had been a talented ballplayer. "We were debating the pros and cons of whether to sign him when Gussie says, 'Well, I know about horses and the bloodline is always important and he comes from a family of ballplayers, so let's go with the bloodline.' "

The pitcher flopped. It would take a while for Gussie to realize that ballplayers weren't horses.

42

"Fire His Ass!"

At a time when black ballplayers were still rare in the big leagues, Gussie was determined to break the color barrier. Before he entered the picture, the Cardinals, which had a strong following in the Deep South, had resisted opening the roster to black athletes. Gussie was so eager to follow the example of the Dodgers, the team that six years earlier had shattered the racial wall with Jackie Robinson, that in 1954 he pushed his front office into acquiring a black first baseman named Tom Alston. A tall, gangly athlete from San Diego, Alston proved to be a washout. More seriously, he later suffered a nervous breakdown.

Although none of Gussie's managers met a similar fate, he might easily have driven them over the edge of sanity. During the first six years the brewery owned the team, Gussie went through five in rapid succession. Eddie "the Brat" Stanky begat Harry "the Hat" Walker, who begat Fred "the Hutch" Hutchinson, who begat Stan Hack, who begat Solly Hemus. Five more followed. Gussie also fired and hired general managers with dispatch. His first was Richard Meyer, a brewery vice president whom Gussie desperately turned to in the early days of ownership, selecting him after he asked his assembled executives whether any of them knew anything about baseball. When Meyer volunteered that he had played first base as a

Lutheran seminary student, Gussie told him, "Okay, you're appointed."

One of Gussie's most celebrated encounters involved Meyer's successor, "Frantic" Frank Lane, who joined the Cardinals in 1956 and immediately started the freewheeling trading that led to his nickname. After two more campaigns fell short of a pennant, Gussie was getting impatient. On the eve of the 1958 season, Joe Garagiola, a former Cardinal turned broadcaster, unexpectedly turned the microphone over to Gussie at a baseball banquet. "Busch," it was observed, "had not expected to speak and therefore did not avoid the cocktail party." Microphone in hand, Gussie uttered a phrase that echoes down through the locker room of Cardinal history: "If Frank Lane doesn't win the pennant this year, I'm going to fire his ass!"

Lane could only mutter that he planned to do his best, but the next day, still distraught, he hopped into his Buick convertible and drove all the way to Florida with the top down in the dead of winter. He wound up with a partly frozen face. Somewhere in Georgia, Lane paused long enough to send a telegram to Gussie suggesting that in view of his embarrassing comments, he should give him a three-year contract extension. The message hit Busch like a water balloon.

Al Fleishman was in Gussie's office when he read the telegram and exploded. Gussie turned to his secretary and offered a slight variation on his earlier remark. "Send a telegram to Frank Lane," he roared. "Tell him to kiss my ass!" When Fleishman deferentially suggested he reconsider, Gussie shouted, "You're fired, too!" As Fleishman put it long afterward, "We were fired every Monday, Wednesday and Friday."

The highlight of the first decade of Anheuser-Busch's ownership of the Cardinals had nothing to do with the team's performance on the playing field. The Cardinals failed repeatedly to make the World Series. Rather, it was the development of a new ballpark. Even though Busch Stadium had been greatly improved by the brewery, with only 30,000-plus seats it was considered too small. In 1959, the city decided to build a new 50,000 seat stadium near the riverfront. It would be within view of the Gateway Arch, a gleaming 630-foot monument to westward expansion under construction along the shore of the Mississippi River. Gussie wanted his company to be the first to contribute to the $53 million building fund for the stadium. When his board of directors balked and suggested kicking in $1 million instead of the $5 million Gussie proposed, he threw a fit. He wanted $5 million.

Someone reminded him that the company had already put up $2.5 million to fix up the old ballpark. A million was fine.

"No, dammit, no," Gussie shouted, banging his fist down on the polished conference table. "Five million!"

The stadium was finished in 1966, two years too late for the Cardinals' first taste of glory under Gussie's reign. The team finally won the pennant in 1964. They had to beat the Mets in the final game of the season. "When the Mets got ahead of us 3–2," Gussie recalled, "I left my box seat and went up to the Redbird Roost high up in the stands. It's my private club, and I walked around for a minute, and then . . . I kicked a hole right in the wall. And then we won. It was wonderful."

The Cardinals went on to beat the Yankees in the World Series, but it was a bittersweet season for Gussie. He had fired his general manager Bing Devine halfway through the year when the Cardinals were struggling. Devine's trade for outfielder Lou Brock had proved to be the key ingredient to the Cardinals' success. Fired, Devine was named baseball's Executive of the Year. His manager, Johnny Keane, who had heard rumors that he was also on the chopping block, dropped a bombshell shortly after the World Series when he announced that he was quitting to manage the Yankees.

The Devine-Keane fiasco was the worst blunder Gussie had made since 1953 when he ordered beer prices raised 15 cents a case and saw sales plunge. In that incident, he had accepted the blame. It was a different story with his firing of Devine. So what if Devine had finally put together the first winning Cardinal team in nearly a decade? The club, Gussie declared to anyone willing to listen, had needed a good shaking midway through the season, and dammit, he had fired him. Reporters like Bob Broeg criticized Gussie for the Devine affair. Broeg had another reason to be occasionally disillusioned by Gussie, a man he liked. He had discovered that Busch could be a tightwad. "If you were with him, he wouldn't mind sticking you for the hot dogs or a bigger check if he thought you had an expense account."

Devine, later rehired as the Cardinals general manager in 1968, likened his experiences with Gussie to handling a powder keg. "You were always afraid that it was going to explode." Fired again in 1978, Devine never really hit it off with Gussie. Harry Caray, for twenty-five years the Cardinals' irrepressible announcer, recalled a black tie dinner he attended at Grant's Farm in 1957 shortly after Devine replaced Frank Lane as general manager. "Gussie kept trying to get me to say something about the deal . . . and I kept trying to avoid saying anything. Suddenly, Gussie said to me, 'Goddamn it, I want you to answer me.' You could hear a pin drop."

Cornered, Caray said, "All right, Bing Devine couldn't carry Frank Lane's jockstrap."

At that moment, the wife of Busch's lobbyist, Tony Buford, blurted out, "Why, I'd fire the son of a bitch."

Mrs. Caray stood up and said, "Did you call my husband a son of a bitch?"

Figuring it was time to leave, Caray and his wife made their exit. They were stopped at the door by Gussie, who told his announcer, "Hey, I would have fired you if you hadn't told me the truth."

Caray speculated that Gussie may not have liked Devine because "Bing didn't smoke or drink or chase around after women." These virtues were often considered weaknesses in professional baseball.

43

"I Was a Bad Son-of-a-Gun"

Cast in the mold of Gussie, August A. Busch III had never been a serious student although, unlike his father, he managed to graduate from elementary school. There were too many distractions—the good life at Grant's Farm, airplanes to fly, trips to Florida, skiing excursions, women to romance, the chance to party with his one or two close friends. A wild boy through much of his adolescence and early adulthood, August admitted that he was unable to attend an Ivy League college because he didn't have the grades. "I couldn't behave myself. I was a bad son-of-a-gun."

But not bad enough for the University of Arizona in Tucson.

August enrolled in the university's business and public administration school in January 1957. He left after two years
without a degree. When he later became a buttoned-down
workaholic, he regretted not earning a diploma. The gap in his
academic background was an embarrassment, and so unnecessary. August was exceptionally bright, but the light had not
clicked on yet. After leaving high school with an indifferent
record, he found himself in sunny Arizona, where diversions
were plentiful. "I think he was playing out here," recalled one
of his instructors. "He had a good time. His father did not
think it was time for him to get into the business. Go out and
have fun for a year or two. He took his classes pretty lightly."

During this rollicksome period before his striking conver-
sion, August was loosely chaperoned by two of Gussie cronies:
Robert Hermann, who had married his daughter Lilly; and
Curt Lohr, who had one of his beer distributorships. A former
Anheuser-Busch executive recalled talking to Hermann about
his experiences. "Bob told me that he had bailed August out of
so many scrapes." Lohr apparently had a similar mission. "At
Gussie's request, Lohr was told to take young August and help
him sow his wild oats."

The oats were plentiful. And one of August's favorite places
to sow them was a dude ranch in the foothills of the Big Horn
Mountains near Sheridan, Wyoming. Eaton's Ranch had been
founded in 1904 to cater to the tastes of wealthy Easterners
who wanted to play cowboy. The Busch clan had often sum-
mered there. On one of these trips, August was fishing with
Bob Hermann in a fast-flowing mountain stream when Hermann badly cut himself on a beer can. What happened next
was described by a family friend as one of the Busches' "manhood rituals."

"Bob was bleeding so badly they had to drive him into Sheridan to see a doctor. When they reached the hospital, August
bet Hermann that he couldn't get the many stitches he needed
without benefit of an anesthetic. Hermann took the bet and
had the stitches sewn in without a painkiller."

August and Hermann later decided to round up some horses
that belonged to a neighboring ranch; it was a joke, but the
practice was "much frowned upon," said the friend. Possibly
in retaliation, someone decided to pay August back during a
packing trip into the mountains. "For revenge they outfitted
him with a small saddle. Halfway up the mountain he was in
agony. The saddle fit him like a vise."

These were August's salad days and his trips to Wyoming also had their pleasant moments. He was regularly approached by "every little waitress in the area willing to spend a night with the heir. Some of them would even show up with their toothpaste."

His position as heir apparent admittedly offered unique opportunities. Few young men had a father with a private, lavishly equipped apartment at a baseball stadium. Martin Quigley, for years a senior executive with Fleishman-Hillard, remembered encountering August shortly before a Cardinal game. Quigley had the keys to the apartment, which was frequently opened to visiting VIPs. August wanted them. He had invited some chorus girls and other cast members from a traveling musical show to spend the evening at the ballpark. Quigley told August he could have the keys only with the approval of his father, brewery executive Dick Meyer or Al Fleishman. "Young August knew damn well that none of those people would authorize him to stage a party in a fully stocked apartment. By fully stocked I mean it had booze, food, beds, whatever the hell you wanted. So he went out and on the way he snarled something at me. He left without the keys."

John Krey III, the son of a wealthy St. Louis meat-packing family, was August's closest friend. Heavyset and affable, Krey and August were often inseparable. They had attended prep school together and shared a room for a while at Grant's Farm. "We supposedly had wild blasts . . . when we weren't even in town," Krey said. He made it clear, however, that they "partied" whenever they *were* in town.

After he settled down to business, August wasn't known for his sense of humor. It was different when he was younger. His playfulness then sometimes had a rough edge. Robert Baskowitz, Jr., the son of Gussie's longtime business associate, remembered the prank August and Bob Hermann played on him when they were water-skiing on the Mississippi. "They were doing jumps. A ski jump should have water on it so you can slide. They wanted me to make a jump, but they didn't tell me that it was dry." Baskowitz hit the dry incline and went flying. "They thought it was funny. It really got me sore. They could have killed me."

During the late 1950s, August spent some time in uniform at Fort Leonard Wood, a U.S. Army basic training camp in the Missouri Ozarks. He was in the Reserves. In 1957, he began working part-time at the brewery, cleaning vats much as his father had done forty years earlier and shoveling the pungent malt in the brewery's cavernous malthouse. "When you finished a shift there," he said, "you knew you were a man."

August also joined the Teamsters. He later returned his union card when he led management in some tough union battles in the 1960s. His early experiences shaped his attitude toward unions. "He must have seen a lot of men sitting around after getting their work done an hour early," said one brewery employee. "He probably thought they were loafing and that fewer workers were needed. That's where he got most of his ideas about labor unions."

Robert Lewis, the president of the brewers' local who got August into the union, recalled that he "wasn't there a lot of the time" as a young man. But a change was coming that would leave family members and acquaintances shaking their heads in wonder. The steel blade in August's personality had been there all along. It was being quietly sharpened. In 1960, he enrolled at the Siebel Institute of Technology in Chicago, the country's premier training grounds for brewers. This time he graduated.

44

Deals With David Beck

The Kennedys—Jack and Bobby—were not Gussie's favorite people. The handsome, well-educated Ivy Leaguers weren't cut in his style, and before the 1960 presidential contest, Gussie was considering supporting Lyndon Johnson or Missouri Senator Stuart Symington for the Democratic nomination. But once Kennedy was chosen to lead the ticket, Gussie opened the moneybags. A fund-raising dinner he hosted in October 1960 raised more than $100,000. One of the Kennedy coordinators was a Massachusetts congressman named Tip O'Neill, who later became Speaker of the House. O'Neill had no trouble raising money with Gussie's help. "All you had to do was tell Gussie that money was getting tight and more was needed," O'Neill said. "In a few days, a package would drop from heaven. Gussie raised it faster and easier than anybody in that era."

One of the reasons Gussie disliked the Kennedys so heartily was because they had exposed what Jack Kennedy called the "abnormal" and "unusual" relationship between Anheuser-Busch and David Beck, president of the Teamsters Union. Beck had obtained an Anheuser-Busch beer distributorship for his son, David Beck, Jr. The company's largest, it covered Washington state and Alaska. It was a smelly relationship, and the Kennedys had held their noses. Gussie never forgot.

In 1946, Beck had taken his son and Irving Levine, president of the K & L Beverage Co. of Seattle, to St. Louis for a meeting with James Carroll, Anheuser-Busch's vice president and general manager. A distributorship was awarded to Levine, and in return for Beck's intercession, Levine took Beck's son into his firm. Beck Jr. later became president of K & L and was able to obtain concessions from Anheuser-Busch unavailable to other distributors—bigger beer shipments and favorable credit terms.

Most of Anheuser-Busch's 8,000 to 10,000 employees belonged to the union led by Beck Sr. While the son received money from Anheuser-Busch, the father went to bat with unions in California to try to head off strikes that might have slowed the construction of Anheuser-Busch's new brewery in Los Angeles. Beck Sr. also supplied Anheuser-Busch executives with information on the bargaining stance of other brewers in California.

The Busch-Beck link was disclosed in May 1957 by the U.S. Senate's Rackets Committee. Senator John F. Kennedy was a member of the committee; his younger brother Robert served as chief counsel. Beck Sr. invoked the Fifth Amendment more than 100 times when he appeared before the committee. Gussie, questioned by committee investigators in Chicago the previous month, did not appear for the hearings. He explained that his mother's illness prevented him from traveling to Washington. The brewery was represented by Dwight Ingamills, general counsel, and John Wilson, executive vice president. Before they testified, exhibits and evidence were read into the record by Pierre Salinger, the committee's staff investigator.

At one point, Senator John McClellan, chairman of the committee, asked Salinger for identification of names introduced in evidence. There had been a reference to "placing Bud in Alaska."

"Who is this Bud?" asked McClellan.

"Oh, that's Budweiser," replied Salinger.

One of the internal Anheuser-Busch documents referred to the elder Beck as "His Majesty the Wheel."

Senator Kennedy sharply questioned Wilson about "your ethical approach and Anheuser-Busch Co.'s toward this whole relationship" with Beck. "In other words, you went to Mr. Beck with whom you had this abnormal, unusual business relationship to find out exactly what your competitors were going to do in regard to wage demands. It would seem to me that Mr. Beck, by discussing this with you, associated himself with you in a limitation on the wage increases of the employees in California. You gave this K & L Co., in which Mr. Beck had an interest, the biggest territory in the country. You had four or five years of great difficulty with him, but you did not break off your agreement, which you could have done as you had no contract. You gave them special orders of beer that no one else could get. You offered to pay $80,000 for the company, even though it had $30,000 worth of debts. Then, at the same time, Mr. Beck was of assistance to you in a strike in Los Angeles. I think Mr. Beck, as you have stated, has engaged in an abnormal relation with you which is neither to Mr. Beck's credit or your company's."

It was rough treatment and after their grilling, both Anheuser-Busch men were, no doubt, happy to get out of Washington. Beck was later convicted in 1959 of income tax evasion and served a prison term of two and a half years.

Another problem Gussie had with the Kennedys was in the area of antitrust. His contributions to the Kennedy campaign did not stop the U.S. Justice Department and Attorney General Robert Kennedy from filing suit in January 1962 against Anheuser-Busch's acquisition of the Rahr Malting Company in Manitowoc, Wisconsin. Kennedy said that by buying the malting company, Anheuser-Busch had violated the Clayton Antitrust Act that prohibited mergers and acquisitions which lessened competition or created monopolies. Anheuser-Busch opposed the government's suit in court. Typical for the brewery, it brought in the best legal talent available: John Stevens, a Chicago lawyer, an expert on antitrust law, and later a member of the U.S. Supreme Court, and William Webster, a St. Louis attorney, who would become a federal judge, the FBI director and director of the Central Intelligence Agency. The antitrust case was eventually concluded during the administration of Lyndon Johnson under very unusual circumstances.

It was soon after John Kennedy's election that Gussie lost the services of Tony Buford, his resourceful, politically connected gofer. The breakup came during an explosion between the two men that had been building for some time.

For years Buford had pestered his friend, Senator Stuart Symington of Missouri, for petty favors for the Busch family and friends. When Frank Schwaiger, Gussie's brewmaster, needed letters of introduction while traveling abroad, Buford secured them. He rushed through the State Department the passport applications for Gussie's daughter Lilly and her husband, Robert; he managed similar one-day service for Gussie's wife, Trudy.

Buford, according to Symington, was "as good a friend as the good Lord has given me on this earth." In writing a letter to Yale in hopes of getting Buford's son admitted, Symington said: "Tony is a friend of all of us in St. Louis. He is Gussie Busch's lawyer and a director of Anheuser." Symington asked Buford to comment on his campaign brochures, and when fellow senators sought Anheuser-Busch beer distributorships or jobs at the brewery or in the Cardinals organization for their friends or relatives, Symington passed the requests on to Buford. Symington also managed to get presidential inaugural tickets for his friend. It was the seating at the Kennedy inauguration in 1961 that led to Buford's abrupt departure from Anheuser-Busch.

Buford had been openly disagreeing with Gussie for more than a year before their blowup occurred. It shocked those who saw it because no one had ever dared dispute publicly the words of the beer baron. The simmering problem finally came to a head during the inauguration. A trainload of Democrats traveled from Missouri to Washington for the festivities, and when Gussie saw where his seat was placed for the ceremonies, he was not happy.

"You're supposed to have a lot of pull in Washington, Buford," Gussie growled. "I want to be up there!" He pointed to the presidential box. When Buford said that was impossible, Gussie shouted that if he couldn't get him a better spot, he would send him back to Jefferson City "where I found you."

Buford, who had had enough, shot back, "You can't send me back to Jefferson City because I quit!" Buford officially resigned as the Anheuser-Busch lawyer on May 2, 1961, citing a doctor's recommendation that he reduce his personal workload.

The uproar did not end there. A man named Walker Pierce was also swept away with Buford. Pierce was the head of the staff of the Brewers' Association. A good friend of Buford's, Pierce told some beer distributors that Gussie had treated Buford unfairly. When word of this got back to Gussie, he arranged to have Pierce fired. He went further. "If you pay him one penny in vacation pay, separation pay or any other money," he told an association executive, "I will consider it a personal affront."

With Buford gone, Gussie made most of his political connections through Symington. One of Gussie's first assignments for Symington was to close down foreign beer shipments to army and air force post exchanges. Symington's help was also sought during the "Communist threat to Budweiser."

Anheuser-Busch had "an extremely serious problem" with a Reciprocal Trade Agreement bill approved by the House of Representatives in July 1962. The bill removed Yugoslavia from the category of most-favored nation status and put it into that of a Communist-dominated nation. Anheuser-Busch was under contract for over 3 million pounds of Yugoslavian hops. The change in the country's status doubled the duty from 12 cents per pound to 24 cents per pound, which meant Anheuser-Busch had to pay an extra $385,000. Beyond the bill's costs, Gussie was more concerned about another matter. "We may be accused of using, as a basic ingredient in our beers, a raw material produced by a COMMUNIST nation . . . a public indictment of this nature could have serious business repercussions," he wrote to Symington.

With Symington's help the Senate Finance Committee later took care of Gussie's problem. The trade bill was amended, knocking out the flat prohibition against trade with Communist countries and giving the president discretion to cut off trade when it was in the national interest.

As Gussie had feared, however, an anti-communist group

issued "The Budweiser Memorandum," which pointed out that
Budweiser was being brewed with Yugoslavian hops. "We believe," it said, "Anheuser-Busch should face reality, just as an
increasing number of good American firms are doing and cease
doing business with the communists." The brewery got worried when several small towns, many of them in Florida,
passed ordinances banning products that originated in Communist countries. To solve that problem, Anheuser-Busch requested a letter from the State Department declaring the
brewery's trade relations with Yugoslavia were "fully consis-
tent with the United States policy toward this country." Gussie wasn't about to let the Cold War chill his beer business.

45

The Beer Taste Test

Gussie found out about Edward H. Vogel, Jr., from his top
brewmaster, Frank Schwaiger. Schwaiger and Vogel had co-
authored a book on beer brewing. Vogel was young and bright,
and Gussie, always looking for new talent, had hired him in
the summer of 1956. It was just another example of Anheuser-
Busch's clout. A graduate of Cornell University and the U.S.
Brewing Academy, Vogel had been a vice president at Griesedieck Brothers Brewing Co., one of Busch's major competitors.
For the next dozen years, there was a love-hate relationship
between Gussie and Vogel. "He had no morals," Vogel said.
"None! What he did have was charisma. Hitler also had charisma. So did Al Capone."

Vogel helped develop the sophisticated marketing strategies
that led to Anheuser-Busch's dominance of the beer industry.
He worked at Gussie's elbow during the brewery's astounding
growth in the 1960s and what he saw sometimes astounded
and disturbed him. "He didn't understand long-range plan-

ning but he liked the results. He had confidence in me, and I
learned early to let him take the credit, let him take the bows.
What you couldn't do with Gussie was razzle-dazzle—the flip
charts and all that—he'd start looking out the window and
you knew someone was in trouble." On the other hand, Gussie
was a born beer man who flew by the seat of his pants. "My
God," Vogel said, "he had hops and barley in his veins."

Vogel discovered that Gussie could be funny, angry, demanding and terrifying all at the same time. He marveled at
Gussie's remarkable sense of taste. During a business trip to
New York City, Gussie and Vogel were in a hotel playing gin
rummy. They took a break and went to the "21" Club. Gussie
had a hankering for "a little smoked caviar on rye toast and a
great big stein of Michelob." The famous restaurant's co-owner
greeted Gussie like visiting royalty and praised his beer, which
he said he proudly stocked. A waiter arrived with a tray and
two glasses of what was supposed to be Michelob.

Gussie took one sip and said, "This isn't Michelob." He
turned to the owner. "You just thanked me for my business
and then you go and give me this? What the shit is going on?"

The owner assured him it was Michelob but Gussie insisted
it wasn't. "If there was one thing Gussie knew it was the taste
of beer, especially his own beer," Vogel said later.

An argument broke out. Gussie finally said, "Do you want to
bet this isn't Michelob?"

"Okay," said the indignant owner.

"I'll bet you the restaurant," Gussie said.

"You're not serious."

"I've never been more serious in my life."

"Fine, you've got a bet. We'll go talk to the bartender."

"No," Vogel said. "We'll go to the cold box and see what's
on tap ourselves."

It wasn't Michelob. "It was Rheingold," Vogel recalled. "The
owner turned white."

Gussie and Vogel returned to their table and the owner followed, profuse with apologies. This only provoked Gussie even
more. "I don't want to hear your goddamn excuses. This is my
restaurant now! What in the hell are you doing in my restaurant?"

"My God, you're not going to hold me to that bet are you?"

Vogel recalled that the owner started to cry. "Gussie laughed
and let the guy keep his restaurant." The bartender, of course,
was fired.

When he traveled with Gussie, Vogel always saw a beer

salesman at work. In the fanciest hotel lounges or the cheapest
bars, Gussie often went behind the bar to demonstrate how his
products should be served. He bought rounds for the house. He
performed and loved every minute of it.

One of Gussie's favorite virtuoso acts involved his "beer
clean glass" routine. His public relations man, Al Fleishman,
saw it often—in restaurants or in railroad dining cars. With
everyone wondering, Who is this nut?, Gussie rimmed the inside of a glass with table salt. If the salt failed to stick to the
sides evenly, the glass wasn't clean enough, and he would send
for another. Finally satisfied, he demonstrated how to pour a
bottle of Budweiser. "He showed that to drink beer you had to
have a head on it. He advised not pouring it down the side, but
to dump it so foam comes out. Then, he would say, 'Now, my
name is Gussie Busch. Why don't you have a bottle on me?' "
He always ordered a bottle for everyone in the dining car or
restaurant. He was famous for that kind of behavior. The
waiter always got a big tip. "He never forgot how to sell beer."

There was a striking variation on Gussie's clean glass routine. He performed it for Ted Schafers, a reporter who accompanied him to a restaurant. "We went there and sat down, and
he ordered beer and they brought a glass and he picked it up
and examined it.

" 'The goddamned thing is dirty!'

"He threw it against the wall, shouting, 'You know I don't
like to see a dirty glass!'

"It shattered into pieces. I heard later he did that sort of
thing quite often."

46

"I Know I'm Curt at Times. But I Just Don't Have Time."

August III, the wild young boss's son with a taste for fast airplanes and exotic getaways, was about to settle down. Business associates recall seeing August dallying at places like Hugh Hefner's Playboy Club in Chicago during the early 1960s or paying attention to a cute waitress at an Anheuser-Busch convention in Houston's Astrodome. But they were also starting to detect a change.

August was beginning to shake off his reputation as a party-loving heir to one of the country's largest fortunes. His mother's death in 1958 might have had something to do with it; he seemed to become more serious. Or it might have been a blunt ultimatum Gussie delivered: mend your fun-loving ways or forget the executive suite. Whatever the reason, August would become, arguably, the most effective executive the beer industry had ever seen. Driven, secretive, obsessed with his company's success and the quality of its products, he transformed himself into a workaholic who thrived on paperwork, round-the-clock meetings and eighty-hour weeks.

An early mentor, Edward H. Vogel, Jr., believed that no one in the industry could carry August's "jock strap" when it came to knowledge of the business. But Vogel also wondered years later whether he had helped create a chief executive who ruled by fear and intimidation. Virtually humorless, August's idea of a roaring good joke was to call a man by his middle name.

Like his father, August started with Anheuser-Busch cleaning out the vats and sweeping floors, but, also like Gussie, he soon got a good promotion. In keeping with family tradition, his career path started near the top. In 1962 he was appointed sales manager for Busch Bavarian, Anheuser-Busch's popular-priced beer. A year later he was named vice president of marketing and joined the company's board of directors. He was twenty-six years old.

Ed Vogel, an Anheuser-Busch vice president, had recommended August for the promotion. He was impressed by his drive and "innate, native ability." To his amazement, he started catching flak as soon as he suggested August for the vice president job. Gussie wondered whether Vogel wasn't bringing his son along too quickly. He had made it clear that there were no guarantees the boy would succeed him. "He has to measure up and prove he can do the job." When asked about his son's prospects, Gussie often responded, "If I've told him once I've told him 1,000 times that the board of directors does the electing. In my book you fall or rise on your own." He had a way of saying that with straight-faced conviction, as if no one realized the board was *his* board, all of its members handpicked relatives, bankers and other businessmen accustomed to doing his bidding.

Vogel, one of the most respected men in the beer industry, was surprised to find Gussie "absolutely mute" when he suggested raising August to vice president. Dick Meyer, Gussie's right-hand man, was dead set against the promotion. Vogel was getting calls morning and night from board members strongly opposed to the idea. That's when he decided to have a heart-to-heart with August. They met for dinner at the Chase Hotel in St. Louis. The conversation shocked Vogel. He learned the dimensions of the gulf that separated father and son.

"I said to him, 'Don't you and your daddy ever talk?' And he looked at me and said, 'I don't have a daddy.' That really took me aback and I said, 'What did you say?'"

August stared at him and said, "You heard me."

Despite the opposition, Vogel convinced the board that August was the right man for the job. Thereafter, August began spending more time at his desk, getting to work at 8:30, then eight, then seven o'clock in the morning. He traveled almost every week. He made enemies. Behind his back, he was called Little Auggie. It wasn't long before there were complaints about his abrasive personality, about his being too rough on people and having little patience with subordinates. August admitted as much. "I know I'm curt at times. But I just don't have time." On another occasion, he said, "If you carry the name management, forget the nine-to-five bit."

One of August's biggest shortcomings was his porous educational background. A college dropout, he discovered that he needed to burn the midnight oil. He devoured reports, often taking a complicated document home, mastering the details, and then asking pointed questions about it at a 7 A.M. breakfast meeting. Despite his willingness to put in long hours trying to make up for the large gaps in his education, August still wanted to learn. With his father's blessing, he hired an expert to give him a crash course in business administration. Russell Ackoff, a faculty member of the University of Pennsylvania's prestigious Wharton School of Economics, had been hired by Vogel to help with the company's advertising. He also signed on to serve as a personal consultant to August. In the beginning, he had his hands full.

Vogel described a meeting he and August had with Ackoff, who often used math equations to explain an idea. August was upset that he was having trouble following along. "Ackoff asked August, how much math have you had? He hadn't had any." Vogel believed August had an "inferiority complex" because of his academic record.

It was a far different matter when it came to August's knowledge of the brewing process. An expert at judging beer, he was listened to and not merely because his last name was Busch. He participated in the crucial beer-tasting sessions and later had samples of beer from the various Anheuser-Busch plants sent to his home so that he could taste them before going to bed. August could pick up the subtle differences in whether a beer was too hoppy, too tart or too sweet. These tasting sessions could be demanding. "It's a wonder the eight tasters don't get intoxicated or eventually become alcoholics," said one observer. "Each puts away more than a sixpack of beer. . . . They say they know how to space the drinks and avoid becoming tipsy."

No one ever recalled seeing August under the influence. His only addiction was work. His preferred beverage was Budweiser. Unlike Gussie, a two-fisted drinker who enjoyed two or three highballs before dinner, August rarely if ever touched hard liquor. Even after the pressures of a day on the road, he was abstemious, having one or two beers with dinner before turning in.

During his early years as a vice president, August often spent over 50 percent of his time on the road, visiting the company's breweries. His out-of-town trips were grueling. An executive recalled working hard with him until well after midnight, only to be told that he was expected in August's hotel room at 6:30

for a morning meeting. "I got up and hauled myself down to his room . . . and he was dressed in a shirt and tie, all immaculate and working."

That same executive traveled with August to California, where he made an impromptu visit to a supermarket. He wanted to check the code on the beer bottles and cans to see whether they were past their shelf life. That was an unforgivable sin. Any wholesaler could expect a strong dressing down if August found old beer in his territory. On this particular occasion, August discovered some old bottles of Michelob. "He went in there and bought all that beer and threw it out. God knows how many cases went down the drain."

Trodding his father's path, August had been an unrepentant playboy during much of his early manhood, a jet-setter who thought nothing of swimming in the Gulf of Mexico one day, then skiing in the Austrian Alps the next. Unlike Gussie, he somehow had found the Protestant ethic while still in his early twenties and settled down to business. No one in the brewing industry worked harder or longer than August; no one matched his relentless ambition. Like Henry V, his riotous youth had been shaken off on the eve of great deeds. There had been a guilty plea to a careless-driving charge, a car wreck that injured two passengers, trouble in school, then, almost miraculously, total commitment.

Gussie, too, had found commitment, but August had none of his father's joie de vivre. He did not run with a glad-handing pack of cronies or attend all-night gin rummy parties. Moody, arrogant, virtually friendless, he had little interest in his father's horses, preferring to fly airplanes, jets and helicopters. He disliked his father's baseball diversions. Given their differences, fierce battles seemed inevitable.

August married Susan Hornibrook, a former model, in an Episcopal service in Beverly Hills in May 1963. His bride was a slender, athletic blonde from an affluent Los Angeles suburb who had attended private schools. August met her through friends in 1962 while on one of his frequent business trips to Los Angeles. Gussie and Trudy traveled to California for the ceremony with a small party of friends. With Gussie in attendance, the wedding must have had its share of raucous gaiety. Lotsie, Gussie's daughter by his first wife, hosted a rehearsal dinner in her half-brother's honor at her home in Los Angeles.

Gussie couldn't resist a little fun. In one of his Peck's Bad Boy moods, he had the fun idea of tossing the guests into the swimming pool, but was persuaded to behave himself by August.

August and Susan lived in Ladue, an exclusive St. Louis suburb, before they moved out to Waldmeister Farm, a 1,200 acre estate that adjoined Gussie's Shooting Grounds in St. Charles County. Their first child, August IV, was born the year following their marriage. Not to be outdone by Gussie, who had insisted that August receive five drops of Budweiser shortly after birth, Susan arranged to feed her son a thimbleful of Busch beer when he was a day old. She did the same when a daughter, also named Susan, was born in 1965. Susan liked to joke that the children's first word was "Budweiser." Both August IV and daughter Susan would later go to work for the brewery. A third child, a boy, died shortly after birth in 1967. Two years later, in 1969, August and Susan divorced. Their marriage, with its share of dark moments and tragedy, had lasted six years.

After his divorce, August suggested that his sixteen-hour days and seven-day weeks had something to do with it. "I learned in my 20s and 30s that it is important to have stability at home." His relationship with his wife, friends said, had often been troubled. The strain must have shaken even a facade as tough as August's. A security guard who worked for him remembered that August sometimes sat in front of a television set for three and four hours at a stretch, not saying a word. "I had to sit there and watch with him, and he wouldn't even talk to me." August never commented publicly on what was widely regarded as another cause for the breakup of his marriage to Susan—her reputed relationship, one she strongly denied, with a party-loving Cardinals baseball announcer, Harry Caray.

After less than two years as a vice president, August had been named general manager in 1965. This time Gussie, obviously pleased with the young man's performance, supported him for the position. As he liked to say, in his book you rose or fell on your own and it was time for his son, then only twenty-eight, to ascend to one of the top jobs at Anheuser-Busch.

The announcement sent shudders through the company. August's reputation for arrogance wasn't reassuring to the troops. "His problem was that he was power drunk," said Ed Vogel.

"He can't remember the distinction between respect and fear. He can't tell them apart. He instills fear and thinks that's respect."

Other executives foresaw problems. They knew August's penchant for getting involved in every detail of the business, for personally taking charge. It wasn't unusual for an executive to be awakened by a telephone call at three in the morning to hear August's crisp voice grilling him with questions.

Ed Vogel realized that the appointment meant his own days were numbered. August was now his boss, a situation he found intolerable. "When August became GM I knew it was the end. . . . He now had charge of me." It didn't matter that Vogel had pushed hard for August's first big promotion. The two had had their share of sharp disagreements. Vogel hadn't scored points with August when he opposed Gussie and his son's support of the "beer tapper" idea. Vogel had waged virtually a one-man war to prevent the company from selling beer in portable aluminum tappers designed to fit in refrigerators. The idea proved a costly bomb for competitors like Falstaff.

There had been other clashes between the two men. Bob Lewis, the president of the brewers' union, got to know Vogel well over the years. "Eddie had called the kid a couple of names and the kid apparently complained to his father about it. Gussie came into Ed's office and told him to stop it."

Vogel left the company in 1968. It was a bitter parting. Vogel and his wife were ostracized by the Busches after nearly twenty years of friendship. Old friends were told not to have anything to do with them. "If you leave the 'Busch family' you're forever out, you're dead," said Vogel. "I even heard after I left that August was going to run me out of town."

August also came to spear points with Bob Lewis, quickly proving that he had little of his father's tolerance for unions. Perhaps motivated by his early recollections of goldbricking laborers, August was concerned about featherbedding in the work force. If Gussie, like the Detroit automobile makers in the 1950s and 1960s, was willing to accede to virtually every union demand to avoid costly strikes, August was of a different persuasion. During a four-week strike in 1969, Lewis blasted August, blaming his "absolute indifference and lack of human understanding" for a national strike. "There has been a complete change of policy and attitude on the part of the company. Unless young Busch's activities are curbed, there will be nothing left of this great company."

Lewis recalled attending a tense meeting between father and son, who were at loggerheads over the labor situation. Gussie, exasperated at August's hardline stance, turned to him and said, "You're either going to get along with Bob Lewis, or you'll never become CEO of this company."

August was said to have been so upset by the settlement with the union that he marched into Gussie's office with a resignation letter. After staring at the paper for a few moments, Gussie reportedly looked up and said, "I'll give you another chance because you're a Busch, but if you ever do something like this again, I'll see that the *Post-Dispatch* has your resignation letter within five minutes."

A far more serious strike was in the offing. The worst in the company's history, it would follow an unprecedented shakeup in the Busch family and its brewery.

47

Offers in Compromise

Of all the presidents he knew, Gussie's true soul mate was Lyndon Johnson. The Texas Democrat and Gussie had similar interests—power and horses—and in that order. Like Gussie, Johnson was an earthy character. Both spoke the same language. Gussie's political operative, Tony Buford, had been the catalyst for the relationship between Gussie and a powerful Texas triumvirate—Senate Majority Leader Johnson, House Speaker Sam Rayburn and Supreme Court Justice Tom Clark. Even after Buford and Gussie parted company, Gussie remained close to his good pal Lyndon.

A young attorney who worked for Anheuser-Busch and later became a United States senator and, briefly, a vice presidential candidate, was on board Gussie's railroad car, the *Adolphus*, in 1955 when it was parked on a deserted siding in Washington,

D.C. Thomas Eagleton, whose father, Mark, was Gussie's personal attorney, learned that Johnson, Rayburn and Clark were joining Gussie on board. "Sure enough, at the appointed hour, I saw the three Texans strolling down the railroad track," Eagleton recalled. "Perhaps for no other private American citizen would these notables walk through the almost abandoned Washington railroad station to have dinner."

Johnson discussed with Gussie his plan to seek the Democratic presidential nomination in 1960. Gussie said Johnson never hesitated to ask him for campaign money. The favors were returned. When Anheuser-Busch was building a new brewery in Houston, Gussie asked his Texas friend, then vice president, to recommend a good public relations firm there. Gussie's publicist, Al Fleishman, had advised him against it, telling his boss, "You don't ask a vice president of the United States for information like that."

"The hell you don't," Gussie shot back. "You don't know Lyndon. He knows everybody in Texas. He's my friend and he likes to do these things. Get him to make a recommendation."

Johnson recommended Jack Valenti, whose firm was hired by Anheuser-Busch. After Kennedy was assassinated in Dallas in November 1963, Valenti was among the first people Johnson called. He later went to work for the new administration.

Gussie liked to impress friends with his relationship with Lyndon. Returning from a horse show on his private bus, he bragged that he knew the president. When a friend didn't believe him, Gussie ordered his chauffeur, Frank Jackson, to get his book of telephone numbers.

"He had the number for the White House, and he had Frank dial right there on the bus. He gets someone on the telephone and hands it to Gussie, who says, 'This is August A. Busch, Jr., and I want to talk to the president.' The next thing we know he's got Lady Bird Johnson on the telephone, and he tells her, 'I got a friend of mine here who doesn't believe I know the president.' He gives me the phone and it really is Lady Bird and she's asking me my name and then she says, 'You take care of Gussie, he's a good man.' "

Gussie had other reasons to like Johnson. The antitrust suit, filed against Anheuser-Busch by the Kennedy Justice Department in January 1962, was dropped by the Johnson administration. The decision in June 1966 was made twenty-four days after Gussie and other brewery executives gave $10,000 in campaign contributions to the President's Club, a Democratic fund-raising organization. Republicans got wind of it from an anonymous letter sent from St. Louis. Accurate in every detail, it convinced its recipients that it had been written by a dissident executive highly placed in the Anheuser-Busch organization.

The White House strongly denied any irregularity in the dismissal of the suit and, in fact, there was evidence that plans to drop the suit were made before the contribution. But more embarrassing developments followed. Donald Turner, head of the Justice Department's antitrust division, took a trip on an Anheuser-Busch airplane from Washington to St. Louis less than a month after the suit was dismissed. Also on the plane were Turner's nine-year-old son and Vice President Hubert H. Humphrey. They were guests at the All-Star Game, where Humphrey threw out the first ball.

Johnson's press secretary, Bill Moyers, declined to comment on whether the White House considered it improper for Turner to travel on the Anheuser-Busch airplane, particularly since the president had issued an executive order prohibiting such activities. Turner insisted the dismissal of the litigation had no bearing on his presence on the airplane. Humphrey had invited him on the junket, and he said he didn't even know it was the brewery plane until he got to the airport. An official in Humphrey's office breezily dismissed any suggestion of impropriety with the comment it was only a series of "striking coincidences."

Republican Congressman H. R. Gross of Iowa thought otherwise. "If assistant attorney general Turner thought that accepting a gratuity in the form of free plane rides from the firm he had just released from anti-trust action was not a conflict of interest, he is hopelessly naive. Perhaps Mr. Turner is now sadder Budweiser." Gross called the whole thing a "Busch league scandal."

After the All-Star Game, Gussie invited Humphrey and St. Louis Mayor A. J. Cervantes out to Grant's Farm. They swam in the pool, then Gussie wanted his guests to see his animals— the elephants, the buffaloes, the zebras. It was a broiling hot, St. Louis summer afternoon. Humphrey and Cervantes declined, despite Gussie's repeated encouragement.

"All right then, by God, I'll bring the animals up here," Gussie snorted. He left only to return later like a circus ringmaster, leading his menagerie around the pool.

Humphrey turned to Cervantes and asked, "Is he for real?"

It was one of the last times Al Cervantes was welcome at Grant's Farm. He became persona non grata in Gussie's book after he saw to it that Falstaff joined Michelob on tap in the bars of the city-owned airport, Lambert Field. Cervantes was a friend of Joe Griesedieck's, president of Falstaff, which in 1967 was the number-one beer in St. Louis. Griesedieck wanted Falstaff draft served at the airport just like Michelob. "The caterer out there was under the control of Anheuser-Busch," Griesedieck said. "I got mad as hell." The brewer went to see the mayor and "eventually, we did get the product out there."

The incident marked the beginning of the end of Cervantes's political career. Gussie blew up. He claimed it was not the brewery's practice to "shut anybody out." During Gussie's tenure there were charges that Anheuser-Busch sometimes arranged for the exclusive sale of its products. "Cervantes said Gussie had him on the telephone that same night and he was raising all kinds of hell with him."

Sue Ann Wood, an editor at *The St. Louis Globe-Democrat*, got a telephone call from Fleishman-Hillard. "They wanted everything I could get on Cervantes. Gussie had said 'Get him!' and he was got." With Gussie always backing his opponents, Cervantes never won another election in St. Louis.

Hubert Humphrey hoped for Gussie's financial and political support during his campaign for the presidency in 1968. Gussie's name was on the Humphrey campaign list as a potential contributor among other well-known Democrats. But the list also said Gussie's "allegiances" were "misleading," an indication that his loyalty to Humphrey was a question mark. There was good reason for the doubt. The Busches were contributing to Humphrey's opponent, Republican Richard Nixon.

The switch of allegiance became highly publicized four years later, in 1972, when Gussie proclaimed his support for Nixon over Democrat George McGovern. Gussie did what he had vowed he would never do—bite the hand that fed him. Nixon was the incumbent and the perceived winner, but there might have been another reason for Gussie's switch—he had a relative working at Nixon's elbow.

One of the powerful, behind-the-scenes figures in the Nixon administration was Peter Magnus Flanigan, a great-grandson of Adolphus Busch. Born June 21, 1923, he was the second son of Aimee Magnus and Horace Flanigan. Aimee was the daughter of Nellie Busch, the spendthrift daughter of Prince Adolphus, and Arthur Magnus, who committed suicide in 1906 while Aimee, then seven years old, practiced the piano in a room next door. Horace Flanigan sat on the Anheuser-Busch board of directors, and Peter's older brother John was a brewery executive who had married Carlota, Gussie's daughter. Like John, Peter also made money from Anheuser-Busch.

Peter Flanigan was a statistical analyst with the New York investment banking firm of Dillon, Read, and Co., which since 1953 had handled bond issues for the brewery. In 1959, Flanigan was chairman of New Yorkers for Nixon and, in 1968, he was deputy campaign manager for Nixon for President, serving under John Mitchell. Nixon's victory in 1968 gave Flanigan the opportunity to enhance his power and influence at the highest levels of government.

At first he served as an unpaid consultant, advising on the recruitment of personnel for the new administration. Eagleton said Flanigan was "a person who works only in the shadows, but only at the highest levels and with the fattest cats." From 1969 to 1973, he was an assistant to the president. In that position, he played a role in the controversial settlement of an antitrust case involving the International Telephone & Telegraph Corporation. Flanigan was also influential in rewriting antitrust policy, which he believed contained an antibusiness bias. He was disturbed about "the explicit anti-bigness philosophy which apparently guides the anti-trust division activities."

In September of the 1972 election year, Gussie deserted his old party and became the national vice chairman of the Democrats for Nixon Committee. In his public explanation, he said he believed Nixon's reelection over McGovern would be in the best interests of the nation. But only a month earlier, McGovern had dropped Tom Eagleton as his vice presidential running mate after it was disclosed that the Missouri Democrat had undergone electric shock treatments for depression. Eagleton and his father, Mark, had long received financial support from the Busches. In 1969, Gussie threw a fund-raiser for Eagleton at Grant's Farm to help him pay off campaign debts from his 1968 election to the U.S. Senate. Whether Gussie's desertion of McGovern had anything to do with his jettisoning of Eagleton was never discussed.

Immediately after Gussie's switch became public, Flanigan

wrote a memo for Nixon marked "administratively confidential." "Among the recent converts to your cause is Gussie
Busch, who will be at the Connally ranch this weekend. This
breaks a lifetime of Democrat habits, starting when Roosevelt
came out for repeal of Prohibition. While the Busches contributed to the 1968 campaign, moving the patriarch into your
column deserved headlines in St. Louis. Should you be greet-
ing Gus and his wife, Trudy, in Texas, he would be susceptible
to any special reference you might make to his joining the
cause."

The switch angered Democrats, especially those who owned
taverns. One bar owner said Gussie was "an ungrateful millionaire who owes the Democrats everything he's got." His
tavern had served Budweiser since repeal, but he registered
his displeasure by switching to Schlitz.

Nixon's second term of office ended abruptly with his resignation in the face of almost certain impeachment for his part
in the Watergate scandal. Peter Flanigan later returned to Dillon, Read. A member of the brewery's board of directors, he
owned nearly one million shares of Anheuser-Busch stock.

Meanwhile, business was booming at the brewery. Between
1950 and 1971, the number of breweries in the United States
had dropped from 407 to 146. The national plants with their
satellite breweries, including Anheuser-Busch, grew larger
while small regional breweries dropped out of existence. And
in their death throes, breweries like Pearl in Texas, Rheingold
in New York and Grain Belt in Minnesota filed lawsuits
against Anheuser-Busch and others alleging anticompetitive
practices.

While the size and number of breweries changed, the business of selling beer had remained essentially the same since
the days of Prince Adolphus. Breweries peddled their products
relentlessly. In the no-holds-barred competition of Adolphus's
time, exclusive sales arrangements were common. Although
Prohibition was supposed to have ended the practice, almost
as soon as beer was relegalized, Anheuser-Busch allegedly
resurrected this time-proven tactic.

At the end of 1934, the company was indicted in federal
court in Louisiana for giving free equipment and fixtures to
seventeen bars and beer retailers with the stipulation that the
bars sell only Anheuser-Busch beer. The indictments repre-

sented an attempt by the U.S. Justice Department to outlaw the old "tied house" system of pre-Prohibition days in which taverns were controlled by the breweries.

Anheuser-Busch fought the indictments contending it was not an unfair trade practice for their wholesalers to furnish equipment to the retailers. A federal judge agreed, and the indictments were dismissed June 7, 1935.

In 1942, the U.S. Treasury Department reported that Anheuser-Busch paid an "offer in compromise" for alleged "trade practice violations." According to a Treasury Department memorandum, the case involved 2,192 separate incidents. To settle the matter, the brewery paid $85,000. There were more problems to come. The Treasury Department filed a complaint in 1969 alleging that the Anheuser-Busch branch manager in Kansas City gave freebies to thirty retailers. The company paid $10,000 to the government to settle that case.

Later, the numbers got bigger. On May 19, 1977, the Securities and Exchange Commission filed a complaint in U.S. District Court in Washington, D.C., seeking an injunction against Anheuser-Busch. The SEC alleged that between 1971 and 1974 the brewery paid more than $2.6 million to wholesalers, retailers, concessionaires, restaurants, airports, ski resorts, arenas and stadiums as inducements to purchase Anheuser-Busch beer. In 1977, the company told its shareholders that the "questionable payments" were prevalent in the brewing industry and that Anheuser-Busch made them "for competitive reasons to maintain its position in the market place." Through a consent order the company did not admit any wrongdoing but promised to discontinue making any payments. It was one of several cases the federal government brought against breweries.

The company wasn't out of the woods. The Alcohol, Tobacco and Firearms Division of the Treasury Department alleged that Anheuser-Busch violated federal law by making the payments. Instead of criminal prosecution, government attorneys accepted Anheuser-Busch's offer of a $750,000 settlement, which was deemed "sufficient to deter future violations."

Nevertheless, there would be more allegations of violations in the not too distant future.

48

"We Never Talked About Baseball. We Talked About Booze, Broads and Cards."

Harry Caray, whose distinctive voice was likened to talking through a mouthful of peanut butter, had a special relationship with Gussie Busch during his quarter century as the Cardinals' rabble-rousing announcer. So did Curt Flood, the team's brooding centerfielder during much of the 1960s. Caray and Flood were both known as ladies' men and lovers of bars and the wee hours. They got along wonderfully with Gussie, who appreciated with the taste of a connoisseur their Rabelaisian lifestyles. "We never talked about baseball," Caray recalled. "We talked about booze, broads and cards." But all that would change dramatically.

Caray was born Harry Carabina in a tough Irish-Syrian section of St. Louis. Orphaned at ten, he was raised by an aunt. At twenty he impulsively wrote to the general manager of a radio station, asking for an audition as a baseball announcer. He got one and in 1944 found himself in the broadcasting booth at Sportsman's Park, describing Cardinals action for Griesedieck Brothers beer, then the team's sponsor.

When Gussie acquired the team, he had grandly announced that he wasn't interested in using the Cardinals as a marketing tool for his beer. Whatever his original intention, he quickly backslid. The year later, Gussie made it clear to Caray that he wanted him to push his product.

The two became friends, and Gussie enjoyed having his own brand of boys-will-be-boys fun at Caray's expense. One year Caray was stopped for speeding in Florida. "I gave him an oral warning," recalled Edward Kelley, a Marino Beach police officer. "He called me a son of a bitch."

Kelley took Caray to jail. Allowed to make the customary telephone call, Caray reached Gussie in St. Louis. Gussie asked to talk to Kelley. "Why are you holding him?" he asked.

"He called me a son of a bitch and I happen to be a police officer and a Southern police officer, and I don't have to take that."

"Well," Gussie answered, thinking it over, "let the son of a bitch stay there overnight."

Kelley, grinning broadly as he told the story, said that Caray spent the night before posting a $200 bond.

Selling beer was something Harry Caray did with the artistry of a master. His broadcasts were punctuated with suggestions to pop open a cold one. A listener could practically taste the brew as Caray praised Budweiser or the virtues of Busch beer on warm summer afternoons and muggy evenings. A peacock in fire-engine red slacks and varicolored sports jackets, Caray was a dedicated beer drinker. His invocations to indulge became as much a part of his persona as such Carayesque expressions as "Holy Cow!" and "It might beeee! It could beeee! It is—a HOME RUN!"

Some members of the Anheuser-Busch corporate family resented Caray, who was known to bruise egos. They didn't like his reputation as a prima donna who ran "amok in taverns." There were frequent attempts to dump Caray, but Gussie stood by him. He was Caray's protector, and never more so than in late 1968, when Caray was hit by a car as he crossed a street on his way to a hotel. He recalled being knocked forty feet in the air and joked later that a woman waiting in his car shouted "Holy Cow!" as he flew by. Caray was almost killed. He had broken legs, a broken shoulder and damaged lungs. Gussie let him recuperate in his beach house in Florida, provided a private plane to fly him there and arranged for a male nurse to stay with him around the clock.

Caray returned to work in typically dramatic fashion. Clutching two canes, he hobbled onto the field to serve as master of ceremonies on opening day. After limping a few yards, he tossed away one of the canes. The crowd broke into wild cheering. Staggering a few more yards, he sent the second cane flying and "fifty thousand people went collectively crazy." After the ceremony, Cardinals pitcher Bob Gibson reminded Caray that he hadn't used the canes for several weeks. "I just looked at him," Caray wrote later, "and said, 'Hey, Gibby, it's like I've always told you, pal. This isn't just baseball, it's show biz.' "

One of Caray's greatest moments, it was also the beginning of the end of his twenty-five years as the Cardinals announcer. His fall came in 1969 amid rumors that he was having a relationship with Susan Busch, the wife of Gussie's son, August. Already general manager, August was the hard-driving heir apparent and a rising power at the brewery, but he did not share his father's enthusiasm for baseball. His disenchantment was said to date from this period.

During Caray's long hospital stay after his accident, one of his visitors was reporter Ted Schafers. "I asked him what about this story that's going around that you had something with the wife of August III."

"I never did chase her," Caray told him.

Soon afterward, August and Susan Busch divorced and Harry Caray's contract with the Cardinals was allowed to expire. He wasn't technically fired. "I thought they were going to give me a gold watch," Caray said, "and they gave me a pink slip." He handled his dismissal with his usual flair, striding into a press conference carrying a six-pack of Schlitz. The official reason for his removal, given in a terse press release, was that he was being booted on the recommendation of the company's marketing division. "That was a lot of crap. Nobody's a better beer salesman than me. . . . No, I gotta believe the real reason was that somebody believed the rumor that I was involved with young Busch's wife."

Over the years, Caray was often questioned about the rumor. In a 1978 interview he said, "Gussie Busch is a dear friend of mine, but August III and I never got along. The rumor that was making the rounds was so flattering that I decided to let it go. Here I am . . . supposedly having an affair with his wife, a 31-year-old woman." On another occasion he said, "I would have rather had people believe the rumor . . . than not believe it . . . that I at 46 to 47 could break up the marriage of a very young and successful executive and his young wife." Asked point-blank whether he was implying that the rumors weren't true, he said, "That's exactly what I'm implying."

In 1989, asked again whether there was anything to the story, Caray hedged, "You couldn't say I did and I wouldn't say I didn't."

He recounted that he had begun hearing rumors in 1969 that he was on his way out and that other announcers were being asked to submit tapes to the Cardinals. Caray decided to confront Gussie about the stories. He told him, "I'm supposed to be breaking up a marriage." The following dialogue, Caray said, then took place.

"You didn't rape anybody, did you?" Gussie asked.

"No."

"If you had a relationship, it was mutual desire, right?"
Caray nodded.

"I've screwed a lot of people because of mutual desire," Gussie said. "So what do you got to worry about?"

Caray was dismissed anyway, prompting the observation, "I guess blood is thicker than water."

Susan Busch, years later, denied the stories of her alleged relationship with Caray. "There were rumors," she said, "not only that he was involved with me, but that he was involved with Trudy. But you know how rumors are. The real reasons Harry was dismissed were highly publicized."

Caray was rehired in 1980 by August III. Happily remarried by then, August wanted him to peddle his products in Chicago, where the sales of Budweiser and other Anheuser-Busch brands had long been disappointing. When Caray was named to baseball's Hall of Fame as a broadcaster in 1989, Anheuser-Busch praised him in full-page newspaper ads.

In that same year of 1969 when Harry Caray was given his walking papers, Cardinals outfielder Curt Flood was traded to Philadelphia. He refused to go, touching off a long, ultimately successful challenge by other players to baseball's most sacred cow, the reserve clause, and opening the door to the era of millionaire .220 hitters. One year earlier, Gussie had paid the first $1 million payroll in baseball history and was starting to complain about rising costs and what he regarded as the ingratitude of athletes like Flood. After dropping over 30 points in his batting average in 1968, the centerfielder had demanded a raise to $100,000, adding, "and I don't mean, $99,999 either."

The crack was like waving a red flag in front of Gussie. Flood was soon gone and was quickly out of baseball, his reflexes shot after a long layoff as he waited for his lawsuit to wend its way through the courts. The U.S. Supreme Court ruled against him, but the damage was done. Owners eventually had some restraints placed on their ability to dictate a player's contract or the terms of a trade. The reserve clause was dead as a result of the challenges brought by other players. Flood, meanwhile, had written a book, *The Way It Is*, that described his skirt-chasing, bar-hopping playing days. Commenting on Harry Caray, he observed that his sometimes harsh criticism of players "never extended to the executive tier of the firm. That is, he 'called 'em as he saw 'em' but he was careful to see nothing

that the front office didn't want him to see." And as for the
reason for Caray's quick exit from St. Louis, Flood quoted an
"oriental epigram": "Broadcaster who antagonize wrong
woman commit Harry Caray."

Flood wasn't the only flashpoint for Gussie. In 1970, when
his star pitcher Steve Carlton refused to sign, Gussie was hop-
ping mad. Carlton wanted his salary raised from $50,000 to
$55,000. Gussie sputtered at one point, "I don't like his atti-
tude, not a damn bit." At another: "I sat with the bullheaded
buzzard for seven hours. . . . We couldn't budge him." Carlton,
like Flood, was shipped in 1971 to the Phillies, where he became one of the greatest lefthanded pitchers in history.

The St. Louis sports media generally went easy on Gussie.
That was especially obvious during the players' strike of 1972
when he was at his bellowing best. Gussie could do no wrong
for the city's large contingent of "homers." Criticism, if it came
at all, was usually muted. How different for the out-of-town
media. During that 1972 players' strike, Gussie was making
big news with his broadsides and the major papers and news
magazines teed off with relish. Gussie, said *Newsweek,* had a
"vendetta" against his players, ordering them to fly in smaller
planes instead of large chartered jets. They once had private
rooms at the best hotels—a lifestyle unheard of in the majors
—but now Gussie directed them to double up. In the cruelest
cut of all, he canceled their free cases of beer during home
stands.

Gussie, New York *Newsday* reported, "has the civic pride of
Fiorello LaGuardia, the largest big-daddy complex since Juan
Peron's and a habit of slamming his hand on the nearest object
while saying, 'Dammit, I said so, that's why!' . . . The good
burghers of St. Louis have grown to accept Busch; they have
been treated to three generations of Busches. They have words
for him: philanthropist, altruist, salt of the earth, and tyrant,
bully, hard headed, overbearing."

It wasn't that Gussie wasn't generous. He paid his players
top dollar and after the rise of the player militancy paid them
even more. In the 1950s, he had made an aging Stan Musial
the highest-paid player in the National League. When Lou
Brock retired, he gave him a yacht. When Roger Maris, the
former Yankee slugger who had helped the Cardinals win a
World Series, hung it up in 1968, he wound up getting a beer
distributorship in Gainesville, Florida.

The players' strike took some of the luster off the sport, some of the fun, and Gussie, the original party animal, knew how to have fun—especially when his boys made it to the World Series. One of his better bashes occurred in Boston during the 1967 series. Gussie and a large contingent of family and friends flew in for the games, taking residence at one of the city's most luxurious hotels, the Ritz Carlton. Ed Vogel, Gussie's executive vice president, recalled what happened. "They were a wild, wild bunch. They were swinging from the chandeliers."

Harry Chesley, director of Anheuser-Busch's largest advertising agency, also made the trip to Boston. Gussie's wife, Chesley said, was in the forefront of the raucous celebration. "Trudy got a fire extinguisher and let people have it when they got off the elevator. Trudy and Gussie both did this." After the series, Vogel got a bill from the Ritz-Carlton. "It was for $50,000 to cover damages and cleanup. I showed it to Busch. He said, 'Pay it.' The money came out of the advertising budget."

During the Boston merriment, the Busches also held one of their famous food fights. John Volpe, the governor of Massachusetts, hosted a luncheon for Gussie and about thirty friends and family members. Gussie's daughters Lotsie and Lilly were in attendance. Lilly, in fine family tradition, fired a roll at Gussie, but hit the governor's wife. Managing to laugh, Mrs. Volpe said she hoped the Cardinals pitching staff was just as wild.

There was little of that kind of amusement to lighten Gussie's gloom during the players' strike, which lasted thirteen days. He was so upset there were rumors he might sell the team. Gussie said he would have to "re-evaluate" the company's continued ownership of the Cardinals. "I assure you I'm certainly going to report to my stockholders that the fans can now see we're not the big, fat pigs making so much money."

He did not sell the team, of course, and although Gussie made his peace with the players, rough seas and more hardball were still ahead.

49

Gin and Honors

The twenty-year period between 1955 and 1975 was a golden one for Gussie Busch. With Trudy, his lovely young wife, he started his third family. It grew large enough—seven children —to nearly fill the reopened castle at Grant's Farm, which had been closed, except on rare occasions, since shortly after his father's suicide. Reopening and redecorating the mansion, Gussie lived and entertained in baronial splendor in the heart of a city. Like his father, August A., he filled his 281 acre estate with animals from all over the world and in a flash of promotional genius opened the gates to tourists.

His new family and baseball diversions gave Gussie pleasure, but his real joy remained selling beer. "My happiness is my business. I eat it, sleep it, dream about it. My family, of course, comes a close second."

Like his grandfather, Prince Adolphus, Gussie's life then seemed in perpetual motion. When he traveled, worked and played, he was always accompanied by a retinue of hangers-on. Gussie didn't like to be alone. "Even in the can, when he went to the can, I'd be in there and he'd be sitting there doing his business," said his friend Robert Baskowitz, Jr.

One of the constants in Gussie's life, no matter what he was doing or where he was going, wasn't beer at all. It was gin. In fact, his life revolved around gin in both its forms—the beverage and the card game. Gussie loved gin martinis.

"Joseph, the butler, told me Gussie drank enough martinis to fill a lake," said Helen Busch Conway, Gussie's second cousin.

"Now you know Gussie puts a fifth of booze away most every day," said brewery union leader Bob Lewis. "Gussie can drink. There isn't any goddamn question about that."

"Gussie liked gin, straight up, and malt liquor, the dark stuff. Gussie liked his martinis—even in the hospital," recalled John Woulfe, who once lived at Grant's Farm.

"Gussie was a good drinker," said Baskowitz. "He liked to have a martini after midnight. After spending a night drinking, he would have a nightcap."

"Gussie would have three martinis and six beers with dinner," said Al Fleishman.

Gussie himself once said he consumed forty-eight bottles of beer during an eight-hour tour of taverns with a distributor. "I had to take a few shots of whiskey to warm up the stomach. That beer sure gets cold."

Gussie liked to start the day on a mixture considerably more potent than oatmeal. A reporter who arrived at Grant's Farm at eight o'clock one morning was invited to the bar and offered a bullshot—beef broth and bourbon. Asked what he drank at night, Gussie said, "Scotch. I only drink beer at lunchtime."

The other form of gin Gussie liked was a card game called gin and honors. The games were played in the motor coach, in hotel rooms, on board the railroad car, at Grant's Farm, in a suite at Busch Stadium and on board his yacht. Gussie played to win, and in the opinion of many of his partners he cheated —brazenly, with flair, redefining the word "cardshark."

"Busch-style 'gin and honors' had lots of special rules and precedents—all of which were instantaneously promulgated by Busch over the years of gin rummy combat," said Tom Eagleton. "Busch was the high commissioner of rules and precedents. In a given evening, he would announce a new rule— always in his favor."

"Sure, he cheated," said former brewery executive Ed Vogel, laughing wildly at a description of Gussie's card playing. "He kept score. His misdealing. His phony totals. Everyone knew."

A family member recalled, "There were penalties for everything—for everything that is but cheating. You could cheat as much as you wanted, and if you were caught, the only thing you had to do was put the money back."

During Gussie's freebooting card games, players pounded the table and screamed at their opponents. Gussie, of course, did most of the pounding and screaming. Sometimes, large sums of money changed hands; if Gussie came up on the short end, he acted as though he had lost the brewery. "You had to play by Gussie's rules, and he cussed the hell out of you while you were playing," said Madison County (Illinois) clerk Butch Portell. "We played a couple of times and I know I won once, oh, about fifty dollars, and that was the hardest fifty dollars he ever coughed up."

During these card games, Gussie talked incessantly. Portell

said he liked to brag about the times he had been arrested for various violations including disorderly conduct, speeding and shooting game violations. "He'd talk about women. He'd talk about drinking. He'd talk about anything."

Gussie used his two favorite pastimes—drinking and card playing—to test the mettle of men seeking employment or advancement in the brewery. It was kind of a litmus test of suitability. He had either Bob Baskowitz, Jr., or another friend, Robert "Piggy" Meyer, and sometimes both, take prospective executives or district managers out to see if they could hold their liquor. Another tactic was to gang up on someone during a card game to see if the person was a good loser. "Let's play cards until somebody gets hurt," was one of Gussie's expressions. "He did that to see how you acted under pressure," Baskowitz said.

Gussie's drinking test was more severe. Whenever he told Baskowitz "you and Piggy take so and so out for dinner," his friend knew what he really wanted. "He meant we were to try to get Joe or whoever it was shitfaced to see if they handled themselves well."

Piggy Meyer, who had a talent for making Gussie laugh, was a frequent escort on these outings. "He liked to have me take them to ten bars and get them drunk. He used to say if you get a man drunk you find out what kind of person they really are."

50

Beer Wars I

Some of the Busches used people and discarded them like crumpled beer cans. If executives flew high, they often crashed hard. Tony Buford was gone; so was Dick Upshaw, Gussie's sidekick for many years. Ed Vogel had also left rather than work under Gussie's son August. Upshaw had been an especially hard case. Union leader Bob Lewis recalled that Gussie wanted to fire his old friend. "He's got to resign or he won't get his pension," Lewis was told.

A very simple formula was applied at the highest executive levels at Anheuser-Busch. Perform and be well rewarded; screw up or cross the Busches and goodbye. Gussie sometimes seemed to relish firing people—especially relatives. A few of the dismissals included those with the blood of Prince Adolphus in their veins. Over the years, Gussie weeded out other family members as well. His frequent battles with relatives sometimes involved brewery operations, sometimes family matters. Sometimes the fights got physical. The arguments were loud and the grudges long lasting. The banished became unmentionable, whose names were no longer allowed to be spoken.

Many of the Prince's descendants began leaving the brewery in the early 1950s after Gussie really started feeling his oats. Eventually Leicester Faust, Adie von Gontard and Adolph Orthwein were forced out or resigned in disgust over Gussie's tactics. Faust, who with his sister owned 352,992 shares, left in 1952. Adie von Gontard followed in 1955, forced out after a series of disputes that included Gussie's suspicion that his German-born cousin was plotting to take his job. The fact that sales were falling and Adie was sales and advertising manager didn't help. Gussie gave Gontard the lofty title of vice chairman of the board and chairman of the executive committee, but in fact he no longer had a job.

Gontard, it was said, was employed *not* to do things. There was an entire list of things he was not to do. He was not to have an office, for example, or use Anheuser-Busch stationery. "Gussie was just furious with Adie," said a longtime family friend. "It seemed like he had unearthed some kind of palace coup. After the blowup, Adie's name was never mentioned. It was like he had died."

Fred Saigh, who acquired a substantial number of Anheuser-Busch shares through the sale of the Cardinals to the brewery, believed Gontard wanted to contest the management of the company. "Actually it was to get more competent people on the board," said Saigh.

And control of the board was Gussie's heaviest hammer. Nearly everyone on the Anheuser-Busch board of directors was beholden to him in some way. "Gussie used to get exactly what he wanted," said a family member. "He had every one of the directors leveraged. He had a way of throwing tantrums and threatening people when he didn't get what he wanted. It almost seemed like when the stags started mating in the Deer Park out at Grant's Farm he started bellowing and acting bullish. . . . He had this terrific fear that we were all after his job. He had a tremendous paranoia about that."

Gontard "retired" on October 1, 1955. He had been spending a lot of time at his estate near Stuttgart, West Germany, and on one particular day this was his undoing. While walking through a brewery building Gussie saw a big empty office and asked, "Who works there? Whose office is that?"

"It's Adie's."

"Well, where the hell is he?"

No one knew and after some hesitation someone said as much. Gussie exploded. "Get this shit out of here. Clean it out."

Gontard was out. The big joke around the brewery was whether he knew it.

"Gussie hated Adie von Gontard because he had more stock," said Helen Busch Conway. Adie "started arguing with Gussie and that wouldn't do. Gussie ousted him. Gussie sent him on an around-the-world tour."

Robert Lewis said John Flanigan told him that during a family reunion Gontard stood up on a stool and began making a speech about how the family needed some leadership. "Gussie ran to a wall and grabbed an axe that was part of a medieval display of some sort and began running around the ballroom brandishing it. Everyone cleared out of the hall, including Gontard."

Gontard's departure coincided with the struggle by Anheuser-Busch to regain the lead among the nation's brewers. For six consecutive years up to 1955, Schlitz had been number one, and getting rid of Gontard showed others that even family members were expendable during troubled times. Gussie's reign was marked by a fifteen-year struggle against "The Beer That Made Milwaukee Famous." The battle was head-to-head with Robert Uihlein, the last of a famous brewing family to head Schlitz. Obviously, Gussie believed Schlitz was his nemesis, just as Pabst had been the main opponent of his grandfather. Once talking about Schlitz, Gussie said: "I'm so goddamn mad at that whole outfit; that son of a bitch Uihlein had swiped our men. They are the worst goddamn thieves on prices."

In 1949, Schlitz had expanded by buying a brewery in Brooklyn. Anheuser-Busch, which had purchased property for a new plant in Newark right after the war, was slow to branch out, and Gussie said later that he had trouble convincing other board members of the need for a new plant. He also had to get approval from his aunts—Clara, Edmee and Wilhelmina. "I had the goddamnedest fight you ever heard of," Gussie said later.

The Newark plant went on line in 1953, delayed because of a construction project fire that killed thirteen workers trapped inside 30,000 gallon vats. Unlike the older Schlitz plant in congested Brooklyn, the new Newark brewery was situated on U.S. Highway 1. It was twice as large, there was plenty of room for expansion and it was within easy reach of the market.

Schlitz's next move was to California; Anheuser-Busch followed, with both building new breweries. The brewers who were going national at the expense of regional companies were following the growth of the baby boom population. After California, the next hot spot was Florida, where Anheuser-Busch built a plant in Tampa in 1959.

Gussie was the company's premier salesman—and he traveled in style. In early 1954 the brewery bought a special, private $300,000 railroad car with luxury accommodations for Gussie. Despite the growing reliability and speed of air travel, he preferred to travel in the style of Prince Adolphus. He hated airplanes because he was claustrophobic. "He couldn't stand being in closed-in spaces," said Al Fleishman.

Some board members complained that the stainless steel car was an extravagance with its oak paneling, four bedrooms, two bathrooms, conference room, observation lounge, kitchen, dining room, television and two-way radio. The railroad car was the first of several of Gussie's purchases that didn't sit well with directors and stockholders. Later there were complaints about boats, a swimming pool and improvements to Grant's Farm. But the railroad car came in handy in 1955. Dick Meyer, a soft-spoken accountant who had worked up through the ranks to become a vice president, suggested a cross-country tour to encourage distributors to beat Schlitz. Gussie and Meyer went coast to coast, meeting with many of the company's 450 distributors.

"Yeah, that famous trip was something," Gussie said later. "We spent seven months on the road, and that goddamn railroad car paid for itself in one trip."

Gussie sold his distributors on the need to beat Schlitz with the same zeal that he used to sell beer over the bar. He also entertained 11,000 wholesalers, retailers and customers during a marathon eleven-night party at Grant's Farm. He shook so many hands that he had to soak his own hand in brine after each night.

Meyer was at Gussie's side for most of these meetings. A former Lutheran seminarian, Meyer was a religious man who, like Gussie's publicist, Al Fleishman, made it a point of keeping a distance between himself and his boss. Unwilling to get caught up in his gin-drinking, card-playing lifestyle, they worked for him, but preferred not to socialize.

Following the trip, Meyer drafted a new agreement with the distributors that gave them equity ownership rights. In effect, Anheuser-Busch promised not to shut them down by denying them beer shipments or setting up another distributor in the same territory. Until then, the brewery had been free to do either. With improved relations with the distributors and the growing capacity of its new breweries, Anheuser-Busch finally pushed ahead of Schlitz in 1957 and stayed there.

Walter Armbruster, an advertising executive, worked on the Anheuser-Busch account when Schlitz was overtaken. He never forgot his first Anheuser-Busch sales convention. It was held in the Chase Hotel in St. Louis. "I was standing in the wings watching the proceedings and the master of ceremonies suddenly says, 'Mr. Busch, will you please come forward.' Gussie marches up the center aisle. And then they make another announcement. 'Mr. Busch, will you take down the Schlitz flag and raise the Busch flag.' There was a big flag pole there with the Schlitz banner flying and Busch lowered it and raised the Budweiser flag. I thought it was all tremendously funny. I thought it was hilarious. I could hardly keep from laughing, but then all of a sudden, I noticed that the guy next to me was crying. He's crying and pretty soon everybody in the place is crying. That's when I realized how seriously they took their business. It was incredible."

Ironically, although Budweiser was number one nationally, it was still not the most popular beer in Gussie's hometown, an embarrassing truth that drove him into rages. St. Louis beer drinkers preferred Falstaff or Griesdieck Brothers. Gussie did everything he could to break in. He cut Budweiser prices below what was charged elsewhere in the country and was promptly sued by the U.S. government for antitrust violations.

He brought out a new popular-priced beer, Busch Bavarian, which flopped. Robert Weinberg, an Anheuser-Busch executive, said Gussie probably didn't think Busch Bavarian was really beer. "If you had Busch Jr. on a psychological couch and asked him about beer, he would say that Budweiser was beer but that 'We had to do that' about Busch."

Local brewers fought Gussie and his hardball tactics to the bitter end. Anheuser-Busch did not conquer the home market until all the other breweries had closed down. A member of a beer-brewing family recalled that the Anheuser-Busch management style was one of toughness. "They did lots of gutsy stuff. There's a lot of aggressiveness there; of picking people and keeping them on their toes. We held on to our share even though . . . the Busches used strong tactics."

Bob Griesedieck, whose family had an interest in Griesedieck Brothers and later Falstaff, said the competition sometimes got expensive. Breweries would pay money to tavern owners to take down a competitor's sign or quit stocking a competitor's product. "We'd have a draft beer stop for 20 years, when suddenly, down would come the signs," Griesedieck said. "The bigs got bigger." Budweiser became the largest-selling beer in America. Gussie was on top of the heap, which was exactly where he wanted to be.

51

The Fight at Grant's Farm

At Grant's Farm, Gussie lived the St. Louis version of La Dolce Vita with the same driving lustiness he brought to the beer business. In his great French Renaissance style château of rose-colored granite, he hosted parties even more lavish than his grandfather Adolphus's. Trudy lit up the big house with a

Jackie Kennedy style. She wore daring, low-cut dresses. And with the experience gained in her father's Swiss restaurant, she made sure the meals were fabulous. "I never have cooked and I don't want to ever," Trudy once said. "But in our home we love to dine well and do."

The dining room table was always set with sterling silver. The walls were decorated with western paintings and an antique Big Ben clock stood in a corner. The mahogany dining table was graced by a golden basket—a fiftieth wedding anniversary gift to Gussie's grandfather from the coffee king, Herman Sielcken—that was filled with fresh flowers. There were other treasures in Gussie's castle. A guest once admired a coal bucket he saw in Gussie's bedroom. "Sure you like it," Gussie said with a laugh. "It's made of solid gold."

The room, the same one in which his father had shot himself, offered a view of the estate and its herds of roaming animals. On moonlit nights when the snows were deep, servants hitched up the dappled gray horses to the sleigh for rides through the Deer Park. Guests returned to the gun room, where a fire roared in the massive fireplace; drinks were brought by uniformed servants summoned by a bell rope. The roebuck Gussie shot with Adolphus in 1911 was mounted on the wall.

On summer mornings, Gussie chose one of the seventeen sleek horses stabled in the air-conditioned Bauernhof for a ride through the grounds. He often carried a brass horn to summon his deer. If he preferred to travel in one of his coach and fours, he had a museum-quality collection to choose from. Many of the Harrimans, pony coaches, German hunting wagons, phaetons and parasol-topped buggies had belonged to his father and grandfather.

Coaching became a daily ritual in which special visitors were taken on tours with Gussie, who wore a carefully creased Stetson, a gift from Lyndon Johnson. The experience, according to one observer, was like riding downhill in an eighteen-wheeler with bad brakes, being on the street during the running of the bulls at Pamplona, or speeding down a ramp on a bicycle missing handlebars and pedals. "To say that coaching can be exhilarating is to say that sky diving is a great way to dry your hair," observed one journalist. His ride with Gussie took an unscheduled detour when the coach careened off the roadway and sailed into a ditch.

Gussie loved his estate. He had walked or ridden over almost every square yard. He made Grant's Farm a public showplace for his baronial way of life—a life of animals, guns, "pals," women and beer. It also became a beer-promoting tourist attraction. Millions of people visited Grant's Farm during Gussie's time, and in return the brewery paid him millions in lease money. With its bison, deer, elephants and other animals, Grant's Cabin, the rustic log house the president built during his hard-luck days; the fleeting glimpses of the castle; and the free beer finale, the brewer's tours of Grant's Farm were superb public relations.

It was from Grant's Farm that Gussie hosted the first color telecast to originate in St. Louis. In 1954, the National Broadcasting Company offered viewers a chance to see Gussie driving a beer wagon. Trudy and her newly born first son, Adolphus, were shown riding with Gussie's other son, August, in an old lumber cart that once belonged to U.S. Grant. They were all smiles. But when Gussie was told that Trudy was hesitant to bring the baby out to ride in the wagon, he had exploded in anger. "He said something to the effect, 'You tell that Swiss bitch to get her ass down here or she'll wind up back in that restaurant,'" recalled Robert Suits, a reporter who covered the telecast.

In that same year of 1954 when *Life* magazine photographer Margaret Bourke-White shot a layout on the Busch family, Gussie and Trudy were all smiles again. The Busches, sandwiched between the Tafts of Cincinnati and the Fords of Detroit, were described as "just about the liveliest, lustiest family dynasty in the country." One photo showed fifty-one family members posing in tuxedos and gowns on the grand staircase of the big house. In the center, wearing an impish grin, was Gussie himself.

A year later, Gussie's picture made the cover of *Time* magazine with an eight-page story inside. When the *Ladies Home Journal* compiled a list of the ten richest men in America, Gussie tied for seventh place. But he seemed to be the winner overall in the vitality class. "Busch of all the millionaires," the magazine commented, "seems to many to get the most fun from his money."

Although Gussie and his family lived in the castle at Grant's Farm, he did not become the owner of the vast estate until after the death of his mother. Alice Busch, August A.'s widow, died in May 1958 during her afternoon nap. She was ninety-two and had been suffering from Parkinson's disease.

As sometimes happened in the Busch family, the death of a

prominent member triggered some nasty squabbles. The fall-out from Alice's passing was fiery. Her will and its seven codicils led to a fight that is still remembered when family members gather and discuss the good old days. The will not only left Grant's Farm to Gussie, but also said: "Because of the deep gratitude I feel toward my son, August A. Busch Jr., who has faithfully served my personal and business interests through the years without compensation or any expectation thereof, I wish to release and discharge him and his estate of all debts owing to me at the time of my death." That paragraph was the spark to the powder keg. Gussie owed his mother about $600,000, money that had helped him cover his $1 million divorce settlement with his second wife, Elizabeth, in 1953. Other family members were angered that their share of the inheritance was in effect reduced by the cancellation of Gussie's debt.

As if she realized her decision might prompt trouble, Gussie's mother tried to explain her decision in the will. "In the first place, he is my only living son and is charged with all of the financial and other obligations which go with his position as successor to my dearly beloved husband. . . . In the second place, I have not provided trust funds for the four children which have been born to him and Trudy as I have for my other children and grandchildren, including his four older children, and I want to assure that he can be helpful to them as I have been to his older children and my other grandchildren."

Gussie and his sister Alice "Pummie" Busch Tilton argued over the will and the fact that Gussie's debts were forgiven. Adolphus "Dolph" Orthwein, Gussie's nephew who had been a kidnap victim twenty-five years earlier, was swept into the dispute. Summoned to Grant's Farm to try to mediate the disagreement, he and Gussie began to argue. Enraged, Gussie grabbed Dolph by his tie. A powerful man, Dolph lifted Gussie and dropped him to the floor, pinning him there with a knee on his chest.

The brief "fight" went down in family history. Gussie offered a revisionist version later, claiming that Dolph fought dirty. That version was heard by union leader Bob Lewis, who believed that "Dolph Orthwein . . . tried to kick Gussie in the nuts in a fight." Dolph, who quit his job at the brewery around this period, smiled when he heard that story. "The only thing I'll say is that I didn't kick him in the nuts."

52

The Man Who Could Talk to the Animals

Gussie loved animals and they were a big part of his life. One family member believed Gussie's behavior ran in the same cycle as the stags he kept at Grant's Farm. Some of those who were very close to him even thought he could talk to animals. "Animals loved Gussie," said Ed Vogel. "He could somehow communicate with them." Helen Busch Conway recalled that Gussie would let out a loud "whoop, whoop, whoop" as they went through the woods at Grant's Farm. The deer, elk, buffalo, and other animals emerged to be fed. She believed they recognized the sound of his voice.

Gussie also understood that people loved animals, and so it naturally followed in his mind that animals could promote beer sales. As a child, he had watched as his father stocked Grant's Farm with wild and domestic animals. Before Gussie was through, he had added enough beasts to make Noah envious. His grandfather Adolphus had transformed an arroyo in Pasadena into lovely gardens for visitors to tour and enjoy beer. Gussie's own gardens became one of the nation's top tourist attractions.

He once invited a female visitor to join him for a dip in the Jacuzzi in the big house's aviary. When their conversation was drowned out by the screeching of the birds, he ordered one of the servants to bring Ralph, the cockatoo. On Gussie's command of "Go get 'em, Ralph!" the bird chased the others to the far end of the aviary and kept them quiet.

Although Gussie loved animals, he never hesitated to show them who was boss. One visitor to Grant's Farm never forgot how Busch treated temperamental hackney ponies, particularly one named Tommy, as the horses were being put in their traces. "He was shouting at them, hitting them. The dust was flying. . . . Busch kept shouting, 'Tommy. Tommy, stop it! Tommy, stop it!' and smacking the horse. There was chaos."

And there was an old story that Gussie had once killed a German shepherd with his bare hands after it attacked him. His daughter Carlota described how he severely beat another dog with a whip because the animal, supposedly part wolf, had turned on him.

Some believed Gussie's close affinity to animals was rooted in his own psychological makeup. "If overall I could think of a word or an idea that captured the soul of this guy," said one observer of the family, "it's a word I would use both positively and pejoratively and that is 'animalistic.' " John Woulfe, who once lived at Grant's Farm, recalled that he and Gussie were sitting on the patio one day when a moose started bellowing in the Deer Park. A smile crossed Gussie's face and he said, "Sounds like someone's going to get a good fucking tonight."

Gussie filled Grant's Farm with elephants, parrots, monkeys, bears, goats, Texas and Scotch Highland cattle, camels, Chincoteague ponies, black buck antelope, European red deer, Japanese Sika deer, swans, sheep, blue swans, watusi, ostriches, zebras, wild mustangs, yaks and llamas, buffaloes and wild burros that were rescued from the Grand Canyon. On one trip he brought back eight baby elephants in a freight car and gave them to the St. Louis Zoo. He named the beasts after members of his family. One was named Trudy and another Alice, after his mother. Al Fleishman recalled another trip. "I still remember sitting in the private railroad car carrying birds back to Grant's Farm from Tampa." The car was "full of vomiting birds."

A visitor got a close look at Gussie Busch in 1976 when an unknown intruder shot four Clydesdales in a pasture adjacent to Grant's Farm. A pregnant mare named Peggy died, and Gussie was on his hands and knees trying to save her foal. The visitor thought Gussie was in mourning or deep shock. "For the first time I saw the famous beer baron in a frame I had never thought of him before. I always thought of him as the guy down there on Pestalozzi Street at the brewery. It reinforced in my mind the depth of his feeling toward these animals, particularly the Clydesdales. Through the morning . . . Gussie was right there with his hands in the horse. . . . While we were doing this, all the rest of the Clydesdales were standing by a fence watching us over our shoulders. I had the awful feeling that I was in the midst of a Grimm's fairy tale or something out of the Black Forest. Here was the famous beer baron . . . ministering to a dead horse trying to save another horse. He wasn't crying or sobbing but he was obviously stricken by the whole thing. And yet he never lost his temper and he never expressed great bitterness or anger at the person who had pulled the trigger. It was the first time I saw him in a personal human context, and it was a context that showed me a guy who was, who had a deep soulful relationship with animals."

The Clydesdales were, of course, a long-familiar Budweiser emblem, but they were not the only horses Gussie used to promote his beer. He bought a champion jumper named Circus Rose in 1950 and changed the name of the gray mare to Miss Budweiser. Then, in perhaps the first involvement of the beer company with the Olympics, he loaned the prize-winning horse to the U.S. Olympic Committee for the 1952 games. The horse went on tour with the U.S. equestrian team. It was a typical Busch advertising coup.

Gussie's promotional use of animals blossomed in Florida. He transformed the grounds surrounding his new brewery in Tampa into a fifteen-acre tropical paradise that even Prince Adolphus would have envied. Hundreds of exotic birds were displayed; herds of wild animals wandered around a replica of an African veldt while visitors got a bird's-eye view from a treetop-level monorail. And of course it wasn't a coincidence that the large $13 million restaurant was nearly identical to the Old Swiss House owned by Trudy's parents. No one seemed to mind the incongruity of a building with a Bavarian motif overlooking an African plain.

Busch Gardens in Tampa—and the other similar parks that followed—began as one of Gussie's seat-of-the-pants experiments at encouraging people to sample his products. Busch Gardens became Florida's second-largest tourist attraction and a constant reminder to the public that there was big money in beer, particularly for Anheuser-Busch. "I told the board and everybody else," Gussie said, "that's what I wanted to do with these Busch Gardens and they thought, well, here, you're a lunatic. So we started slow on 'em and you know what they're doing today, for godsakes. We're having millions of visitors." Like his grandfather, everything Gussie touched, it seemed, turned to gold.

53

Gussie and a Different Cardinal

His marriage to Trudy led Gussie into a colorful relationship with the Roman Catholic Church. Trudy was a Catholic, and after Gussie married her, he was eventually baptized in that faith. The church welcomed such a prominent and wealthy new member. In the early 1950s, Father Paul Reinert, the president of the Jesuit St. Louis University, believed that the Holy Spirit led him to Gussie to head up a fund drive for the school. It was a hard job convincing him, but he eventually agreed and the school raised $18 million. "He realized that he was being respected for what he was doing. He was very active then in raising money for the Democratic Party, but this was a different kind of respect, a different kind of feeling and he liked it. It changed him from being someone who was, to put it frankly, somewhat self-centered and engrossed in his business activities and Grant's Farm to a much higher philanthropic interest."

In gratitude, the university showered honors on Gussie, who was named to its board of trustees and received an honorary doctorate of laws degree. Father Reinert even agreed to offer a prayer for his new brewery in Tampa. "Gussie couldn't believe it. He found out that he couldn't get a minister in Florida to say a prayer over a brewery, and so he called me and I said your wish is my command and I flew down there and said the prayer."

Father Reinert later discussed with Gussie the idea of a memorial to the Busches in St. Louis. Their talks led to the construction of the Busch Memorial Union, the student center on the St. Louis University campus. The family did not bear all the costs. The building was funded with the help of Anheuser-Busch's wholesalers, who had been pressured by Gussie. They were asked to contribute a sum based on the number of barrels of beer they received from the brewery. "It was a tax on that production, a kind of surtax," Reinert recalled.

Although Father Reinert believed Gussie was a generous man, others did not share that opinion. Gussie, they said, might have been generous with the brewery's money, but not with his own. "He is tight with his own money, as if he didn't have anything," said Al Fleishman. "He was not generous," Ed Vogel confirmed. "He'd never spend his own money." Vogel recalled a time when he and Gussie were at Al Lang Field in Florida watching the Cardinals. A woman told Gussie she was broke, and Gussie asked Vogel to give her fifty dollars. When Vogel later asked for his money, Gussie smiled and said, "You know how to get that back, Eddie."

"What he meant was put it on your expense account," Vogel said. "Nothing comes out of their own pockets. I never heard of Gussie giving anything to the city. It's the brewery that gives the money." Gussie did, however, give about $25,000 a year in stock to St. Louis University from 1959 to 1963. He later donated more of his stock to the school—$25,000 to establish the Mark Eagleton Memorial Scholarship fund for the law school in 1971. In 1976 he gave an additional 750 shares of common stock valued at $24,900. According to Reinert, Gussie contributed hundreds of thousands of dollars to the university.

Whatever Gussie's personal altruistic motives, there were always two other underlying reasons behind his charitable contributions. To a certain extent, they were a cost of doing business. Since the time of Prince Adolphus, philanthropic endeavors brought favorable publicity that didn't hurt a business so dependent on the public's good will. Secondly, there were income tax advantages.

When changes were proposed in 1963 to limit business income tax deductions for charitable contributions, Gussie wrote his old friend, Missouri senator Stuart Symington. He was "terribly upset" about the proposed changes. "As you know, I and the other executives of our company have made very liberal contributions to our great universities, to the United Fund and to almost every worthwhile organization in this area and in many other parts of the country. Our interpretation of the proposed new law would cause us to reexamine all of our activity in the light of what is proposed. It is not often that I write to you so strongly about matters of government affairs, but the possible far-reaching effects of this action by the government should not be allowed to go unchallenged."

If Gussie's involvement with a Catholic university gave him good publicity and generous tax deductions, his relationship with the church also enabled him to fulfill Trudy's long desire to have a personal chapel built at Grant's Farm. She wanted one of those quaint little chapels that clung to the mountainsides in her native Switzerland. Gussie thought Father Reinert could help him get one. He asked him for a small favor. "Do you know how those rich families in Switzerland have those private chapels? Well, I want a private chapel for my wife and children out at Grant's Farm and I want you to go to Cardinal Ritter to get permission."

Father Reinert was astounded. He knew the church in America frowned on such private chapels. He pointed out as diplomatically as possible that the cardinal had already closed a couple of them. Swallowing hard, he finally said, "Gussie, I don't think I can do that for you."

"You go out," Gussie replied gruffly, "and you get permission, Father."

Father Reinert dutifully visited Cardinal Ritter and explained his dilemma. "The cardinal thought about it a moment and said, 'Well, now wait a minute. It's true we don't want Catholic families to have their own chapels, but in the first place, Mr. Busch isn't a Catholic, and in the second place, I can put restrictions on how it is used.' "

Gussie and Trudy got permission to build their chapel. They sent an architect to Switzerland to research the project. They called antique dealers who furnished paintings, a crucifix, an altar and other fixtures—most of them centuries old. Trudy's parents donated the bells. And when the chapel was built after about six months, Gussie called Father Reinert again.

"Father, the chapel is ready. I want you to get Cardinal Ritter to come out here and bless it. I'd like him out here next Saturday morning at eleven A.M. The place will seat thirty-five people. I'm going to have my board of directors out here and the family and I want the cardinal to come so you go talk to him and have him out here Saturday."

Father Reinert froze. "Gussie, I don't think you quite understand. Cardinal Ritter really doesn't want the world to know that this chapel is even out there."

"Well, this is an exception," Gussie boomed back. "You go out and get the cardinal!"

So Father Reinert paid another awkward visit to Cardinal Ritter, who astounded him a second time. "You know," he said, "I've never been to Grant's Farm and I'd kind of like to see it."

Before the big day arrived, Gussie called Father Reinert with a question, "What do you call this guy?" Father Reinert told Gussie to call the cardinal "your eminence." "And he must have practiced a week getting that straight because when the cardinal showed up, it was your eminence this and your eminence that."

On the day of the chapel dedication, it snowed five or six inches in St. Louis and Gussie drove the cardinal to the chapel in an electric golf cart. "For the first time possibly in the history of the Catholic Church," Father Reinert said, "a fully attired bishop went off into the woods in a golf cart." Cardinal Ritter suggested the chapel be dedicated to Saint Humbert, and Gussie later sent antique dealers scurrying to find a statue of the obscure German, the patron saint of hunters.

The blessing went off without a hitch. Gussie even cried during Cardinal Ritter's homily. Later, back in the big house for lunch, he sat next to the cardinal. "Have you ever ridden in a coach and four, your eminence?" he asked.

"Mr. Busch, I'm a farmboy from Indiana. I've ridden behind a plow and on clapboard wagons, and I can tell you we didn't have a coach and four."

"Would you like to ride in a coach and four?"

"Mr. Busch, I'd love to."

Father Reinert described what happened next. "Right away Gussie's voice booms out. 'Get out the coach and four.' You know he had an intercom in every room but he was always shouting. Everyone went outside into the snow and there was another first in Catholic history, possibly. The cardinal was lifted up into the coach and sat there in the front driver's seat next to Gussie. He was wearing the big red robe of a cardinal. It was an incredible sight. Gussie whipped the horses and off we went, the cardinal sitting up there with his robe flowing in the wind. There were some visitors at Grant's Farm that day and they looked up at us and some of them started applauding. They thought it was part of some show."

Later, when Trudy wanted the bells in the chapel to ring the Angelus, an expert was brought over from Europe to set it up. One morning Gussie asked him when the bells would ring. He was told 6 A.M., noon and 6 P.M.

"What time do you ring those bells in the morning?" Gussie demanded.

"At six in the morning," the craftsman repeated.

Gussie frowned. "Not around here they don't ring at six in the morning. You fix my Angelus bells to ring at nine in the morning."

54

"Dawn Patrol"

In 1971, Gussie, seventy-two and thinking of his succession, took a step widely regarded as a slap in the face of his energetic son, whose vision of the company's future had veered sharply from his own. He named one of his trusted retainers as president, not August as many had expected. The decision, as usual, was rubber-stamped by his compliant board. Gussie retained power as chairman and chief executive officer. Dick Meyer, at fifty-four, became the first non-Busch to ascend to the presidency in the company's history.

The move prompted sighs of relief among Gussie's old guard, who regarded August as brash, pushy and impertinent. They didn't like his style and they didn't like the well-educated MBAs he had been assembling at the brewery. They had good reason to be apprehensive. Mistrustful and unsure of himself, even Gussie felt challenged and so he asserted his dictatorial authority: Meyer was in and August was left waiting in the wings. "The talk," *Business Week* reported, "was that the elder Busch was teaching his chilly, tough-minded son some humility."

Gussie felt comfortable with the efficient, quiet Meyer, who had started with the company as an office boy. He had accompanied Gussie on his famous whistle-stopping journey across the country in 1955—the trip had been his idea—and he knew how to get along with his mercurial boss. As a kind of consolation prize, August was named executive vice president.

Meyer might have been the right man to head up the brewery, but he wasn't a Busch and some family members gingerly questioned Gussie about his unprecedented decision. He told them that he felt his son still had to show he was qualified for the job, confiding that August's day would come and that they should all trust his judgment.

August seriously doubted that. So did the band of executives he was gathering around him, most of them fresh from Ivy League business schools. They thought that Gussie had lost his grip, that he had grown too cautious and was afraid to expand the company to meet the growing challenge from Schlitz. But there was no appeal from his decisions, which could be delivered with a pounding fist and the sputtering cry, "Because I said so, dammit." "The old man," said Russell Ackoff, "was a king. He did not manage the company, he ruled it."

Gussie's relationship with August's team was occasionally frosty if not downright hostile. Dennis Long, who started with Anheuser-Busch as a part-time elevator operator, had risen in the company to become August's lieutenant. He received an incredible welcome from the beer baron. A former executive recalled the story of the day August introduced Long to Gussie. "They were out at Grant's Farm one afternoon. Gussie didn't like to sit still and so they decided to go out and look over things. They hiked all over the place and then got into a car.

"At one point during their drive, Gussie, who was in the front seat, turned and says to August, 'What happened to Thing?'

"August said, 'What do you mean? What thing?'

" 'I said, what happened to Thing.'

"Then August realized what his father meant. 'You mean what happened to Denny?'

" 'Yeah, Thing.' "

Long was still in the back seat, ears burning no doubt and silent.

"If Gussie liked you, he called you pal. If he didn't like you, he called you Thing!"

For many of these new hires, Anheuser-Busch and the volatile brewing industry was a brave new world unlike anything they had encountered in business school. The textbooks had never described anyone like Gussie Busch. An executive who joined the company in the early 1970s remembered attending his first wholesalers convention, a typical Busch extravaganza held in Houston. Senior managers were making their presentations from a stage before several hundred wholesalers assembled in a great hall. A vice president for marketing dropped dead from a heart attack halfway through his presentation. "They just closed the curtain . . . and then went on with the convention."

Robert Weinberg was one of the first executives recruited by August. The two met in 1965 at the Wharton School in Phila-

delphia, where both were on the board of directors. Trained in
economics at Columbia University, Weinberg had been chief
technical planner for IBM. At first Weinberg was skeptical of
August. He thought he was "a snot . . . who talked too much."
Then he began to have second thoughts. The more he listened,
the more August impressed him. "Here was a young man with
no particular formal education who was asking extraordinarily good questions." August finally asked Weinberg to work for
Anheuser-Busch; he wanted him to help the company get
started with computer-based planning, a field totally alien to
his father and men like Meyer. Weinberg joined Anheuser-
Busch in 1966 and stayed five years. His experiences with Gussie were often rocky.

Gussie and Meyer offered virtually no encouragement to
Weinberg and August in their attempt to develop long-range,
computer-assisted planning. Other MBAs came on board,
many of them also handpicked by August. "I think," said Weinberg, "that August, at an early age, recognized that the cheapest thing you can buy in the business world are brains."

August's men, many of whom were assigned to Weinberg's
planning department, began to question virtually all of the
brewery's practices, which increasingly set Gussie on edge. He
often didn't understand what these new whiz kids were talking
about and when he did understand, he often didn't like what
he was hearing. "In the heat of over-enthusiasm," *Fortune*
magazine commented, "one daring fellow, forgetting Busch's
love of tradition, suggested that the company dispense with its
teams of Clydesdales." How Gussie must have roared when
that proposal crossed his desk.

Weinberg had his own unforgettable moment with Gussie.
He had commissioned a chemical analysis of beechwood-aged
beer, for generations a key ingredient of the Budweiser brewing process. Weinberg had the temerity to wonder whether
those belt-sized chips of beechwood really made any difference
to the taste of the beer. In the temple of Busch that was a
breathtaking apostasy. When Gussie found out, he exploded.
"I don't think in my entire career," Weinberg said, "I have ever
been chewed out like that man chewed me out."

The problem, as Weinberg and others saw it, was that Gussie
had gridlocked the brewery's decision-making process. Nothing was approved without his authorization. He became adept
at stalling, at pigeonholing proposals for further study. "They
were paying me a lot of money, but I couldn't give my secre-

tary a twenty-five dollar a week raise without the old man approving it," Weinberg said. "The company was run like a corner grocery store. The management system was phenomenally inflexible."

Gussie was deathly afraid of incurring debt to build more breweries, even though men like the departed Vogel had long recommended expansion. He was loath to hurt his profit margin by building excess capacity. The new guard, led with increasing sureness by August, favored expansion and an emphasis on more advertising. The old guard, led by the ever-irascible Gussie, favored standing pat. The two camps clashed repeatedly.

The cerebral Weinberg, who had enjoyed "baiting the old man" with graphs, charts and computer printouts, all of which he detested, was one of the first to lose his head. His demise occurred when he brashly disagreed with Gussie over a market share projection during a board meeting. He was called to his office by one of Gussie's assistants and shown two letters. The first, addressed to all the board members, was a confession that he had made a mistake and that, upon somber reflection, he now realized Gussie was right. The other was a letter of resignation. Weinberg chose to sign the letter of resignation.

Weinberg's departure was widely viewed as Gussie's way of telling his son who was still in charge. But while August was intensely disliked by many in Gussie's executive corps, the men he had personally recruited were solidly loyal. He gave them uncommon freedom, and his rules were uncommonly simple. "He was pretty clear-cut," said one executive. "If you did what you were supposed to do, you got a lot of money. If you didn't, you got fired."

Virtually all of August's executives were molded in his own image. None smoked, for August had kicked a chain-smoking habit—"it was no problem"—and was intolerant of those who were still addicted. Haircuts were close, even during the covered-ear era, for August, it was remarked, looked as if he parted his thick brown hair "with an axe." A twelve-hour day was the rule. The cadre was uniformly young, white and male. "I don't know why they even bothered with a personnel department," one of the band observed. "I mean it would have been so much easier just to go seek out the most conspicuous workaholics you can find. Those were the only ones who seemed to stick around."

It gradually became apparent both within the company and

among analysts that it was time for a change in leadership at
Anheuser-Busch. New management techniques were long over-
due, and the company faced ever-stiffening competition. Many
felt Gussie should have considered stepping aside in favor of
the new generation of aggressive MBAs led by his son. The
problem was that the patriarch was still very much in the
saddle. Some insiders thought that at Gussie's advanced age
"he should have quit."

In the meantime, August's staffers considered themselves his
private army. They were confident that Gussie would eventually be deposed. They planned in secret, crawling out of bed
on many a Saturday and driving to August's farm at 6:30 in
the morning for a meeting. There were so many of these sessions they began calling themselves the "dawn patrol."

The planning went on methodically. Dennis Long, August's
assistant and Gussie's Thing, once showed a member of the
inner circle a secret organizational chart, which detailed who
would be doing what when the coup finally occurred. "Denny
told me that we were the chosen few," the man said. "We were
to be the new team when the revolution came."

There was a story that August and Long had drawn up loyalty lists, ranking all the chief executives according to their
loyalty to either the father or the son. It wasn't unusual for
Gussie to summon to his office someone who had accompanied
August on a business trip and ask for a detailed summary of
everything his son had said. The undercurrent of suspicion
bubbled and boiled.

August rarely loosened up. One of his new hires was a man
he had known since elementary school. "I was ushered in for
the final interview with August," he recalled. "It was striking.
Here was a guy I had known all that time and he acted like he
didn't know me. He called me Mister." Flying was a rare form
of relaxation for August. He was an excellent pilot, first of
airplanes and jets, and later helicopters. He flew a stub-winged
stunt plane, landing it on a dirt airstrip on his estate. Fellow
pilots admired the skill it took to take off and land in such a
short distance. Less impressed, the company's board of directors made August get rid of the airplane, apparently considering it a needless risk.

Weinberg remembered a trip he took with August at the
controls of the corporate jet. They were landing when a strong
updraft almost flipped the plane. August managed to regain
control and land. Walter Armbruster, an advertising executive,

was flying to Los Angeles in a Lear jet with August, who suddenly disappeared into the cockpit. Armbruster began to worry when the pilot emerged and sat down next to him. "When I asked him whether August knew what he was doing, he smiled and said, 'It's kind of embarrassing. We took the pilot's test together and August came out with a higher score than any of us.'"

As August prepared for the day when he would take over, his reputation as an ice-cold executive with a voracious appetite for work was firmly established. He did not like to go out at night, or go to a restaurant for dinner. "I doubt if August ever went to the symphony," said Henry King, former president of the U.S. Brewers' Association. "I doubt if he's read many of the Great Books, but he sure as hell devotes himself day and night to the business." His prickly demeanor, some felt, was meant to keep people at a distance. There was no small talk with August. Executives who accompanied him on business trips were exposed to a steady stream of questions. Their fatigued brains were picked mercilessly. A two- or three-hour flight with the man could be a wracking experience. "It was like," recalled one executive, "being in a speeding torture chamber."

It was almost impossible for August to have close friends. "I've never met a Busch yet I didn't think was paranoid," said one associate. "They are all phenomenally suspicious people, but I'm not sure whether running a company like that wouldn't make anyone paranoid . . . you're always wondering whether someone is being friendly because he likes you or because he wants something."

August continued to be solicitous of his father—at least in public. He tried to avoid confrontations, even over seemingly trivial matters that he knew could drive Gussie into one of his formidable rages. Henry King recounted a trip he took in the corporate jet. On the way back, thirsty for a beer and unable to find any Anheuser-Busch products, he bought a six-pack of Coors and put it in the plane's refrigerator. A few days later he got a call from August. He wanted to know what that Coors was doing aboard the plane. "I explained what had happened, and he said, well, I'm not upset but if my father saw that beer he'd have both our asses."

It wouldn't be much longer before August could stop worrying about such paternal pique.

55

Heads Roll

Early in 1974, in possibly the worst corporate massacre in Anheuser-Busch's history, over 120 executives and office workers were fired. "Heads Roll," read the newspaper headlines. "New Guard takes over Reins of Anheuser-Busch." Alarmed by falling profits, Gussie had gone on the warpath to try to reduce costs. In the ensuing reign of terror, employees were canned by the dozens. Cutting the fat, Gussie called it.

Serious problems at the brewery were already apparent late in 1972 when Gussie was forced to take the unpalatable step of announcing that earnings were down. The unprofitable Busch Gardens in Houston were partially closed. Anheuser-Busch stock plunged, dropping from $55 a share to as low as $28. The trend continued in 1973 when profits fell nearly $11 million. The irony was that the company continued to set sales records, but the price of rice and other essential ingredients had skyrocketed, driving down the profit margins.

To make matters worse, the company also was being pressed hard by Schlitz. The Milwaukee brewer, in a daring move to boost profits, had cut its brewing process to fifteen days. Gussie wasn't about to follow suit; Budweiser took nearly forty days to brew, which meant that Schlitz could turn out beer almost three times as fast with far lower costs. Schlitz's president, Robert Uihlein, a millionaire's son cut in the Busch mold, had stabled his polo ponies in his mid-thirties and settled down to business. In that regard, he was similar to August. After reformulating his work habits, Uihlein had ordered the controversial reformulation of his beer.

It would prove one of the biggest disasters in brewing history. A tidal wave of beer drinkers abandoned Schlitz; it took years to win them back. Ultimately, Gussie would be vindicated for refusing to tamper with his product. But early in 1974, it looked as if Schlitz had a shot at toppling the king of beers. Gussie was worried and he was getting some uncharacteristically bad national press. "It is hard," *Forbes* magazine observed, "not to sympathize with Gussie Busch, with his pride in tradition and in his product. Yet if the job of management is to make money for its stockholders and to assure the long-term health of the company, it is fair to ask whether Busch should not begin paying more attention to the dollar sign. Will Gus Busch's pride yield to economics?"

Gussie responded with a meat cleaver. Dick Meyer, his president, opposed the slashing cuts. So did some of his senior advisers. At one tense meeting in which the personnel reductions were discussed, Gussie turned to a reluctant executive and snapped, "If you don't know who to fire, give me a list of the organizational chart and I'll do it myself."

The cuts were so severe that Meyer resigned in protest. He summoned Al Fleishman to his house and told him that Gussie "was going too far. He won't listen. Maybe if I resign that will stop him." Fleishman dutifully prepared a resignation announcement, which noted only that Meyer had had a disagreement with Gussie. The problem, observed Fleishman, was that Gussie's "mind was beginning to wander."

The firings weren't the only means of cutting costs. Even August's helicopter had to go. He had been using the chopper to commute from his estate to the office, but the aircraft was sold in the economy move. August leased an apartment in the city, so that after one of his marathon sessions at the office he wouldn't have to face the thirty-mile drive back to his farm.

Gussie accepted Meyer's resignation, and August was named president, a move quickly approved by Gussie's always obliging board of directors. And in the vacuum that followed the shake-up, August wasted little time moving many of his own men into key positions. The new president began to leave an even wider mark. He received a prestigious award from the American Marketing Association and had recently been named to the board of overseers at Wharton, which continued to provide him with a steady stream of bright MBAs. "This is fun," he said of his new job. "This is my life. This is what I like to do."

In public, August was careful to keep up the proper facade. He continued to call his seventy-five-year-old father the Chief. But a new lion had padded into the den. As he sat in his baronial office with the gilt-framed portraits of Prince Adolphus and August A. staring down at him, Gussie, who had never been a reader, might have done well to pick up *King Lear*.

56

The Beer Fleet

Other forces—both impersonal and personal—were closing in
on Gussie Busch. During his reign the value of Anheuser-Busch
stock, much of which he owned, had soared in value—at least
until the precipitous drop in 1972. But even then, as Dick
Meyer had pointed out to shareholders during the 1972 annual
meeting, 100 shares purchased in 1950 for $2,400 were now
worth $62,832. It sounded good, but some believed the stock
would have been worth more if Gussie had not been in charge
of Anheuser-Busch. Fred Saigh always thought the Busches
profited personally at the expense of the company and its
stockholders. Long a thorn in Gussie's side, Saigh believed the
stock would have been worth two or three times more "if they
hadn't found so many ways to milk the company. They have
milked the company for years."

Saigh's lawyer, Lon Hocker, filed lawsuits which the courts
rejected, and questioned Gussie openly during testy stockholder meetings. At one such meeting in 1963, Hocker wanted
to know, among other things, about deals that allowed Gussie
to receive income for the brewery's use of Grant's Farm,
income he received from a Clydesdale breeding farm and
the arrangements that permitted him to buy stock at lower
than market prices. "I'm not unhappy about the progress of
Anheuser-Busch," Hocker charged. "Its success is not due to
Mr. Busch but to thousands of loyal and competent employees. My fight with the Busch-controlled board of directors is
that too much money and fringe benefits are being lavished
on Mr. Busch and his family."

Hocker was disturbed about stock options worth $1,960,000
to Gussie, a 1964 salary of $140,000 plus a bonus of $68,150
and the $194,623 he received from the brewery for the rental
of Grant's Farm. Gussie answered that the stock option plan
was granted by the board of directors and approved by the
stockholders.

"What about Goat Mountain?" Hocker asked in frustration during one Anheuser-Busch stockholder meeting. "Who paid for that?" As a replica of a mountain near Trudy's hometown of Lucerne, an artificial hill had been constructed on Grant's Farm to provide a natural habitat for Gussie's mountain goats. The cost of $31,000 was paid by the brewery. Gussie said that at any time when Grant's Farm was no longer leased to Anheuser-Busch, he would pay for the unamortized remainder.

The expense of Goat Mountain was nothing compared to the costs of Gussie's "fleet," one of his most lavish perks. Tied up near his beach house at Pass-a-Grille and floating on beer money were the *A & Eagle*, a 119 foot yacht; the *Miss Budweiser*, an 84 foot yacht, and the *Miss Bavarian*, a 41 foot fishing boat. The brewery had bought the boats, which Gussie claimed were used for business purposes—to entertain clients, distributors and retailers.

The *A & Eagle*, his luxurious flagship, was a million-dollar vessel of 235 tons. It was built at a shipyard in Lemwerder, Germany, and outfitted by interior decorators in Tampa. Filled with custom-made furnishings, the yacht had teak-paneled living and dining rooms, four double staterooms, each with a private bath, and, of course, a well-stocked bar.

One of Gussie's most expensive traditions was to take his fleet to the Caribbean. Invitations were sent to executives, VIPs and relatives. "The letter . . . invited them to a special conference," said Robert Baskowitz, Jr. "It was just a cover because it was really a big party. We'd head for one of the Keys and have a ball."

Women were also invited on these so-called business trips. "There were a lot of broads on board," said Harry Chesley, an advertising executive, who sailed with Gussie to Bimini aboard the *A & Eagle*. At one point, Gussie called back to Florida over the ship's radio and complained that "the ship hasn't arrived with the new broads."

On another trip to Bimini, he sent a different message. "Gussie radioed to 'Send over some fresh bait. I want white bait and some of that brown bait. I'll send a plane over and have them come to Bimini.' The person he was talking to comes back on the radio and says, 'Do you want the bait to take a taxi when they get there?' "

Chesley also recalled that he and his wife were aboard the *A & Eagle* when another boat blocked their entry into a mooring slip. A crew member named Rawlins "shouted out, asking the boat to move, but nothing happened. Gussie said to try again, and Rawlins cries out, but nothing is done. The other boat is still blocking us. Finally, Gussie says to poor Rawlins, 'Tell those sons of bitches to get their goddamn boat out of the way.' Whereupon Rawlins says, with a slight stutter now, 'But Mr. Busch, aren't you forgetting that making friends is our business?' Gussie did a double take, smiled and said, 'Fuck you, Rawlins, you're fired.' "

For years John Dowling was captain of the *Miss Budweiser.* Originally hired to take Gussie tarpon fishing, he followed the *A & Eagle* to the Bahamas and Cozumel, Mexico, and points in between. There was fishing, dining, card playing and skeet shooting off the back of the boat.

In September 1965 Gussie was aboard the *A & Eagle* bound for Cozumel when Hurricane Betsy hit. His flotilla pulled into a port and planes were dispatched to pick up the party. "Gussie flew back with them. He wouldn't ride in rough weather. He didn't like it," said Dowling. "Gussie was a calm-water man. . . . He didn't like open water. He would always stick to the intercoastal waterways if he could. He didn't want to go out."

Even after the big storm passed by, the *A & Eagle* ran into heavy seas on the way back to Florida and was damaged. "We worked our way up to Key West," Dowling said. "We wanted to tie up at Navy Pier there, but they wouldn't let us in." He called Gussie, who by that time was back in St. Louis. Gussie telephoned his old friend President Johnson. Permission to tie up at Navy Pier was promptly granted. A navy captain "came down and it was all very nice. It was 'Yes, sir, what can I do for you, sir?' "

Gussie sometimes steered the boat. It didn't matter that as he got older, he couldn't see the channel markers. "If someone tried to outrun us, he'd open it wide open. He loved to go fast." He also loved to spend the brewery's money on a lavish scale.

Gussie had never hesitated to call the president when he needed help, no matter who the president happened to be. Other important politicians got similar calls from his executives. In June 1974, Gussie's wife, Trudy, was in a jam and Stan Fike, administrative assistant to Senator Stuart Symington, received a desperate telephone call from Fred Kuhlmann, an attorney for Anheuser-Busch. After being hospitalized in Lucerne for a concussion, Trudy wanted to return to the States with her mother, Martina Buholzer. The problem—and the reason for Kuhlmann's urgent call—was that Mrs. Buholzer was a Swiss national whose passport had expired. She was also without a visa. With a long weekend looming, Kuhlmann wanted to know whether anything could be done to arrange for the untroubled entry of Martina Buholzer into the United States?

No problem.

Fike was a very able and resourceful senator's assistant. It was shortly before quitting time on a Friday evening, but within minutes he was on the telephone to William Honan of the Immigration and Naturalization Service. A few more telephone calls were made informing others of the importance of the parties seeking help. Honan contacted the airline, Swissair, waiving the customary $1,000 fine which normally would have been levied for bringing a foreign national into the country without a valid passport. The officer on duty at Kennedy was alerted that Mrs. Buholzer's passport and visa had been waived. Within twenty minutes, the arrival of Trudy and her mother was greased through the airport. Whereafter Honan politely suggested that Mrs. Buholzer contact the Swiss Embassy in the United States at her earliest opportunity to get her passport extended.

The reason for the urgency of Trudy's return was that Gussie had collapsed with what was thought to be a heart attack. It soon proved to be a false alarm. But Gussie was now seventy-five and his lavish lifestyle and intemperate habits had taken a heavy toll on his health.

57

Old Blue Eyes

If Gussie was adept at self-promotion, he had long been a genius at promoting his beer. Early on in his reign, Anheuser-

Busch realized the advantages of using celebrities to sell its
beer. In the 1950s, when Eddie Cantor toured the country
doing a one-man show, he hawked Budweiser from the stage.
In return, Gussie gave money to Cantor's favorite charity.

Princess Grace of Monaco was another star Gussie used to
advantage. When the famous actress gave birth to her daughter Caroline in 1957, he had ten cases of Budweiser flown to
her palace because somehow he had "heard" that she was on a
beer diet while nursing. The flap that ensued generated plenty
of free publicity for the brewery. The managing director of the
Monaco Modern Dairy protested, saying: "The good Lord has
given us milk for babies and that is the only liquid nourishment they or their mothers should get." Gussie, no doubt, disagreed.

The best-known entertainer he hired to peddle his product
was Frank Sinatra. In 1965, the singer approached Ed Vogel
and Harry Chesley while they were vacationing with their families aboard one of the Anheuser-Busch yachts near Cape Cod.
Sinatra's boat was moored nearby. Aware that the brewery
had reserved an hour of prime-time television on Thanksgiving, he wanted that kind of exposure himself and so arranged
an introduction. It proved to be a shrewd move.

A deal was worked out. Sinatra got $750,000 for the first
television broadcast to be sponsored by Anheuser-Busch. He
also was required to do two appearances a year at conventions.
The program, called "Frank Sinatra, a Man and His Music,"
was a hit. A second show followed, but this time there was a
flap. The program featured Ella Fitzgerald, the famous black
vocalist. The problem for the brewery was that Sinatra kissed
her. "You've got to remember that we had about three hundred
distributors in the South that were pissed at us because of Ella
Fitzgerald on that show and that Sinatra kissed her," Vogel
said later. "A lot of them were raising hell."

So was Gussie. "You fucked it up, didn't you?" he raged at
Vogel. "We've got 300 wholesalers raising hell. What do we
do?"

"We don't do a goddamn thing," Vogel replied.

Gussie agreed it was the best policy. "And he did back us,"
Vogel said later. "In something like that, he had guts."

A meeting was finally arranged between Sinatra and Gussie
on the West Coast. The two men sat down at a restaurant.
Gussie wanted to know the format for an upcoming show, and
Frank said, "I'll sing it for you." "And he goes in to 'Chicago.'

He sang it for Gussie," Chesley said. "Then he sang another song, and another and Gussie said, 'Oh, this is fabulous.' "

Sinatra eventually landed an Anheuser-Busch distributorship in Long Beach, California.

The use of television advertising in shows like Sinatra's fueled Anheuser-Busch's meteoric rise. Beer advertising and television grew up together in the early 1950s. Jackie Gleason, Milton Berle and Budweiser. Anheuser-Busch and other brewers were the earliest supporters of the new technology. In 1951, although it ranked eleventh nationally in point of sales, the beer industry was number eight in money spent on television advertising. And while the average national advertiser put only 3 percent of his budget into television, the brewers poured 8 percent of their national advertising dollars into TV commercials. In the 1950s, these messages were as bland as flat beer. But television helped make beer a national business and dictated the demise of smaller, regional breweries.

Gussie understood how television sold beer. But there was yet another hallmark of his reign. He knew the importance of emphasizing quality. His commercial messages about quality had the ring of truth because Gussie so clearly believed in it. That message had been drummed into him from childhood. Prince Adolphus had preached it to his son, and Gussie still remembered how his father, August A., had resisted efforts to change the taste of Budweiser immediately following repeal.

Gussie had had to fight a similar battle when in the late 1960s Schlitz made its cost-cutting move. No quarter was asked or given. Gussie showed a film to his distributors in which a bum off the street entered a Schlitz brewery, threw filthy rags into a brewing vat and said, "That ought to give it some gusto." When Schlitz crept to within five percentage points of Anheuser-Busch, pressure began to mount on Gussie to cut costs by shortening the brewing time for Budweiser and Busch. He refused.

Frank Sellinger, an Anheuser-Busch vice president, suggested using corn instead of more expensive brewer's rice and to discontinue the beechwood-aging process. No way, Gussie roared.

In many breweries the sales departments dictated when beer left the plant. If demand went up, the beer storage time was shortened. But at Anheuser-Busch, the brewing division determined when the beer was sold. Gussie and his brewmaster, Frank Schwaiger, saved Anheuser-Busch, Ed Vogel believed, by firmly resisting efforts to shorten the time it took to brew beer. "You can say what you want to about Gussie Busch. He was a wild man and all that, but he stuck with Frank Schwaiger when the stockholders, his whole goddamned family and everybody else wanted him to make beer like everybody else. He knew quality. He knew that in the long run, and he took a lot of heat—Pabst, Schlitz, Rupert—were making beer the shortcut way. He was getting heat from stockholders, bankers and his family."

Gussie put "an iron curtain" around Schwaiger to protect him. No one was allowed to interfere with the brewing process. Schwaiger designed the new breweries the company built so that they could make beer only one way. The point was significant. While other breweries used engineers to design their new plants, Anheuser-Busch turned the job over to its chief alchemist, the brewmaster.

Almost at the same time, Gussie was under tremendous pressure to keep building new plants to expand capacity. But after building half a dozen breweries, he had become too cautious, some thought. He was reluctant to borrow more money, they argued.

Before he resigned, Vogel had been one of those pushing Gussie to build bigger breweries. He raised the subject again during a trip to St. Petersburg. He and Gussie were driving to Al Lang Field to watch the Cardinals, and all the while Vogel pressed his point. He talked debt-to-equity ratios and how they could justify borrowing more money. Gussie remained unconvinced. In a passion, Vogel finally blurted out, "Don't you think Anheuser-Busch is bigger than you are, Mr. Busch?"

Gussie ordered the car stopped. He was livid. He glared back at Vogel. "The answer to your question, you son of a bitch, is no! And don't you ever forget it."

58

Honeybee

When Gussie's final child, Christina, was born in 1966, Gussie called her "the last of the Mohicans." He was sixty-seven and his daughter was very special to him, perhaps because he realized he might not have much time left to spend with her. He called her his little honeybee. Gussie and Trudy now had seven children. The first, a son named Adolphus August Busch, had been born in July 1953 when Trudy was twenty-six and Gussie fifty-four. Others rapidly followed: Beatrice on July 5, 1954; Peter on December 5, 1955; Gertrude on July 6, 1957; William on August 22, 1959; Andrew on February 8, 1963; and then finally Christina on April 25, 1966.

Gussie was still having children eighteen years after he became a grandfather for the first time. All together, he had eleven children by three wives and liked to compare his fathering abilities with his grandfather Prince Adolphus, and his great-grandfather Ulrich. "My great-grandfather had twenty-one children and my grandfather had fourteen. Or was it fifteen?"

Christina was clearly the most special. "Her baptism was a big, big deal," said a family friend. "Gussie realized that it was the last. It was like the coming-out party for a princess. She was his youngest, his last child and he loved her. She was always in his lap, or he was walking around holding her hand."

Much of the child-rearing duties fell to Yolanda Gloggner, whose family knew Trudy's in Switzerland, and who came to the United States to take care of Gussie's growing brood. The Busch children grew up at Grant's Farm. Beatrice called it a fairyland. Among their toys was a storybook playhouse complete with a wood-burning fireplace. Beatrice recalled her father's impulsiveness. "One day he brought home twelve parrots to our beach house in Florida."

Their world was carefully protected. Fearing kidnappings,

Gussie made sure security at Grant's Farm was tight. Some of the men who worked there were off-duty police officers. The children were taken to school by chauffeurs, and when they traveled any distance, they were accompanied by Yolanda. Often there were long stretches when either their mother or father, and sometimes both, were not present. But in their absence, no one in the household let down his guard.

"I was struck by the separateness of the family from the world around them," said a public relations executive who dealt with the Busches. "The children were being ministered to by nannies, servants, helpers, women who traveled with them. In particular there was one woman . . . who was very muscular. She served not only as a nursemaid, nanny, but also as a bodyguard. . . . She never took her eyes off the young man I now believe was Peter. Whenever he asked for something she got up and got it for him—a sandwich, a soda, whatever, and I was struck by the sense . . . that he was sort of like a young lion and was very conscious of his own inherited power."

The executive found it sad that the children, who were "part of a family with considerable history of influence in America," a family that got "large numbers of people to drink large amounts of beer," could be so "terribly separate. And I think that's probably true of wealthy, powerful business people in general—that people at that level are in fact separate from the rest of the world. They protect the guy from a very early age and if the shit hits the fan they really have precious little to understand the feelings of those outside of themselves."

Gussie's daughters blossomed into women with their mother's beauty, and he was still able to escort them to debutante balls fifty years after attending his first. Gussie's sons grew up to be handsome young men. But because of his age, he was not able to play with them. He had slowed considerably. A disk operation forced him to wear a corset, and he had to watch his movements to guard against reinjury.

Gussie monitored the development of his sons and daughters, and, like other fathers, criticized such things as the length of his boys' hair if he thought it too long. But he sometimes had difficulty remembering the order in which his children were born. When that happened, he turned to his secretary, Margaret Snyder, for help. "Adolphus is the oldest, by this marriage, he's sixteen," he once said. "Beaty, her real name is Beatrice, is second. Who's the third one, Margaret? Peter, yes. Then Billy. No, Trudy, then Billy. Oh, there are eleven all told and how many grandchildren, Margaret? I've got to have help to keep track of them."

Gussie's three sets of children were not close to one another. A gulf separated them and at times there were arguments—especially between August and Gussie's children by Trudy. Acquaintances and friends quickly learned the differences among the various factions of the family. Gussie and Trudy's children had "a strict loyalty to themselves."

Two of them—Beatrice and Gertrude—were belles of the St. Louis balls. Beatrice was a special maid at the Veiled Prophet Ball of 1972; five years later, her sister Gertrude was named queen. The Veiled Prophet Ball was the St. Louis society event of the year and its Queen of Love and Beauty was invariably a member of one of the city's richest and most influential families. Gertrude seemed almost embarrassed by the event. "My parents really wanted me to do it."

The real queen of Gussie's life, however, was Christina, his youngest daughter. A blue-eyed blonde, she was treated like a china doll by her brothers and sisters. Gussie spoiled her. If he had survived a lot in his life—the death of a wife, his father's suicide, an ugly divorce—none of it compared with the event that took place December 6, 1974.

It was the feast of St. Nicholas, a big day in the Busch household. Trudy had hired someone to play Santa Claus, and was waiting at Grant's Farm for Christina and her brother Andrew to arrive from school. The gifts were all wrapped and waiting. Then the telephone call came. There had been an accident.

Eight vehicles had slammed together on Interstate 44. The pileup began when a tire blew on a tractor-trailer truck. Out of control, the huge rig crashed head-on into a Volkswagen van carrying eight-year-old Christina and eleven-year-old Andrew. The family chauffeur, Nathaniel Mayes, was killed instantly. Andrew survived, but Christina suffered brain damage and internal injuries. She did not regain consciousness.

At St. John's Mercy Hospital, the sisters let the Busches use the first floor of their convent as a command post. Extra telephone lines were installed, and people stayed there overnight. The vigil lasted eleven days. Relatives flew in. Gussie and Trudy conferred constantly with specialists—all to no avail. Christina died December 17.

After she learned of her daughter's death, Trudy went riding

for two hours. She had done this before in moments of crisis.
Gussie, unable to mount a horse for years, had no similar release. The child's death crushed him. Friends said the tragedy
sent him into depths of grief from which he never recovered.
He doubled over at the news and couldn't stop crying.

Sisters of Mercy spent the night praying for the child. Cardinal John Carberry said the funeral Mass in the great hall at
Grant's Farm the following day. Christina was buried at Sunset Cemetery near the grave of Gussie's first wife, Marie, and
his father, August A. Every year thereafter, a Benedictine monk
said a special Mass in her memory at a family gathering at a
retreat house on the Mississippi River, where the chapel is
named after the little girl. Trudy later called her chalet high
in the Eigenthal near Lucerne Chalet Christina.

After his daughter's death, Gussie became a Catholic. "I
think it . . . really moved him to consider questions of eternal
life and being with her," said Monsignor Jerome Wilkerson,
who participated in his baptism.

Christina's death changed Gussie's personality. The power,
the spark, the vibrancy were gone. He often acted as though
there was nothing else to live for. "When his daughter was
killed that's what broke his heart," said Al Fleishman. "He was
never the same after that. He aged quickly. . . . He lost a little
of his zest for life."

59

"Papa Is Out!"

It wasn't unusual for Brother John Woulfe to get telephone
calls from Peter Busch. He liked to think of himself as a friend
of young Peter's, one of Gussie's brood of children by Trudy.
Woulfe, stocky and friendly, was a member of the Brothers of

Mary, a Catholic religious order. He had been Peter's high school guidance counselor. On this particular day in May 1975, Peter wanted to talk to him about Gussie and about his half-brother, August. Woulfe could tell that the boy was badly upset. He never forgot Peter's first few words: "August has stabbed my father in the back."

What had happened at the brewery still wasn't public knowledge, but it was a bombshell. August had finally forced Gussie out. He was now the new chief executive officer. The board, for so long Gussie's compliant gang of yes men, had supported the son in ousting his father. Planned for years, the deed had been done. Gussie was raging.

He had found out about the coup only the night before it occurred, friends said. It couldn't have come at a worse moment. Gussie still hadn't got over the loss of Christina. Her death continued to torment his days and nights. The fire that drove him had been partly extinguished. He had long since been losing his grip on his business, and after Christina's death the pattern accelerated. His mind wandered. Garrulous in his prime, he now began to ramble; business discussions took embarrassing turns when he veered off the subject; meetings that should have lasted minutes dragged on for an hour or more. When he found out that the board and August planned to force him out, he was unable to focus or respond effectively.

Gussie had been deposed. There was nothing he could do about it, and his rantings were terrible. "He reminded me of Peter O'Toole in *The Lion in Winter*," said a family friend. "He was raging at his fate, raging against the traitors. It went on for months, the anger and the fury. It was like a medieval drama. He was the raging king."

August had had no trouble convincing the board of directors that it was time for a change. The company's profits were slipping; they were under pressure from competitors and Gussie was seventy-six years old and fading. August offered a dynamic plan for the future. He had a young staff; he had the will to succeed. No one doubted that his moment had finally arrived. It was also, some said, payback time. Whatever resentments board members may have harbored over Gussie's roughshod manner of dealing with them bubbled to the surface. August had lobbied them assiduously. His second cousin, James Orthwein, the president of D'Arcy Advertising and a board member, was a key man in the coup. August needed him badly. "Jimmy Orthwein was pivotal," recalled one executive. "The

story was that August agreed he'd never fire D'Arcy" in exchange for his vote. Orthwein's sons, James Orthwein, Jr., and
Percy Orthwein III, later acquired a lucrative beer distributorship in the Miami area.

Another important board member in the shakeup was Wal-
lace "Buck" Persons, the acerbic president of Emerson Electric
Company. Tall and lean with the ramrod erectness of a military officer, Persons took the lead in convincing the board that
Gussie had to go. When they finally met behind closed doors,
the showdown was fiery.

"I thought you were my friend," Gussie shouted to Persons.

"I am your friend," Persons answered. "That's why I'm telling you it's time to go."

Gussie's inability to deal with the competition from Miller
was cited as one reason for his removal. August, it was said,
"was able to show the board in very concrete, black and white
terms how Miller was a serious threat. His father would not
recognize it. There was only a window of time within which to
deal with Miller. There was no way August could take over in
time if he had waited his father out. Through a very orderly
presentation he was able to show how his father's time was
passed." David Callahan, a former district manager for Anheuser-Busch, said August had little choice in removing Gussie
from control. "He saw that his father was letting the company
slip away. . . . The old man wasn't looking to the future. He
wasn't prepared to see what was right around the corner. He
either had to catch the train or get off the platform. August
somehow manipulated him aside and took over the operation."

Substantial pressure was applied. Gussie reportedly was
told that if he didn't step down, he would lose control of his
favorite diversion, the Cardinals. "They wanted him to sign a
torch-is-passed statement," said a friend. "If he signed it, he'd
get the Cardinals. If he didn't sign it, he wouldn't get the Cardinals." It was also suggested that threats were made to disclose the murky circumstances surrounding Gussie's huge
divorce settlement with his second wife, Elizabeth. "The old
man got an awful pushing around by the threat to go public
[with the settlement] if he didn't get out," said Robert Lewis.

Another version was offered by Ed Vogel. "They did threaten
Gussie, but it wasn't over the loss of the Cardinals. They got a
lot of people on the board and others in the company . . . to
sign a petition that unless the board agreed to kick the old man
out, they'd resign in a body. That was the threat."

August had learned his lessons well, observed one family member. "Young August used the same tactics on his father that Gussie had used for years. . . . He went to every member of the board and used the same power play, telling them that if you want to continue doing business with the brewery, you'll vote for me against my father. It worked wonderfully."

Not long after the final vote, Lewis was playing golf at a private country club. He was interrupted on the eighth hole when a messenger said an important call was waiting for him in the clubhouse. Thinking it was union business, Lewis hurried back. When he picked up the telephone, it was August's secretary. A few moments later, August himself came on the line. The two men had clashed sharply over the years, but there had been a thawing in their relations after August became president. "Robert, papa is out—o-u-t!" August told him. "I'm the chief executive now."

Some family members were angered by Gussie's ouster. Trudy was livid. She believed Gussie should have stayed in charge until his death. Adolphus, Gussie's oldest son by Trudy, had a stormy meeting with August. It occurred at the border between August's estate and Gussie's Shooting Grounds, where Adolphus was living. A quiet, serious-minded young man, Adolphus had briefly tried to work for Anheuser-Busch, but the experiment hadn't turned out well. Bitter words were exchanged. "Adolphus and August had a falling out," said a friend. "They had many nasty confrontations after Gussie was forced out."

Family members like Lotsie, Gussie's daughter by his first marriage, reserved the full heat of their anger for the board. She said their action was cowardly and without justification. Others were inclined to agree. Robert Baskowitz, Jr., a friend of Gussie's and the son of his principal bottle supplier, said the old man had made some enemies on the board. "He had made the mistake of hurting a few people . . . and they found a chance to get him. I just think Gussie should have been allowed to bow out with dignity. . . . There was no need to bludgeon him out of there."

Forced to give up control of the company, Gussie was also stripped of some of the expensive perquisites that went with the job. He had grown to love these trappings, which he regarded as his personal possessions. Their loss only made his anger more explosive. "The yacht, the *A & Eagle,* was a bone of contention between Gussie and the board and August," said a former executive. "August decided the company would keep the yacht, but that it would be used only for corporate promotions. That really pissed off Gussie. He always looked at it as his boat."

This same executive had been involved earlier in another sore subject between Gussie and August—Busch Gardens in Tampa. "Before we cleaned it up, it was sort of a playground for Gussie and his entourage. It was notorious for all the beautiful women on the staff who entertained the gentlemen who came down there on their vacations." Like the rest of August's men, he wasn't sorry to see Gussie leave. "The public perception is that Gussie is a good guy and that August is a son of a bitch. My view is the reverse of that. . . . Gussie was one of the most ruthless, immoral, terrible despots who ever lived."

In addition to being told he couldn't use the *A & Eagle* and other corporate yachts as his personal playthings, Gussie was denied permission to use the boat house in Passe-a-Grille or the corporate airplanes. Gone were the days when he or Trudy could hop on a company plane. With Gussie out, they suffered the indignity of flying commercial. Trudy had to make her own arrangements when she wanted to fly to Milwaukee for the funeral of a friend, recalled Vogel. "She couldn't use the Busch plane because of August's edict."

After the coup, August was scrupulous in not using company property for his private pleasure, a concept totally alien to Gussie. John Dowling, the captain of the *Miss Budweiser*, said that on those infrequent occasions when August went out on the boat, he wrote in the log that he was to be billed personally for its use.

Little of the intrigue and plotting that surrounded the coup was ever reported. On the surface the public perception was that Gussie had graciously yielded the top job to his son, who would carry on in the fine tradition of Anheuser-Busch. At a shareholder meeting the following spring in Williamsburg, Virginia, the site of a new brewery and a theme park, August took pains to speak of his father in glowing terms. "Since relinquishing the position of chief executive, Mr. Busch Jr., has received a great deal of richly deserved recognition for his many achievements. He continues to serve as board chairman."

He was a board chairman without portfolio who plotted his revenge. In the months after his fall, Gussie began to think the unthinkable. What if he sold out? It was heresy even to consider it, but Gussie did more than merely ponder the unsettling thought. He owned 14 percent of Anheuser-Busch stock and had voting rights on a huge block of shares; August owned less than 1 percent. Gussie's lawyer, Lou Susman, was in the thick of these proceedings, recalled Vogel. "They had an offer from R. J. Reynolds to buy the company. R.J. offered Gussie $34 a share, but he wanted $38. Susman was for the deal and R. J. Reynolds wanted to buy. Paul Sticht, the CEO for Reynolds, negotiated with Susman. . . . They should have paid him what he wanted. Gussie was definitely tempted."

The secret talks between Sticht and Gussie took place at Gussie's shooting lodge in St. Peters. A few close friends of the family were aware of the possible deal. "They had every member of the family there to discuss it, but it fell apart. That's how serious it was."

Under August a new era had begun at the brewery, and he wasted little time removing most of Gussie's lieutenants. "The kid disliked anyone who was close to his father," Vogel said matter-of-factly. "With a few exceptions, he got rid of all of them." One of the casualties was Al Fleishman, for nearly thirty years Gussie's spokesman and confidant. Fleishman's public relations firm, Fleishman-Hillard, was hugely dependent on the Anheuser-Busch account. Fleishman, heavyset and slow moving, looked like an avuncular, slightly disheveled academic. Well connected and shrewd, he had managed to stay in his fickle boss's good graces and was largely responsible for the public image of Gussie as a benevolent merchant prince, charmingly crusty, but basically generous and warmhearted. Fleishman had saved Gussie from numerous gaffes. He sanitized Gussie and made him fit for public consumption. But now that he was out, it became apparent that Fleishman would have to depart as well. August didn't like him. "Fleishman-Hillard only kept the account because Al disassociated himself from the company."

Secretive and mistrustful of reporters, August filtered every public pronouncement through Fleishman-Hillard. Curt "no comments" became the rule. August and his executives rarely granted interviews. If a new product was introduced, FH handled it. The company also took on the family tragedies and scandals. One newspaper columnist waggishly began calling the PR firm "The Great Satan."

In 1977, two years after Gussie's departure, August was

elected chairman of the board. His father, then seventy-eight, was named honorary chairman. It was perhaps symbolic that August did not move into Gussie's grand two-room suite with its towering walls and portraits of glowering ancestors. He chose a smaller, more functional office. He was thirty-eight when he deposed his father, and he was about to face the greatest challenge of his career—a disastrous strike and a frontal assault by the Miller Brewing Company, which would largely change the beer business.

August started off on the run, setting a blistering pace and rallying his troops to follow his example. He had won the war with his father and was ready to do battle with the unions and Miller. Reacquiring his old habit, he flew to work every morning in a Bell Ranger helicopter, usually landing by seven o'clock on the roof of his corporate headquarters. The chopper became the unofficial clock for his executive corps. If it was already on the roof when you arrived for work, you were late.

As a role model, August was daunting. David Callahan, the former district manager, met him only a few times during his career. But that was a few times too many as far as Callahan was concerned. "I was always just careful to stay the hell out of his way," he said. Callahan recalled how he and fellow executives would prepare white papers for August. "He always asked more questions than you thought. . . . The guy's mind is a steel trap. He is very, very together, very much a Type A behavior. The kind of guy who loves to work twenty hours per day, seven days a week. He thrives on it. The challenge is to be smarter than anyone else in the industry."

As had happened repeatedly in the brewery's history, a new leader had presented himself at a crucial hour. August was sensitive to criticism that he was running the company because he was a Busch and not because he was the best man. "For people who inherit their jobs, it's a burden," said Walter Armbruster, an advertising executive who worked closely with August. "You're never sure whether you deserve the job or not. . . . August had grown up with the business. He had heard about the history and the heritage from his earliest years. . . . It was more than just a business. It was a personal responsibility, almost a sacred trust."

Only once did Armbruster see August's anger flame out over what he perceived to be an imputation that he wasn't fit for the throne. "He must have taken something the wrong way and he exploded. He said something to the effect, 'I'm good enough to run this company. I deserve it.' "

60

"*Have One for the Ditch!*"

History is rarely kind to dethroned kings. If fortunate enough to survive with their heads intact, they suffer in the shadows. Soon forgotten, they vanish from view only to be resurrected, for good or evil memory, in death when biographers write about them. So it was with Edward, Duke of Windsor, who lived out his long life as a roving dinner guest. So it was for Henry VI, Louis XVIII, Napoleon, and Kaiser Wilhelm. Gussie Busch was more fortunate. After the palace coup that drove him from the kingdom of Anheuser-Busch, he still had the Cardinals.

Gussie's long reign as the king of beer may have ended, but the Cardinals kept his name ablaze in lights. There would be more angry exchanges with his players and the commissioner of baseball, more pennants and more occasions to mount a beer wagon behind a team of Clydesdales for a triumphal ride around Busch Stadium. If in extreme old age he was almost strapped in place like the dead El Cid tied to the saddle of his horse, it hardly mattered. Gussie Busch had become a legend.

After his forced departure from the brewery, he was allowed to keep his favorite distraction—a consolation prize from August. "Busch ran the ballclub," said sportswriter Bob Broeg, "like his personal toy, given virtual autonomy by son August." No one at the brewery doubted for a moment, however, that August was in the driver's seat. This became clear later during the relentless attempt to remove Bowie Kuhn as baseball commissioner. Gussie may have slammed his cane on the table and shouted four-letter expletives, but the commissioner admitted that the shadow of "Young August" and the advertising clout of the brewery darkened almost every exchange.

Although the rancor between father and son was muted by Gussie's retention of the Cardinals presidency, baseball matters still precipitated explosions. It didn't take much to set Gussie off, as Bob Lewis discovered when Gussie invited him to Grant's Farm. Gussie respected Lewis for his hardboiled negotiating skills. The union leader was shocked to find out that Gussie wanted him to help the team negotiate with the Major League Players Association and its aggressive president, Marvin Miller. During the meeting at the Big House, Gussie's anger with his son spilled out. He called him a "son of a bitch," Lewis said. "I swear to you. That's what he said." Gussie told him that August had taken to calling him "Junior."

Such outbursts never made it into print. As far as the baseball-loving St. Louis public was concerned, Gussie still had the Cardinals so all was well. With the elder Busch so readily identified with the team, it was widely assumed that he was the owner. "You always hear that," said Ed Vogel. "The fact is, the brewery owned the Cardinals."

The myth of Gussie's ownership was similar to the popular belief, Vogel went on, that Gussie was quick to dig deep for a worthy cause. "My God, there's hardly been anyone alive to match him . . . the private railroad car, the private airplanes, the private boats. He was a modern baron."

Gussie's reluctance to open his wallet became apparent not long after his ouster from the brewery when he tried to purchase the Cardinals. It was a lackluster attempt at best, and it introduced to the stage a lawyer who would play an increasingly important role in Gussie's life—Louis B. Susman. Shrewd, tough, well connected and persuasive, Lou Susman would variously come to be called "the Cardinal Richelieu of baseball," a threat to baseball and Gussie's "Luca Brassi," the Godfather's bull-necked enforcer. "Mess with Gussie," one columnist said, "Lou could make you sleep with the fishes."

Susman had long been active in Democratic politics as a fund-raiser. Tall with guarded blue eyes, he was one of those "magical characters in Savile Row suits and manicured nails, people whose tracks led unerringly to money." A "rainmaker" who rarely saw the inside of a courtroom, Susman was a friend of Senator Edward Kennedy's, who was a tennis partner during visits to St. Louis. He raised money for such Democratic luminaries as Walter Mondale, Hubert Humphrey and Richard Gephardt, whose congressional district in St. Louis included the brewery. He also raised campaign funds for another friend, Thomas Eagleton. After leaving the Senate, Eagleton went to work for Susman's silk-stocking law firm. It was through "Senator Tom," some believed, that Susman made his important connection with Gussie.

Susman was soon serving as Gussie's principal legal adviser.

He represented him during the time he was considering a proxy fight to retain control of the brewery and was involved in Gussie's aborted discussions over a proposed sale of his shares to R. J. Reynolds. He also helped Gussie hang on to his presidency of the Cardinals. As a reward Gussie named him to the team's board of directors. Susman became the club's principal contract negotiator and was Gussie's point man in his efforts to fire Bowie Kuhn. "I loved Gussie," Susman said, "like a father."

Late in 1975, the year he was removed as head of Anheuser-Busch, Gussie made a stab at buying the Cardinals. A public relations spokesman for Anheuser-Busch declared: "Gussie Busch loves to be in the limelight. Since he left the brewery, he needs something to be in charge of, have an organization to run, trade players when he wants." The brewery agreed to negotiate the sale, but it wanted an independent appraiser to determine the value of the team. When the price came in—$11 million to $13 million—that ended the discussions. Gussie balked at the price. It was far cheaper to keep the title and the perks.

Gussie remained as the team's chairman of the board and president. More a figurehead than an owner, he still got a kick out of running the Cardinals even if he had to do it with August's advice and consent. In fact, he had become highly knowledgeable about the business of baseball. And what he saw happening in the sport began to bother him more and more. In 1976, the same year he balked at buying the team, Gussie clashed sharply once again with Marvin Miller, the head of the Baseball Players' Association. The two men began exchanging salvos from the moment the baseball owners locked the players out of their spring training camps in 1976 after negotiations failed for a new collective bargaining agreement. The lockout lasted three weeks before the camps were ordered reopened by Bowie Kuhn, a decision that marked the beginning of Gussie's festering displeasure with the commissioner.

When an agreement was finally reached around midseason, he said the owners had been "kicked in the teeth. . . . If anyone does not believe that we had our ass kicked in this labor matter, they are dead wrong." The owners had been "jackasses" for agreeing to proceed with the season without a signed contract with the players. "We have lost the war and the only question is can we live with the surrender terms."

The 1970s were one long doldrum for the Cardinals. There

were no pennants and to Gussie's mind his high-priced players weren't putting out. By 1978 he was "getting damn mad" at their performance. His bluster didn't help. The Cardinals foundered to the sorry end of the decade. More managers came and went and so did the commissioner of baseball.

The turbulent career of the magisterial commissioner of professional baseball led some to compare Bowie Kuhn with the captain of the *Titanic*. And for Kuhn the shipwreck came when he collided with Gussie, Lou Susman and August, a formidable iceberg. The Busch-Kuhn feud was widely reported while it raged during much of the 1970s and into the 1980s, but it wasn't until the deposed commissioner brought out his book, *Hardball*, in 1987 that the collision was revealed in all its spicy detail.

During his fourteen years as commissioner, Kuhn had crossed swords repeatedly with Gussie, even though he admitted that he liked him, "for all his imperious and curmudgeonly ways." Gussie had blasted Kuhn for reopening the baseball camps after the 1976 lockout. That same year Kuhn fined the Cardinals $5,000 for some of Gussie's comments. "I suspect," Kuhn said, "that Busch had never been disciplined before in his long life."

There were more serious problems. In 1981 Kuhn refused to intervene with NBC and ABC to win advertising rights for Budweiser. He also had "foiled" a bid by the brewery to buy an ad package with fifty-two Yankee and Cardinal broadcasts on the ESPN cable network. These, he admitted, were his major problems with Gussie and August, a "hard, tough-minded little guy." There was no longer any question in his mind "that young Busch and the brewery interests were calling the shots in St. Louis." Then, too, there was the occasion Kuhn had complained about profanity during a meeting of major league owners. Gussie leaped to his feet and growled, "Listen, Commissioner, I'm an American citizen who fought for the freedom of speech, and I'll be damned if you or anybody else is going to change me."

Kuhn was reminded of a warning he had received many years earlier from Walter O'Malley, owner of the Los Angeles Dodgers. "Because Anheuser-Busch sponsored the local broadcasts of a majority of major-league clubs, he asserted their potential for mischief was enormous, given the leverage those substantial dollar commitments made possible," Kuhn wrote. Anheuser-Busch sponsored broadcasts of twenty-three of the twenty-four American-based major league teams. O'Malley bluntly told Kuhn, "Watch out for Anheuser-Busch; they have too much power."

Those words came back to haunt the commissioner as he tried to keep his job in the early 1980s in the face of Gussie's all-out push to unseat him. Gussie's hatchet man, as always, was Lou Susman. In his book, Kuhn reserved some of his sharpest bolts for the lawyer. He was later told that Susman wanted to be commissioner of baseball himself, which Kuhn regarded as "rather devastating news."

Kuhn had his supporters. A majority of club owners favored keeping him in office. There was so much bitterness in the air that Peter O'Malley, Walter's son and a Kuhn backer, removed Budweiser from Dodger Stadium in Los Angeles, replacing it with Miller High Life. In the end, however, Kuhn still got the axe. He needed a three-fourths majority of votes from the owners to win reelection in 1982. He fell two votes short in the National League. He had carried eighteen of the twenty-six clubs but had lost. Kuhn was told that after the decisive vote was taken, Gussie pounded the table with his cane, saying, "He should clean out his desk tomorrow!"

After Kuhn's departure, Gussie had the good luck to enjoy an abrupt turnaround in his team's fortunes. If the Cardinals were a bust in the 1970s, the 1980s were their decade. The team won three National League pennants, and in 1982, the year of the commissioner's ouster, they took the World Series. Much of the credit went to manager Whitey Herzog. White-haired, portly, and moon-faced, he became Cardinals manager in 1981. Herzog looked and talked like a good ol' boy from the country, but his cunning earned him his nickname—the White Rat.

Herzog and Gussie were soul mates from the start. Gussie gave him complete control to clean house and try to salvage a sinking franchise. They met often at Grant's Farm. Herzog brought sausage, Gussie supplied the beer and the bullshots. "The two," it was reported, "would talk baseball, drink beer, talk more baseball and drink more beer." One afternoon after a long pouring session, Herzog declined another of the bouillon and bourbon bullshots, saying he had to get back to the ballpark.

Gussie forced the final drink on his manager with the comment, "Have one for the ditch."

61

". . . They Can Buy a Life."

The Busches were sometimes compared with the Kennedys. It was a comparison both flattering and disturbing. The Busches had little taste for the Kennedys' dedication to public service. They brewed beer or sold it or played polo or trained animals. But both families were enormously rich, enormously self-centered and there was that same remarkable drive, that same unflagging élan. Both families, accustomed to winning, were "ruthlessly competitive," and both families—here the comparison turned sinister—were visited often by tragedy.

An undercurrent of violent death seemed to be entwined with the Busches' birthright. They were "almost cursed with it." Their estate at Grant's Farm had often been a scene of mourning. August A., Gussie's father, had shot himself there in 1934. Gussie's youngest child, Christina, had been laid out at the mansion after she was killed in a highway accident in 1974. Seven years earlier, in 1967, a fourteen-year-old friend of Gussie's son Adolphus died after a horse fell on him as he was riding on the estate. A trainer at Grant's Farm was crushed to death in 1933 when the rear gate of a horse trailer hit him.

Suicide, fatal accidents. And always bubbling beneath the surface was the family's long infatuation with firearms. Gunfire at Grant's Farm was hardly unusual. Gussie and his sons routinely thinned the herds that roamed the property, dispatching the animals with rifle shots. This practice occasionally became troublesome. When the Busches picked up their rifles, neighbors sometimes picked up their telephones. On one occasion, a woman complained to police about bullets whizzing dangerously close to her home.

A far more serious shooting incident at the estate—one of the worst tragedies in the family's history—involved Peter Busch, Gussie's second-oldest son by Trudy. When it came to guns, Peter could be scary. Growing up at Grant's Farm, he regularly carried a rifle, shotgun or pistol. He was a "cowboy" with firearms. "You have to understand that all of that group were raised with guns," said a family friend. "Peter adored guns. They have that shooting lodge near St. Peters and go hunting all the time. They drive around that place in that crazy Jeep shooting at tin cans." Peter's love for guns frightened his mother, who had seen her son walk around the Big House with a pistol in his hand. "I was always scared to death for the other children," she said. He had as many as ten guns in his bedroom, "an arsenal" of rifles, shotguns, "about six handguns" and a fully loaded AR-15 that his father had given him when he was fifteen or sixteen.

Gussie had also given the boy a snub-nosed .38-caliber Police Special when he was fourteen—his first handgun. Among other weapons, Peter owned a .45-caliber single-action Colt revolver and two .22-caliber Derringer pistols. He slept with a loaded pistol within easy reach on the nightstand next to his bed. He wasn't unique among Gussie's sons for his attachment to weapons. "All of us," said his brother Adolphus, "have guns close to us at all times."

Trudy knew that Peter enjoyed shooting pigeons off the roof of the Bauernhof with a shotgun, sometimes with his father as they toured the estate in a golf cart. He had permission to shoot only black pigeons, not the rarer white ones. Trudy was aware that some of the employees at Grant's Farm were "afraid of Peter." One of them, William Pike, was the manager of the property. Pike believed that Peter had a "fantasy for guns" and admitted he was afraid of being around the boy because he was "very careless" in handling them. Besides pigeons, Peter also shot sparrows, and in the evenings he shot at the rats that infested an animal feed shed. One day Pike heard Gussie shout, "Pete, be careful of that damn gun." Peter answered, "Yes, Dad," then shot "a pigeon or two on the Bauernhof roof."

The worry about Peter's love affair with guns became serious when he shot himself in the leg. He was practicing quick draws with his .45 revolver in a creekbed in the estate's Deer Park. The remote spot with its high banks served as Peter's private shooting range. He was seventeen. "I was by myself. And as I pulled the gun out of the holster, my finger slipped off of the hammer." The bullet tore through his calf. Peter made nine trips to the doctor to treat the wound and for a while hobbled about the farm with a cane. Trudy hoped that her son had "learned a lesson." She asked Gussie to tell Peter to be more careful. In the Busch household that was the father's responsibility, not the mother's.

Gussie had taught Peter how to fire a .410-gauge shotgun when his son was nine. He took pains with the lessons. It was part of the Busch ritual of manhood. Every male learned how to ride—and to shoot. Gussie himself had learned from his father. Gussie's oldest son, August III, was a superb marksman and had taught his own two sons to handle weapons. A dedicated and sophisticated collector, Gussie was proud of the firearms that were arrayed in the mansion's gun room. "I have plenty of guns, I'll tell you that."

The word "plenty" might have been an understatement. His collection numbered eighty-two rifles, shotguns and pistols, including a repeating shotgun named the Miss Budweiser and a gold-plated Winchester carbine with Gussie's signature engraved on top of the barrel.

Gussie was clearly ready for any shooting contingency. So was Peter. Asked once why he felt compelled to carry a loaded gun, he answered, "Well, we have always been brought up in the kind of atmosphere . . . where people had been giving my father threats about kidnappings and that sort of thing. . . . The other reason was . . . for any kind of wild dogs or coyotes."

Coyotes, admittedly, were a rarity in the densely urbanized environs of Grant's Farm. The fear of kidnappers and other threats was another matter. Everyone remembered that Adolphus "Dolph" Orthwein, August A.'s grandson, had been kidnapped as a boy. Gussie often told Trudy and his children at the dinner table that he had received threatening letters. Three days before Christina was killed, the FBI had discussed with Trudy a threat to kidnap the girl. Peter himself had been the subject of threats that were reported to his father by the FBI. While in his late teens, he was shown photographs of two men who allegedly had plotted to kidnap him. The family took these warnings seriously. They had their round-the-clock security guards, their kennel of dogs—and they had their guns.

By his twentieth year, Peter was another of Gussie's strapping sons. Just over six feet tall, he was sturdily built with dark blond to brown hair and blue eyes. He had attended several elementary schools before entering Chaminade, a Catholic high school for boys. Peter was not a good student. In college—he wouldn't graduate—his grades hovered between C + and D.

John Woulfe, the former Brother of Mary who was Peter's high school guidance counselor, recalled the troubles the boy had as a student. As a sophomore, Peter astounded Woulfe by announcing he wanted to drop out of school and join the Marine Corps. He said that his father would sign the necessary papers. Gussie exploded in anger when Woulfe called him. "What the hell's wrong with that kid?" Gussie asked. "Doesn't he know that he'll need an education?"

While still in high school, Peter had met David Leeker, a theology student at St. Louis University. David was a slender six foot three inches, quiet and thoughtful. He lived near Grant's Farm and was three years older than Peter. His parents, Doris and Elmer, owned the So-Good Potato Chip Company. They were not part of the Busches' social circle, but their son and Peter became good friends. Trudy Busch approved. Their relationship, she thought, was nicely balanced because Peter was "aggressive" and David more "passive." William, David's younger brother, had a different perspective. Peter, he believed, respected David because he wouldn't "yield to Peter's every wish as other friends did."

When David graduated from college, he went to work for his father. He continued to see Peter regularly, often spending the night at Grant's Farm in a sleeping bag in Peter's bedroom, sometimes after an evening sparring at karate. David's younger sister, Leslie, briefly dated Peter, who drove a silver-gray 1976 Pontiac Firebird equipped with a CB radio. His handle was Silver Bullet. Leslie recalled that Peter was prone to temper tantrums. One evening he got angry when she refused to ride in his car. "It was Peter being Peter. He was set in his ways."

He was also living in a household that was becoming increasingly strained as Gussie and Trudy's marriage began to break up. There was already talk of divorce, and David tried to help Peter cope with that prospect. "You've got to feel sorry for him," he said to his parents. "David told us you have to have compassion," said Doris Leeker. Peter has "been raised in a very strange home. His mother is never there and his father is different. . . . He screamed and yelled a lot at him. . . . He wasn't raised normally."

Leslie was also aware of the strange, often tense atmosphere at the Big House and how difficult it must have been for Peter and the other children. "It was as if they didn't have parents. They had people running the household. They had people who cooked for them. They had people who drove their cars. They had people who opened gates for them. It was so different from any other family. . . . Gussie seemed so out of touch with everything much less with his kids. . . . They just got anything they wanted."

Doris and Elmer Leeker worried about their son's friendship with Peter. There were aware of an argument between the two young men over David's girlfriend. She had gone to a party at Grant's Farm with David, but refused to leave with him, preferring to stay with Peter. "David was upset that Peter abused a friendship," said Doris Leeker. "Peter's justification was, 'Why would anyone want to be with you when they can have me? I'm a Busch.' "

More troubling was the Leekers' fear about Peter's fondness for guns. They knew he had accidentally shot himself. Their concern was heightened when David told them that on the same night his girlfriend had disappointed him, Peter had flourished a pistol. "He was waving it," Elmer Leeker said. "Somebody had taken the gun away from him." He was told that "Peter had one too many to drink." The story was denied by Peter and couldn't be proved.

What was proven, however, was that on Sunday, February 8, 1976, Peter and David went shooting at the Deer Park at Grant's Farm. They used a new pistol Peter had received a month earlier from an old family friend, Robert Baskowitz, Jr. The weapon was meant as a combined Christmas and graduation present for Peter, who had just finished high school and had enrolled, like David, at St. Louis University. It was a Colt .357-magnum Python blue-steel revolver with a four-inch barrel.

Peter had practiced with the Colt six or seven times, firing an estimated 500 rounds. On that Sunday he fired maybe fifty to 100 shots. David even tried a few rounds himself. A day later, on the evening of Monday, February 9, David drove his white and beige 1972 Mercury Montego to Grant's Farm. He arrived at 7:30 P.M. Half an hour later, he and Peter left in Peter's Firebird to pick up Yvonne Moorad, one of their friends. Vonnie Moorad, an attractive, twenty-year-old brunette, lived at B&B Farms, the Busches' horse farm. Before Peter pulled off the estate, he stopped near the gate. Knowing that it was against the law to take a loaded weapon off the property, he carefully laid his new .357-magnum behind a tree. With Vonnie and David in his car, he drove to a supermarket. David bought a six-pack of beer. For the next hour and a half or so, they cruised. "We weren't doing nothing," Peter said later. "It wasn't a very exciting night." Peter drank two beers; David, who didn't like beer, took only a few sips.

Shortly after ten o'clock, Peter returned to Grant's Farm, stopping to retrieve his pistol, After visiting with a horse trainer who lived in a trailer near the Big House, Peter and David drove Vonnie home. This time Peter took his pistol with him, wedged between the driver's seat and console. Peter and David were back at Grant's Farm soon after midnight. David was going to spend the night. Before turning in they played several hands of gin rummy in the kitchen. Peter laid the Colt on the table as they played cards.

At one o'clock in the morning, deciding to turn in, they ascended the long flight of stairs to Peter's second-floor bedroom, which was next to Gussie's. Peter placed the pistol on the double bed and changed into his pajamas. Then he took a sleeping bag out of a closet and laid it on the floor next to the bed for his friend. David, seated at the desk in the corner of the room, asked for a pillow. Peter, who had picked up the Colt from his bed and was carrying it, got a pillow from a linen closet and dropped it on the sleeping bag.

"Thanks for the pillow," David said. Holding his shirt, he was standing in front of a chest of drawers. He was looking straight at Peter.

"I was going to throw the .357 onto my bed," over his left shoulder, Peter said later. "And as I was coming up to throw it, the gun somehow discharged."

The sound exploded. One of the most powerful of handguns, the Colt roared in the tight confines of the bedroom. The slug smashed into the right side of David's face just above his lip. Traveling slightly upward, it destroyed his brain before embedding itself in his skull. David fell backward. Blood streamed from his mouth, nose and right ear, pooling on the carpet.

Peter froze and stared at his friend, who lay dead at his feet. Running to his brother Adolphus's bedroom, he screamed that he had just shot David. Adolphus, already awakened by the shot, hurried into the room with Peter. Gussie, who had also heard the weapon fire, was coming down the hallway to investigate. Peter's mother was not at home. For the past ten days, Trudy had been in Lucerne, Switzerland.

"Dad, don't come in here," Adolphus told him.

Gussie entered anyway. He checked David for a pulse. Not getting one, he told his sons to call the police and returned to his bedroom.

Peter telephoned St. Louis County Police at 1:05 A.M. and asked for Major William Owens, the chief of detectives. Peter knew Owens because he worked part-time as a security guard at Grant's Farm. Told that Owens was off duty—he would arrive later—Peter reported the shooting to the officer in charge. He tried to get a pulse from David. As his panic increased, he beat on his friend's chest five times and tried mouth-to-mouth resuscitation in an attempt to revive him.

The first squad car arrived at 1:12 A.M., followed five minutes later by a fire department ambulance. When paramedic Joseph Minnella entered the bedroom his first thought was that David had committed suicide. A strong odor of gunpowder lingered in the room. David had lost three to four pints of blood and was still bleeding badly. Minnella's partner, Michael Frank, wasn't able to get a pulse or heartbeat. Because David's body was warm and there was a slender chance that he might still be alive, he was taken to a hospital. He was pronounced dead at 1:45 A.M.

After the police and ambulance were summoned, other telephone calls began to ricochet from Grant's Farm. Adolphus telephoned Margaret Snyder, an Anheuser-Busch vice president. During Trudy's frequent absences, Gussie had come to rely more and more on the talents of the sixty-one-year-old widow. Dressing quickly, she called Lou Susman's home. Susman, Gussie's personal lawyer, was in Clearwater, Florida. His wife told Margaret that she would call one of his partners. Two lawyers from Susman's office, Richard Sheehan and Ronald Lurie, were dispatched to Grant's Farm.

Margaret arrived at the Big House at 1:30 and hurried to Gussie's bedroom, where she remained throughout the early morning. Gussie, who was later given a sedative, asked her to help Peter. There wasn't much she could do; he was crying in his father's bathroom.

Susman, reached in Florida, wasted little time in calling Al Fleishman, Gussie's longtime public relations man and confidant. Fleishman, then seventy-one, tried to explain that he had recently retired from the firm he helped establish—Fleishman-Hillard. Susman asked him to get out to Grant's Farm anyway. Leaving immediately, Fleishman met with Gussie, Margaret and Peter in Gussie's bedroom. The lawyers, Sheehan and Lurie, were also present.

Fleishman knew that reporters had already begun to gather outside the gate to Grant's Farm. That was trouble. "I said that there was going to be publicity and notoriety . . . because even if a deer was killed at Grant's Farm, that somehow made its way to the front pages of the paper." At about three o'clock Fleishman went down to face the press. It was to be, he said later, the worst experience of his life. Standing in the glare of television cameras, he explained what had happened.

It turned out that the story, as he presented it, "wasn't the right story." After he finished his statement, he got a taste of the controversy that would quickly surround the shooting. After the klieg lights were turned off, a television reporter ventured an opinion: "I guess you know nobody's going to believe this."

The Leekers didn't find out what had happened until well after Snyder, Susman, the lawyers, Fleishman, and even the news reporters. They were the last to be told. Sergeant McCrady, the detective handling the investigation, arrived at their comfortable two-story home with attorney Ron Lurie at 3:15 A.M. It was less than a mile from Grant's Farm. Elmer Leeker, a tall, husky man of fifty-two with graying hair, answered the bell. His wife, Doris, was still upstairs, as was their youngest son, Jason, who was sleeping in his bedroom. Two other children, William and Leslie, were at the University of Missouri. A third, Suzette, was married and living in St. Louis.

Elmer Leeker was surprised to see Lurie, who happened to be his lawyer. He didn't know yet that Lurie also was working for the Busches and that he would soon be told he needed to find another attorney. Lurie broke the news. There had been an accident. David was dead. Somehow Peter had shot him. They still didn't know how it had happened.

The words almost crushed Elmer Leeker. Joined by his wife, he was told their son's body had already been sent to the morgue. The lawyer and police sergeant left a short time later, promising to return when they had more information. The couple was advised not to discuss the incident with reporters. The Busches, they were instructed, "had already taken care of everything."

The family waited that morning for someone to call them and tell them what to do. They still didn't know where David's body was. "We kept wondering when the Busches would contact us," said Leslie, who had returned home from the University of Missouri with her brother Bill. Her sister, Suzette, was also there. "We kept thinking about that, that no one from their family had even called us. Later that afternoon, around three, my sister and I were fit to be tied. We decided we were going over there and try to get some answers."

Leslie and Suzette drove to Grant's Farm. Peter wasn't there. Accompanied by his lawyers, he and Adolphus had gone to police headquarters so that Peter could take a lie detector test. While they waited for him to return, the two sisters were ushered into the gun room. "It was incredible," Leslie recounted later. "All those heads of animals on the walls and guns, and that's where they decided to sit us."

Gussie came into the room. He told them what a "terrible tragedy" it was. Badly shaken, he kept repeating the phrase, mentioning that the last tragedy to occur in his family was when his daughter Christina was killed. He began to cry.

"Why didn't you call us?" Suzette asked, unmoved by the old man's tears. "Wasn't that simple courtesy?"

Still crying, Gussie didn't answer.

Peter returned. He had passed the lie detector examination. Police were convinced he was telling the truth when he said the shooting had been an accident.

"You have to come over to our house and face my father," Leslie told him angrily. "My God, what are you waiting for? You haven't even called us."

Peter agreed to go to their house. His lawyers and his brother Adolphus went with him. "We got back home," Leslie said, "and we went in and Dad and Mom were there. . . . Peter waited in the front hall with his two or three lawyers. He finally came into the room. He was just standing there, staring down. We were in the family room. His lawyer was right behind him."

"Forgive me," Peter told Mrs. Leeker.

"Peter, don't you know you never aim a loaded gun?" she asked.

Peter didn't answer.

"Why didn't you come get me?" Mrs. Leeker said. "Why didn't you call me?"

"They wouldn't let him," Adolphus said.

The awkward visit lasted ten or fifteen minutes. On the way out, Peter told Elmer Leeker, "David was my best friend."

He returned later that night, invited again by Leslie, who still wanted to try to understand what had happened. They drove to Grant's Farm and went for a walk around the lake. "I remember asking him what happened. He said it was an accident. At one point, he even held me and was crying on my shoulder. . . . Peter showed me how he threw the gun. I tried to get him to show me. It didn't make sense to me."

Peter insisted he didn't know how the gun could have fired. "I tried to explain it to her," he said later. "I don't know if she believed me or not."

Elmer Leeker finally saw his son. The body had been taken to an undertaker. Steeling himself to look at David's face, he noticed the small indentation over the lip where the bullet had entered. He noticed something else—his son's face was pock-marked with powder burns. He was shocked. He had been told that the gun had fired as Peter was placing it on his bed. He had been led to believe that the pistol was some distance from David when it went off. How could there be powder burns, he wondered. He called the coroner's office. "They said the gun was from two or four inches from his face," Leeker said. The news hit him like a hammer blow.

Leeker was determined to find out what had happened in Peter's bedroom. So were the police. Their investigation had already been criticized by the St. Louis County prosecuting attorney for discrepancies. The accuracy of some of Al Fleishman's comments to the press was being questioned. Everyone, it seemed, wanted to talk to Peter about how his gun had fired. The only exception was his father. Gussie never asked him about the shooting. "I never wanted to know."

The problem was that Peter had given several conflicting stories of what happened in the moments before his Colt went off in David's face. He originally said he had drawn the pistol from the waistband of his pajamas when it discharged. He later said he was carrying the pistol in his right hand and that, when he attempted to toss it on the bed, it went off. "He explained the difference," a police investigator said, "by stating he was upset and confused and at first it was hard to remember exactly what occurred."

Other discrepancies emerged. Fleishman had told reporters that the gun fired when Peter tossed the pillow on the sleeping bag. Police investigators determined, however, that the gunshot had occurred a few seconds later and had nothing to do with the pillow toss. Peter had told detectives that David was "within five feet or closer" when he was shot. The muzzle had actually been within a few inches of David's face.

Question were also raised about the propriety of Major William Owen's presence at the Big House on the morning of the shooting. Owens, a twenty-eight-year veteran of the St. Louis County police force, worked as a security guard at Grant's Farm, but his superiors said there was no conflict of interest. Owens had taken no active role in the investigation and as chief of detectives was required to be there. Besides, there wasn't anything unusual about police officers working for the Busches, who were considered "the largest single employer of off-duty policemen apart from shopping centers."

No one disputed that the shooting had been accidental. The question was whether Peter had been negligent and whether he should be charged with a crime in his friend's death. Courtney Goodman, Jr., the prosecuting attorney, made it clear he was dissatisfied with the early police investigation, which was clouded by unanswered questions. He ordered that all the witnesses be reinterviewed. The inquiry became one of the most exhaustive in St. Louis history. The lawyer handling the investigation for Goodman's office determined that "Peter's final version is significantly inconsistent with the earlier version. You simply don't get flustered and make a mistake about pulling [a gun] out of your waistband unless you're lying." The weapon had been pointed in David's face. There was a strong case for negligent manslaughter. Peter, according to assistant prosecuter Sam Bertolet, was "at least guilty of killing David Leeker without justification or excuse—manslaughter."

The case was presented to a grand jury, and in late March, Peter Busch was indicted for manslaughter—a felony. The indictment charged that he "unlawfully and feloniously handled a gun in such a manner as to show a reckless disregard for human life." On April 1, Peter returned from a trip to Florida and surrendered to police. Wearing a blue sweater and slacks, he calmly walked past a mob of reporters, ignoring their barrage of questions. Fingerprinted and booked, he was released on a $5,000 bond.

In the long interval between the shooting and Peter's appearance before a judge, Leslie Leeker met with Trudy at the Big House, in her "huge drawing room." Trudy had returned from Switzerland to attend a memorial service for David. They talked for over an hour. Trudy said that things might have turned out differently had she been in St. Louis. "Gussie had no control over the children," Leslie said. "Trudy knew that the boys did as they pleased. She was the only one in the family who was sympathetic. She was the only one who seemed sorry."

One other shock was in store for the Leekers. Police investigators had determined that David "apparently was homosexual or at least bisexual." Their report on the shooting added that "no information was found to indicate that Busch was homosexual." The Leekers were stunned, their dismay giving way to outrage. They were convinced their son wasn't gay. So were David's friends and acquaintances. And so was Peter. Questioned closely by police who wondered why he often slept in the same room with David, Peter denied that they had had a "homosexual affair." But he added that during a party at Grant's Farm "a man I know . . . who is a queer, took some sort of advantage of David because David was drunk."

David had mentioned the episode to his father. The man had propositioned him, nothing more, Elmer Leeker said of their conversation. "He thought it was a joke." As a matter of fact, the police had interviewed a young man in Chicago who admitted he had had "a sexual experience" with David, but that he didn't regard David as a homosexual. The allegations about David's homosexuality, which the Leekers regarded as a smear, later influenced their decision about whether to pursue a civil lawsuit against the Busches.

Peter's trial on manslaughter charges never occurred. On January 17, 1977, just over a year after the shooting, he pleaded guilty. His lawyer was Norman London, a prominent St. Louis criminal attorney. London and Lou Susman met with Goodman, the prosecuting attorney, to ask whether his office would "recommend suspended sentence or probation" if Peter pleaded guilty. Goodman refused.

Wearing a pinstriped suit, Peter faced Circuit Court Judge Harry J. Stussie and pleaded guilty. In a soft, low voice, he answered the judge's questions. Yes, he was changing his plea at his own request. Yes, he understood that he could face imprisonment. "I am very sorry," he said. "Dave and I were the best of friends. . . . I know now that I had to have my finger on the trigger because there was no other way of the pistol going off. . . . I was very careless in that regard."

Stussie gave Peter a suspended sentence and placed him on probation. A report prepared for the judge had recommended two years probation. Stussie increased it to five. He also added the provision that during that period Peter was "not to handle firearms of any kind."

Judge Stussie had occasion to intervene in Peter's life one more time. In January 1978, Peter was riding his father's championship horses and announced that his goal was to make the U.S. Olympic equestrian team. He had even been invited to take several of his jumpers to Europe that summer. As soon as he read an account of the proposed trip in the newspapers, Stussie fired off a strongly worded leter to Peter's probation officer. "I do not feel that it is proper for a person on probation for five years on a plea of guilty of manslaughter to be traveling around the country and to Europe when he apparently is unemployed."

Peter didn't go to Europe.

Peter Busch once summed up his "underlying philosophy" with the comment, "What comes around goes around." And what came around after he killed David Leeker was a happy marriage, four children and the eventual acquisition of an Anheuser-Busch beer distributorship in Florida. In May 1978, instead of going to Europe, he married a nurse. Setting up a new household in St. Louis was simple. A telephone call to Lou Susman sufficed. "He just told him he wanted to buy a certain house and Lou took care of it," a friend recalled. Hanging up, Peter remembered something else. He called a charter airline. He needed a Lear jet for a few days.

Peter dropped out of St. Louis University and managed Gussie's B&B stables. He later went to work for the brewery, starting as a bottler. He took a year-long management training program. Peter was serious and studied hard. After a stint in Stillwater, Oklahoma, he returned to corporate headquarters as a marketing manager. He liked the work, but wasn't optimistic about his prospects. His half-brother, August, stood squarely in his path. "He was very disappointed with how he was treated," said one family friend. "He was disappointed August III wasn't nicer and didn't include him" in the decision-making process. It was said that Peter knew that his rise would be blocked and that he had no chance of running the company.

He began casting about for other opportunities. His wait was short. John Woulfe was with him the day August III called. "He told him a distributorship was available in Florida." With the help of a bank loan—the decision to grant the money took forty-five minutes—Peter acquired Golden Eagle Distribution in Fort Pierce, Florida.

He moved there in 1984. By then he had three children. Against the wishes of his father, he named his first child David in memory of his dead friend. "Gussie was angry about that," recalled an acquaintance. "He was very adamant that Peter not do this, that every time he looked at his son he was going to remember what had happened. . . . Peter successfully stood up to his father on that one."

Peter admitted he had changed since the days he used to stroll around Grant's Farm carrying a loaded pistol. One of his greatest accomplishments since coming to Florida, he told a reporter, was becoming a Christian. He was also interested in helping abused children and advocating responsible drinking. A short profile in a Miami newspaper listed Peter's "Ambition": to play on the same polo team as his brothers "and compete on a good enough scale and every once in a while win one of them." The profile offered this "Quotation": "I can handle it."

The Leekers did not have an easy time learning to handle their grief. They were never satisfied with Peter's explanation of what had happened. In February 1978, they filed a $3 million lawsuit against Peter and his parents, claiming that Gussie and Trudy were negligent in letting Peter have a loaded weapon without proper supervision or training. In 1981 they were prompted to settle their lawsuit out of court for considerably less than $3 million—published reports indicated they received somewhat more than $150,000—partly out of fear that David's alleged homosexuality would become an issue had there been a trial. Afraid that their son would be slandered in death, they were also worn out by their long ordeal. They wanted to try to put it behind them. As the years passed that proved impossible.

The memory and the anger continued to fester. Elmer Leeker initially accepted Peter's version. But he was of a different mind years later. Now, he refuses to believe Peter's story about what happened. His youngest son, Jason, who had grown into a tall young man with a strong resemblance to his dead brother, found it difficult to live in St. Louis, where the Busch presence weighed so heavily. Jason recalled selecting the bouncing Anheuser-Busch theme song, which is played at every St. Louis Cardinals home game, for the subject of a college speech. "It has a different meaning for me. It's more of a stabbing, painful song."

It was the same with Leslie, who still had nightmares about her brother's death. Like her father, she was convinced that the law applied a different standard for the Busches, that if David had killed Peter he would have been quickly jailed. She clung to a single, unvarying belief: "The Busches own St. Louis and they can buy a life."

62

Divorce

In the wake of Christina's death and Peter's shooting of David Leeker, Gussie's marriage underwent severe strain. Trudy had grown tired of her husband's boorish habits such as whistling for her in public. Gussie had a way of putting two fingers to his lips and letting out with an ear-piercing blast to summon his wife. Trudy finally had had enough of it.

Their arguments became more frequent. It was as if Gussie looked for opportunities to start fights. Trudy nagged him to cut down on his drinking, but his binges seemed to last even longer. There was a story that he deliberately dropped a pair of her emerald earrings down the toilet, and then in front of the servants accused her of losing them. His second cousin, Helen Busch Conway, recalled a party in which Gussie had too much to drink. Trudy "got up and put on her wrap and went out because she didn't want him to drink anymore. He was drinking too much. She stood outside while he sat inside, drinking."

There were other embarrassing moments. During a trip to New York City for a horse show, Trudy wanted Gussie to take her to an expensive restaurant. She liked such outings; Gussie hated them. When Trudy ordered wine, Gussie responded explosively. "What the fuck do you want wine for? Get some Budweiser!" Trudy went ahead and ordered wine, "a damn good wine, as good as you can get," said Robert Baskowitz, Jr., a friend who was present. "Well, the waiters were going around pouring it into glasses. A Houston beer distributor was paying for the bash, not Gussie. The guy keeps pouring glass after glass for Gussie and he's pouring it on the fucking floor. . . . These are the things about Trudy that pissed him off about her. She liked restaurants; he didn't like restaurants. He didn't like to go out to eat. If it was business that was different. He could hit ten to fifteen bars if it was work. . . . He was jealous. She was a flirt and he could get awfully jealous."

Like Gussie's previous wives, Trudy received expensive gifts from men who did business with the brewery. One businessman gave her linens from an expensive shop on Fifth Avenue, a gift that he said cost him $11,000. Gussie was furious. "He was pissed at what I spent," the man said, "and now he's thinking that I've got something going on with Trudy. That kind of thing could scare the shit out of you."

Gussie also lavished gifts on his wife, but even that could backfire. Helen Busch Conway attended an anniversary celebration at Grant's Farm, where Gussie gave Trudy a choker of gold and jade. "Instead of taking it out of the box and putting it on, she threw it across the table to the wife of an architect who was attending the party."

During one of Trudy's frequent absences, Baskowitz and another friend, Bob "Piggy" Meyer, visited Grant's Farm with their wives. Gussie took them up to Trudy's room and opened several closet doors. "All those clothes racks. It was like Sears . . . no . . . like Saks," recalled Meyer. "Pick out whatever you like," Gussie told them. "The bitch won't miss the stuff. Go on, take a couple of dresses. Take anything you want. You want a couple pairs of shoes?"

Gussie grew to hate Trudy's long trips. He was seventy-five, his wife a young-looking forty-eight. He was afraid that she would remarry after he died. "He was worried that she would marry a nobleman and that his kids would not get their share of his estate," said a family friend. Related Al Fleishman: "It was a paranoia that fed on him. He was getting older and more irritable, and she was spending more time in Europe. He was a very domineering person, and by then she . . . didn't like him ordering her around. It wasn't that Gussie missed her, but his pride was hurt. That's all there was to it."

There were times when Trudy must have felt like a prisoner

at Grant's Farm. Gussie refused to let her go back to Switzerland for her brother's wedding. "The last two years were very bad," said her mother, Martina. "He would not let her go anywhere. She was like a slave."

In September of 1977, Trudy began living in the Cottage, the smaller mansion near the Big House at Grant's Farm, where Gussie's mother had lived before her death. Gussie continued living in "the castle." Unknown to anyone but their closest friends and relatives, the separation continued throughout the fall while quiet, behind-the-scenes negotiations took place to reach a reconciliation or settlement. The hope was to avoid an expensive divorce.

Proposals and counterproposals were exchanged. There were suggestions that Trudy live in the Big House "in the manner expected of the wife" for twenty-five years. Yolanda Gloggner, Trudy's companion and the children's governess, was to be allowed to live in the Bauernhof. Gussie offered to pay off a $75,000 loan Trudy had received from a St. Louis bank and cover up to $30,000 of her outstanding bills at Saks, Montaldo's, Cartier's and Nieman-Marcus.

One of the proposals suggested that Trudy be warned in advance whenever Gussie's secretary, Margaret Snyder, and his lawyer, Lou Susman, paid a visit: "It is known that the relationship between Gertrude Buholzer on the one hand and Margaret Snyder and the attorney for August Busch on the other is extremely strained and adverse. Therefore, if August Busch insists upon their presence from time to time at Grant's Farm, then August Busch shall notify Gertrude Buholzer in advance of their intended presence or the intended presence of either of them so that any unpleasant confrontations may be attempted to be avoided."

The negotiations focused on how much of Gussie's wealth Trudy could claim. In 1977, this amounted to $15 million from a 1932 trust, $8 million in Anheuser-Busch stock, $6 million in real estate and tangible personal property, $1 million in profit-sharing accounts and another $500,000 in cash. Late in the year, the negotiations collapsed, and Gussie and Trudy were headed for a divorce.

Helen Busch Conway learned of the impending breakup during a New Year's Eve party at Grant's Farm. She believed one of the reasons was Gussie's drinking. "He'd get crocked," Conway said. "He drank so much."

Their parents' estrangement became a bad dream for the

children. Some of them still lived with their father in the Big House while Trudy was in the Cottage. Gussie reportedly threatened to cut them from his will if they even saw their mother.

After twenty-six years of marriage, seventy-eight-year-old Gussie and his fifty-year-old wife agreed that their marriage was "irretrievably broken." Trudy asked for a lump sum settlement, alimony, all the property jointly held and custody of their fourteen-year-old son, Andy. Her lawyer, Paul Schramm, argued that Trudy was the victim of "harassment, abuse, intimidation, oppression, molestation and a disturbance of the peace." He charged it had "caused trauma" to their children's lives and got a judge to issue an order preventing Gussie from throwing Trudy off the property.

Lou Susman, Gussie's lawyer, requested that the entire case —the divorce and the custody question—be heard in juvenile court, which would have kept the proceedings secret. Trudy wanted the matter heard in open court.

The preliminaries had their lighter moments. A deputy sheriff named Minnie Mitgang took extraordinary measures to serve divorce papers on Gussie. She got past the security guards at the gate at Grant's Farm by hiding on the floor of Trudy's car. Once inside the grounds, she knocked on the front door of the Big House, brushed passed the butler and found Gussie, who was sitting in the dining room. As Minnie handed the startled brewer the divorce papers, she said, "We all love you." Gussie replied true to form. "Would you like a beer?" he asked, smiling.

His good humor did not last long. The divorce was bitter. Trudy remained a virtual prisoner at Grant's Farm. A guard checked the trunk of her car when she entered or left the grounds to make sure she wasn't taking any money or jewels. Gussie also prevented her brother, Kurt Buholzer, from visiting her at the Cottage. Buholzer had come from Switzerland to be with his sister. "I was horrified to understand when I came to the gate that my brother was not allowed in," Trudy said. "I need someone from my family to help me. I cannot understand. To me, refusing him entrance is just totally . . . it's diabolic." Gussie was in Florida where the Cardinals were in spring training and offered a familiar Busch answer: "I have no comment."

In January 1978 Gussie issued a written order to Trudy "to vacate the premises which you are currently occupying, commonly known as 'The Cottage.' No other living quarters will be available to you at Grant's Farm. At the time you move from the premises, please take only those personal items of clothing which you feel you will need immediately. I will make arrangements to have the balance of your personal clothing and effects delivered by appropriate means to the location you designate."

Gussie told Trudy she could "drive the white Lincoln pending the divorce," but was no longer entitled to the services of any of his employees. He fired her friend, Yolanda Gloggner. He also informed Trudy he had "advised all department stores, restaurants, airlines, etc. that I will no longer be responsible for any debts incurred by you, whether incurred in my name or your name, effective January 9, 1978."

The divorce was finally granted February 27, 1978. Trudy got joint custody of Andrew, a house in the St. Louis area and "a few million dollars" in alimony, cash, securities and other property. The settlement also called for the maintenance of two trusts in her behalf, one of which had been arranged in a premarital agreement. At first Trudy said she was satisfied, but she later filed a lawsuit seeking more than $25,000 in cash, a horse named Coffee Break, china, silver and riding equipment. She claimed that Gussie had broken the divorce settlement.

For twenty-six years, Trudy Busch, the former Swiss restaurant hostess, had lived like a queen with the king of beer. After the divorce, many of her old friends avoided her. There were places where she was no longer invited, people who no longer called. "That first year after the divorce," a friend said, "was a real revelation to her." But Trudy grew to enjoy her independence. She traveled to exotic places, riding horses along sunny beaches in Portugal, yaks in China and camels in Egypt. She divided her time between her homes in St. Louis and Switzerland. A portrait of Christina, a pretty girl in a yellow dress, hangs in her living room. A statue of the lost daughter stood in her Swiss chalet, a rustic cottage in the Eigenthal.

"Everybody has hard times in life and good times. This is a very good time in my life," Trudy once said. Her advice to her children: "Don't take yourself too seriously, be optimistic and cheerful, don't carry a chip on the shoulder—above all, don't rely on your name."

63

Beer Wars II

With Gussie removed from the captain's chair, August was confronted by two of the greatest crises of his career—an all-out attack by the rejuvenated Miller brewery and the worst strike in his company's history. Of the two, the encounter with his Milwaukee rival would have the greater repercussions. The Miller War, it was said, made August.

Miller, acquired in 1970 by the Philip Morris Company, had promptly turned the industry on its ear with a high-voltage marketing strategy and the introduction of the most significant new beer of the century—Miller Lite. The hugely successful brand was introduced in 1975, the same year August took command of Anheuser-Busch. Miller's gregarious president John Murphy had worked for Philip Morris and had made the switch from peddling cigarettes to beer without changing stride. "After all," he liked to say, "we're not in the brain surgery business." Red haired and mischievous, Murphy quickly proved adept at getting under August's wafer-thin skin. He had a rug embossed with the Anheuser-Busch eagle under his desk to wipe his feet. He also had a voodoo doll named August.

In what was likened to a Darwinian struggle, Anheuser-Busch and Miller fought each other with a blizzard of lawsuits, name calling and dirty tricks. Advertising budgets exploded. In the midst of an awkward change of regime, Anheuser-Busch had been caught flatfooted by the Miller challenge. August, who proved himself an able street fighter, set the tone when he addressed his employees and wholesalers, telling them, "There is little choice for either of us for we are at war." Workers took to wearing red T shirts emblazoned with the words "Miller Killers." Baseball caps and office stationery carried the acronym ASU, for "A Sense of Urgency." SWAT teams of young, eager salesmen were sent to work with wholesalers to drum up new accounts and hold on to old ones. To his arch-rival, August offered the challenge: "Tell Miller to come right along, but tell them to bring lots of money."

One of the opening shots in the beer wars was fired, fittingly, near Boston. This time the provocation was from the Joseph Schlitz Brewing Company, which piously announced it had dropped plans to build a new brewery on the Merrimack River near Merrimack, New Hampshire, because the water was much too polluted for its "fine, premium brews." Anheuser-Busch already had a brand-new plant on the Merrimack, and as soon as Schlitz made its announcement, Budweiser sales in Boston plunged 90 percent.

There was near panic in St. Louis. Everyone on Pestalozzi Street knew that their plant in New Hampshire got its water from crystal-clear wells, not from the river. The company counterattacked, chartering a fleet of buses and hauling scores of Boston beer drinkers from their favorite taverns to the Merrimack brewery, treating them to an afternoon of free beer. The tactic worked. Sales picked up in Boston.

It was much more difficult to deal with Miller and the runaway popularity of its new Lite brand. At first August denied there was a problem, or that his company even needed a light beer. "It's just a matter of time until Miller Lite falls on its face," he said. A half year later, with Lite sales still booming and Miller with a virtual corner on the hot new low-calorie market, August decided to get into the fray and fast. His brand originally was called Anheuser-Busch Natural Light Beer, a name that he admitted "was too damn long." It was quickly shortened to Natural Light.

Another salvo was fired soon after Anheuser-Busch entered the light beer sweepstakes. Miller filed a complaint with the Federal Trade Commission asking it to stop Anheuser-Busch from claiming that its beers—Budweiser, Michelob, Busch and Natural Light—were made solely from natural products. Miller argued that Anheuser-Busch used a chemical additive, tannic acid, in its formula. The cruelest cut of all, however, was the attack on Anheuser-Busch's cherished beechwood-aging process. Beechwood aging, Miller charged, was nothing more than "dumping chemically treated lumber" into the beer tanks.

"Sour grapes" from a company that couldn't use the same description for its own products, countered Anheuser-Busch. It gleefully added that Anheuser-Busch used no foam enhancers, preservatives, antioxidants or artificial flavorings, unlike other brewers it declined to name.

Losing round one with the FTC, Miller came out swinging at Michelob Light, another Anheuser-Busch entry into the less-is-more competition. It wasn't really a light beer at all, the brewery claimed. At 134 calories, a bottle of Michelob Light had only a few calories less than Budweiser. "We understand," Miller argued before the Bureau of Alcohol, Tobacco and Firearms, "that Anheuser-Busch produces Michelob Light simply by brewing a batch of regular Michelob and then diluting it with carbonated water." It cheekily added, "Although it has watered down its beer, Anheuser-Busch has not reduced the price."

Miller lost that round, too. Anheuser-Busch fared considerably better in the skirmishing, leveling its guns at Miller's Löwenbräu super-premium brand. Anheuser-Busch told the FTC that Miller was misleading consumers with its Löwenbräu ads. Although Löwenbräu was brewed in the United States, the ads implied that it was an imported beer brewed according to the original German formula. Not true, said Anheuser-Busch and the FTC largely agreed.

Perhaps in a fit of pique Miller applied for a trademark for a new beer. They were going to call it Gussie. Asked why, a Miller spokesman said, "I guess we're just not nice guys."

One of the more curious sidelights of the beer wars involved a persistent rumor that August and other Anheuser-Busch executives were adamantly antigun and had donated to various firearms control causes. It was a red herring, but "from hunting regions as far apart as the Rockies and the Upper Peninsula of Michigan, rod and gun clubs threw out the Budweiser and Busch."

Anheuser-Busch lost significant business, but was reluctant to confront the delicate problem publicly, said a former executive. "The irony was that, if anything, the Busch family was enraptured with guns. August was one of the top shooters around and loved to shoot . . . but they were afraid to promote that fact. If they ran around saying, 'No, you don't understand. We love guns!' they would have the entire antigun lobby on their ass. . . . There are a lot of gunners out there in America who drink beer. I mean that's a real connection in the demographic profile. Beer drinkers and hunters are frequently the same people. . . . The corporation's clear intent was to locate and prosecute anyone involved in that story. The attitude was if we can find the fuckers, we'll sue them, but they could never find anybody. . . . They were bothered by that problem, but they never went after it in a forceful way that showed, by God,

Budweiser supports shotgun people in America. August went out to his lodge more than one night and had his rocks off shooting clay pigeons, wishing somebody knew the real him. But no one ever did."

The Miller assault obsessed August. Sensitive that he would be compared unfavorably with his father and eager to carve out his own record, he drove his staff relentlessly. An inspirational leader, he whipped his troops into a war fervor. Sixty-, seventy-, eighty-hour work weeks became common during the mid- to late 1970s. Shredding notes and papers was routine practice. August worked harder than anyone. His helicopter was usually parked on the roof of his corporate headquarters shortly after dawn. He expected extraordinary effort from his senior executives. "The minute they're out of bed in the morning, I want them immediately thinking about making their areas of work better."

August's mournful intensity led to some bizarre incidents. When a news story appeared describing an in-house film Miller had put out that poked fun at Budweiser's beechwood aging, "August hit the roof," recalled the reporter who wrote the piece. "He absolutely lost it . . . I found out from people who worked there . . . that there was big, big trouble. . . . They even found out that I had a neighbor who worked for the company and they called him onto the carpet, thinking he had leaked something to me about beechwood aging."

In a similar episode, August launched an investigation when a trade magazine printed a story he didn't like. Certain that someone had leaked to the magazine, he went to any lengths to find the source. Even a dentist was grilled: the man was suspected of passing on information he had gathered while drilling an Anheuser-Busch executive's teeth.

No quarter was asked and none given during the beer wars. The animosity between Anheuser-Busch and Miller drove Miller to drop out of the United States Brewers' Association. The euphemism given at the time was that it had withdrawn for policy reasons. The real reason, it was speculated, was that Miller couldn't abide a proposal, supported by Anheuser-Busch, that the industry voluntarily list the full ingredients on beer labels although Miller denied this. The bitterness of the struggle even extended to hotel accommodations. When a group of Anheuser-Busch executives checked into a Washington, D.C., hotel for a meeting and learned that Murphy and other Miller people were staying there, they immediately turned on their heels and walked out.

Applied to Miller and other rivals, August's bulldog aggressiveness would pay big dividends. But when it was directed toward his company's unions, it had disastrous consequences. August hadn't finished his first year as CEO when he was embroiled in the longest, costliest strike in Anheuser-Busch history. The Teamsters strike in the spring of 1976 lasted nearly 100 days. Production was slashed almost 50 percent; the company's market share plunged from 23.7 percent to 19.4 percent. Its stock sank to a nine-year low of $18, down from $69 a share in 1972. The strike cost the company more than market share and earnings. It also cost good will. August's tactics recalled a needling comment that Robert Lewis, the president of the brewers' union, had once made about the youthful executive. During an earlier strike, Lewis had said that August was "biologically incapable" of doing his job.

Gussie had repeatedly proven that he hated strikes. "But now," said August, "the union pushed us to the cliff. They wanted written into the contract that they would have the right to approve or disapprove any changes in production before we could implement them. They would manage our production, not us. It was the first time they had dealt with me on the front line."

It was a firing line—literally. Rifle shots knocked out a transformer at an Anheuser-Busch brewery in Jacksonville, where police called it guerrilla warfare. Trucks were peppered with gunfire. A man with a baseball bat smashed about two dozen automobile windshields in a company parking lot. Anheuser-Busch offered a $25,000 reward for the arrest and conviction of anyone involved in the shootings. The union complained that St. Louis police, always on friendly terms with the brewery, were providing armed escorts for the city's Anheuser-Busch distributor.

The strike ended with the union accepting Anheuser-Busch's original economic package. It was an expensive victory. Labor relations were soured and the strike cost Anheuser-Busch an estimated $30 million in profits. But August hadn't blinked. If he had lost some beer drinkers, it hardly mattered. He was already planning a $2 billion expansion to increase capacity. He was also in the midst of the most expensive, boomingly successful advertising program the industry had ever seen. Total marketing it was called.

August was going to bombard the public with messages about his beer. Leading the charge would be cowboys, movie stars, recycled jocks, rock stars—even a dog. He would dominate professional and collegiate sports advertising, everything from the World Series and the Super Bowl to car and speedboat racing. He would make Budweiser a piece of Americana. He would win back those beer drinkers he had lost and then some. It was a beer blitzkrieg.

64

Red Neck in the Morning—Executives Take Warning

The word came crackling down the long corridors of the D'Arcy advertising company that August wanted a new Budweiser campaign and wanted it fast. If the ad agency executives heard the ring of cash registers in their ears, they also knew they had to produce. August was on a rampage and he could extinguish careers; the luckier were merely banished. One executive had a name for him. Darth Vader.

At war with Miller in the 1970s, August had stopped at nothing. Money was no object. Gussie had opposed heavy spending to match the expensive Miller campaign, which was one of the reasons August had deposed him. The message was clear: he was in no mood to be told what he couldn't do. He would spend record millions to bury Miller and woe betide anyone who bungled or got in his way. Wary advertising and marketing executives took to watching his neck. If he strode into a meeting with his neck burning red, there was a good chance someone would be sacrificed. If his neck was only pink, they might all hope to collect another paycheck.

In one of his first major efforts, August wanted a full-blown Bud campaign immediately. D'Arcy threw 100 people into the task; they worked seven days a week, practically living in their offices until they hit a bull's-eye. Following Miller's example, they focused the campaign on the beer-drinking blue-collars, the roughly 20 percent of the population that drinks 80 percent of the beer. They were the guys who worked hard to support their families and whose only pleasure was maybe two or three beers with the boys after the whistle blew.

Some agency people thought the campaign would be copying too closely the successful Miller commercials, which also zeroed in on blue-collars. "We brought in this independent research man, who had data that it would be a big mistake to copy that ad and August still wouldn't accept the results," an executive recalled. "He practically kicked the guy out of the brewery for telling him the truth." August knew what he wanted. He wanted blue-collars and he wanted to know how long the campaign would take to produce.

"This was one of those days when he came in with a red neck," the executive said. "He was mad, you could tell it. That's when he asked me how long would it take to do these commercials. Our creative director was standing next to me and he was sweating bullets. . . . You could see the perspiration just beading up. . . . Other people were slouched under the table. I mean these are big executives and they're just hiding. They could see it coming. Our creative director said the normal production time was six to eight weeks. And with that August hit the goddamn ceiling. He just blewwwwww! He hammered the table and said, 'Goddamn, I'm tired of this shit! You guys telling me it takes this long. We're going to do this whole package in four weeks! And I don't give a shit how much money it takes.' And, man, he went on for twenty minutes."

August got what he wanted. The commercials were shot in four weeks without actors. They used real factory workers at a meat-packing plant in Houston. August didn't like actors in his commercials; he wanted the real thing. He liked the series and the tag line, "For all you do, this Bud's for you." With his unerring eye, he had personally selected the slogan from a list of about twenty possibilities. When the session was over, he curtly thanked everyone. Turning to leave, he paused and said, "It just proves one thing. You guys can't work unless I put the pressure on."

No one could put the pressure on like August. There were trips to plan advertising campaigns from which some men figuratively didn't return. A reporter who covered Anheuser-Busch knew a D'Arcy executive who had suffered this fate. The man had worked on the Bud account. "They would have these annual trips down to Hilton Head or some other plush spot to discuss the upcoming campaigns with August. It was the kind of exercise where they all knew, every man on the plane, that one of them wouldn't be coming back, that one of them would be sacrificed to the great god August.

"They would be sitting around the table and his blue eyes would be searching the faces and he'd start boring in on someone, grilling them and you'd start to breathe easier, but the wiser hands knew that was only to throw you. At the last minute he'd suddenly turn to someone else and say, 'I thought your proposal was terrible. You're through!' . . . Every year you got this. You always knew that one of you would get the axe."

Sometimes men were sacrificed accidentally. An executive who worked on the Anheuser-Busch account described a trip to Williamsburg to make a presentation to August. "He looked over the proposals and didn't like anything. He was there only two or three minutes, pronounced them all bad and blew out of the room, but not before he said something like, 'Fire that guy with the yellow tie. I don't like him.' And so they fired the poor son of a bitch and then they redid the ad campaign and showed it to August again and he liked it. But he tells one of his people, 'I thought I told you to fire that guy.' And his man looks over and sees the guy and says, 'Oh, Jesus. You meant fire *that* guy.' They had canned the wrong man."

August insisted on realism in his commercials. Long an admirer of Philip Morris's Marlboro ads, he used horses and real cowboys to promote Busch beer. A Busch ad was expected to have a bubbling spring, a shot of a rearing black stallion, a distant shot of snow-peaked mountains and the popping Buschhhhhhh of an opening tab top. "Consistency of message," August called it.

In his quest for just the right commercials, August started inviting perhaps forty blue-collar and other employees to some of the major advertising campaign presentations. "He sits in the first seat in the front row and he's got a sheet of paper with the names of the rank and file on it," the same executive recalled. "Right in the middle of some guy's presentation, he might suddenly stop him and yell out, 'Starbuck, did you understand that?' Now Starbuck, some guy from the malt room or bottling line is . . . afraid of looking like a fool, so he says, No, he doesn't understand it. And the guy on the stage sort of freezes and dies. August wants to know if the average man 'gets' what these agencies are trying to do. . . . Some big agency has had a dozen people working for months on some program and then it's scrapped all because Starbuck from bottling doesn't 'get it.' My God, it was so unbelievable.''

Miller got a big jump on Anheuser-Busch by leaping into sports advertising. During the 1970s, the reinvigorated Milwaukee brewer gobbled up virtually every one of the major network sporting events. The highly popular Monday Night Football package went to Miller; so did the College Football Game of the Week, the Moscow Olympics, the World Series, the Indianapolis 500, and dozens of college football games. Miller also pioneered the recycling of superannuated jocks like former footballer Bubba Smith, who was shown ripping off the top of a Miller can with his bare hands. August admitted that Anheuser-Busch had made a mistake in letting Miller open a lead on them. "We were," he said, "simply unsmarted."

Realizing it had to get into the game and fast, Anheuser-Busch approached the networks about buying sports programming. August's marketing chief, the Jesuit-educated Michael Roarty, put it this way: "They looked at us like we had just come to town on a bus and they said, 'Where have you been? We've been sold out for years!' "

August was willing to pour hundreds of millions of dollars into sports advertising because Miller had demonstrated it worked and because he knew the average American beer drinker worshipped at the altar of sport. As Roarty observed, "Sports figures are America's heroes."

While he waited for a chance to take the plunge with the big sports shows, August focused on the next best thing, "alternative sports." Everything from softball games, jogging and hot air ballooning to hydroplane boat races and touch football games. More significantly, he entered the college sports market. He ordered his staff to assemble a book listing every college in the country that played sports. August was interested in buying a piece of the radio or television sponsorship of each team. If there was going to be a beer commercial during a collegiate game—any game—he wanted it to be an Anheuser-Busch commercial.

"That book was about five or six inches thick," recalled an executive who participated in the exercise. "One day we got together and August said, 'Well, let's go. Read 'em.' We had a media guy reading them off. . . . August would say, 'What about Albion? What do they do?' And we'd say, 'Naw, that's just a very small liberal arts college and they don't do anything.' August would say, 'Okay, what about Albuquerque A&M?' We'd say, 'Yeah, they play football.' And August would say, 'Buy 'em!' "

On and on it went, one school after another. The litany rolled on until they reached the schools that started with Z. August didn't care whether they were inefficient buys or not. "He had the money. He wanted to dominate."

It was domination in sports advertising unlike anything ever seen before. In 1976, Anheuser-Busch sponsored twelve professional baseball teams and seven National Football League teams. A little over a decade later, the company would hold sponsorship rights with all twenty-four United States–based major league baseball teams, twenty of twenty-eight NFL teams, twenty-three of twenty-four National Basketball Association teams, thirteen of fourteen domestic National Hockey League teams, nine of the eleven Major Indoor Soccer League teams, and more than 300 colleges. The alternative sporting events, including the Bud Light Ironman Triathlon World Championship and the Michelob Night Riders cycling circuit, numbered "about a thousand." Anheuser-Busch also became the exclusive beer advertiser for the ESPN sports cable network. The beer company even pried away a piece of the Monday Night Football package. Eventually, Anheuser-Busch and Miller would have a virtual monopoly on sports beer advertising through what are known as exclusivity clauses, which, after other breweries complained, were ruled completely legal by the Justice Department.

The National Catholic Basketball Tournament was a typical example of Anheuser-Busch's drive to push its product through collegiate sports. The little guys got bought as well as the big boys. By no means a major postseason tournament, the small-college National Catholic Basketball Tournament, held in Dubuque, Iowa, had a strong Midwest following, and Anheuser-Busch made its presence known as the principal sponsor. During the 1990 contest, the words "Budweiser" and "Bud Light" were plastered all over the gymnasium; the same brand names appeared no less than six times on the front cover of the official program, and the back cover, which showed two foaming cups of Budweiser, was dedicated to "One Team That Never Fails to Make Points."

The tournament's halftime festivities showcased an appearance by the Bud Light Daredevils, "the most unique slam dunk act in the country." Members of the five-man gymnastic team, wearing bright red and blue uniforms with bold Anheuser-Busch lettering, were so many flying billboards. Bouncing off trampolines, they performed such "daring feats of agility" as "Dial 911" and "Shake Down the Rafters 'Til the Morning After." Students and parents were informed that the Daredevils had performed at over 200 colleges and universities in forty-five states, not to mention Europe, the Middle East, Japan, Latin America and Australia. In a single year they appeared at some 125 events before more than one million fans.

August put about 70 percent of his estimated $400 million budget for broadcast advertising into sports programming; that was more than the combined budgets of Miller and Coors. *Advertising Age* pegged Anheuser-Busch's total ad spending at over $600 million a year. The account for Budweiser alone, the world's best-selling beer, was worth $125 million. Anheuser-Busch's commercials seemed to be everywhere fans gathered to watch a sporting event no matter how humble. The bow-tie-shaped Budweiser logo appeared on the helmets of the U.S. Olympic hockey team when it faced the Soviets. Budweiser cars ran in the big auto races; Budweiser boats roared in the big boat races. A St. Louis lawyer even told the story of the night he turned on the television and saw a photograph of a duck race. "And by God, right there by the finish line of the duck race was a Bud sign."

August had achieved a place in history with his saturation approach to sports advertising. "He's made his beer part of the fabric of America," said one observer. "He's made it a part of Americana. He's done it by making it part of every sporting event in the country. He's done it by money."

"When they decide where they're going," observed Russell Ackoff, August's scholarly mentor, "they're like an army on the march." As commander in chief of the world's largest brewery, August led that march. He had learned Miller's big lesson well. Following the proven success record of Philip Morris, Miller had segmented the beer market as never before, pegging different brands and sales pitches to different consumers. It was a radically fresh idea in the industry, and for an exhilarating moment it drove Miller to within a few percentage points of overtaking Anheuser-Busch. The company rocketed from seventh place to a strong second.

August pushed Miller's winning idea even further, developing a fragmented marketing approach that blitzed the country city by city, neighborhood by neighborhood, street by street, even bar by bar. Using sophisticated demographics, August's team divided beer drinkers by race, income, sex, age, even ethnic origin. It was called target marketing and there were targets everywhere. The Latino segment alone was broken into Mexicans, Puerto Ricans and Cubans. There was one approach for Irish beer drinkers in Boston and another for Poles in Chicago. Ads focused on racing fans, blue-collars, jocks, yuppies and computer nerds. One Bud commercial cheered bartenders and waitresses; "This Bud's for everyone that serves them up cold." Another was aimed at immigrants, still another went after "all the men and women in uniform who proudly serve this great country." The country was carved into some 210 markets with the focus on big cities like New York and Los Angeles where most of the beer was consumed. The result was an incredible number of different sales promotion programs— as many as 10,000.

The command post for this saturation bombing was a conference room on the ninth floor at August's corporate headquarters, Number One Busch Place, once the address of his great-grandfather's mansion. It was called the war room and the walls were plastered with charts and graphs indicating the company's performance against its competitors. August's marketing staff churned out over thirty new promotional programs a day. They did their work exceptionally well; it was estimated that the typical city resident was exposed to the word "Budweiser" almost ten times a day.

Nothing was left to chance. "We want to be here," August once said, pointing to his wall charts. He pointed again. "We want to be there. We want to be everywhere. We are going to target every segment." And cost be damned. "In the 1970s they were so intent on beating back Miller's challenge that it was said if you could dream up a $250,000 bartop tiddlywinks campaign, you could take it down there and sell it to somebody," said an advertising executive.

Miller had forever changed beer advertising by putting the beer drinker smack in the commercial and appealing to his ego. That was a radical message and August jumped on the bandwagon. He was given a big assist by a watershed analysis of beer drinkers by Ackoff, his friend from the University of Pennsylvania's Wharton School. Every year Anheuser-Busch paid the university $200,000 to $300,000 for computer studies on everything from plant construction to what makes someone drink beer. During the 1960s, Ackoff's team had studied data on drinking behavior. Refining the information, he developed a theory that there were four types of drinkers. Two of the four drank to escape social or personal failures. The idea was to zero in on the "target market segments" to be reached by Anheuser-Busch advertising and to tailor the message accordingly. The approach worked splendidly, said Monty Roberts, a former Anheuser-Busch marketing executive. Ackoff's marketing strategies "were the bible at AB."

Undeterred, Anheuser-Busch steamrolled the land with advertising campaigns that resembled Sherman's March to the Sea. There were inevitable complaints from competitors. "Theyre tough, tough, tough, really ruthless," said Paul Lohmeyer, a beer importer. "They seem to have the absolute intention of running everyone else out of the business."

Early in the 1980s, August coolly predicted that Anheuser-Busch would have a 40 percent market share by the end of the decade. He got it. In 1980, the brewery was the first to produce 50 million barrels in a year and August marked the occasion by bunging the historic barrel with a silver hammer. In 1987, with beer sales flattening, Anheuser-Busch still managed to sell 76 million barrels and increase its share. When August said he wanted 50 percent by the turn of the century, few experts were willing to dispute the possibility.

With such a gargantuan slice of the beer market, August was aware of potential dangers. "We've seen others in this business get to the top and get in trouble because they got too big for their britches. We're scared to death of that. . . . It makes us live on the razor's edge."

By the later half of the 1980s, the razor's edge had become dangerously sharp. Vocal opponents of the brewery's marketing tactics and critics of alcohol abuse were making serious charges against Anheuser-Busch in Congress and in the market place. The company had become "the big gorilla." The brewery, said one critic, had long had things its own way. "And with that kind of concentration of power, bad things can happen. The federal regulators are afraid of them, afraid of their lawyers. Nobody should have unlimited power, but they are getting it. All sports are dominated by Mr. Big, all television, all markets . . . . I'm afraid that the future holds simply more and more Budweiser and less and less of everything else."

With the prediction of a 50 percent share of the market by the year 2000, Mr. Big wanted to get bigger.

65

The Missing Heir

When the great-grandson of Adolphus Busch mysteriously disappeared in 1981, there was hope that he had simply gone into hiding for some unexplained reason. It had happened before. Sometimes he wasn't seen for months. But as the months turned into years, the fear was that he might have been murdered. Others weren't so sure and wondered whether this elusive man had simply dropped out to start a new life.

Adolphus Harvey Gert von Gontard was named after his great-grandfather and grew up in the typically opulent lifestyle of a Busch descendant. He was the son of Paul C. von Gontard, who was born to Clara Busch and Baron Paul von Gontard in 1897 in Hagen, Germany. A big-game hunter and horseman, Paul was a globetrotting adventurer who had written books about hunting in Africa.

When Paul died of a brain tumor in 1951 at the age of fiftyfour, Adolphus was a sixteen-year-old student at Country Day School, the prestigious private academy in St. Louis. His father left an estate valued at $519,946, including about 15,000 shares of Anheuser-Busch stock. Then in 1959, his grandmother Clara died leaving $6 million, including 250,000 shares to her descendants, one of whom was Adolphus. The stock split several times in the 1960s, and Adolph, as he was called, became a very wealthy man.

In 1954, he had married Christa Kluge, the daughter of one of his father's hunting partners. Adolphus was nineteen years old, his bride twenty-one. They were married quickly because

Christa's permit to visit from Germany had nearly expired. The couple had four children and lived in St. Louis County and Germany. In 1961, they separated and Adolphus moved to Munich. They were divorced in 1970.

Marrying again in Germany, Adolphus moved to New Mexico and established an estate he called La Barbaria in a remote cluster of hills near Santa Fe. Born in Czechoslovakia, his new wife was named Jutta. This marriage also ended in divorce. They separated in January 1981. Adolphus was forty-six years old. Two months later he disappeared.

A daughter reported Adolphus missing fifty-three days after he was last seen alive. His disappearance touched off a search that extended from the United States and British Columbia to West Germany. Private detectives hired to look for him later turned over a briefcase full of documents to David Corey, an investigator for the Maricopa County district attorney's office in Phoenix. Corey got the case in August 1981 because the missing man was last seen in a lounge in that city's Sky Harbor International Airport. "I don't want to say the guy's dead," Corey said many years later. "I don't want to say that at all. But you put everything together."

When everything was put together, the investigation pointed to Rick Allen, who had been seen with Adolphus in the airport lounge. Allen was a graduate of the University of Santa Clara and its law school. In 1974, he was suspended by the California bar for two years for commingling clients' funds. In 1977, he was disbarred for a variety of offenses.

Adolphus was supposed to meet with Allen in Phoenix to collect $200,000 from the sale of a piece of property in British Columbia. Shortly after he disappeared, Allen established a chiropractic clinic in Sparks, Nevada, outside Reno. He was later convicted on nine of ten charges stemming from the operation of the clinic, including practicing medicine without a license.

Adolphus also knew another unsavory character. His former wife, Jutta, told investigators that after meeting with Allen in the Phoenix airport, Adolphus was supposed to fly to Las Vegas to see Benjamin P. "Pat" Callahan, a high-stakes Nevada gambler. Corey, the Arizona investigator, learned that Allen and Callahan were longtime associates. One year after Adolphus was reported missing, Callahan was arrested by U.S. Customs Service agents in Louisiana when his airplane was found to contain 1,500 pounds of marijuana worth about $1 million. En route from Colombia to Oklahoma, it had landed in Louisiana because of fuel problems. Callahan was later convicted of drug smuggling and sentenced to federal prison.

Over the years Corey continued to send Adolphus's dental records to police every time an unidentified male body was found in Arizona or Nevada. He never forgot the case. "Here's a guy who had a lot of money, but who never really held down any kind of job of his own. It seemed like he had a very boring life. It's as if he wanted desperately to get his life together. . . . Technically, the case is still open. Our files are still here, extensive files. I feel like I know everything there is to know about him. Everything but where he is."

On the day Rick Allen was found guilty of practicing medicine without a license, he told *The Reno Evening Gazette* that he thought Adolphus's disappearance was tied to alcoholism and religion. He said Adolphus went into hiding "knowingly and willingly. I don't believe anything happened to the guy at all. I think he did what he had to do and had his own reasons for doing it." Allen said he had refused to discuss the disappearance with authorities because "I'm not going to say anything to jeopardize this man. If they want to know what he's done, I'll leave that for him to explain."

In March 1986, the Santa Fe County District Court declared Adolphus von Gontard legally dead. His estate, valued at between $1.2 million and $2 million, was divided among his four children, although a sixteen-year-old German girl later filed a claim. She said she was his illegitimate daughter.

66

A Beer for Prince Philip

On a winter's afternoon in February 1984, a cement truck slammed into a van on a four-lane highway not far from St.

Louis. It was a nasty wreck. A tangle of metal, the van was knocked over 100 feet. The driver of the truck, which snapped down a traffic signal, later died. A fifty-five-year-old woman who was driving the van was critically hurt. Her passengers, four young children, were injured. Two of them were the son and daughter of Virginia and August Busch III. The children's governess had made a left turn in front of the cement truck in rural St. Charles County, where August's estate was located. Steven Busch, then seven, and his sister, Virginia, five, had been incredibly lucky, suffering only minor cuts. The two other children had internal injuries.

It was yet another of the tragic accidents that seemed to plague the Busch family. There were the inevitable comments that the family was cursed, that the power and influence of the Busch name also carried a dark baggage of appalling bad luck and fatal carelessness. It was not likely that a man as unsentimental and coolly rational as August would have entertained such a notion, but he must have been jolted when death brushed his children so closely. He was strongly attached to the pair of sons and daughters he had had by his two wives.

August's attentiveness to his children's welfare showed clearly when he and his first wife, Susan, were divorced in 1969. August insisted in the divorce decree that his daughter, Susan, and son, August IV, be raised in the St. Louis area, where "the Busch family prestige and social position" would help them. He also insisted on the sole right to select their nurses, schools and doctors.

Not surprisingly, no mention was made in the divorce papers of Susan's alleged relationship with Cardinal broadcaster Harry Caray. Susan accused August of "general indignities." She charged that he "quarreled . . . nagged and criticized her conduct and found fault with her without just cause; exhibited bad temper . . . and used profane and humiliating language toward her causing her embarrassment and humiliation." On numerous occasions, she said, August left the house for long periods, displayed "a cold and indifferent attitude" toward her and often said he was no longer interested in her or their marriage. She also said he refused to travel or to attend social engagements with her.

Five years after his divorce, in December 1974, August married Virginia Lee Wiley in Cabo San Lucas, Mexico. Ginny Wiley had grown up in Buffalo, New York. After attending Boston College, she worked in television advertising in New

York and Miami. A blonde like Susan, she was a willowy, vibrant woman who shared August's love for flying. As he had done with his son August IV, he taught her himself and she held both private and commercial licenses. Their son, Steve, also took flying lessons. Airplanes, not the horses so dear to Gussie, took precedence in August's household. "In this family," Ginny said, "everyone flies."

After her children were older, Ginny went back to school to earn a law degree at Washington University. If becoming a lawyer might have been considered a remarkable midlife undertaking for the wife of a powerfully rich executive, Ginny also astounded friends when she went to work for the St. Charles County public defender's office. A colleague recalled that she dressed elegantly if conservatively, arrived for work in a black Mercedes, was intellectual and serious about the law. She knew the cases and worked hard at her job. "You can't forget that she's rich and a Busch," said the fellow lawyer, "but she certainly won't bring it up."

Ginny's connection with the president of the world's largest brewery sometimes led to awkward moments. A lawyer remembered that she was in court one day when a man pleaded guilty to a charge of driving while intoxicated. She smiled uneasily when he admitted that he had drunk about a twelve-pack of Busch. "She was sort of embarrassed," said the lawyer.

Ginny and her husband spent every hour they could at their farm in St. Charles County. Surrounded by fields and stands of trees, August loved the isolation and the wildlife. You could walk for miles, he liked to say, and not hear a car or see anyone. He enjoyed slipping into a Western shirt and jeans and plowing the ground on a tractor. His farm was in the middle of the Mississippi flyway and in the fall the ducks came by the hundreds on their way south. The hunting was superb. Like his father, grandfather and great-grandfather before him, August was a dedicated hunter and marksman. So were his children. His two sons, August IV and Steve, had their own weapons. "August IV is quite adept with a shotgun and a very good pistol shot," *The American Rifleman* reported. "Steve, too, is at home with a smoothbore at his shoulder and proved a steady shot with a .22 rimfire rifle."

Anheuser-Busch sponsored a variety of shooting matches and championships, including the National Rifle Association's Junior Olympic Shooting Program. In one year, 1986, the company provided financial aid for fifty-seven shooting events held in forty states. August was a Benefactor Member of the NRA; his sons were members as were many of Anheuser-Busch's senior executives. August was also an avid conservationist. His company quietly chipped in half a million dollars to buy ranch land in Montana considered crucial habitat for elk. Anheuser-Busch took similar steps to protect the bald eagle, its corporate symbol; its financial assistance helped establish the Ferry Bluff eagle sanctuary in Wisconsin.

Jerry Clinton, the president of Gray Eagle Distributors, an Anheuser-Busch distributorship in St. Louis County, hunted with August in Scandinavia. But even during a pleasure trip, August erected a high-walled privacy zone. "It's very hard to get personal around August. He gets very guarded. It's almost scary, those blue eyes. He won't tolerate small talk. There are very few people he can relax with . . . . You can count the people who have had close contact with him on one hand."

One of these was Bernard Little, Jr., a former Lear jet salesman, who sold planes to August and whose two sons now run three Anheuser-Busch distributorships in Florida. Another was John Krey III, a friend from his school days. Krey acquired an Anheuser-Busch distributorship near August's home in St. Charles County. August rewarded his friends generously. It didn't matter, a family friend said, that the decision to let Krey have the distributorship upset Gussie's son, Adolphus, who also lived in St. Charles County. "That got Adolphus mad as hell."

When Krey was stricken with cancer, August was distraught. "Whenever someone mentioned to August that Krey was dying, he would just lose it," said an acquaintance. "He'd say, 'No, he's not sick. I don't want to hear that he's sick.' " August went to great lengths to make Krey's last days as comfortable as possible; he fitted out a plane as an ambulance so that his friend could make a trip to Europe. After Krey's death at forty-nine, his wife, Mary Ann, was allowed to take over the distributorship.

August rarely attended civic or social functions, usually sending an Anheuser-Busch executive in his place. When he did show up, he didn't stay long. "You could hear," joked one businessman, "the beating rotor blades outside." An exception was when Prince Philip stopped in St. Louis to promote wildlife conservation. This time, the king of beer was willing to meet a prince. When the Busch family hosted a gala dinner in Philip's honor, there was a flap over whether beer or wine should be served. "August wanted beer," recalled a guest. "The prince sat at August's table and August wound up ordering wine in glasses that had Anheuser-Busch engraved on them. After the first course, they drank beer for the rest of the evening."

Another exception to August's civic aloofness was his involvement with the Boy Scouts. As president of the local scouting chapter's board of directors, he was especially interested in helping Scouts from the inner city and boys with handicaps. He provided planes to fly Scouts to camping jamborees and was known to slip into a pair of hiking shorts and leggings.

Unlike his father, August was a true-blue Republican. He liked to recall that Gussie had become a Democrat because President Roosevelt had supported repeal. "The Democrats did a helluva job—then." He backed Republican candidates because he thought they were more attentive to the business community and less tolerant of the powerful labor unions he mistrusted. "I'm concerned about the will to do a day's work for a day's pay, which we've lost sight of," he said. "That's what made this country great, wasn't it?"

It took years, but August's strained relationship with his father slowly improved. Friends said that a sign of their reconciliation was when August occasionally attended baseball games with Gussie. In 1987 August was chosen St. Louis Man of the Year, an award bestowed by the city's civic elite. Gussie, then twelve years out of power and in his dotage, had some kind words to say about his son to mark the occasion. "He's a great kid, but more than that, he is doing a great job of keeping up the traditions of the family and the company."

When August's daughter Susan and his son August IV went to work for the brewery, the tradition continued. August IV, whom his father hoped would succeed him, was the man Anheuser-Busch watchers kept their eyes riveted on. If he did well, his future was assured. If he fouled up, the betting was that August would give him a lucrative beer distributorship as he had done with several of Gussie's sons by Trudy, and wait for son Steve to grow up. But if August IV, a lively, dark-haired young man who preferred blondes, had a promising future, he also had inherited a taste for guns and fast cars.

67

"Party Animal"

A narrow road snaked through the dusty northeast corner of Tucson, hugging the base of foothills from which, late at night, the lights of the city were visible. It was called the River Road, taking its name from the Rillito River, which it followed with all of its twists and turns.

At one spot, the road zigged and zagged in a sharp S bend. Not far from where Camino del Celador crossed it, the bottom seemed to drop out of the pavement. Taking the curves at high speed was a stomach-lifting experience. Local hot-rodders in Pima County called this most dangerous stretch of concrete Dead Man's Curve. A twenty-five-mile-an-hour speed limit sign was posted among the scrub trees and bushes that lined the roadside.

Early on the morning of November 13, 1983, a gleaming black 1984 Corvette hurtled through this turn on the River Road. The driver could not control the powerful sports car. The vehicle leaped into the air, crashed into a dirt bank and corkscrewed in a roll. As the sun roof flew off, a woman was thrown through the opening, her body caught beneath the tumbling car. Pitched free, she hit a palo verde tree, snapping some branches. The Corvette came to a stop, resting on the driver's side, seventy feet from the pavement. For several hours, the smashup went undiscovered.

In the light of a pink Arizona dawn, motorists driving along the River Road early that Sunday morning noticed a dazed man walking west along the shoulder more than a mile from the wreckage. Despite the chill of the late fall morning, he wore no jacket. Three drivers stopped to help. The disoriented young man had blood on his head, shoulders and clothes. A nurse offered him first aid and a trip to the hospital. He refused. Instead, he accepted a ride to his townhouse in Tucson. None of these Good Samaritans reported their discovery to police— at least immediately.

It wasn't until 8:30 A.M. that the Pima County Sheriff's Department was notified about the accident. One of the first investigators to arrive on the scene was Ronald Benson, a deputy sheriff. Benson was a tall and trim six foot two with reddish-brown hair and a mustache. Accident investigations were his speciality. He was one of the few automotive engineers in law enforcement.

By the time Benson arrived, some evidence around the car had been obliterated by firemen who walked over the footprints near the wreckage. The woman's body was cold to the touch. In her pocket he found a half-smoked marijuana cigarette and an expired driver's license. The face of the dead woman matched the photo on the license. She was Michele Frederick, a brown-eyed, brown-haired, 125 pound Tucson resident who had celebrated her twenty-second birthday two months earlier.

Scattered nearby and underneath the smashed Corvette, Benson found several empty Bud Light cans, which he bagged for fingerprint checks. A radar detector was also found and inside the car was a .44-caliber Magnum revolver. A check of the car's Missouri tags, MWL-933, showed the registration had been issued on a 1983 Audi Quattro to August A. Busch III, the chief executive officer of Anheuser-Busch. The label of a brown tweed jacket read: "Designed for August A. Busch IV in April, 1981 by Demetre's, St. Louis, Missouri."

A wallet was brought to Benson's attention. It contained credit, identification and membership cards. There were also two Missouri driver's licenses for August A. Busch IV. One of them stated he lived at Waldmeister Farm in St. Peters, Missouri. It showed his birthday as June 15, 1964, which would have made him nineteen years old at the time of the accident. The other license gave his birthdate as February 15, 1960. That would have made him twenty-three and eligible to drink in states like Missouri where the legal drinking age was twenty-one. In Arizona, the legal drinking age was nineteen, which was Busch's actual age. One of the licenses was a fake.

Also in the wallet was a membership card to the Tucson Rod and Gun Club. It had been issued just three days earlier to August A. Busch IV of 1900 East Campbell Terrace, Tucson. Two deputies were dispatched to the address, a townhouse that hugged the bluffs in a fashionable part of Tucson. The deputies repeatedly knocked on the door, but got no response. They could hear music inside. They tried the door. It was open.

"Mr. Busch?" one of them called.

"Yes," came an answer from the bedroom.

When deputies finally found the heir to the Busch brewing empire, he was naked, except for a sheet covering his midsection. His head, face and upper body were covered with dried blood. Blood had dried on the pillow and his bloody clothes were nearby. At the foot of his bed was a semiautomatic AR-16 rifle. A loaded sawed-off shotgun was on the kitchen table.

The blue eyes of the great-great-grandson of Prince Adolphus were glassy and he appeared dazed, but he was able to answer questions. August IV told them he was not sure what had happened. Checking with their superiors, the deputies were instructed to read him his rights. They did so and then again asked him what happened. August IV said he remembered driving the night before. He said he had grown tired. Getting out of his car, he had fallen to sleep by the side of the road. He suggested he might have been run over.

An ambulance was summoned. As the deputies waited, one of them noticed a wall mirror that contained a logo for Anheuser-Busch. "Are you related to the Busch beer family?" he asked.

"Yes," August IV responded. He was the eldest son of the chairman of the company.

From that point on, the Pima County Sheriff's Department was aware that it was dealing with something that was, as Deputy Prosecutor Thomas Zawada put it, "a high-profile case." Deputy Benson wanted to leave no stone unturned. He did not want to leave any lingering doubts or unanswered questions like "Chappaquiddick," the accident in which Ted Kennedy had driven his car off a bridge and a young woman was drowned. Benson vowed to do everything possible to see that the investigation was thorough and objective. The county's reputation was at stake, and Benson did not want it said later that there was any favoritism or special handling of the case involving the violent death of Michele Frederick.

The fatal accident was not the first for a Busch. Deadly automobile wrecks occurred periodically in the family's annals. There had been accidents in which Busches were seriously injured, and multicar pileups that left a family member and others dead. Also, their chauffeur-driven limousines had run down pedestrians with fatal results.

In December 1974, Gussie's daughter Christina had died after an accident that killed the family chauffeur, Nathaniel

Mayes, and injured her brother Andrew. Five years later, his son Andy, then sixteen, escaped injury when the car he was driving was involved in a four-vehicle accident in which the driver of another car was killed.

August's first wife, Susan, suffered minor injuries in 1968 when she lost control of her car, struck several small trees and ended up in a ditch. In 1954, when August was seventeen years old, his car ran into a telephone pole, injuring two of his passengers.

Gussie's daughter Carlota suffered serious head injuries, and his future bride, Trudy Buholzer, had a kneecap broken in 1950 when a car driven by Carlota struck another car. The driver and a passenger in the other car were also injured.

With a chauffeur driving Gussie's wife, Elizabeth, and his daughter Carlota, their car struck and killed a man in 1942 in St. Louis County. No charges were filed. As early as 1910 a chauffeur-driven car carrying Gussie's father, August A., ran over and killed a man. A coroner's jury ruled that death an accident.

August IV's accident was part of a long, unfortunate history in the Busch family. As the young man was being transported to the Tucson General Hospital, he "indicated he remembered drinking the night prior and that he had had quite a bit." August IV told the sheriff's deputies he had consumed one or two vodka collinses and some light beers. At the hospital, he was treated for a skull fracture and loss of blood.

Usually in cases where driving while intoxicated is suspected, police order medical people to take a sample of a suspect's blood or urine, or both. The deputies wondered whether there was justifiable cause, at that point, to have the samples taken to determine whether August IV was under the influence. Several hours had elapsed since the accident, but the samples might still have been useful evidence. If they showed that alcohol or drugs were currently present in August IV's blood, an estimate could be made on the levels several hours earlier. Such data could prove helpful if authorities determined when the accident occurred and whether August IV was involved.

Deaths from driving while intoxicated were a serious problem in Arizona. It was referred to as the state's "deadliest street crime." More than one-fourth of all fatal accidents in Arizona involved a drinking driver. Over 25 percent of the arrests were for DWI, ranking Arizona 81 percent above the national average.

As the case involving August IV got under way, legal advice was requested from Ed Nesbitt, a deputy county attorney. Although Nesbitt seldom handled DWI cases, he had been called out on Sunday to supervise the gathering of evidence. Well aware of the Busch connection, he suggested that everyone proceed cautiously.

Blood and urine samples were finally drawn from August IV at about 11 A.M., but they were held at the hospital until authorities got a search warrant to have them tested. At the hospital, August IV told deputies George Heaney and John Himes that he did not think he had had too much to drink and drive the night before. He claimed that he had a high tolerance for alcohol because he had been drinking beer since he was a little kid. That was very true. Like his father, August IV had been given beer at a very early age. His mother, Susan, had fed him a thimbleful when he was a day old.

August IV also told the deputies that he did not make it a practice to loan his car to others, but that if he were too drunk to drive, he would sometimes let a girl drive it. He also said that the last thing he remembered was lying down about forty feet off the road at about two o'clock in the morning. August IV gave the deputies the names of people who, he said, could account for the events of the previous night. Then the deputies left. It was the last interview with August IV the lawmen got.

Before the accident, August IV had led an idyllic life on the campus of the University of Arizona. He had entered the university in the fall of 1982 after graduating from Parkway West High School in St. Louis County. He was in the School of Engineering in the fall of 1983 and was still listed as a freshman. He had friends, a fast car and a townhouse in Tucson.

August IV was seen frequently in Dirtbag's, a hangout on the edge of the university that was a popular watering hole for students. A sign on the outside said it was "Part of Growing Up." Michele Frederick worked there full-time as a bartender. She did not attend the university.

The fire code limited the number of people who got into Dirtbag's to 250, so, on busy nights there was usually a line of young people out in front waiting to enter. August IV never had to wait. One of the co-owners let him jump ahead in line. An acquaintance said of August IV: "He was a popular guy. He never hurt for friends. People knew who he was. When you have money it's easy to attract a crowd. People gravitate to you."

Michele had met August IV one month earlier through a girlfriend who worked at Dirtbag's. Michele's family was originally from Ottumwa, Iowa. Her father, Kenneth, and stepmother, Judy, still lived there. Her mother, Gretta, and stepfather, Ernesto Machado, lived in Nogales, Arizona. Michele had graduated from Sahuarita High School in Tucson and had worked at Dirtbag's for two months prior to the accident.

Those who knew Michele said she was a nice young woman with a pleasant personality. They said she was attractive, but not outgoing. In the months following her death, Michele's mother never quit crying, according to close friends. But they also said she felt that her daughter's death was not the type of thing to be angry or bitter about. Benson, the Pima County sheriff's deputy, said the family was not interested in revenge or restitution from the Busches. "All the mother wanted was her daughter."

The Sheriff's Department invested 400 man hours in the investigation of Michele's death. Friends and associates of August IV and the dead woman were questioned. Twenty-nine people gave detailed, tape-recorded statements and another forty were interviewed. A picture gradually emerged of the activities of August IV and Michelle the day before the accident. That Saturday, November 12, began with August IV meeting Ronald Karstens, a close friend, for breakfast at a local bar and restaurant. Later, he worked out in a gym, went jogging, slept for an hour and met Karstens again for dinner. The two young men had pizza together before heading into Tucson for a night on the town. August IV drove his Corvette while Karstens sped along in his Camaro Z28. Karstens was clocked by police radar doing sixty-five in a forty-five-mile-an-hour zone and was issued a ticket. Unlike August IV's car, his Camaro was not equipped with a radar detector. August IV's driving record showed he had pleaded no contest three months earlier to a speeding charge and paid a $65 fine.

By 9 P.M., August IV and Karstens ended up at Viola's, a popular discotheque where people were jammed in elbow-to-elbow. Michele Frederick was also there. Waitresses and witnesses interviewed by police said August IV drank between four to seven vodka collinses. One waitress said she had served him five or six of the drinks. A close friend said it was six or seven. Michele, who arrived later than August IV, had two White Russians.

At about the 1 A.M. closing time, a group of diehards assembled in the parking lot. Their plan was to drive to one of their homes and continue the evening. About ten people loaded into five cars. Michele got into the Corvette with August IV behind the wheel.

Deborah Harrold, Michele's roommate, had gone to the bar with her. She was told to follow August IV's car. She pulled out behind the black Corvette, but August IV took off so fast that she could not keep up. She told deputies later that he sped away at about sixty-five miles per hour or more, passing cars on the way. He "was not driving safely," and she could not follow him. That was the last time Deborah saw her friend alive.

Dr. Thomas Henry, who performed the autopsy on Michele, found that her death had been caused by blunt force trauma of the head and chest. A nasal swab test turned out positive for cocaine, as did urine tests. But investigators determined that the probable source of the cocaine was at a place and time when Michele wasn't with August IV. However, according to an affidavit filed by police, August IV was identified as "a user of cocaine" by a man who had known him for several years.

Five days after the accident Deputy Benson filed a affidavit with the Superior Court of Pima County requesting a search warrant for the samples of blood and urine that had been taken from August IV the day of the accident. In the affidavit, Benson stated there was probable cause to believe that "the crime of manslaughter was committed on or about November 13, 1983, by means of a motor vehicle." The affidavit said Frederick was the victim and that "the suspected driver was August Adolphus Busch IV." An examination of the samples was necessary to "provide relevant information regarding Mr. Busch's state of intoxication and further assist in the determination of the cause of this accident."

Benson's request was approved by the judge, but there was a problem. In the five days it had taken to get the search warrant, the urine sample had been lost at the Tucson General Hospital. Even worse, the blood sample had been placed in a centrifuge and spun, reducing it to its basic components and making it almost useless for testing for alcohol content. The deputies questioned members of the hospital staff, but no one could explain what had happened. A key piece of evidence in the case had been obliterated.

Pressing on, Benson obtained two warrants to search the Corvette and remove parts of it for analysis to determine the cause of the accident. Experts were brought in to study the wrecked car and examine the fibers, hairs and bloodstains. Part of the car was dismantled. Samples of glass and undercoating were removed for examination.

The sheriff's deputies were not the only ones busy on the case. Elaborate preparations were being made to build a strong defense in case August IV was charged with a crime. Two prominent Tucson law firms were hired to represent the Busch interests in the city, and Norm London, a well-know St. Louis defense lawyer, was also brought in. London had represented August IV's uncle, Peter, after he killed David Leeker at Grant's Farm.

Private investigative agencies, Rainbow Forensics and Investigations and Foresight Investigation and Evidence Research, looked into the accident as agents for the Busches. Highway safety experts and accident investigators from St. Louis, Texas, California, Illinois and Colorado were hired. Authorities soon realized that the Busches had more resources to pour into the defense of August IV than Pima County had to prosecute him.

Sometimes Benson and Zawada, the deputy Pima County prosecuting attorney, met with August IV's large defense team to discuss the case and such things as young Busch's request to leave the state and return to Missouri. "Zawada and I would sit down for some of these different interviews and things, and it would be he and I at this nice big table, plenty of room to spread out our papers and books. And the other table was real crowded with lots of attorneys and lots of investigators."

Two weeks after the accident, the experts assembled by August IV's defense team gathered at the wreck site. The River Road was blocked off and a brand new Corvette, nearly identical to the one August IV had, was driven repeatedly through Dead Man's Curve. Numbered signs were placed beside the road as reference points. Cameras mounted on the roadside and a movie camera operated by a passenger recorded the runs through the dangerous S bend. The tests went on most of the day. They were repeated at night. It was clear that if August IV went to trial, the county's highway engineers would probably be called as defense witnesses.

August IV's father, August A. Busch III, held daily 7 A.M. meetings with the lawyers, investigators and experts asking for updates on the case. His rapid-fire questions often came with the flick of a finger as he pointed around the table, asking, "What have you done?" or "What have you got?" Carmine Brogna, the Tucson lawyer, was later flown to St. Louis to give August III briefings.

As his own investigation proceeded, Benson noticed something strange. His progress was being monitored. "This case was doing all kinds of weird things. I had people I would interview and as soon as I left their house the investigators for the other side would show up. Sometimes within minutes. So, we had to assume that somebody was using a scanner, tracking what was going on."

A week after the accident, August IV had been released from Tucson General Hospital and returned to St. Louis to spend Thanksgiving with his family. Authorities said his return to Missouri would not hamper the investigation because August IV, through his lawyer, agreed to make himself available in Tucson if additional evidence was needed.

In the weeks that followed, Benson combed Tucson looking for anyone who might have seen the accident. Every Saturday night for a month, he sat in his car on the River Road writing down the license numbers of passing cars. He tracked down all the drivers, hoping they might have passed the spot the night of the accident. He was unsuccessful.

There were other dead ends. The empty Bud Light cans found at the scene had no usable fingerprints. The only identifiable footprints around the wreck belonged to firefighters. A check with the Alcohol, Tobacco and Firearms division of the Treasury Department revealed that the .44-caliber Magnum found in the car had been purchased by August A. Busch III on May 11, 1982. The weapon was in a case and was not loaded, although there was a small amount of ammunition with it.

During the investigation, a letter was sent to the Pima County Sheriff's Department from a woman in St. Louis County, encouraging the deputies to pursue their investigation. "We (some of us, that is) . . . are awfully tired of reading about the Busch family and what they get away with. . . . Too bad that money thinks it will buy its way to heaven irregardless of what our behavior is on earth. My sincerest wishes are that you pursue this to the end."

On December 29, 1983, Benson filed a petition with the Pima County Superior Court. He wanted samples of blood, saliva and hair from August A. Busch IV. He also sought fingerprints and palmprints. Benson said he had probable cause to believe that the crimes of manslaughter and leaving the scene of an accident had occurred in the death of Michele Frederick, and that Busch "has been tentatively identified as the perpetrator of this crime."

In his petition, Benson recounted the witnesses' recollections of August IV's drinking the night of the accident. He reported that R.J. Karstens said August IV was extremely particular about his vehicle and allowed no one else to drive it. He included the testimony of a witness who said August IV drove off at a high rate of speed with Michele as a passenger. He also reported that deputies had interviewed a man, "who stated that Mr. Busch was a user of cocaine." The samples and palmprints, Benson said, would "contribute to his identification as the individual who committed the crime because they could be compared with physical evidence obtained from the vehicle." A judge approved the petition the same day. August IV was ordered temporarily detained to provide the samples.

His lawyers, Brogna and London, fought the warrant on constitutional grounds. They argued that there had been no finding of probable cause that August IV had committed a crime. The state, they said, had only established that a fatal accident had occurred. The lawyers, two of the best in the business, also challenged the statute allowing the search as unconstitutional and pointed out that the state had already collected one blood sample from Busch.

Pima County Judge William Druke ruled on January 16, 1984, that there was reasonable cause to believe that the felony of manslaughter had taken place, and that taking evidence from August IV might contribute to the identification of the individual who committed the crime. He ordered August IV to give authorities the samples. His ruling was appealed to the Arizona Supreme Court, which suspended the judge's decision until it could hold a hearing on the matter February 28 in Phoenix. A day later, the state's high court agreed with Judge Druke. August IV was ordered to submit the samples.

But instead of August IV coming to Tucson, Deputy Benson flew to St. Louis to collect them. August IV's lawyers had argued that a plane trip might be dangerous, because of his head injuries and the possibility of future surgery. Arizona officials agreed to the plan as long as the state was not required to pay for the trip. August A. Busch III picked up the tab.

On March 14, Benson flew to St. Louis to collect three test

tubes of blood, twenty hairs, fingerprints and palmprints from August IV. Benson often found himself looking over his shoulder. He knew of the strong connection between the St. Louis police and the Busch family, and he was concerned about his own safety. "I felt there was a possibility that something was going to happen after I got the samples—that something would happen to me. I felt that real strongly. So, I took a lot of little precautions."

A representative of the Busch family was to meet Benson at the St. Louis airport and take him to the hospital where samples would be drawn. "When I got off the plane . . . it was interesting. They had somebody there with a big sign that said 'Deputy Benson' on it. I'm thinking to myself 'Right, like you expect me to walk up to this,' which I didn't. So I went on down to another gate and waited and watched who was there and tried to figure out how many people were working with this guy and all that kind of garbage that you do, and then finally met up with the man."

The man who met him was a security agent for the brewery and a former St. Louis police officer. Benson was out of his jurisdiction and away from any backup help. He felt uncomfortable. "And you are dealing with somebody who by this time I knew had lots and lots of money and lots and lots of power."

With Benson in his car, the security guard called ahead to St. John's Mercy Medical Center where the blood samples were scheduled to be drawn. When they pulled up, Benson thought he had interrupted the arrival of a visiting VIP. "There were all kinds of people in the parking lot, not people milling around but people at the intersections of streets around the hospital itself like they were controlling who's coming and going. All these people were apparently connected with Busch because we drove up to the back entrance after being waved through the successive little barriers of people into this little back area which I assumed to be some back floor of the hospital. And it was all Busch people. As a matter of fact, I think Mr. Busch III and his son, plus Mr. Norman London, pulled in either just before or after. So it became apparent that all of this was connected with the case, which was a trip."

At the hospital, the vials of blood were drawn and the hairs plucked from August IV's head. A doctor supervised the procedure. From there, Benson was taken to the St. Louis County police department headquarters where August IV was to be fingerprinted. "The interesting thing about that was that as we entered this building, as I recall, some of these people were in uniform and some weren't," Benson said. "But the curious thing was that as we went through the door, everybody was saying, 'Hi, Mr. London,' 'Hi, Mr. Busch,' 'Hi, Auggie.' " Benson received a different reception. He was told, "You, stop, let's see some ID."

After he collected the prints, Benson turned down an offer of lunch at the Busch farm. Returning to the airport, he had his driver drop him off "at a different gate from the one I was leaving on so I could check to see whether or not I was being followed. Sounds funny in retrospect, but it wasn't funny that day. And I flew back to Tucson."

It took a long time for the samples to be analyzed and a report prepared. It was July before the findings came back from the Arizona Department of Public Safety. August IV's blood type showed up on the driver's door, the driver's visor and other parts of the wrecked Corvette. For that reason Benson concluded that August IV was driving the car when it ran off the road. He estimated the speed between 42 and 52 miles per hour and that no brakes had been applied before the sports car went airborne. But putting August IV behind the wheel would not be enough. In addition to proving that he was operating the car at the time of the accident, the state would also have to show that he was driving it in a criminally reckless manner.

For the Pima County prosecuting attorney's office, it was too great a burden. Eight months affter the accident, the office announced that it did not plan to prosecute August IV. In a prepared statement, authorities said it could not be proven that he was under the influence of alcohol at the time of the accident. Although he might have exceeded the speed limit going through the curves, that alone was insufficient to support a homicide charge. Unless additional evidence developed, the county attorney's office considered the matter closed.

The death of Michele Frederick and August IV's involvement in it remains open. Some officials still hope to get additional information some day. "In Arizona,'" explained Zawada, "there is no statute of limitations for homicide."

Benson reflected on the incident years later. "In retrospect, if anything, this case has made me more obnoxious. I mean, I put more nails in every coffin now because there are so many little quirks that come up in dealing with these people—that now I'm inclined to overnail a case."

After the Arizona accident, Benson and other deputies involved in the case thought August IV was "on the fence." They agreed he was not "a dyed-in-the-wool little jerk," but neither was he a choir boy. "I remember the thought at the time, wondering where he will go," Benson said. "He's got all this power and all this wealth and which way is it going to take him? And we were curious about what kind of effect this case would have on him, one way or the other."

Their curiosity was satisfied within a year of the decision to drop the case against August IV in Arizona.

Traveling at eighty miles per hour, the 1985 Mercedes came screaming down the boulevard like a shiny streak of silver metal. Just behind it, an aging sedan struggled to keep up. Through the quiet, darkened streets of St. Louis, the race went on in the early-morning hours of May 31, 1985. The windows of the $47,000 luxury car were as dark as sunglasses, and the police officers in the pursuing car could not see who was behind the wheel. Some of the officers thought that they were chasing a well-known drug dealer.

For approximately fifteen minutes the two cars raced through the Central West End, a gentrified area of elegantly rehabilitated old homes that still had some rough edges. At times, the unmarked police car lost the Mercedes, but then another car of undercover narcotics detectives spotted it. The chase ended when Detective Dwaine Wilhite, riding shotgun in the pursuing car, shot out the left rear tire of the fleeing car.

When the Mercedes stopped, officers quickly surrounded it. The driver was pulled out, handcuffed and forced to lie on the pavement. "Why are you doing this to me?" the driver said to Wilhite. "Do you know who I am?"

In a few minutes, the police discovered that they had been chasing August A. Busch IV, the son of one of the city's richest and most powerful men.

"It's going to be a long night," said one of the four police officers who arrested him.

It had been quite a chase. Robert Thomure and Nicholas Frederiksen, two undercover narcotics detectives, had started to trail August IV at 1:30 A.M. when his speeding Mercedes nearly hit their unmarked police car. They pursued the car for fifteen minutes, lost it and radioed that they were giving up because of the high speeds involved.

A second unmarked police car, occupied by Wilhite and Junius Ranciville, picked up the chase. The officers said that they used their siren and red light in an attempt to stop the fleeing vehicle. At one point the car slowed enough for Wilhite to get out of his police car. As he approached the Mercedes, it suddenly accelerated, nearly hitting him. During the chase, Ranciville twice pulled up next to the Mercedes. Each time it swerved toward him. That was when Wilhite fired at the tire.

When they searched August IV's car, they found a .38-caliber stainless steel Smith & Wesson revolver on the floor behind the driver's seat. One cartridge was in the handgun and five were on the front floor. August IV was arrested on suspicion of two counts of assaulting police officers, carrying a concealed weapon and six traffic violations.

When they realized who it was they had just arrested, the police officers did something they might not have done if the driver had been a drug dealer. They changed the flattened tire. And one of the officers joked with August IV, telling him how he thought Grant's Farm was such a wonderful place, with its animals, train rides and free beer. August IV replied that he hadn't been on the train since he was twelve years old.

The officer was astonished. "Really? No, you should go back out there. It's a wonderful place, and I really love that little train you ride around in."

"You get me out of this," August IV said, "and I'll fucking give you that train."

Since his troubles in Arizona, August IV had enrolled in St. Louis University. His father, August, had asked university president Father Paul Reinert to keep his presence quiet. "No news," he said. "No news. You know what I mean?" But Reinert pointed out that it would be hard for the students not to know that a member of the Busch family was one of their classmates.

August IV was doing very well at St. Louis University. He received three As, one B and an incomplete during his spring classes of 1985. He had an overall average of 3.5 in the school of Business and Administration. But it was not all work for August IV. At the time of his arrest, he was returning from a bar in Sauget, Illinois, that featured topless female dancers. Then twenty years old, he was too young to drink legally. He said he did not stop for the pursuing cars because he did not know they were occupied by police officers. The men after him were not wearing uniforms, and he believed he was the target of a kidnapping attempt. He disputed the policemen's statements that they had used their flashing lights and siren.

Not surprisingly, police handled the case very gingerly. The department's top brass were called at home and hurried in to deal with the crisis. Arresting officers were ordered not to discuss the case. The official police report of the incident was kept under wraps. August IV was eventually charged with three misdemeanor counts of third-degree assault. Each count carried a maximum penalty of one year in jail. As he awaited trial, August IV was arrested again. He was cited by St. Louis County police for driving a black 1984 Porsche at sixty-five miles per hour in a thirty-five-mile-per-hour zone.

August IV's trial on the assault charges began in St. Louis on April 14, 1986. He was defended by Norm London, who had represented him in the Arizona case. A top defense attorney, London seldom dealt with misdemeanors. While the prosecutor attempted to prove that August IV had intentionally tried to run over two police detectives who showed him their badges as they approached his car, London argued that the officers had not used their lights and siren. He claimed that it was understandable that August IV could have mistaken them for kidnappers.

Throughout the three-day trial, August A. Busch III, his wife, Ginny, and his former wife, Susan, August IV's mother, sat in a rear bench, listening intently to the testimony. Wearing cowboy boots, August III glared at reporters and refused to answer questions. He stared intently at the police officers who had arrested his son. One of the officers never forgot August III's reddening face as he testified. "He was so mad, I thought he was going to explode." The only light moment occurred when witness Penny Coleman, a waitress at a St. Louis restaurant, was asked what August IV's favorite drink was. Bud Light, she answered. The Busch delegation smiled broadly.

The closing arguments were rough. "You have seen lies" in this courtroom, London said. "You have seen perjury committed. You have seen coverup." Prosecutor Eric Banks countered that young Busch was "a party person, who plays by his own rules." Banks was black, and with blacks on the jury there were knowing smiles among courtroom veterans when a young black attorney appeared at London's side at the defense table.

The jury acquitted August IV. Afterward, one of the jurors, Benjamin Davenport, said he was impressed with one of London's comments that encouraged the jurors to "walk a mile in the shoes of August Busch." Davenport said, "You have to walk in someone else's shoes, and sometimes those shoes are a little tight."

A few months later, August IV was placed on one-year's pro-
bation after pleading guilty to the speeding charge in St. Louis
County. The probation was ordered by Associate Judge Daniel
J. O'Toole, at the request of Busch's lawyer.

Because of the clout the brewery and the Busch family had
with the St. Louis police department, one of the officers who
had arrested August IV feared that his career would be ruined.
But he never saw any evidence of that as the years went by.
"There were no repercussions," said the detective.

August IV's mother, Susan Busch, said of her son, "There are
so many good things I would want to say about my son, things
no one knows about. I know my son to be a wonderful person,
but because of his name, he has suffered a lot."

August IV's encounters with the law did not slow down his
rapid rise at Anheuser-Busch. He got a bachelor of science degree in business and administration with a major in finance at
St. Louis University in January 1987. Then he worked as an
apprentice brewer and line foreman at the brewery. It wasn't
long before he was named an executive assistant for the vice
president of brewing.

August IV lived in a St. Louis townhouse and was served by
a maid and a personal valet whom a visitor found to be snob-
bier than Busch. He kept a busy schedule, flying in and out of
St. Louis, serving as a public relations representative for the
rock concerts that promoted Budweiser. When he was in St.
Louis, he worked out in the afternoon with weights. In the
evenings, he played the field. A young woman who dated him
thought he was open and friendly, but "pompous." He liked
blondes. "He's always with a blonde. When we first met and
talked, people and friends pulled me aside and said, 'Do you
realize who he is?' as if he were the prince or something. He's
pretty much of a party animal."

August IV often called her on short notice for a date, expecting her drop everything to meet with him at a restaurant.
"When he was running late, he would call up the restaurant
maître d' and say to him to tell me he would be late. He would
never give out his home telephone number. Instead, he used a
beeper. This was because an ex-girlfriend had constantly
called his home and used his answering machine to take messages off the answering machine."

The young woman knew she wasn't interested in August IV.
"I could never stay with him. He is very dominating."

68

"Tell Anheuser-Busch to Leave Our Kids Alone."

August IV's involvement in the car wreck in Arizona couldn't have come at a worse time for his father. The alcohol industry was embroiled in the most serious antidrinking campaign this country had seen since August A. wrestled with Prohibition. As head of the world's largest beer producer, August III was acutely sensitive to unfavorable publicity that linked his product to the drunken-driver menace and to society's rampant drug abuse. It didn't help that August III's son had been drinking before his Corvette careened off the road, killing Michele Frederick.

It infuriated August that his product was compared by some with cocaine, heroin and other hard drugs. "That is so ridiculous we can't even respond to it. What they're doing is sanctifying the use of crack, cocaine and heroin. When I go home tonight at dinner, I'll have a beer. My children will look at me drinking a beer. These critics would say that my children should look at that the same as me snorting cocaine. Beer is legal, legal, legal!" He grudgingly admitted that alcohol was a drug. "But the word drug is not a bad word. Is caffeine a drug? Yes. Is aspirin a drug? Yes."

August lumped the critics into what he called the "neoprohibitionist" movement. The company was forced to deal with an increasing array of public interest groups, congressmen and other officials who wanted to ban or restrict beer commercials such as Anheuser-Busch's Spuds MacKenzie, the piebald English bull terrier nicknamed the "Party Animal." They successfully got Congress to mandate warning labels on beer, wine and liquor containers and pushed to curtail the potent beer-sports connection and increase taxes on alcoholic beverages.

By the early 1990s, when alcohol consumption was declining, the ghosts of Carry Nation still walked the land. Instead of carrying hatchets, they were armed with facts and figures about the health risks and social costs of drinking to excess. The drunken driver—responsible for an estimated 26,000 deaths a year—received special attention. The yearly death toll laid on alcohol's doorstep was said to reach 100,000.

The statistical avalanche was chilling. Vocal, well-prepared groups like the Center for Science in the Public Interest, the National Parent-Teacher Association and the American Automobile Association Foundation for Traffic Safety claimed that between the ages of two and eighteen, the average child was exposed to as many as 100,000 television beer commercials. "By the time kids start kindergarten, they've already watched 2000 hours of beer and wine commercials. They see look-alike athletes, look-alike rock-stars and look-alike actors. Incrementally, they become comfortable with drinking." A former Anheuser-Busch executive put it this way: "They essentially create an environment where every kid in America thinks it's okay to drink beer."

Alcohol-related traffic crashes were the leading cause of death among Americans between the ages of fifteen and twenty-four. Of special significance to August, beer was the beverage of choice among the majority of those convicted of drunk driving. The AAA Foundation for Traffic Safety concluded that beer commercials were linked with male machismo, creating "a powerful, distorted and dangerous message." A study by the foundation and the Marin Institute entitled "Beer and Fast Cars: How Brewers Target Blue-Collar Youth Through Motor Sport Sponsorships" stated that highway crashes were the major cause of death for teenagers.

Beer brewers annually spent $50 million on racing events largely aimed at the "very population at greatest risk of drinking and driving." The study argued that the breweries had linked beer and fast cars "in a carefully crafted effort to promote beer, especially among working class youth and young adults who are part of the 'car culture.'" Anheuser-Busch had long promoted racing with its Budweiser Indy 500 car, its *Bud King* dragster and its *Miss Budweiser* hydroplane.

Alcohol, not cocaine and heroin, was the undisputed drug of choice for most young people. "Kids aren't doing crack," said Pat Taylor of the Washington-based Center for Science in the Public Interest. "Kids are doing beer." It was a message echoed by the National Commission on Drug-Free Schools, which identified alcohol and tobacco abuse as the most serious drug problems for those in school. The commission's twenty-six members blasted the alcohol and tobacco industries for targeting youths through expensive advertising campaigns. Their 1990 report, "Toward a Drug-Free Generation: A Nation's Responsibility," noted that nearly one-fifth of all high school seniors had been drunk as early as in the eighth grade. Alcohol was also blamed for more than half of the rapes, assaults and other incidents of violence on college campuses.

The commission viewed alcohol as a "gateway drug" in the sense that an overwhelming number of young drug abusers tried alcohol first. In their broad indictment, the members concluded that the alcohol industry often targeted those under the legal drinking age with "highly attractive and persuasive advertising and promotion techniques." Because most young people began drinking in their mid-teens, alcohol manufacturers stood "to increase their market share by establishing an early loyalty to their brand and few seem to have any compunction about such targeted advertising."

"Long before the debate exploded on Capitol Hill, August had recognized the sea change. For a start, he corrected an abuse that had gone on for decades under the corporate nose, namely the long-cherished right of brewery workers to swig free beer whenever they wanted, the so-called sternewirth or beverage privilege.

A relic of an era when nineteenth-century brewery workers had to put in eighteen-hour days in broiling heat or cold cellars, the free beer helped them get through their grueling shifts. By the 1980s, however, such widespread drinking on the job wasn't considered a suitable corporate image. In a regulatory climate, it was no longer acceptable to turn loose thousands of workers at quitting time with who knows how many of them under the influence. August convinced the unions to give up the practice. They still got their free beer—two cases a month—but they were to drink it at home, not at work.

There was no question in the mind of Bob Lewis, the former president of Anheuser-Busch's brewers' union, that free beer was dangerous. He had seen many "juiced" workers in his career. He had been juiced once himself. After drinking too much at the plant, he had wrecked his car on the way home, slamming into the back of a truck.

A more serious accident occurred in a tunnel beneath the brewery. St. Louis police would gather there late at night to drink as much free beer as they wanted. Cops from all over the city knew about the perk, but it was usually men from the Third District—their station house was just up the street—who assembled, glasses and cups in hand, after their shift ended. As many as thirty officers crowded around the spigots that tapped directly into the huge beer vats. One patrolman recalled that before the practice was ended, a cop who had had a few too many leaped onto a moving freight elevator only to scrape the side of his face against a scaffolding. He lost an ear.

A departed Anheuser-Busch executive, who admitted drinking beer while driving a forklift during the strike in 1976, said August also cleaned up the corporate offices. "They stopped providing beer to all the refrigerators for all the salaried personnel. . . . There were a lot of people depending on that beer to get them through the day." Russell Ackoff, August's mentor from the Wharton School, reportedly played a major role in convincing him to eliminate the free beer. "I think Ackoff told him," recalled one executive, "that if you don't clean up the brewery, you're going to get hit with another Prohibition."

A chorus of angry voices also wanted him to clean up his commercials. Spuds MacKenzie, with his nubile Spudettes and his party hardy message on behalf of Bud Light, came in for special attention. Spuds, a macho dog who was actually a she, had a way of sparking debate. In 1987, Strom Thurmond of South Carolina rose on the floor of the U.S. Senate, clutching a Spuds MacKenzie stuffed toy. The senator said he worried about the impact such a lovable-looking beer symbol had on children.

The National Council on Alcoholism, among many others, charged that Spuds irresponsibly encouraged underaged drinking. In New York, the state's alcoholism and drug abuse division called for a federal investigation of the Spuds campaign. "The commercials and marketing of Spuds MacKenzie as being cute, adorable and a 'party animal' encourage children and adults to drink beer." In one of his frequent assaults on alcohol advertising, Surgeon General C. Everett Koop wanted to muzzle Spuds and other ads for telling "youth that alcohol consumption leads to athletic, social and sexual success."

Faced with such a backlash, August put Spuds in the doghouse. The company claimed Spuds was a victim of overexposure, not scathing criticism. But when the pooch reappeared on the airwaves after about a year's absence, he was suddenly offering a more sober image, becoming August's "Know When to Say When" spokesdog. Anheuser-Busch's "Know When" program was launched in 1985. It was aimed at stressing moderate, responsible drinking, and when Spuds was unleashed again, he was suddenly barking up a new tree. "The message has been that Spuds knows how to party responsibly," said an Anheuser-Busch spokesman. "He knows when to quit drinking."

The company's new message brought to mind the days when August A. and Adolphus himself had defended beer as the drink of moderation. Critics didn't buy the message then just as their modern successors attacked the recycled version. Anheuser-Busch's tactics were slammed by Representative Thomas Luken of Ohio: "The whole purpose of drinking is to get a buzz on so you don't know when to say 'when.'"

Even the powerful National Association of Broadcasters, long an opponent of any regulatory limits on alcohol, began to get skittish. Its president admitted that congressmen were worried about the "sexy and youthful lifestyles" portrayed in beer commercials. "There is," he warned, "an ill wind blowing."

The wind had long blown the strongest from the office of Surgeon General Koop. An outspoken critic of beer and alcohol advertising, he had stopped short of calling for an outright ban, favoring voluntary restraints. But when two members of President George Bush's cabinet went even further, the ill wind suddenly looked like a hurricane.

Transportation Secretary Samuel Skinner and Health and Human Services Secretary Louis Sullivan aroused the ire of the alcohol lobby when they suggested that stricter regulation, even a ban of alcohol advertising might be needed. Groups like Remove Intoxicated Drivers wanted beer and alcohol ads pulled from television just as cigarette ads had been outlawed. When Sullivan announced that he "fully supported" that sentiment, the battle lines were drawn.

The new climate was illustrated by the fierce debate over the nomination of John Tower as secretary of defense. Tower, whose drinking habits were questioned, was forced to take the unprecedented step of promising on national television that if confirmed he wouldn't touch a drop. That was unheard of on Capitol Hill, where elected drinkers had long staggered down the halls of Congress only to be politely ignored by an indulgent press corps. Another unmistakable sign that public attitudes toward alcohol were shifting was the decision by a London securities firm to advise clients to reduce their holdings in Anheuser-Busch stock. "Claims against alcohol companies now raise the possibility," it warned, "that the beer industry could face a series of product liability claims similar to those faced by the cigarette industry."

The first major victory of the rejuvenated temperance movement was the requirement in 1989 that all alcoholic beverages carry a warning label about birth defects and other potential dangers. There was also a move to make the warnings even more inclusive by requiring them in broadcast advertising as well.

The breweries reacted to this proposal as if they had been gored. Do it and we'll pull our ads, they threatened. There were dire predictions—as if anyone really believed them—about the ruinous effect this would have on the sporting world, which floated on beer money. Jobs would be lost, they warned. Entire industries wiped out. As the beer lobby huffed and puffed, Gallup polls indicated 42 percent of the public supported a total ban of all beer, wine and liquor ads.

Anheuser-Busch, said Pat Taylor of the Center for Science in the Public Interest, had made a mistake by trying to portray critics of beer advertising as "crazies" and by continually raising the specter of Prohibition. "The fact is they underestimated the power of the public health movement in this country." Faced with the ability of companies like Anheuser-Busch to dominate the airwaves, Taylor admitted that it was difficult for the public health message to get through. "The power of the Busch family is so great. No matter where you go, you encounter the overwhelming influence of this family."

Public interest groups wanted equal television time to counter the relentless, channel-to-channel beer commercials. They also wanted to stop the breweries from promoting their products through sports and ads aimed at college audiences. Some of their most voluble complaints were over that blowout of all beer blowouts—Spring Break.

The annual spring migration to the beaches of Florida was one of the rites of passage for the nation's young people. Sun, sex and suds—so much suds that the international symbol for Spring Break could be a beer bottle.

If students saw this interlude as an opportunity to have a good time, the brewers saw it as an opportunity to sell beer. During one bash, Anheuser-Busch had set up an inflatable two-story Bud six-pack on the beach at Daytona, where employees distributed Bud T-shirts and hats among the 400,000 students who descended on the community. In 1978, the Florida Beverage Commission sought $18,000 in fines from Anheuser-Busch for ordering rounds on the house for college students. The brewery objected and three years later a Florida appeals court reversed the decision, ruling that the fines were inappropriate. No one disputed that the brewery had sponsored free beer parties in sixteen bars and taverns in Daytona Beach during the 1978 spring break. A spokesman admitted then that the company did "set up the house" on occasion. "The young adult market is very important to us. And this is the time to get them loyal to your product. . . . The kids loved it."

Beyond a doubt, the fuzzy-cheeked collegiate market was big and important. College students spend $2 billion to $3 billion a year on beer. But in a changed environment, Anheuser-Busch and other breweries started stressing moderation and sensible drinking at week-long beach parties like Daytona. Free breakfasts were offered along with free doughnuts and coffee.

Admittedly, the "Know When" and other messages were a hard sell when hotels and bars bombarded the students with free drinks, happy hours and two-for-one specials. The breweries, some argued, were targeting their message to those under the legal drinking age. "Spring break has gotten defined as a drinking holiday and the beer industry isn't doing anything to discourage that," said Christine Lubinksi of the National Council on Alcoholism. Many, if not most, of the revelers were under twenty-one. If the breweries were really concerned about underaged drinking, the argument went, why weren't they preaching abstinence instead of "responsible" drinking?

It was a question that Bobby Heard, a student from Texas, wanted answered. "If the alcohol industry is so concerned with our young people, why don't they just come out and once and for all tell young people under the age of twenty-one, because we care about you, we don't want your business." The thought was echoed by Anne Meyer of the National Federation of Parents for a Drug-Free Youth. Her message to the breweries: "We would rather have you use your expertise to advertise to young people not to drink at all, and why they shouldn't drink—not that they shouldn't drive drunk, because that isn't even a message for kids."

Another brewery practice that came in for heavy sledding was the use of students as company representatives on college campuses. Anheuser-Busch's youthful drummers were called the "brew crew." "They tried at first to have the wholesalers maintain a full-time rep in the college community, somebody who was going to school there," recalled a former Anheuser-

Busch district manager. "They got their tit in a wringer in a number of locations because a lot of these reps were under twenty-one, and of course the reps . . . might pass out coupons good for discounts on kegs of beer or free cups to encourage people to sample your product. . . . College administrations got wind of this and have plugged up a lot of those holes and a lot of those people have faded away."

The former manager said he received $100 to $150 a week to buy people beer. The money was called "spendings." He was expected to spend all of it to promote his products. "For nine and one-half years I did this in two states. You had to be very careful that the liquor commission did not find out. You had to use very roundabout ways to do it."

Florence "Jerri" Beardslee, who once owned a distributorship near San Francisco, recalled the letters she received from Anheuser-Busch encouraging her to sponsor a beer man on campus. She declined and complained about the practice, even to August himself. She was told that the company wasn't after the underaged drinker. She believed otherwise. "I said, well, your advertising materials don't promote what you are saying. It's a direct contradiction. . . . You say you are after adults but all the stuff that you have is geared toward the youth market."

Even one of the nation's largest brewers wondered whether things were getting out of hand. William K. Coors, chairman of the Adolph Coors Company, worried about the industry's "outrageous" lack of ethics in promoting beer sales among college students. Coors admitted that his company pushed its product hard on campuses, paying 250 college students to get the word out through wet T-shirt contests and beer parties. "We do this not because we think it is right, but because other brewers do it," Coors said frankly. "They will steal our lunch —they'll eat our lunch if we don't do it."

The breweries also pushed the sports-booze connection, a cozy relationship that likewise sparked protests. When National Collegiate Athletic Association executive director Richard Schultz suggested banning beer ads during television broadcasts of the annual NCAA basketball tournament, he might as well have doused himself with gasoline and lit a match. Schultz had pointed out the absurd paradox of allowing beer commercials to follow the NCAA's own public service announcements about alcohol abuse. "College and high school administrators have said the No. 1 problem on campus and in school is alcohol abuse. We are concerned that we are sending mixed messages by having drug-education spots followed by beer ads."

It was no surprise that Schultz was pilloried. There were howls of protest from college athletic directors, the brewing industry and the television networks—bedmates who feared their huge revenues would dry up with the beer. An NCAA spokesman, using a practiced form of newspeak, declared that Schultz "never proposed a ban in the first place." Schultz won a battle, if not the war, when the NCAA cut the maximum time for beer commercials during its popular postseason tournament from ninety seconds to sixty seconds an hour.

Divorcing sports from beer would be a daunting task. The ties have become too close, the symbiotic relationship too deep-seated. Only a handful of countries, Austria among them, outlaw public references to alcoholic beverages or tobacco during sporting events. It was a similar rarity when Stanford University, after a beer brawl at one of its games resulted in thirty arrests, proposed banning alcohol at all sports events.

Anheuser-Busch and the major breweries also received brickbats from African-American and Latino groups over their marketing tactics, especially with regard to such high-octane beverages as malt liquor. In Chicago's inner city a man known only as Mandrake had taken to whitewashing billboards that depicted sultry black women smoking cigarettes or men with matinee idol good looks clutching a can of malt liquor. A coalition of twenty-two ethnic and health groups argued that Anheuser-Busch was hyping the alcoholic potency in its King Cobra brand in ads that said, "The bite that's right." That line, the company insisted, referred to taste, not kick. Anheuser-Busch was "outraged" by a report that accused it and other breweries of "offensive" target marketing aimed at the Hispanic community.

The criticism began to take on ominous tones as more and more health officials, public interest groups and congressmen proposed limiting beer commercials. Some of the most extensive recommendations were offered by the National Commission on Drug-Free Schools. The commission's hard-edged suggestions included requiring equal time for what it called "counteradvertising." Paid for by the alcohol and tobacco industries, this campaign would try to curb drinking and smoking among the young. Another recommendation would require additional health and safety messages on all products and ad-

vertising. The commission also proposed raising taxes on cigarettes and alcoholic beverages, "especially beer."

One of the most controversial proposals would ban the advertising and promotion of alcohol and tobacco at colleges and
universities—and at their sporting events. Another called for a
total ban if advertising continued to target youth and glamor-
ize the use of alcohol and tobacco. In possibly one of its most
insightful recommendations, the commission proposed that
students be taught "the basic concepts of marketing alcohol
and tobacco." The idea was to show how companies try to
entice them through such seasoned practices as audience targeting and celebrity endorsements.

One Anheuser-Busch celebrity endorsement had to be
shelved when rock singer Eric Clapton cut a commercial for
Michelob, then later went into treatment for alcoholism. Clapton told *Rolling Stone:* "I was actually in treatment in Minnesota when that came on the TV. I was in a room full of
alcoholics, myself being one of them, and everybody went, 'Is
that you?' " Michelob halted the Clapton ads before the interview was published.

As the criticism and pressure mounted, Anheuser-Busch took
the lead in trying to defuse the crisis. It pumped more money
into its moderation ads and funded programs to combat alcohol abuse. It introduced low-alcohol and no-alcohol products.
It began fighting back. Just as his grandfather had done sixty
years earlier, August set up a consumer-awareness department
to reach the 80 million Americans who drink beer. Stories were
circulated about George Washington, Thomas Jefferson and
John Adams—Founding Fathers who had brewed beer. The
budget for the "Know When" campaign was increased from
$10 million to $35 million. Anheuser-Busch supported programs as diverse as the Alcoholic Beverage Medical Research
Foundation and Students Against Driving Drunk. Its "Pit
Stop" program was aimed at students headed for Spring
Break. In addition to the coffee and doughnuts, Anheuser-
Busch also offered "a message of personal responsibility" at
highway rest stops.

Taking a cue from its critics, the company played the statistics game, pointing out that the death toll from drunk driving
accidents had dropped steadily and the polls indicated the
number of adults who say they drive after drinking had declined 24 percent. Anheuser-Busch also hammered at the fact
that there was no persuasive scientific evidence suggesting

that beer advertising contributes to alcohol abuse. There were, as August himself mentioned, a number of scientific studies that associated moderate beer drinking with such health benefits as a lower risk for cardiovascular disease.

August kept fighting back. He made sure his company's point of view got through to political power brokers, the media and the public. When the National Commission on Drug-Free Schools issued its report, one of his executives was ready with a written, critical response. When public hearings touched on the beer business, Anheuser-Busch's representatives were in attendance—and often on their feet, asserting their company's position.

Little escaped them—not even the alcohol and drug talks delivered to school audiences by Ed Moses, a forty-five year-old sergeant with the Missouri Highway Patrol. The former undercover narcotics officer described the beer industry's marketing tactics during a lecture at a St. Louis high school. He mentioned Coors, Miller, Anheuser-Busch and Spuds MacKenzie. A few days later, Moses recalled, an Anheuser-Busch executive called the superintendent of the highway patrol. The executive wanted Moses to talk more generically about alcohol and not single out the St. Louis brewery.

The call upset Moses, who told his bosses that the young men and women killed in Driving While Intoxicated accidents did not have generic names. "Tell Anheuser-Busch to leave our kids alone," he remembered saying.

A few days later, Moses delivered the same speech—this time with his supervisors watching. They complimented him afterward. "I didn't get any pressure from within, but pressure was applied by Anheuser-Busch," Moses said.

Pressure was something August understood. Above all, he insisted on a "stronger, more vocal stance in defense of our products." He wanted to convince the public that beer was as American as apple pie and baseball. "We must promote the consumption of alcoholic beverages as a part of normal, everyday life."

The risks were that the public was starting to take a close, critical look at how August and his beer brethren promoted their products. As the biggest of the big, Anheuser-Busch got more attention than anyone else—and some of the sharpest criticism. The situation called to mind the final years of his great-grandfather Adolphus, as he tried to beat back the winds of national prohibition. There were fires wherever he had

turned, the abuses of his industry too conspicuous to be overlooked. These same fires were again burning hotly.

No one really believed that beer would be banned as it had
been earlier in the century. But the advertising and aggressive
promotions of companies like Anheuser-Busch were another
matter. Unless they toned down their message all that just
might have to go, some warned. Similar warnings had been
leveled at Adolphus. Correct the abuses of the saloon and other
excesses or risk prohibition. Unwilling to listen, the brewers
had been forced to swallow nearly a generation of bitter medicine. The experience had killed most of them.

August knew all that. He also knew that the potent issue of
drunken driving was something Adolphus had been spared.
The auto was still in its infancy when the Prince died in 1913.
How different was today's climate and how incredible that in
a state like August's native Missouri it was perfectly legal to
drink a beer while driving a car. With drunken drivers considered a national menace, every fatal accident involving his
product became a corporate scar.

When *Newsweek* reported the death of a pretty high school
homecoming queen in a car wreck near Honesdale, Pennsylvania, it noted that "a bloody six-pack of Michelob Light" was
found by her side in the wreckage. The article, "Pennsylvania
Gothic" said that the dead woman's twenty-one-year-old
brother was accused of shooting to death the driver of the car,
who survived the crash. Ironically, the dead girl had been an
active member of the local chapter of SADD, Students Against
Drunk Driving. So how had it happened? *Newsweek* suggested
an answer. Court testimony had indicated she "more likely fell
victim to the very equation she so frequently warned against;
the search for fun through alcohol, a fast car and a winding
mountain road."

For August all this must have seemed to be a no-win situation. By every measure he had reached the pinnacle of success.
But the more his products dominated the American market,
the more his commercials engulfed the airwaves, the louder
became the criticism. Some said that he did not know when to
say when.

69

The "Archetypal Playboy"

William Kurt "Billy" Busch was a piece of work. At six feet one inch and 215 pounds, his chest and arms rippled with muscles sculpted by diligent iron pumping. In many respects Billy was just a beer-drinking good ol' boy with a taste for cowboy boots, pickup trucks and fistfights. His passion was polo. Billy had a string of eight ponies and every winter traveled to Florida to match his skill against the best riders in the world.

By most accounts, Billy was an exceedingly friendly young man who had the uncanny ability to get into jams. The third oldest of Gussie Busch's sons by his marriage to Trudy, he was born August 22, 1959, and named after Trudy's Swiss father, William, and her brother, Kurt. Like his older brother Adolphus and his younger brother, Andrew, Billy attended the Priory, an exclusive boys' high school run by an order of Catholic monks in St. Louis. Billy graduated in 1978. The caption under his yearbook photo said, "You can't budge me an inch."

After trying out for the University of Missouri's football team —he was an all-conference linebacker in high school—Billy enrolled at St. Louis University. Gussie favored the Jesuit school. Presided over by his old friend, Father Paul Reinert, it was the university of choice for the Busch clan. Seven of them attended at various times. Gussie's son Adolphus graduated with a degree in business administration in 1976; daughter Trudy received a nursing degree in 1980. Beatrice and Peter, two more of Gussie's children, also took courses but didn't graduate. Andy, enrolled in 1981, had spent nearly a decade working toward a degree. Billy earned his BA in psychology, graduating *cum laude* in 1988, ten years after he left high school.

Polo was the main reason for Billy's long delay. He was dedicated to the sport, which has been likened to hockey on horseback. Billy and Andy usually dropped out of school in January to compete in the three-month winter polo season in Florida. With all that time spent in the saddle, there wasn't much time left for sitting in a classroom.

Among the most dangerous of sports, polo was part of the Busch heritage. Gussie had played and had seen to it that his sons learned the fine points early. The raw speed and power of the game were appealing to his offspring. Eight men on horseback, wielding bamboo-handled mallets like sabers, charging up and down a playing field three times as long as a football field. Slamming into an opposing rider at full-tilt on horseback was perfectly legal as long as it was done properly. Serious injuries and even fatalities were not unheard of. Adolphus, who had once scored three goals in a match with Prince Charles, had his nose smashed. Other family members had had shoulders crushed and arms broken. All had friends who died in horrible spills. "I would imagine," said Gussie's nephew Adolphus "Dolph" Orthwein, Sr., a devotee, "that statistically more people are killed playing polo than any other sport."

Along with its strong aroma of danger, the sport also had the undeniable cachet of wealth. Rich men with their strings of polo ponies. Lush playing fields in exotic places. The Rolls-Royces and Bentleys pulled up to tented pavilions. Servants in white jackets serving chilled champagne—or Budweiser. Polo stars imported from Argentina, the "Argies," the best in the world. Unrepentant playboys and the rich and beautiful women who attached themselves to the sport and its players.

Every winter, Billy rode for a team in Boca Raton sponsored by Michelob. During his playing career, which started while he was in his mid-teens, he had purchased about twenty-five horses ranging in price from $1,500 to $25,000. The average price tag was $10,000. One recent string of eight ponies was valued at $80,000, money that had come from his $2 million trust. He was "known for his long ball and aggressive play." It was a style of play that carried over into his personal life.

In December 1981, Billy was spending a quiet Saturday night at a St. Louis bar called H.P. Cassidy's Saloon. He later bought a part interest in the place. But on this particular evening, he was playing Foosball when someone challenged him to an arm wrestling contest. Billy obliged, his grip and biceps made powerful by hours of bench pressing and dumbbell curls. A group of young men gathered to watch. "I don't believe you can beat us farm boys," one of them told Billy.

"It was late," Billy recalled. "It was about twelve-thirty, one in the morning. This one fellow wanted to arm wrestle me, so he did and I beat him; and he said I was cheating. . . . I said, We'll do it again. So we did it again, and I beat him again; and he got very upset and asked me to step outside with him. So we went outside, and we started fighting. I had him on the ground, and I thought we were going to end it right there."

The spectators started shouting, "Bite him! Bite him!"

With his arms pinned behind his back, Billy's nineteen-year-old opponent gave it a try. A mistake.

"I bit him back," Billy said. "And his ear came off."

Only the lower lobe was left. The upper half of the ear came cleanly off in Billy's teeth.

Later, a judge involved in another of Billy's escapades was intrigued by the incident and wanted to know how much he had paid his victim.

"Twenty-five thousand," Billy answered.

Efforts to reattach the ear were unsuccessful. No charges were filed against Billy because he hadn't started the fight.

He wasn't as fortunate eight months later when he was arrested on charges that he had assaulted a nineteen-year-old employee at a Mexican fast-food restaurant. Billy had pulled his pickup truck into the parking lot around three in the morning. Words were exchanged with several employees as Billy and two friends ate on the restaurant's patio. About to leave an hour later, Billy heard one of the workers behind the drive-up window say "something vulgar . . . something to the effect that your mother sucks." Billy reacted swiftly. "I reached in on him. I barely grazed him." His young antagonist filed a $500,000 lawsuit, claiming he suffered spinal column injuries and was forced to wear a neck brace. It was a felony charge, but Billy was acquitted during a nonjury trial. He dressed for the occasion in a blue suit and brown cowboy boots. The prosecuting attorney for St. Louis County, George R. "Buzz" Westfall—perhaps remembering that Billy had sarcastically said, "I'll buy my way out of this"—called the verdict a disappointment. Seven years later, Westfall would have occasion to intervene again in a matter involving Billy Busch.

"One gets the sense not that they are barons who rule the peasantry," wrote *Post-Dispatch* columnist Bill McClellan, "but that they are, at heart, peasants themselves. Filthy rich

peasants, but peasants. Nothing prissy about the Busch clan."
He was commenting about Billy, "a regular beer-drinking,
truck-driving, bar-fighting guy," who had met his perfect
match in Angela Teresa "Boo" Whitson, a willowy, full-
breasted young woman with a hard-luck background. "Mixed-
up soulmates," they were called. The two, appropriately, met
in H.P. Cassidy's, the same bar where Billy had performed
masticatory surgery on the ear.

Billy and Boo were introduced in 1981 by a friend, another
young woman with an intriguing past who was dating Billy's
brother Andy. Her name was Connie Hanna, and Andy, who
apparently shared his brother's tastes in women, dated her for
five years. When they split up in 1987 she fled to California
because "I had a broken heart." She would later plead guilty
to burglary and robbery charges.

Angela Whitson was seventeen, married, and the mother of
an infant son named Ashley when she met Billy Busch. A year
earlier, she had dropped out of high school after getting pregnant. She and her husband lived in a house trailer without
running water or electricity. It was a "Tobacco Road," or to
use the local vernacular, a "hoosier" existence. Billy—he was
twenty-one when he first beheld Angela in the noisy bar—soon
changed all that.

In the beginning, it was anything but love at first sight for
Angela. "He repulsed me," she said. "He was a slob and he told
dirty jokes." Billy had his own peculiar brand of slumming.
He liked bars, boots and blue jeans and had the money to
indulge his taste for horses. He could also be witty, considerate
and persistent. Changing her mind about the strapping millionaire, Angela began to date him. Billy wasn't so bad once
you got to know him, she thought. "He charmed the pants off
me."

Soon there were trips to what she called "the castle" at
Grant's Farm. It was quite a change for the teenager, who had
had a tough life as a child. Her father died when she was two
years old. Angela grew up in a small house with her mother,
described later by a judge as an alcoholic. Also living in the
house were her grandfather, described as an alcoholic by Billy
in court testimony; her grandmother; her mother's eleven
brothers and sisters; assorted aunts and uncles of her own age;
and Robert Whitson, a boy raised by the family whom she later
married.

Billy offered Angela a Cinderella glimpse of another world,

of butlers, mansions, riding stables and travel. But even though their affair looked promising in the beginning, this was no fairy tale. He swept her off her feet with those visits to Grant's Farm, where she remembered that the bedroom rugs were made of furs and the elevator had a bar stocked with sherry. For three years Angela and Billy "were quite an item." In May 1983, Angela and her husband were divorced. She kept custody of her son, Ashley. A month later she had her second child, a girl. Angela, who loved the movie *Gone With the Wind*, named her Scarlett.

Playing polo at St. Louis Country Club, Billy was two hours late for the birth of his daughter. It wasn't a planned pregnancy. In fact, Angela had been pregnant once before by Billy and had also had a miscarriage. When they found out she was expecting the first time, he drove her to a clinic for an abortion. After Scarlett was born, Billy never denied he was the father of the child, who bore a strong resemblance to him. She had the same blue eyes, the same light blond hair, the same full face. Within a month of Scarlett's birth, Billy moved Angela and Scarlett into an apartment and provided $150 a week for expenses. He later bought and furnished an $80,000 condominium for her. He visited at least once a week. And Angela and her two children were frequent visitors at Grant's Farm, where Gussie apparently accepted the somewhat remarkable situation with aplomb, as did Trudy.

Money to support Angela and her children was, of course, no problem. Billy merely had to tap his trust fund. His yearly income from his trust was about $120,000. He later acquired a one-sixth interest worth $12 million in the Silver Eagle Anheuser-Busch distributorship in Houston. Joining him in this enterprise were his brothers Adolphus and Andy. Billy's fees as a director of Silver Eagle were $50,000 a year. Rounding off his income was the $4.50 an hour he earned for his labor at Grant's Farm, where he lived with Gussie and Andy.

Billy loved working outdoors. His tasks at Grant's Farm were varied. He trained the elephants; he trained "a pooch and monkey to do tricks." He built fences, cut down dead trees and split wood. He helped build new houses for the workers who lived on the estate. He helped build animal feeders and pens and laid down grass seed and painted. He also attended classes at St. Louis University.

For diversions, Billy lifted weights, rode his polo ponies, partied and drank beer "three maybe four times a week . . . sometimes I drank a lot at one time and didn't drink for a few days after that." On occasion, he also used drugs, often with Angela. They smoked marijuana six to a dozen times, he calculated. Billy admitted using cocaine "approximately six times," including once at a New Year's Eve party at Grant's Farm. He tried a Quaalude.

Angela was a much heavier user, according to court testimony. Her drug of choice was crystal—an amphetamine. By 1986, she was snorting the stuff on a daily basis, sometimes in front of her children, and selling it to her friends. Under the influence of drugs, her life unraveled. She had heated arguments with Billy. She frequently left her children for long periods. Once, after saying she was going to get some milk, Angela drove to Memphis with two men for the tenth anniversary of the death of Elvis Presley. She was gone nearly a week. At various times, Angela modeled bikinis and lingerie at bars and restaurants; she danced at bachelor parties. Competing for a $1,000 prize in a swimsuit contest, she was arrested for lewd and lascivious behavior. She was also arrested and placed on probation for endangering the welfare of her son by leaving him unattended.

During this roller-coaster period, Angela met Karla Stratton, a dancer at PTs—a bar featuring topless dancers. It was a place where men came with fistfuls of dollar bills suitable for stuffing under G-strings. Karla was dating another of the Busch boys—August IV, the son of Anheuser-Busch's president, August A. Busch III. They dated for about four months in 1986. Karla remembered that Angela joined her for a topless dance one evening.

Billy and Angela's relationship began showing the strain. Their arguments became more heated. He didn't like her "promiscuous behavior," the way she wore shorts "that were cut up very high" and her "very, very tight pants . . . and small halter tops." He didn't like the fact she dressed Scarlett the same way. Angela used to taunt him by telling people they were engaged. "He hated that. The guy was so heavy into his freedom." She claimed that he broke her ribs during a hayride at Grant's Farm. Billy's version was that a girl "stuck some straw" down his back and Angela "just threw a complete fit . . . she jumped on me and started pulling my hair and punched me." Billy held her until she calmed down. The hayride continued, "but it wasn't much fun after that."

Billy finally stopped seeing Angela. "I knew she had a drug

problem, and I couldn't help her." Angela had a different version of their breakup. She started hearing stories about Ginger. At first she thought it was one of Billy's horses. Ginger turned out to be a new girlfriend.

In September 1987, Angela took her two children to the small town of Hesperia in the Mojave desert of southern California where she had relatives. She wanted to get away from Billy and away from her family. She also wanted more child support—a great deal of it, $10,000 a month. "Our daughter Scarlett," she explained, "has developed a close and intimate relationship with the Busch family including her grandfather, August (Gussie) Busch and her grandmother, Gertrude (Trudy) Busch." The family has "almost raised her in the lifestyle of a princess. Scarlett was baptized in Gertrude's family mansion and has taken weekly coach rides at the Busch family castle. . . . Scarlett is a precocious five-year-old who has her own horse and has been riding horses since she was two years of age. Her grandparents have impressed upon her that she should wear $200 riding boots and to do her clothes shopping at Saks Fifth Avenue where her grandparents often take her. Scarlett has had her hair done along with her grandmother at fancy salons. She has enjoyed riding on the family elephants . . . . She has her own bedroom in the family castle." Ashley, she stated, had received the same treatment. Angela suggested "that $10,0000 per month would not be unreasonable" especially considering that she believed Billy's income exceeded $200,000 a month and that he had been paying her $3,500 a month "plus clothes and other fringe benefits."

Thus an ugly fight began between an heir to one of the world's largest fortunes and a young woman who had once modeled lingerie. Billy went to his father's lawyer, Lou Susman, who was also general counsel for the St. Louis Cardinals. Lawsuits began flying. Angela accused Billy of threatening to have her killed, a charge she later withdrew.

Even with her life now under a microscope, she continued to neglect her children and use drugs, according to a judge who later examined the case. Neighbors reported seeing Scarlett playing in an abandoned, glass-strewn car or sitting by the roadside, crying, looking for her mother. In eight months Angela lived in five different places in California, including a motel room. She worked as a bartender and she astounded Billy by telling him she had a job as a gardener. He had never seen Angela "do anything that resembled gardening." Then she explained. "I'm the type of gardener that goes to guys' houses and does things for them in a sexual type of way." Not "a call girl gardener." Just a "kinky gardener."

Angela started seeing a man who also used cocaine and crystal. Her new boyfriend—his name was Gino—had a "sociopathic personality" and on occasion "drank too much." In a rage, he struck Angela, but that didn't stop her from leaving her children with him. There were reports that he struck them, too. Billy, meanwhile, had cut off Angela's living expenses. "I was bouncing checks all over the desert," she said. "I woke up one morning and my car was gone." Her 1987 Ford turbo-coupe had been repossessed. In fact, Angela went through cars —five of them were purchased by Billy—as if she drove in a demolition derby. She wrecked two, including the Thunderbird that was repossessed.

On July 4, 1988, Billy decided to rescue the children after receiving a telephone call from Angela's great-aunt in California. Angela, he was told, was in bad shape. She was living with Gino, who was described as a drug dealer. More ominous, the children were in trouble. Ashley was bruised. Scarlett reportedly had been sexually molested by a young girl who lived next door. Billy flew to California. He called Angela, who told him in tears to come right over, that Gino was a "lunatic psycho" and that she was afraid he would beat her up.

Billy arrived just as the police were handcuffing Gino and putting him in a squad car. He asked to talk to Angela's new boyfriend. "Gino told me that . . . Angela was spending most of her time away from the children and that she was using drugs and that he was very upset with her because now she wanted to go out with some guy that came from New York who drove a black Corvette. . . . He told me that this guy is the biggest drug dealer in New York. . . . He said I had to get the children out . . . of the environment."

The next day Billy returned to Grant's Farm with Scarlett and Ashley. Angela followed him to St. Louis when he refused to return them. With the help of her attorney, Michael McAvoy, she started fighting to get the children back. Billy's flock of high-priced lawyers, which included Susman, hired private investigators to explore Angela's background. They also began to represent Robert Whitson, her former husband, who suddenly filed for custody of eight-year-old Ashley.

Billy kept the children for two months. He got a break from a sympathetic juvenile court commissioner who awarded him temporary custody without holding a hearing. "Busch wasn't even required to come to the courthouse. All [the commissioner] needed to know was what Busch wanted."

Even with court papers in his hand ordering Billy to release the boy and a sheriff's deputy to back it up, McAvoy was halted by guards at the gate to Grant's Farm. A police officer, allowed on the grounds, was told by a lawyer that Billy wasn't at home. After a frustrating two-hour wait, McAvoy finally left. It was an example, he said, of the family's ability to obstruct the legal process. "Who else in this country," he asked, "can pull what he has pulled?"

McAvoy's exasperation increased when Susman walked into the newsroom of the *Post-Dispatch* and asked senior editors to kill a column that had been prepared about the custody fight. The story was spiked. The editors for the paper, which subsequently covered the affair in detail, said they were trying to protect the children. McAvoy said it was just another example of buckling under to the Busches' influence.

Angela's lawyer had his hands full. He was badly outmanned by Thompson & Mitchell, the legal firm that employed Susman, and three other lawyers handling Billy's case. McAvoy convinced the county's prosecuting attorney, Buzz Westfall, to order Billy to return Ashley. Billy complied and the boy was turned over to his mother. McAvoy won another round when the Supreme Court of Missouri overturned the juvenile court ruling giving Billy temporary custody of Scarlett. Then, unexpectedly, the court announced it had taken jurisdiction of the case. Until a final ruling was made, Billy and Angela were to share custody of Scarlett.

The decision was unprecedented. No one could recall the last time the Supreme Court had taken jurisdiction in a custody fight. It often took years for such cases just to reach the circuit court level, but here was one that in a matter of weeks sailed right to the top. "Being a Busch," observed one writer, "means never having to stand in line."

The Supreme Court appointed a retired circuit court judge named Frank D. Connett, Jr., to hear the case and report his findings. The hearing occurred in St. Louis in early April 1989 behind closed doors. McAvoy objected to Connett's decision to close the proceedings to the public. It wouldn't have happened, he said, "except for Billy's last name."

It quickly became apparent that the fundamental issue was whether Angela was a fit mother to have custody of her daugh-

ter, then six years old. "This will be, at minimum, a lurid tale,"
Billy's lawyer, David Wells, cautioned the judge shortly before
the hearing began. Angela made her courtroom entrance,
carrying a baby, which she placed on a table before the bench.
It was her third child, an infant daughter. Gino was the father.

Billy came in for some rough moments during his long inter-
rogation by McAvoy. Earlier depositions became part of the
court record, including testimony about the ear-biting episode.
The grilling was merciless. Billy was forced to name all the
women he could recall sleeping with.

"Go ahead, fire away," he said when the subject turned to
his girlfriends.

What about Ginger, for example, the girlfriend Angela had
mistaken for a horse? "Do you recall her last name?"

"No."

"Was Ginger one time, or more than one time?"

"More than once."

"About how many times?

"Fifteen."

And on and on until he was asked, "Is there any other woman
you have had sexual relations with?"

"Yes, I can't recall their names."

Asked about his parenting skills, Billy said, "Well, I haven't
read the whole thing, but I started to read a parenting psychology book."

Angela appeared in an even more unfavorable light. "Pregnant six times by three men to whom she was not married at
the time of conception, twice by Robert Whitson, three times
by [Billy] and once by Gino. . . . From this she has had three
children, two abortions and one miscarriage." Angela admitted to sexual affairs with four other men after the birth of
Scarlett, one of them with Donny Houghton, an escapee from
a prison in Indiana. Then there was the long litany of her drug
use and the neglect of her children. Connett, a crusty, no-non-
sense judge from St. Joseph, Missouri, found that she was "absolutely unfit" to have custody of Scarlett. He recommended
that Billy get complete custody of the child with only limited
visiting rights for the mother. Angela, who once said she was
fighting a "monster" in dealing with the Busches, was devas-
tated. "In my heart, I believe that this whole thing was fixed."

The Supreme Court later affirmed Connett's findings and
awarded custody of the child to Billy. But not without some
blistering observations by Charles B. Blackmar, the chief jus-

tice. "I cannot say very much in Busch's favor. He is the archetypal playboy. He lives and 'works' at Grant's Farm, helping to train elephants and dogs for the public shows there and tending crops and gardens. He spends considerable time in Florida playing polo. He has experimented with cocaine and other illegal substances, but there is no evidence that he has done so recently, or is a substance abuser. He is the beneficiary of a family trust to which he resorts when he needs money. He has a current flame whom he visits regularly and sometimes brings to Grant Farm. His counsel have stipulated to his ability to pay whatever expenses may be charged against him, possibly to avoid further inquiry into his resources. . . . I doubt that he will allow his daughter to stand in the way of his pursuit of transient pleasures."

In a final shot, Blackmar ordered the entire record of the proceedings opened to the public, and not kept under seal as Billy's lawyers had so strenuously requested.

Not long after the verdict, Billy moved to Houston with Scarlett. He wanted to attend to his distributorship, no doubt in part to try to defuse a legal dispute that challenged the Busch boys' right to own a Texas beer distributorship without living in the state.

Billy made the papers again when he delayed a TWA flight in Chicago so that Domino's could deliver his pizza. Billy had some advice for one of the flight attendants. "If anyone drinks other than Anheuser-Busch products, ask them to leave the plane."

Angela, for her part, tried to get a book contract and began making the rounds of the television talk shows. When she appeared on *Geraldo*, she cried. Finally, in one of the more bizarre epilogues to a bizarre story, Angela won custody of Ashley. She was ruled completely unfit to have custody of her daughter, and yet was considered fit enough to raise her son.

70

Horses and Horses' Asses

At the age of eighty-one, Gussie Busch drove a coach and four at the Royal Agricultural Show in England. He met Queen Elizabeth II and impetuously invited her to visit Grant's Farm. He later told friends that the monarch was much prettier in person than in her pictures.

In his ninth decade, Gussie had become a St. Louis icon. He was named the city's outstanding citizen of the last half century. When he attended civic meetings, the guests stood as he entered. He walked with a cane because of arthritis made worse by the replacement of a hip joint. "That hip joint," he joked, "can forecast bad weather faster than the weather bureau."

Gussie was a legendary figure who went out of his way to look the part. His cane with a ram's head handle was a family heirloom. He usually wore a Western style string tie fastened at the neck by a jeweled A-and-Eagle clasp that had been the Prince's watch fob. At baseball games, he wore a red jacket and red cowboy hat. Superstitious, his right boot always went on first, and he was never caught without his two buckeyes and lucky coins.

He could still put them away. When one of his daughters, Beatrice, was married, someone asked him about a scratch on the cheek of one of his in-laws. "That crazy son-in-law of mine drank 15 martinis last night, while I had 17. I got a little tight and we fell all over each other trying to stand up."

Gussie's physical problems worsened. He was hospitalized for twelve days with gastrointestinal bleeding. His nights were restless. He increasingly relied on his secretary, Margaret Snyder. "Goddammit, get over here," Gussie told her on the telephone. "I don't know which pills to take." Margaret invariably obeyed, playing gin rummy with him until he fell asleep.

Margaret Snyder had joined the company in 1942 and became the first woman named to the board of directors of Anheuser-Busch. Although a certified professional secretary, she became a vice president and director of the brewery. She was also a director of the Cardinals and Busch Properties, a real estate development subsidiary. Her husband died in 1974, the same year she was named vice president.

Gussie leaned more and more on Margaret for help, companionship and advice. By 1980, he began discussing with family and friends the idea of marrying his longtime secretary. A family friend described the twosome as "a brother-sister relationship." But his desire to marry Margaret imperiled his relationship with the Catholic church. Gussie had been divorced from Trudy in civil court; he was still married to her under the laws of the church. He asked his old friend, Father Paul Reinert, to see whether his marriage could be annulled. This time the priest wasn't able to help. Gussie took the plunge anyway. There had never been any doubt.

Hosting a private party at his winter home in Pass-a-Grille on March 16, 1981, Gussie announced that he had married his former secretary in a private ceremony a few days earlier. Just days short of his eighty-second birthday, he had embarked on his fourth marriage. Margaret was sixty-four. The couple moved to Phoenix and bought a big home. Some thought Gussie went west to relive the happier days of his youth. "But it was a bust," said a family friend. "They just sat there. They didn't know anyone." The couple returned to Grant's Farm, but things were not the same. Margaret built a wall around Gussie that few penetrated. Old friends, even family members, were cut off from him. They called her "the sheriff." Some thought Gussie was her prisoner.

It was during this period that Gussie and Al Fleishman got the idea to write a book on his life. The idea fascinated him and his enthusiasm bubbled over after Fleishman showed him the first few chapters. "Oh my God," Gussie cried out, reading the material. "We'll make a fortune." "He almost had an orgasm," Fleishman said later. The book was never written. When Margaret found out, the idea was shelved. "Margaret's entering the picture pretty well killed the book deal," Fleishman said.

When the Boy Scouts wanted to name a camp after Gussie, officials approached Fleishman, who called Margaret to try to arrange an appointment.

"Why?" Margaret asked curtly.

"They want to name a camp after him."

"We don't have any money!"

"Margaret, they don't want money."

"Then they'll want stock."

The meeting, like the book, never got off the ground.

Margaret also estranged Gussie from his niece Sallie Wheeler, the daughter of his late brother Adolphus III. "She was very hurt for a long time." A family friend said Margaret also seemed to look for opportunities to be critical of Gussie's children by Trudy. He said she had a "what can you expect?" attitude toward them.

None of these children was involved directly in the brewery's operations. Adolphus IV, the oldest son, became a stockbroker and lived on the Shooting Grounds. Peter operated a beer distributorship in Florida, while his brothers Andy and Billy took care of Grant's Farm and dabbled with their Houston distributorship. Trudy became a nurse after completing her degree in 1980. Beatrice studied languages in Lucerne, traveled in Africa and tried her hand at writing. She married three times. Following a tradition set by some of her ancestors, she chose a relative, Adalbert von Gontard III, for her most recent husband. He was her second cousin once removed.

Gussie's children were present when he celebrated his eighty-sixth birthday at his beach house at Pass-a-Grille. They were joined by a friend, Peter Palmer. "Gussie and I, well we both got a little loaded," Palmer recalled. "He does that from time to time."

Gussie wanted to sing, so they gathered around the piano in the living room. "We all sang," Palmer said, "including August." It was the only time Palmer ever saw Gussie's oldest son let his hair down. Gussie lustily sang a favorite of his, "Bad, Bad Leroy Brown."

During a visit to Grant's Farm, Palmer and Gussie watched the horses drink at a pond. " 'Gussie, how does it feel to be looking over all these horses' asses?" Palmer asked.

Gussie smiled. "I know a lot more horses' asses than I've got horses."

Aging quickly, the beer baron still insisted on royal treatment. When he took a carriage tour of his estate, the staff and grounds keepers stopped whatever they were doing, removed their hats and stood stiffly at attention. When Francis Barnes, a visitor, witnessed this, he thought he had gone back 100 years to see the passage of a Prussian noble.

Although Gussie had long since retired from the active management of Anheuser-Busch, he continued to own and control enormous blocks of stock because of the trusts created by his mother and father. As the brewery's profits grew under his son's relentless energy, Gussie's wealth doubled and redoubled until he was far richer than his grandfather Adolphus had ever been.

He also continued collecting $202,000 a year for the rental of Grant's Farm from Anheuser-Busch, $177,000 for concessions and $1 million reimbursement to cover expenses. On top of that, he received $12,600 as annual rent for the eighty-four-acre Clydesdale breeding farm and $300,000 for expenses.

In 1988, *Forbes* magazine ranked Gussie thirty-sixth among the 400 richest Americans. Worth $1.1 billion, he held 13 percent of all Anheuser-Busch stock. His holdings were so large that he lost or gained hundreds of millions of dollars with fluctuations of the stock market. During a bullish period in 1983, he made $111 million. When the market crashed on October 19, 1987, he lost $189.4 million in a single day. To prevent wide fluctuations in Anheuser-Busch stock prices after his death, the brewery announced there was a plan to dispose of Gussie's 35.6 million shares. It was revealed—without details, of course—in September 1987, two months after Gussie completed his will.

His health grew more fragile, and frequent bouts with pneumonia often led family and friends to believe he had only weeks to live. But each time Gussie astonished them by rallying and recovering. He seemed indestructible.

Margaret was not so fortunate. She died from complications following surgery on August 4, 1988. For six or seven weeks prior to her death, she had been acting strangely. Medical tests revealed a malignant brain tumor. She died of a pulmonary embolism at the age of seventy-two.

After Margaret's death, Gussie called Trudy. "He even went so far as to ask her to come out and go coaching with him," said a friend. "That was as close as he could get to a reconciliation with her, but for Gussie, that was quite an effort."

Trudy did not accept his invitation.

71

"Get a Bad Apple at the Top and You've Got Super Trouble."

The glittering nature of Anheuser-Busch's beer business came to light during the revealing, often entertaining trial of two vice presidents and another man on charges that they had bilked the company and the IRS through a kickback scheme. The president of the brewing division, Dennis Long, resigned. Five key executives were either fired or ordered to leave. August was said to be "mortified" when he learned about the scandal. That he learned about it first from a journalist who had got wind of the affair probably mortified him all the more.

The federal trial in 1988 offered an intimate look at corporate excess as practiced at Anheuser-Busch. Described as perhaps the most public airing of dirty laundry in years, the spectacle provided a peek behind the company's guarded doors. And it was soon apparent that Anheuser-Busch's gold-plated marketing tactics were on trial as much as the three defendants. Top executives had routinely accepted such expensive gifts as Rolex watches, computers and televisions. So many gifts flowed into Anheuser-Busch's corporate offices that it was likened to a warehouse. At Christmas the presents were so plentiful they had to be piled up in the halls.

The vaunted sales and promotion departments, which had helped Anheuser-Busch dominate the industry, proved to be its Achilles heel. Plenty of opportunities existed for clients to give gifts to Anheuser-Busch executives, some of whom were more than willing to accept them. "This is a soft, squishy area," said Robert Weinberg, a former executive, "and there is enough money floating around that it would create an opportunity for chicanery."

As usual, August ordered no comment, no interviews. But in a letter to employees, he said the questionable activities were thought to be "inconsistent with corporate policy." He promised "additional guidelines" on ethics practices and conflict of interest. Trying to cauterize the damage, he launched an inhouse investigation. Heads rolled in what was described as an "inquisition atmosphere." One executive said company lawyers grilled him not only about his business dealings, but also about his personal life. Some blamed the excesses on the tradition of lavish spending set during the beer wars, which one former marketing executive called "our Vietnam." August's attitude was captured in a remark he had made years earlier: "If you get a bad apple anywhere in the lower executive levels, you've got trouble. But get a bad apple at the top and you've got super trouble."

The trouble involved, if not a barrel, at least several bad apples. Rising stars at the brewery, Joseph Martino, vice president for sales, and his friend, Michael Orloff, vice president for wholesale operations. Both were Wharton graduates, August's favorite MBA factory. Bright, aggressive and in their mid-thirties, they were fellow workaholics. Both earned well over $100,000 a year and had rocketed through the ranks. They were accused of engineering a kickback scheme with Mark Shyres, a principal in a St. Louis ad agency that had provided advertising and promotional services for Anheuser-Busch. By faking inflated Anheuser-Busch invoices over a five-year period, they were said to have raked in thousands of dollars, not to mention expensive clothing, airline tickets, auto repairs and club memberships. All three got three-year prison sentences and $10,000 fines for defrauding the brewery and the IRS. The judge also ordered the defendants collectively to make $30,000 in restitution to Anheuser-Busch.

What fascinated observers was that Martino and Orloff insisted there was nothing unusual about accepting extravagant gifts from companies that did business with the brewery. They were only doing what everyone else did, so why pick on them, they argued. "It was," Martino wrote two years later, "part of the corporate culture." During eight years at Anheuser-Busch, the young executive said he had "witnessed incredible greed and corruption at the highest levels of the company. I saw illegal activities and I saw flagrant personal misuse of corporate and thus shareholder funds. . . . There is a lot hiding behind the polished corporate image of Anheuser-Busch."

At the trial, a string of Anheuser-Busch executives had raised their right hands and testified about receiving gifts from vendors and company bigwigs. Some of them got gifts all year round. From Fleishman-Hillard, the brewery's public relations firm, one vice president and half a dozen other executives received $600 robots that could pour Budweiser. Michael Roarty, Anheuser-Busch's leprechaun-faced chief of marketing, allegedly gave one executive a big-screen television, a portable television, a camcorder and a video cassette—all gifts that had been given to him. Roarty reportedly had so many to hand out they were stored in a large closet across from his office. It was like a treasure vault, with one executive testifying that he was allowed to take an Apple computer from the cache. He said he was advised to thank Roarty—but not in writing.

Shyres, glib and cheery and a good friend of Martino's and Orloff's, offered a glimpse of how some of Anheuser-Busch's advertising decisions were made. When he learned that the brewery planned to have Michelob sponsor polo matches, he was opposed. "Polo—you can get nosebleeds, it's so upscale." He changed his mind as soon as a square-shouldered young man took credit for the idea. "He said, 'My last name is Busch,'" Shyres recalled. "I said, 'Great idea.'"

Dennis Long, then fifty-one, was the most serious casualty of the mess. When the company was reorganized some years earlier to make diversification easier, Long had been named president of the brewing subsidiary. The number two man at Anheuser-Busch, he was also August's valued friend and colleague. Although not implicated in the scandal, Long was cut loose because the stink bomb had exploded on his watch. Friendship or not, August wanted a major house cleaning. "Augie does not forgive," said one former Busch executive. But unlike Martino and Orloff, who were escorted off the property by security guards, Long was given ample time to clean out his desk. August even let his old friend retain one small beneficence. He was allowed to handle the launch of Budweiser in Ireland and run the Irish Derby. In honor of its new sponsor, the famous horse race had been renamed the Budweiser Irish Derby.

The scandal demonstrated that nepotism was alive and well at the brewery. Long reportedly had eight family members on the Anheuser-Busch payroll, including a son-in-law who managed the Clydesdales and a daughter who worked in the communications department. His brother owned a firm that supplied promotional items to the company. Long was only said to be following the example set by the Busch family. "You get into the question . . . of what impelled Denny Long to hire his relatives," said one industry observer. "And then you look at Anheuser-Busch, and the Busch family has relatives all over the place." The difference, of course, was that their name was over the door.

August's son and daughter by his first wife worked for the company. But there were many other Busch relations who also had close ties to the brewery. Besides Gussie and August, three other relatives were members of the board: James Orthwein, August's first cousin and the former president of D'Arcy Masius Benton & Bowles; Peter Flanigan, a great-grandson of Adolphus, a former Nixon White House aide and managing director of Dillon Read & Co., an investment firm that provided investment banking services for Anheuser-Busch; and, finally, Walter Reisinger, another great-grandson of Adolphus, who was on the Anheuser-Busch payroll to develop "contacts with the PGA golf community on behalf of the Michelob brands." Gussie's wife, Margaret, received $50,000 a year as a consultant.

August had once said he hoped that any Busch who was qualified and interested would want to work for the brewery. He also had made it clear that he wasn't going to hire someone based on bloodlines alone, which might have explained why none of Gussie's sons by Trudy—Adolphus, Peter, William and Andy—had found a permanent job at Number One Busch Place. If there were any disagreements with August, it didn't stop Gussie's boys from latching on to lucrative beer distributorships. Peter bought one in Fort Pierce, Florida. Adolphus, Billy and Andy got a huge distributorship in Houston despite charges that a "token Texan" had been appointed as the principal owner to get around a residency requirement to qualify for a state liquor license. A number of other relatives and former Anheuser-Busch executives also wound up with distributorships.

The delicate issue of how the brewery acquired some of these distributorships was the subject of a lawsuit by the "beer baroness" of northern California. Florence "Jerri" Beardslee, a petite blonde, was also called the "Bud Lady" by customers in her area, the picturesque coastal region of Mendocino County. Beardslee alleged that Anheuser-Busch had prevented her from selling her small, two-delivery truck operation so that it could force her out and take over her business. "They are buying distributorships all over the United States and putting their own people in," she said. Her attorney, the flamboyant

former mayor of San Francisco, Joseph Alioto, charged that
the company was following a pattern of acquiring distributorships "at bargain prices" and then giving them "to folks who
were basically insiders."

A former Anheuser-Busch distributor in the Deep South
agreed. "Just about every one of them who retires ends up
taking over a distributorship. . . . If they want it bad enough,
my friend, they gonna get it. You can book it."

Scandals like the kickback affair were a rarity at Anheuser-
Busch during August's tenure. But when they did occur, they
were often big. In 1978, the company had made a then record
$750,000 settlement—it was not called a fine—with the Bu-
reau of Alcohol, Tobacco and Firearms. Anheuser-Busch admitted it had made $2.6 million in "questionable payments"
to increase beer sales. After promising to tighten up ship, the
brewery found itself in the same tub of boiling water barely
six years later.

In 1984, Anheuser-Busch reached another settlement, or
"offer in compromise," with the Treasury Department's Bureau of Alcohol, Tobacco and Firearms investigators. This time
it shelled out $2 million, another record, to settle charges of
attempting to monopolize beer sales at ballparks, racetracks
and stadiums by inducing retailers to buy only its products in
violation of the Federal Alcohol Administration Act. The alleged inducements, which recalled hardball practices dating
to Adolphus's era, included accusations of "renting, lending,
or selling" to retailers money, fixtures, signs and other supplies
—some of the very abuses that led to Prohibition. Anheuser-
Busch was also accused of that venerable beer industry practice of enticing retailers to stock their products by "paying or
crediting" them "for advertising, display or distribution services."

The alleged violations were said to have begun in 1979, only
one year after Anheuser-Busch paid the earlier settlement for
similar allegations. The company, regulators charged, "engaged in what can be characterized as predatory trade practices." Anheuser-Busch denied any wrongdoing. The alleged
violations, officials insisted, were contrary to company policy
and top management was not involved. The Bureau of Alcohol,
Tobacco and Firearms admitted that Anheuser-Busch had a
policy of "strict compliance" with the law and blamed the
breakdown on "field-level omission and inattention."

Investigators cited ten instances of alleged violations involving Anheuser-Busch sales at such places as Comiskey Park, the home of the Chicago White Sox; Arlington Stadium in Arlington, Texas, home of the Texas Rangers; the Charlestown Motor Speedway in Charlestown, Indiana; and the 1982 World's Fair in Knoxville, Tennessee. About forty other alleged violations were examined at other sports facilities around the country, but weren't pursued reportedly because of lack of funds. In a brief statement when its $2 million settlement was announced, Anheuser-Busch breezily asserted that the beer it sold as a result of these practices was "immaterial" when compared with its total sales during the period under investigation.

As long as Anheuser-Busch stuck with beer it was without rival. Problems cropped up only when it strayed into new ventures. One effort in particular blew up with a loud bang. For sparking criticism that often bordered on the irrational, nothing compared with August's brief fling with the "not-so-soft drink" called Chelsea.

The lemon-lime beverage with the snap of apple and spicy ginger had been August's baby from the start. The company wanted to branch out into the booming soft drink market. August was keen on diversification and the move made sense. Beer sales were flattening and he was well aware of the increased demand, by health-conscious consumers, for nonalcoholic beverages. His answer was Chelsea. It contained no chemical preservatives, caffeine or artificial sweeteners, and had one-third less sugar and one-third fewer calories than competitors' products. In the Anheuser-Busch tradition, it was all natural.

With less than one half of one percent alcohol, Chelsea was the direct descendant of another famous Anheuser-Busch soft drink that bombed, the Prohibition-era Bevo. It was meant to appeal to the adult palate. "It would have given," said August, "the American consumer a socially acceptable product that you could not physically become intoxicated with no matter if you drank a whole case."

In the late 1970s, the product turned out to be a multimillion-dollar lemon and was pulled off the market—the victim of negative press and the newly found strength of alcohol industry critics. Anheuser-Busch was accused of marketing a "kiddie beer" in a pernicious attempt to lure children and young adults into the beer habit. Critics almost foamed at the mouth about the "not-so-soft drink" ad line. They blasted the clear container and foil wrapping, which they said was cunningly designed to resemble a beer bottle; they railed at the fact that the beverage was amber-colored and left a head of foam when poured.

"Disgusting and disgraceful," proclaimed Senator Orrin Hatch, a Utah Republican who was a Mormon and a member of the Senate subcommittee on alcoholism and drug abuse. Ban its advertising, declared Joseph Califano, Jr., then secretary of health, education and welfare. "A seemingly insidious effort to pre-condition children," added the American Automobile Association, sentiments that echoed those of the Seventh-Day Adventists and the Virginia Nurses Association.

The chorus was loud and devastating. One of the problems was that Chelsea was made by a beer company. "As long as that's the case," said one Anheuser-Busch executive, "there'll be people who'll suspect it's a training bra for Budweiser." An industry analyst put it this way: "Being slightly alcoholic is like being slightly pregnant." It didn't matter that August, with typical stubbornness, changed the bottle from clear to green, eliminated the robust head and rewrote the ad line from the "not-so-soft drink" to "the natural alternative." The damage was done. Chelsea was dead.

So it happened with another of August's soft drink ventures, a root beer called Root 66, a clone of an earlier Anheuser-Busch product. There were other flops as August tried to diversify. He got into the sparkling water business with his Sante and Saratoga brands, only to sell them later. August's low-calorie wine cooler, Dewey Stevens, also fizzled. "When a smart company does something that dumb, you wonder why the hell they did it," said one bemused expert. "I think they were trying to convince the consumers that wine coolers are a dumb product. Look at Dewey Stevens. Good Lord, that sounds like a wimp acrobat."

August's similarly ill-fated entry into the natural-soda business showed his grinding perseverance and, in the opinion of one competitor, his willingness to play for keeps. When Sophia Collier created Soho Natural Soda in her Brooklyn kitchen in 1977, she knew she had a winner. Soho took off, but she soon began to detect the large footprints of Anheuser-Busch, which had just entered the natural-soda market with an entry called Zeltzer Seltzer.

The product's label looked remarkably similar to her own brand's checkerboard design. Lawsuits and countersuits flew with Collier charging that Anheuser-Busch had violated trademark protections, pressured distributors to stop carrying her sodas and had acquired her recipes and customer lists. Anheuser-Busch retaliated, accusing her of defamation. Collier, who was thirty-one, took her story to the newspapers and hired a silk-stocking lawyer. "They think by this kind of hardball they can scare me into not exercising my first amendment rights," she said. "They have millions of dollars to promote their product. We have only my lone voice."

In May 1987, the night before a court hearing, Anheuser-Busch settled the case, dropping its suit against Collier and agreeing to stop using the checkerboard label. The brewery later sold Zeltzer Seltzer.

Sophia Collier wasn't the only person to face a legal challenge from Anheuser-Busch. The company was never afraid to take people to court—even little people like a college student at the University of North Carolina. The brewery sued the young man for alleged trademark infringment after his fledgling T-shirt company started selling a hot number that caught the fancy of the seashore crowd. His design featured a red and blue can and the captions: "Nags Head—the King of Beaches" and "This Beach is for You." The student's lawyer said it was only meant as an amusing parody.

Back in St. Louis, Richard Balducci, the editor and publisher of a tiny humor magazine called *Snicker*, used similar language to describe his own run-in with the brewery. Balducci, who published the magazine from his home, had some fun with an oil spill that briefly shut down the company's flagship brewery. Anheuser-Busch didn't laugh. Balducci was sued in federal court—the issue, again, was alleged trademark infringement—after he ran a parody of Michelob Dry's ad slogan, "One taste and you'll drink it dry." Balducci's version said, "One taste and you'll drink it oily." When the lawsuit hit, Balducci said the brewery's executives couldn't take a joke. "They may need to have an X-ray taken of their funny bone, because I don't think they have one."

Then there was the case of Owen Ryan, sued by Anheuser-Busch when he tried to market a line of crackers called Party Animals. The brewery argued that people would confuse his sesame seed crackers, which were shaped like ducks, deer, pigs and rabbits, with its mascot, Spuds MacKenzie. Ryan admitted he had his hands full. "Can you believe that pooch can bite so hard?" he asked. "But every dog has its day."

Anheuser even sued the Florist Association of Greater Cleveland for trademark infringement and unfair competition. The reason? It sold flowers with the slogan: "This Bud's for You." In a rare defeat, the brewery found the courts siding with the florists—and their buds.

It appeared that August had suffered a more bruising defeat when he launched his Eagle Snacks subsidiary and then shelled out over half a billion dollars in 1982 to acquire Campbell Taggart, the nation's second-largest bread and bakery company. Both lost millions for years, but he hung tough and slowly began to turn both ventures around. Year after unprofitable year, it seemed foolhardy to pit his Eagle snack chips and salted nuts against a giant like Frito-Lay, but he was going to make it work. If sales didn't support the brand's "Everybody Loves Them" slogan, then by God, the day would come when he would *make* everybody love them.

Such commitment notwithstanding, critics found August's performance outside the familiar realm of beer to be disturbing. Some questioned whether he would have survivied such a litany of flops if he weren't a Busch. "Before I'd give August another star," said one executive who left the company, "I'd like to see him do something successful that doesn't rely on Budweiser, Busch and Michelob. The question is can he grow out of the old AB?"

72

More Hardball

August flew airplanes and helicopters. He did not, in any emotional sense, fly with the St. Louis Cardinals. Baseball had never been fun for him. He was not a fan. The game was business, albeit a very important one to the brewery. His tepid attitude toward the sport was readily apparent to Robert Weinberg, a former Anheuser-Busch executive. A color photo-

graph of August hung on the wall of Weinberg's office. The
signed photograph showed August standing and applauding
while he watched a game from his box seat during the 1985
World Series. Uncharacteristically, he was smiling. The picture was "a private joke" between them, said Weinberg, because it depicted August apparently enjoying himself at a
baseball game.

His indifference did not extend to making sure he could get
his product on those rare occasions when he actually attended
a game. William Smith, the former president of Pabst, recalled
watching August and his father through a pair of field glasses
during the 1982 World Series when the Cardinals played the
Brewers in Milwaukee. County Stadium did not serve Budweiser, but there was plenty of Pabst on hand. "The old man
was there and August the Third. They had a runner who was
going outside to pick up Budweiser. He was sneaking it down
to these people. . . . See what happens when they come to Milwaukee? They won't even drink our beer."

August may have given his father a loose rein in running the
ball club, but no one doubted that any major expenditure had
to pass his desk for review. In 1979 when the Cardinals tried
to sign Pete Rose, August was actively involved. Rose paid a
visit to Gussie's hospital room, where he was preparing for a
hernia operation. Gussie's offer, approved by August, was for
$750,000 a year for four years and possibly more if Rose agreed
to do a few beer commercials. That was ruled out because Rose
didn't drink. Gussie suggested another possibility. If Rose
signed, he might have a chance of getting a beer distributorship just as Roger Maris had done nearly a decade earlier.
There were no guarantees, of course. Rose would have to buy
it, but everyone knew the skids could have been greased. Rose
wound up in Philadelphia.

In ripe old age, Gussie had mellowed considerably about
paying top dollar for athletes. What was three-quarters of a
million dollars a year for Pete Rose if he could help turn the
franchise around? The value of the team to the brewery's profits was self-evident. Gussie had admitted as much many times,
but never more clearly than during a 1978 interview in which
he reflected on his twenty-five years as president of the Cardinals. "Let's face it, we not only made money most of the years,
but the ballclub ownership was good for the brewery's image
and mine, too. We went from under 6,000,000 barrels a year to
35,000,000 now."

A decade later those barrels had more than doubled, due in

part to the fact that every Cardinals broadcast was a nine-inning advertisement for Busch and Budweiser. In the new Busch Stadium there were signs that flashed, signs that revolved or fluttered, and if you caught the game on radio or television, the team's beer-selling sports announcers never let you forget that Budweiser, Busch and Michelob and an assortment of lights and drys were the finest brewed in the world. When the Clydesdales were flashed on the mammoth instant replay screen and the fans started clapping and stomping to the Bud theme during the seventh-inning stretch, it was the ritual's high moment. "There were the endless, shameless, tawdry Budweiser jingles and Clydesdale horses," commented one writer after the 1982 World Series. "That made Busch Stadium the most appropriately named park in America."

Long forgotten was the day in 1953 when the brewery bought the Cardinals and Gussie proclaimed he would not use the team as a vehicle to sell beer. The promise had faded from memory in a Niagara of suds. Fred Saigh, who sold the team to Anheuser-Busch, had known the score for years. "The ascendancy of Anheuser-Busch dates with the acquisition of the ball club. Since then, when beer drinkers think of beer, they think of Anheuser-Busch."

None of this meant that the brewery wasn't interested in improving its financial picture with the Cardinals. There had been a few years, after all, when the team operated at a loss. The biggest financial drain was the arrangement the Cardinals had with Civic Center Redevelopment Corporation, the quasi-public entity that owned the stadium. When Gussie agreed to support a new stadium and move the team there, he also had agreed to forgo any parking and vending revenues. It was a sizable concession worth nearly a million dollars a year by the early 1980s. Later Anheuser-Busch set out to gain control of Civic Center. The wrangling that ensued was the kind of game August excelled at. He may not have been a baseball fan, but he knew how to play hardball.

Thanks to what was described as a "skillful public relations effort," the battle for control of Civic Center was portrayed as an effort to improve the prospects for the Cardinals. If they had parking and concession rights, they could afford to pay more to improve their lineup. But that was only a smoke screen. The battle "was essentially a real estate deal, a very big real estate deal. And, for Anheuser-Busch . . . a very good deal."

The opening gambit was the brewery's offer to pay $33.5 million for Civic Center, which, in addition to the stadium, also owned four parking garages, a hotel on the riverfront, two undeveloped parcels of land and $15 million in investments. The property covered thirty-four acres in downtown St. Louis. Civic Center's board of directors declined the deal. The price was far too low. A Wall Street investment firm pegged the value of the property at between $75 million and $90 million. The brewery came back with another lowball offer—$40 million. This, too, was rejected. That was when things turned interesting. Another firm, Apex Oil, entered the picture with an offer of $52.4 million. When Anheuser-Busch matched that figure, Apex raised the ante to $59.9 million.

At that delicate point, Anheuser-Busch began making ominous noises it might have to sell the team if it couldn't reduce its operating losses. The company even offered to sell the Cardinals to Apex for $23.5 million. Behind the scenes, however, Anheuser-Busch was privately buying up Civic Center securities and ultimately wound up with enough stock to win voting control. Apex realized the game was over and withdrew its offer.

It was estimated that Anheuser-Busch paid $53 million for Civic Center, which was quickly made a brewery subsidiary. That would have been $17 million less than the lowest appraisal. A lawyer familiar with the transaction called it "one of the most stunningly successful real estate deals in St. Louis history." Gussie, by then in his early eighties, had little to do with the buyout. But his son August, indifferent to baseball, had hit another home run.

Once Anheuser-Busch controlled Civic Center, it set out to clean up another bit of unfinished business. For years vendors had hawked baseball caps, pennants and other souvenirs outside the stadium. With their small carts and boxes piled up on the sidewalks, these low-overhead salesmen created an unpleasant atmosphere and caused traffic problems, the brewery argued. More to the point, they competed with vendors peddling the same stuff inside the stadium. At Anheuser-Busch's request, the city's Board of Aldermen obligingly passed an ordinance that banned the independents unless they had a contract with Civic Center. In exchange for the favorable vote, the company agreed to spend $1 million for landscaping and other improvements around the stadium.

Two vendors filed suit, alleging that Civic Center was involved in a price-fixing scheme to restrain trade and limit competition. One of the men, Richard Yackey, was the unofficial spokesman for the vendors. He recalled being summoned to a meeting with Lou Susman during the height of the controversy. Susman, Yackey said, started the conversation by lighting a cigar, settling himself comfortably behind a desk, and pointing out that Yackey had plans to open several outdoor restaurants on city property. Yackey had the impression that his plans could be jeopardized. Recalling his experience later, he said, "I knew they had the juice and they could do it."

Gussie Busch continued to take an active role in the Cardinals until well into his eighties, and whenever he climbed up on a bright red beer wagon to be pulled around Busch Stadium by a team of Clydesdales, the place went wild. A gate would swing open in right field, the horses pranced out and the Budweiser theme, "Here Comes the King," suddenly blared from loudspeakers. Gussie, decked out in a red cowboy hat and red jacket, received a standing ovation, and if in his later years he no longer held the reins and seemed propped in place while public relations flacks trotted alongside, no one seemed to notice.

Gussie's last hurrah came with the 1987 World Series against the Minnesota Twins. The Cardinals lost in seven games, but the team drew over 3 million spectators that season, boosted by the brewery's aggressive promotions—T-shirt days, bat days, book days, mug days, straight-A student days, days without end. Gussie's health, precarious for years, began to fail seriously after that, a fact carefully concealed by the brewery's publicists, who kept issuing reports of his vigorous good health almost up to the moment he died. Gussie was portrayed as fit as a fiddle, so hale that, nearing ninety, he still took up the reins of a four-in-hand out at Grant's Farm. The truth was that he had been slipping badly. After the 1987 season, Gussie was no longer actively involved with the Cardinals and things began to change.

Some said the bean counters took charge, the brewery's businessmen. The team failed to re-sign slugger Jack Clark after the 1987 series. In following years the management likewise failed to sign many of the high-priced players manager Whitey Herzog requested. Why bother? The fans—the majority of them white and affluent—kept breaking attendance records and clapping on cue to the Bud theme. And if the players occasionally were an embarrassment, no one minded as long as they were stars. Pedro Guerrero, the team's leading hitter, missed a game in 1989 in Houston, claiming that he had eaten some bad fish. Two women, according to authorities, were invited to his hotel room and had slipped him a Mickey Finn. They stole his $14,000 Rolex and $12,000 in other jewelry. In the current atmosphere of professional sports, the story hardly created a ripple. Herzog, who finally quit in 1990, let it be known he had reason to lament Gussie's departure from active management of the Cardinals. The old man was colorful and he knew how to win.

73

"He Can Hurt You Badly."

August was upset and irritated. It was almost 7:30 in the morning and, seated at the head of a large table in the conference room that adjoined his office on the ninth floor of Number One Busch Place, he was finishing breakfast. He had scheduled a meeting with some fellow executives but only Father Paul Reinert, the chancellor of St. Louis University, had arrived on time. August kept impatiently tapping his wrist watch. "You know, it took twenty-nine minutes today," he said, still troubled that the Jesuit priest was the only one to show up for the early meeting. "Twenty-nine minutes!"

Reinert wondered what he was talking about. Then August explained. "It's never taken me more than twenty-seven minutes to fly in from the farm. But there were some strong headwinds today." He tapped his watch crystal again. "It took twenty-nine minutes!"

Remembering the incident later, Reinert still shook his head in wonder. "He was upset that it had taken two minutes longer than usual to fly in on his helicopter. And now he would have to make that up somehow."

Another episode provided an insight into the flinty character of this dynastic ruler who had made his brewery the most powerful in the world. When Anheuser-Busch opened a new Los Angeles brewery, August halted a procession of golf carts shuttling dignitaries through the plant. He had seen something terribly wrong, something unforgivable.

A gum wrapper.

There it was smack in the middle of an expanse of floor clean enough to eat off of—a wad of crumpled paper and foil. Retrieving the offending wrapper, August found the manager in charge of housekeeping. For one awful moment, it seemed that August planned to fire him on the spot. Instead, he stuck the wrapper into the man's breast pocket.

August could intimidate. It was part of his mystique, part of his professional persona. When a journalist, with ranking Anheuser-Busch executives seated around him, happened to tell August how intimidating he could be, nervous laughter broke out, but only after the boss smiled first. There was something almost frighteningly machine-like about his personality. He never let up. Never. If he noticed a dirty Anheuser-Busch truck on one of his frequent business trips, the wholesaler could expect a scorching memo. If he found a bottle or can of old beer —a capital offense—the wholesaler would be made to sweat hard.

The pressure was relentless and filtered down through the ranks. Beer truck drivers could get physically ill when one of August's executives rode with them on an inspection. Some got so uptight they threw up. Wholesalers were also subjected to the "treatment." "They have a way of chewing on wholesalers that is a remarkable thing to see," said David Callahan, a former Anheuser-Busch district manager. "You just keep pushing the wholesaler's head under water until he pays attention to you. You stay in his face all the time." And as far as encountering August himself? "I was always careful to stay the hell out of his way."

Ed Vogel, a former senior vice president, described August as a "monster" who could still be charming when the mood was upon him. "It would be a horrible way to have to work. To be scared to death. It's his way of doing business."

August also had his admirers, former and present executives

who appreciated his managerial skills and his willingness to pay top dollar for talent. He gave his people yards of rope and if they hanged themselves, there were plenty of MBA hatchlings in the woods.

Appearing regularly on lists of most-admired CEOs, August was also richly compensated. A *Business Week* survey ranked him tenth among the twenty highest-paid executives in the country. His compensation in a typical year was nearly $9 million, including salary and bonuses. Only when that huge salary—$22.5 million in total compensation between 1987 and 1989—was compared with return to shareholders did August receive bad marks. *Business Week* gave him its lowest grade in the pay versus performance category, placing him at the bottom of the pile when stacked up against his peers in the beverage industry. A poor report card like that, however, was a rarity. Anheuser-Busch invariably appeared on *Fortune* magazine's list of most admired corporations; a recent ranking placed it ninth out of 305.

One of August's rarely broken rules was that no one talked to the press without his approval. That applied both within and without the company. When *Business Month* tried to do a profile on August, a string of prominent St. Louis executives declined to talk. "You never want to get on the wrong side of August Busch," one of them said. "He can personally kill any project you want. He can hurt you badly."

The code of silence extended to such normally outspoken politicians as Thomas Eagleton, the former United States senator from Missouri and briefly George McGovern's vice presidential running mate. Eagleton's father was an Anheuser-Busch lawyer. The senator's first job was with the brewery, which continued to pay him as a consultant even after he was elected lieutenant governor. He now works for a St. Louis law firm that represents Anheuser-Busch, Thompson & Mitchell. The usually chatty Eagleton declined to discuss his long association with the Busches. "Our firm represents the estate and various family members," he said. "They've requested we not be interviewed."

With August, the dynasty had produced a remarkable if chilling specimen. Each of his predecessors would have had difficulty matching his consummate dedication. Adolphus, for all his robber baron skills, liked to hobnob with rich friends in Pasadena or shoot stag on his estates in Germany. During the depths of Prohibition, August A. liked playing the gentleman farmer at Cooperstown or Grant's Farm. Gussie liked extravagance and fun whenever and wherever he could find it. August liked to work.

He was driven, some said, by the desire to match the successes of the Busches who had preceded him. His yardstick was always Gussie, who, by building the first new breweries and developing the wholesaler network, created the modern Anheuser-Busch. August's record couldn't compare with that kind of achievement, said Vogel. "August is very envious of his father. . . . Gussie gave him a finely honed machine. He really-would have had to work at it to screw up. . . . Everything he's done has followed in a path laid out by his daddy."

His record, nevertheless, was remarkable. As the company entered the last decade of the twentieth century, it controlled 42 percent of the American beer market. Miller, the number two brewery and once Anheuser-Busch's greatest challenger, was a distant second with 22 percent. Budweiser alone, with 27 percent, was bigger than any of the company's competitors. When August calmly said he expected to have 50 percent of the market by the middle of the decade, he was taken at his word. "We look at 50 as something that is attainable. But I don't think we should limit our vision to 50 percent."

Nowhere was Anheuser-Busch's influence more apparent than in Washington during the often paralyzing struggle by Congress in late 1990 to come to grips with a runaway budget deficit during an election year. Anheuser-Busch had long taken a leading role in beating back even the most modest suggestion to increase federal taxes on beer, wine and spirits. The excise tax for beer and wine—16 cents on a six-pack—had last been raised in 1951 when Gussie's old pal, Harry Truman, was in the White House. When President George Bush suddenly proposed a fivefold increase in the excise tax to try to come to terms with the ballooning deficit, another Busch read his lips.

In what was described as "one of the most extensive and visible campaigns in the history of the U.S." Anheuser-Busch whipped together a multimillion-dollar "Can the Beer Tax" advertising blitz. More than 30,000 beer trucks carried the message and a toll-free number, urging angry drinkers to voice their complaints. The company's 950 wholesalers were exhorted to distribute petitions and gather signatures to send to Washington. Briefing books were distributed by the score on Capitol Hill; television, radio and newspaper ads peppered the country with the same theme. It didn't matter that opinion polls showed 75 percent of the public supported higher alcohol and tobacco taxes. The Anheuser-Busch campaign generated more than 2.4 million petition signatures and 1.6 million letters.

Congress got the message. It approved only a modest doubling of the beer tax—to 32 cents on a six-pack. If not exactly canned, the original version was certainly dented. It was not surprising. The alcohol industry had showered legislators with millions of dollars in campaign contributions and speaker's fees. Common Cause pointed out that two of Anheuser-Busch's "friends on the tax writing committees," Senator John Danforth and Representative Richard Gephardt of Missouri, had benefited handsomely from political contributions from the brewery's executives.

In one year Danforth received $40,000. And during the 1990 beer tax brawl, Gephardt admitted that he had been given nearly $50,000 during a two-year period. The house majority leader and former presidential candidate, Gephardt was a longtime opponent of higher excise taxes on beer. He had good reason to be more than sympathetic: his congressional district included Anheuser-Busch's corporate headquarters. Gephardt was widely considered a key player in canning the beer tax.

In its ceaseless effort to beat back a tax hike, Anheuser-Busch helped sponsor a group called Beer Drinkers of America, the brainchild of a public relations firm that worked for the beer industry lobby. Beer Drinkers, naturally enough, opposed higher taxes on beer as well as any restrictions on advertising. The group flooded the mails with more than one million letters, bearing the signature of former St. Louis Cardinals slugger, Stan Musial. "Working America has always paid our fair share of taxes," said Musial, a typical working American, who was paid for his endorsement.

The prospect of higher taxes promised to remain a thorn in August's side as more consumer groups, economists and even a few congressmen climbed on the bandwagon. So did the explosive issue of open container laws. Anheuser-Busch consistently opposed them. In a few states, a minority that included Missouri, where the company's largest brewery is located, it was perfectly legal to drink a beer while driving a car. Year after year state legislators like Chris Kelly introduced bills to stop the practice. And year after year the powerful Anheuser-Busch lobby opposed and helped to defeat them. In one memorable exchange, the company's lobbyist, John Britton, offered what might be called the peanut butter defense.

The real problem, Britton deftly suggested, had nothing to

do with driving while drinking an alcoholic beverage that
might impair reflexes. The real problem was the fact that the
driver's hand is wrapped around a beer can instead of the
steering wheel. In that context, a peanut butter sandwich was
just as dangerous as a beer, Britton argued. The Missouri leg-
islature bought the argument.

Taxes, open container laws, attacks from critics who wanted
to muzzle its advertising. They all clouded Anheuser-Busch's
future. So did August's disappointing diversification record.
He had never received good marks for efforts to broaden his
company's product base during an era of falling beer consumption. A favorite avenue had been the theme park business,
which was laid out by Gussie. Again, August followed his father's footsteps. The company, late in 1989, paid $1.1 billion
to Harcourt Brace Jovanovich for four Sea World complexes
and two other amusement parks. The deal made Anheuser-
Busch, which already owned the Sesame Place and Adventure
Island theme parks as well as Busch Gardens in Tampa and
Williamsburg, Virginia, the second-largest operator of such
parks in the country, trailing only Disney. (The Busch family
never threw anything away. Visitors to Williamsburg could see
the fountain and nude statue cast in honor of Adolphus Busch,
but banned in St. Louis.) The Sea World purchase was expected to increase the number of people the company entertained from 5 million to 21 million a year. "We get a feel for
what the consumer thinks," August said. "We get a pulse on
that. So we like the entertainment business."

Unfortunately, it could be a notoriously fickle business—
especially if public attitudes changed about keeping dolphins
in captivity at places like Sea World. Loud protests had been
raised by conservationists and animal rights activists, one of
whom referred to Sea World and other marine parks as "dolphin abusement parks." Although many experts praised Sea
World for its breeding programs, it was roundly criticized for
keeping killer whales in captivity.

Such criticism notwithstanding, Anheuser-Busch professed
to be pleased with Sea World and similar ventures. In fact, it
had plans to build a $300 million theme park and resort near
Barcelona on Spain's Mediterranean coast. Five years in the
making, it was one of August's boldest ventures. With American beer consumption down 4 percent since 1981, the idea was

to give Anheuser-Busch a toehold in the tough European beer market. August liked to call the Spanish park Anheuser-Busch's "footprint in Europe." It was a shrewd move, for the brewery's traditional marketing approach wouldn't work in Europe. "We think this," he said, "is the way to enter Europe —not by television because European beer commercials are restricted to certain times of the day and certain segments of a program."

August planned to go all out to expand overseas. The company was licensed to brew in six countries and exported to forty others. There were disappointments. The big beer-consuming countries of Europe, particularly Germany and Great Britain, had proved tough nuts to crack. England was especially inhospitable. Despite heavy marketing since 1984, Budweiser claimed less than 1 percent of the world's fourth-largest beer market.

One of the problems with breaking into Western Europe involved the lock that the centuries-old Budvar Brewery in Ceské-Budějovice, Czechoslovakia, had on the trademark Budweiser in that coveted area. More court battles were touched off. August proposed dividing the world into three parts, like Caesar's Gaul, with Eastern Europe going to Budvar. Anheuser-Busch would get the rest and there would be coexistence in Western Europe. August reportedly offered $2 million for the right to use the Budweiser trademark and suggested a joint venture in Europe. The matter remained under dispute. In the meantime, Anheuser-Busch sold Budweiser in Finland, the Netherlands and Great Britain. It was also sold in France, Italy and Spain, but only as Bud.

An entry into Europe was crucial for August. Despite his dominance of the domestic beer market, all was not well. The scent of potential trouble was in the air. Rumors that Anheuser-Busch could be a takeover target surfaced periodically. August admitted his company wasn't immune from a takeover. "The secret," he said, "is to keep this company growing and keep the stock price high."

More serious was the reported dip in sales of Budweiser, the flagship brand. A story was bannered in *Advertising Age* in late 1989 with the headline, "Budweiser's Sales Slipping," and the lead, "The king of beers is starting to look less regal." After years of steady growth, sales had declined only slightly, but considering that Budweiser accounted for 64 percent of Anheuser-Busch's volume, that was disturbing news. August, of course, refused to comment, but some analysts wondered whether the success of Anheuser-Busch's new light and dry beers was coming at Budweiser's expense. "The sheer size of Budweiser makes it vulnerable,' said one. "You have to have some cannibalization."

With a lineup of sixteen different brands, including three imports, August was without peer at rolling out superior new beers whenever he smelled a market. After a late start getting into the light game, he rarely erred again. He became heavy with lights; one light after another was put on the market. If Michelob sales were down 31 percent, no matter. He introduced Michelob Light and Michelob Dry to prop them up. If Michelob Dry slipped a tad, there was always Bud Dry or Busch Draft to pick up the slack. It was the same with LA, August's entry in the low-alcohol market. When LA—some wags said the letters stood for "Little August"—took a nosedive, Anheuser-Busch was already planning an entry into the promising nonalcoholic field. No sooner was LA's imminent demise reported than, presto, the bright green bottles of O'Doul's were on the shelves and selling well. The nonalcoholic brew, 22,000 cases, was even shipped to the American troops stationed in Saudi Arabia during the Desert Shield–Desert Storm deployment. Alcohol was not permitted in the Islamic nation, which suited many military commanders who reported fewer discipline problems.

On occasion Anheuser-Busch followed its competitors into the marketplace with new brands. The company brought out Natural Light, Michelob Light, Bud Light and Busch Light after Miller Lite took off. When the brewery introduced Busch Draft, it again was following Miller's lead even down to using a clear bottle. This prompted a spokesman for the Milwaukee brewer to comment, "Some companies have consistently followed Miller into the marketplace with me-too products and packaging." Miller was flattered by Anheuser-Busch's imitation.

Putting it out, August called it. Putting out more beer than anyone in the world. Oceans of beer, as if sheer volume alone could drown both his critics and his competitors.

74

The Last Beer Baron

"I don't ever remember a dull moment," Gussie once said. "And if there were such moments, I seem to have been able to stir things up and make things happen."

That held true down to the beer king's final hours. He celebrated his ninetieth birthday on March 28, 1989, about the time his former executive Ed Vogel visited him at Grant's Farm. Vogel asked him how he was getting along with August.

"All right," Gussie said. "But I'll tell you one thing, he isn't in my will."

Vogel's last memory of Gussie was of him sitting in the gun room, surrounded by family mementos—horse trophies, photos of the rich and famous, the mounted heads of animals his ancestors had shot, one of them the buck Gussie himself had killed in 1911 with his grandfather, Prince Adolphus. "He was sitting there with tears in his eyes. Then, he said, 'Goddamn it. I love this place.'"

Vogel said later: "I loved Gussie. I had my problems with him business-wise, but I loved him anyway."

During the summer there were persistent reports of Gussie's rapidly failing health, stories invariably denied by Anheuser-Busch's publicists. He wasn't too bad at all, they said. And the old boy still managed to climb up into a coach for a spin around Grant's Farm. The image of Gussie in vigorous health was kept up almost to the end, even though friends and family knew better. Helen Busch Conway, his second cousin, paid a visit that summer. When she arrived at the Big House, the butler told her Gussie had fallen asleep at the dinner table while eating. Before she departed, she walked quietly up to his room. He was asleep with an oxygen tube in his nose.

Gussie's slide to death began to steepen in August. He had pneumonia. His nights were restless and he slept very little. He was taken to St. Luke's Hospital, and when Father Reinert visited him, Gussie recognized his old friend and begged him to get him out. Medical equipment was installed in his room at Grant's Farm, the same room where his father had died.

In the last week of his life, Gussie lost control of his bodily functions. His oldest son, August, helped the nurses attending his father, doing everything he could to make him as comfortable as possible. Their battles forgotten, the son now carried out his father's bedpan and joined in the prayers at his bedside.

The day before he died, Gussie spoke to Trudy by telephone. His estranged wife was traveling between India and China. He told her he was sorry and asked forgiveness.

All ten of Gussie's surviving children were in his room on the morning of September 29, 1989. Before he lapsed into unconsciousness, he whispered that he loved them. At 12:25 P.M. Gussie died. Moments earlier a brilliant red bird had landed on the feeder at his window and then darted away—a cardinal.

Unlike the elaborate, publicly announced funerals of his father and grandfather, Gussie's burial was a private, almost secret affair. Gussie's son Billy and his grandson August A. Busch IV were upset about the press release the brewery issued when he died. They thought it sounded too much like an Anheuser-Busch promotion, and since it was prepared in advance of Gussie's death, they argued it gave the appearance that the family could not wait until he died.

Although the funeral at Sunset Cemetery was private, a public memorial Mass was held four days later in the St. Louis Cathedral. Shuttle buses brought employees from the brewery and loudspeakers were installed outside the church for the overflow crowd. Six priests celebrated the Mass. The death of his last wife, Margaret, made the service possible. No longer married, Gussie could be buried in the faith he had come to late in life.

At the time of his death, Gussie was worth approximately $1.5 billion. He had 13.5 percent of Anheuser-Busch's stock. His extensive property holdings included the 281 acre Grant's Farm estate with its Big House, Bauernhof and other buildings. He owned an additional 140 acres near the estate, property that included his horse farm and the breeding farm for his beloved Clydesdales. He also owned the Shooting Grounds in St. Charles County, for generations the family's happy hunting land.

Gussie's seventy-seven-page will was a marvel of muddied language, intelligible only to the lawyers who prepared it. His huge stock holdings were parceled out in private trusts, the size of which could only be estimated. However, an indication of their value became apparent several months after his death when eight million shares of Anheuser-Busch stock went on the market under the agreement reached by his heirs several years earlier. Peter Busch was allowed to sell 85,000 of his 422,087 shares. With a share then valued at about $37, his inheritance from the shares of stock was worth nearly $16 million.

Another measure of the size of Gussie's estate became apparent in the summer following his death. The state of Missouri reported that the estate taxes it received had jumped by $15 million in July 1990, the month they were due. Ed Molotsky, director of taxation for the Missouri Department of Revenue, said that if someone paid $15 million in Missouri estate taxes, the taxable assets of the estate would be about $100 million. In addition, the federal tax would be about $40 million, Molotsky said.

In addition to stock, Gussie bequeathed money and land to his children by Trudy, who were his principal beneficiaries. He left $250,000 each to his daughters Gertrude and Beatrice. His sons received property. The breeding farm and other property surrounding Grant's Farm went to Peter and Andrew. The Shooting Grounds went to Adolphus and Billy.

To his son August, who had forced him from the throne, Gussie left very little in the way of personal property. August received the solid-gold telegram that employees had given to his great-grandfather Prince Adolphus to mark his fiftieth wedding anniversary. It was inevitable that some wondered whether Gussie had slighted the son with whom he had feuded for years.

There was no question however that August clearly benefited by the trust agreements after his father's death. The year before Gussie died, he owned about 680,000 shares of Anheuser-Busch stock; the year after, he was worth nearly four million shares. If August didn't receive much of Gussie's personal property, he got something far more valuable—control of Anheuser-Busch.

The servants and caretakers who had spent decades taking care of the beer king received only modest sums. "Gussie left most of his billion plus bucks to people named Busch," wrote one observer. "He left a grand total of $92,500 to five of the 'little people' who waited on him hand and foot for decades.'' There were no charitable bequests in the will.

Gussie's lawyer, Lou Susman, did far better. Susman was named executor of his estate. For letting Gussie's vast wealth pass through his hands, he received two percent of the trust income and one percent of the sale of Gussie's personal property. He was soon worth millions. Gussie's rainmaker had been rained upon.

The will also included a bombshell. Gussie left Grant's Farm to all six of his children by Trudy. His hope was that one of them would buy the others out and keep up the place just as he and his father had done. It was an optimistic hope. Arguments among his sons and daughters broke out almost as soon as the document was read. They were shocked and angry. Adolphus promptly announced that he was moving his family to Grant's Farm and that if Billy and Andrew, who already lived there, didn't like it, that was too bad. Billy and Andy, a friend said, didn't like it at all. "There was a lot of anger and confusion." Friends of the family recalling the words of August A. over seventy-five years earlier, predicted the arrangement would brew trouble.

There was also trouble over the Clydesdales. For years the brewery had leased its breeding farm near Grant's Farm from Gussie. August upset Trudy's children when he moved the breeding operation to Los Angeles. According to friends of the family, he saw no reason to continue paying Gussie's kids for a lease when the brewery already owned a good horse farm in California. For public relations purposes, August agreed to breed a few of the animals in St. Louis, but most were sent out West.

If Trudy's children didn't like the decision, they didn't complain publicly. They didn't dare. With August it was prudent to hold one's tongue. But they knew Gussie would have been boiling mad. He would never have gone along with any plan to pull the Clydesdales from St. Louis. "Dad would just never stand for this," one of them said. "He wouldn't believe it."

One could hear him bellowing, "Over my dead body!"

75

"He Might Wind Up Running the Company—if He Can Stay Out of Trouble."

Early in 1990, August A. Busch IV, the great-great-grandson of Prince Adolphus, was put in charge of the national launch of the brewery's newest label, Bud Dry. He was given the title senior brand manager. To make sure both he and the brand got off to a booming start, $70 million was set aside to promote Bud Dry—the most money ever spent to kick off a new beer. "It's an extremely aggressive program," said a smiling August IV.

At age twenty-five, the young man was hurrying along the career track of his father, who was already general manager of the brewery at age twenty-eight. Beer industry watchers had long kept their eyes on August IV, the heir apparent. August's hope undoubtedly was that his son would succeed him. Not soon, of course. But someday. He might have been embarrassed by August IV's fatal car crash or by his disturbing encounter with St. Louis police, but it hadn't stopped him from giving his oldest child a giant shove up the corporate ladder. When August IV led his first pep talk with distributors, his proud father stood at his side. If the boy somehow found the same workaholic religion that had changed August's life in his early twenties, all would be well. He would prosper and, based on history, so would the company and stockholders.

Adie von Gontard, Jr., a family member who had long ago moved to Connecticut, once commented on the Busches' propensity for scandal. "If they could run their private lives like they run the brewery, they'd be Jesus Christ." The truth, however, was that personal disasters didn't count as setbacks in the Busch scheme of things. They hadn't stopped Gussie and they hadn't stopped his son August, or August's son August IV. For that matter, they hadn't stopped Peter or Billy either. Peter wound up with a lucrative distributorship after pleading guilty to manslaughter. So did Billy, the handsome heir, who admitted using cocaine, sired an illegitimate daughter and had the distinction of being branded a consummate playboy by the chief judge of the Missouri Supreme Court. The Busches have always overcome even the most tragic difficulties with money, influence and grit. And through every individual setback, Anheuser-Busch has prospered.

With August IV, the Busch heritage promised to endure. Considered the most intelligent of his generation, he appeared to be the best candidate to lead the world's largest brewery through the early decades of the twenty-first century. "He's a very bright guy and very aggressive," said a family friend. "He might wind up running the company—if he can stay out of trouble."

Even if there were trouble—big trouble—the odds were great that the Busch dynasty would continue to flourish. When you said that, you have said it all.

76

Bottoms Up

The gray mansion stands on a bluff overlooking the Mississippi River at St. Louis. The home, some say, is haunted by the querulous ghosts of two brewers who committed the "Dutch Act" there—William Lemp, who shot himself in 1904, and his son Billy Jr. who followed in 1922. Their brewery is a ghost of a different kind. Once the city's largest and ranked among the top ten in the nation, it didn't survive Prohibition. Today, their huge plant, which resembles a walled medieval city, stands desolate half a block from the Lemp mansion. Beer hasn't been brewed there in nearly seventy-five years.

Less than a mile up the river, white smoke rises in clouds above the brewery that left the Lemps and so many other competitors in similar straits of abandonment. A basilica to beer, it is the home of the most resplendent brewer in the world—Anheuser-Busch. Atop the massive Bevo plant, spelled out in blazing red neon letters a story tall, the word "Budweiser" is followed by a mark of neon punctuation. A period.

In 1991, as other brands slipped badly or fought to hang on to their market share, Anheuser-Busch reported its fourteenth straight year of record earnings. The company sold nearly 44 percent of all the beer brewed in the United States, and many experts believed it would claim 50 percent within a few years. No one else was even close. The Busches have vanquished the field by playing tougher and smarter than anyone else and by brewing what is arguably the most consistently excellent beer ever mass-produced. The word "quality" has never been merely a public relations buzzword with them. It is the gospel according to Busch.

Over the last century and a half, the Busches have earned the right to be called one of America's great families. The progeny of Adolphus didn't drop the ball or sell their birthright. Few industrial giants are still run by the descendants of the rough-edged buccaneers of the Gilded Age. While many scions and heirs of other huge fortunes have disappeared or have dissipated or squandered their fortunes and their companies, the Busches have endured through five tumultuous generations. The best among them have matched anyone's standard of hard work and pride of product. They have minded the store. Above all, they have remained true to their calling. They made beer—and if anyone thought that was too common or plebeian, to hell with them.

While they cannot measure up to the Fords, Rockefellers, Kennedys and others for the importance of their product or their service to country, they are a genuine American phenomenon, a reflection of all that is both commendable and disturbing in the national character. Enormously rich, the family has often set a shocking standard of behavior—fights, fatal accidents, sex scandals, boorishness, unabashed extravagance. Some of them have acted as if nothing more was expected of them, that they deserved the best of others while exhibiting the worst of themselves.

They are not known—many of them—for their personal contributions to the arts or to charity, although over the years
Anheuser-Busch has donated generously to these and other
causes. Often bestowed with an eye to the corporate image,
these donations can appear unseemly, as when the company
announced that it was giving money to a center for Native
Americans, a minority ravaged by alcohol abuse. Complaints
about the linkage between the relentless advertising of their
product and alcoholism, fatal accidents and juvenile drinking
have been handled deftly in state capitols and in the halls of
Congress. If not silenced, the critics often have been neutral-
ized. Few have played this delicate game better than Anheuser-
Busch. Once again, his heirs have proven Prince Adolphus
right. They have, used their considerable money and influence
to make most Americans "look upon beer in the right light."

While August III is as capable a corporate head as this country has ever produced, there is a slavishness to his dedication
to the task of making and selling beer. Lacking that dedication,
many of his relatives, Gussie's children in particular, have
been content to live off their considerable incomes, as if that
were justification enough for their existence. Some thought
that Lotsie, who once toasted her father, Gussie, as the greatest
stud of them all, might have made a superb company president. She had to settle, instead, for designing the company
float for the Rose Bowl parade.

Branches of the family like the Orthweins have managed to
hang on to a good deal of their wealth. James Orthwein, who
recalled how his grandfather August A. swore after President
Hoover asked him for a drink in the depths of Prohibition,
wanted to buy a piece of a professional football team. A world-
class sportsman, he has set three records for catching bonefish
with a fly rod. The Florida yacht business in which he was a
part owner turned out a sleek model that fetched more than $1
million. Orthwein owned one of them himself, running out to
Bimini on fishing expeditions. Safe to say he could afford it.
His 1.3 million shares of Anheuser-Busch stock were worth
about $56 million. Orthwein's older brother, Dolph—kid-
napped over sixty years ago—played polo well into his hale
seventies. After leaving the brewery following his stormy dispute with Gussie, he ran a successful electrical supply business, living in St. Louis, West Palm Beach and Cooperstown.
Dolph did not attend Gussie's funeral.

At the Sunset Cemetery near Grant's Farm, cut flowers were

placed regularly on Gussie's grave. An American original, he had a full, lusty life—with his wives, with his children, with his company, with his extraordinary wealth. A lucky man, he made the most of his good fortune. But the monuments to his achievements are ephemeral—baseball and beer, entertaining the public and himself with so many World Series pennants, so many upended bottles and cans. If he had higher aspirations, he did not act upon them.

The same pattern seems to prevail in his son, August III— the "beer god" in the words of one writer—who once suggested that his own life had been preordained. "He said that his job was something that he had to do, that he had no choice," recalled Andrew Brandt, who had two memorable meetings with him. "He suggested that just possibly there might have been something else he would have liked to do with his life." Brandt had introduced himself to August in rural Missouri, where August had landed his two-seat helicopter in a field to talk to a farmer about soybeans, a crop he also raised. August took a liking to Brandt—a college student—and later gave him a ride in his helicopter, flying him from his estate near St. Louis to the brewery. They had a rare, unguarded conversation. At the controls, August spoke openly, giving the young man an unforgettable glimpse of the face behind the mask.

"I was struck by his isolation," said Brandt. "He lives far away from everyone on a farm and then he flies in to work far above everyone. . . . I said something about how relaxed he seemed and that in all the photographs I had ever seen of him, he always looked so stern. He glanced at me and said it was funny that I had mentioned that. He said that when he went to a meeting, people usually sat there and stared at him. 'They won't come up and start a conversation. That's something I usually have to do,' " Brandt said August told him. " 'It sometimes makes me feel like there's a barbed wire wall in front of me, or that I'm wearing a suit of armor.' "

Brandt asked August what he thought about as he piloted his helicopter to work every morning. "Sometimes about my father," he replied. "I always felt that I had to excel, that I had to do something to get my father's attention and respect." August said that he always made a point of telling Gussie that he had done his chores. It was a revealing comment. A lonely young man striving to impress his father and later pushing himself and the company to a plateau Gussie could never have dreamed of reaching. Then Brandt asked him about his own son, August IV. "He said," Brandt recalled, "that he had done a lot of crazy things in the last few years, but that he felt his son had finally realized what he was supposed to do. He felt that in the past his son really didn't understand his role, but that . . . he had matured a lot. He understands now that he is a lot different from other people."

The Busches, to paraphrase F. Scott Fitzgerald, whom they would have fascinated, are different from other people. An American dynasty with shadings of the tragic and the trivial, the grand and the petty, they have enriched themselves by providing the masses with cheap alcohol. That alone hardly makes them different in the pantheon of other rich American families. Vast fortunes have been made in the sale of whiskey, cigarettes and asbestos, to name only a few. What makes the Busches unique is that they have survived.

How then is such a family to be judged, their contributions measured? Does it really matter, in a society that reveres success and riches, how the Busches have made their money or how they have chosen to spend it? Not everyone would agree. What is indisputable is that their beer and influence have helped shape—sometimes subtly, often blatantly—popular culture. They have chiseled their message into the nation's psyche. For their tenacity and singleness of purpose, they deserve admiration, if not awe. But if their power and their legendary fortunes—and the uses to which they have been put—are unsettling, some justification must be left to future generations of this singular family.

Notes

The sources of *Under the Influence* include interviews with eye-witnesses, published accounts, letters and official documents. The authors tried as often as possible to encourage sources to speak on the record. However, a number of those interviewed requested anonymity. While some of their observations and recollections were confirmed by a second source or documentation, it occasionally was impossible to obtain more than one recollection. Before the information was used, the credibility of the source was carefully weighed before his or her account was included. Not all of the interviews were conducted by the authors.

The most frequently used sources are identified by a key, which follows:

AA	*Advertising Age*
AAB	August A. "Gussie" Busch, Jr.
AF	*Gussie*, manuscript by Al Fleishman
BW	*Business Week*
CD	Congressional Digest
CHE	*Chicago Herald-Examiner*
CR	Congressional Record
CS	Charles Sitton Collection
CT	*Chicago Tribune*
FB	*Forbes*
FM	*Fortune*
GD	*St. Louis Globe-Democrat*
EHV	Edward H. Vogel, Jr.

HAB   "A History of Anheuser-Busch, 1852–1933," Ronald J. Plavchan, doctoral dissertation, 1969.
HBC   Helen Busch Conway
LAT   *Los Angeles Times*
LBG   *Gussie*, Lotsie Busch Giersch, 1985
NP   Nagel papers, Yale University Library
NYT   *New York Times*
PD   *St. Louis Post-Dispatch*
SI   *Sports Illustrated*
SLC   *St. Louis Star-Chronicle*
SLR   *St. Louis Republic*
SLS   *St. Louis Star*
ST   *St. Louis Star-Times*
WP   *Washington Post*
WSJ   *Wall Street Journal*

Chapter 2: Mud Clerk

Page
19   "Don't tell your father": Interview, AAB.
20   "I was a big man": PD, Aug. 25, 1975.
20   On a summer afternoon: Parish records of St. George's Catholic Church of Kastel, Germany; Busch family history by AAB, July 25, 1940, Missouri Historical Society; Wilhelmina Busch Woods family tree, Bernried, Germany, Archives.
21   In fact, there had been: Adolphus Busch birth certificate, Kastel, Germany, Archives; family tree assembled by Johannes Westerkamp, Ginsheim, Germany.
22   He also worked: Interview, Carola Wagner Wallenstein, granddaughter of Anton Busch.
22   In 1856: HAB 22; *Dictionary of American Biography* (New York: Charles Scribner's Sons, 1944), 141.
22   He was probably recruited: Interview, Ulrich Busch, grandson of John B. Busch.
23   "hunting, loafing": Walter B. Stevens, *Eleven Roads to Success* (St. Louis: self published, 1914), 21.
23   "He could pick": Ibid.
23   After working in: HAB, 24.
24   The first lager: Thomas C. Cochran, *The Pabst Brewing Company* (New York: New York University Press, 1948), 15; PD, June 9, 1974.
24   "They don't drink it": Mark Twain, *Life on the Mississippi* (Minneapolis: Dillon Press, 1967), 117.

Chapter 3: A Beer Baron and a Beer Princess

Page

25   He was well educated: PD, May 3, 4, 1880; Deposition, Lilly Busch, June 29, 1918, U.S. Justice Department files, National Archives.

25   When a small brewery: Roland Krebs and Percy J. Orthwein, *Making Friends Is Our Business* (St. Louis: Anheuser-Busch, Inc., 1953), 18; HAB 11–13.

26   "It is true": PD, Sept. 30, 1906.

26   As Anheuser gained control: Stanley Baron, *Brewed in America* (Boston: Little, Brown, 1962), 231.

26   "der Lockenkopf": *Frank Leslie's Illustrated Newspaper*, Jan 11, 1890; Deposition, Lilly Busch, June 29, 1918.

26   Three days after: SLR, Oct. 11, 1913; PD, March 8, 1911; Alice Busch Tilton, *Remembering* (St. Louis: self published, 1947), 1 & 2.

27   Numbering 5,000: Robert J. Rombauer, *The Union Cause in St. Louis in 1861* (St. Louis: St. Louis Municipal Centennial Year, 1909), 441–445.

27   One of the survivors: PD, Sept. 30, 1906.

27   By an odd coincidence: *Memoirs of General William T. Sherman* (Bloomington: Indiana University Press, 1957 edition) 172–75; *Personal Memoirs of U. S. Grant* (New York: C. L. Webster & Co., 1885), 236–38.

28   During the war: Stevens, *Eleven Roads*, 26.

28   "I wish we": Adolphus Busch to William D'Oench, Feb. 2, 1899, CS.

Chapter 4: The Birth of an Empire

Page

29   "a super-salesman": Gerald Holland, "The King of Beer," *American Mercury Magazine*, Oct. 1929.

29   "pleasure and agreeable": Adolphus Busch to Charles Nagel, Dec. 8, 1909, NP.

30   "was so inferior": Holland, "The King of Beer."

30   "All brewers": Ibid.

31   "After my experience": Stevens, *Eleven Roads*, 26.

31   He renounced allegiance: Deposition, Lilly Busch, June 29, 1918, Justice Department files, National Archives.

31   Pasteur, in a makeshift laboratory: Rene J. Dubos, *Louis Pasteur* (Boston: Little, Brown, 1950), 146–48.

31   Many years later: *Denver Post*, Oct. 29, 1990.

32   It was a decisive moment: HAB 68–69; Baron, *Brewed in America*, 259; Cochran, *The Pabst Brewing Co.*, 73.

Chapter 5: The Birth of a Dynasty

Page

32   True to his: Busch family history by AAB, Missouri Historical Society; PD, May 22, 1905.

33   The first to go: Bellefontaine Cemetery records.

33   There were 480 shares: Edwin Kalbfleish, "Anheuser-Busch Financial
      History," Sept. 18, 1951, CS; HAB 38.
33   By that time: *Anzeiger des Westens*, May 3, 1880; PD, May 3, 4, 1880.
33   Anheuser's stock: Bellefontaine Cemetery records.
34   "The story was": Interview, not for attribution.
34   "Adolphus Busch and my grandmother": Interview, AAB.
34   "Well, the Busches": Interview, Mabel-Ruth Anheuser.
34   In the years: Maxine Sylvia Sandberg, "The Life and Career of Adol-
      phus Busch" (MA thesis, University of Texas, 1952), 68.
34   While Adolphus consolidated: HAB, 75–80; Baron, *Brewed in America*,
      259.

Chapter 6: The Monks' Recipe

Page
36   Soon after: Adolphus Busch to Rowland Cox, a New York attorney,
      March 29, 1894, CS.
36   "be easily pronounced": Ibid.
36   "scoundrels": Adolphus Busch to Charles Nagel, July 26, 1897, CS.
36   "The 'Budweiser' beer": Ibid.
37   "was an inspiration": "Gentlemen: The Creator of Budweiser," *Bevo
      Tattler* (Anheuser-Busch newsletter), Aug. 1921.
37   "conceived the name": "Origin of Budweiser," undated information
      sheet distributed by Anheuser-Busch Companies, Inc.; *Budcaster* (An-
      heuser-Busch newsletter), Sept. 1953.
37   The true story: Invoice of C. Conrad & Co., May 23, 1882, CS; PD, Jan.
      16, 1883.
37   In 1911: legal opinion by Paul Bakewell, June 21, 1937.
38   "seriously affect": Ibid.
38   The cloudy origins: CT, May 15, 1989; PD, Sept. 11, 1989.
38   In December 1990: PD, Dec. 11, 1990.

Chapter 7: Dealing with Pabst

Page
39   "My Dear Friend": Adolphus Busch to Frederick Pabst, Jan. 3, 1889,
      April 27, 1881, in Cochran, *The Pabst Brewing Co.*, 151.
40   Under Adolphus's sole control: HAB, 42.
40   Sometimes Adolphus bought: Baron, *Brewed in America*, 266.
41   Adolphus also controlled: HAB, 52–72.
41   "It's a hell of a story": Interview, AAB.
42   "because they did": Adolphus Busch to August A. Busch, Sept. 20, 1890,
      CS.
42   On a typical day: Adolphus Busch's letterbook, May 1893, CS.
43   The St. Louis brewers: Mary Jane Quinn, "Local Union #6 Brewing,
      Malting and General Labor Department" (MA thesis, University of Mis-
      souri, 1947).
43   "There go": PD, June 9, 1974.
44   "we will cease": Adolphus Busch to August Busch, June 12, 1894,
      CS.

Chapter 8: The Blue Ribbon

Page
44 During his frequent: GD, Nov. 23, 1912.
45 "The family residence": *Frank Leslie's Illustrated Newspaper*, Jan. 11, 1890.
45 "inhabited mausoleums": PD, Oct. 13, 1923; W. Robert Niske and Charles Morrow Wilson, *Rudolf Diesel: Pioneer in the Age of Power* (Norman: University of Oklahoma Press, 1965), 193.
45 A wrought iron fence: Alice Busch Tilton, *Remembering*, 1947, 5–15.
46 "The carriage approached": "Lights on Pestalozzi," Edna Huth, Missouri Historical Society.
46 "the grandest place": *San Francisco Call*, April 13, 1906.
46 The garden eventually: *House and Garden Magazine*, Aug. 1909.
46 "The place is": SLR, Oct. 11, 1913; ST, Nov. 30, 1912.
47 For his German residence: Johannes Westerkamp interview with Egon Anheuser, godchild of Adolphus Busch, Bad Kreuznach.
47 "Let us meet": Adolphus Busch telegram to Charles Nagel, April 18, 1910, NP.
48 "Vell, vot to drink": Holland, "The King of Beer."
48 "It may be said": Ernest Gordon, *The Wrecking of the Eighteenth Amendment* (Francestown, N.H.: The Alcohol Information Press, 1941), 147.
49 "You will find": Adolphus Busch to William Howard Taft, Nov. 28, 1905, Taft papers, Library of Congress.
49 Adolphus was such: GD, July 2, 1916, June 27, 1927: PD, Sept. 30, 1906, Nov. 14, 1949; SLR, Oct. 11, 1913.
50 "I have you": Adolphus Busch to Nagel, July 29, 1911, NP.
51 Adolphus's major competitor: Cochran, *The Pabst Brewing Co.*, 135–38.
51 "You know there" et seq.: Adolphus Busch to August A. Busch, June 12, 18, 1894, CS.
52 "Prizes are not": Adolphus Busch to August A. Busch, June 18, 1894, CS.

Chapter 9: Prince Adolphus

Page
52 "The prince!" PD, Oct. 13, 1913.
52 "I am disappointed": Adolphus Busch to Charles Nagel, April 4, 1910, NP.
53 "See, just like": Holland, "The King of Beer."
53 "Are you German": Jack Ryan and H. W. Lanigan, *Happy Days Are Here Again* (St. Louis: Con P. Curran Printing Co., 1933), 19.
53 "beautiful cane": Simon Wolf to Nagel, Oct. 30, 1913, NP.
54 "You look good": PD, Oct. 12, 1913.
54 "Ladies, one thousand dollars": GD, Oct. 30, 1913.
54 "Here, Pecky" et seq.: GD, Oct. 21, 1913.
54 When Adolphus became interested: Niske and Wilson, *Rudolf Diesel*, 125–26. Morton Grosser, *Diesel: The Man and the Engine* (New York: Atheneum, 1978), 61–62.

Chapter 10: Princes and Princesses

Page
55 "Fight at Faust's": PD, Nov. 8, 1895; GD, Nov. 9, 1895.
55 The suspected cause: FM, July 1935.
56 "a cheap screw" et seq.: PD, Nov. 8, 1895; GD, Nov. 9, 1895; Samuel Levy v. August A. Busch, St. Louis Circuit Court records, Dec. 5, 1895.
57 Adolphus Jr. rose: HAB, 107–8.
57 But like his oldest brother: PD, April 15, 1898; GD, April 17, 18, 1898.
57 "the most impressive": GD, April 18, 1898.
58 "During a year": PD, May 22, 1905.
58 "The boy cannot": Adolphus Busch to August A. Busch, July 22, 1898, CS.
58 "an accident" and "wounds": Adolphus Busch to August A. Busch, June 12, 18, 1894, CS.
58 One descendant: LBG, 6.
58 "appendicitis, nephritis": Peter Busch death certificate, Bureau of Vital Statistics, St. Louis Division of Health.
58 "We are heartbroken": SLR, May 21, 1905; PD, May 22, 1905; GD, May 21, 1905.
59 Apollonia was Adolphus's sister: *Dictionary of American Biography* (New York: Charles Scribner's Sons, 1935), 492; family tree supplied by Johannes Westerkamp.
59 "I have written": Adolphus Busch to August A. Busch, June 12, 1894, CS.
59 "Mr. Magnus has been": PD, Jan. 24, 1906.
59 During one of: Maxine Sylvia Sandberg, "The Life and Career of Adolphus Busch" (MA thesis, University of Texas, 1952), 113.
60 "wore a most exquisite": PD, March 21, 1897.
61 "reared in surroundings": PD, Dec. 31, 1905.
62 "I do not believe": PD, Dec. 28, 29, 30, 31, 1905, March 3, 4, 1906; SLR, Dec. 30, 1905; GD, Dec. 31, 1905, March 4, 1906.

Chapter 11: "The Child We Love Most"

Page
63 "are very handsome" et seq.: *Frank Leslie's Illustrated Newspaper*, Jan. 11, 1890.
63 Lilly's jealousy: LBG, 11.
64 "Our whole welfare": Adolphus Busch to August A. Busch, March 10, 1905, CS.
64 "If we should permit" et seq.: Adolphus Busch to August A. Busch, July 22, 1898, CS.
65 "You are a chip": Ibid.
65 "I would give": Adolphus Busch to August A. Busch, March 10, 1905, CS.

Chapter 12: Fighting "Fanatics"

Page
67 "A great many": Adolphus Busch to Charles Nagel, July 29, 1911, NP.
67 The Committee of Fifty: Francis G. Peabody, *The Liquor Problem: A Summary of Investigations* (Boston: Houghton Mifflin, 1905), 125.
67 "show the Prohibitionists": Otto Koehler to Adolphus Busch, Jan. 2, 1904, CS.
68 "sober and temperate": *From Steerage to Congress* (Philadelphia: Dorrance, 1930), 206–7.
68 Because breweries financed: Perry Duis, *The Saloon* (Urbana: University of Illinois Press, 1983), 232.
69 "This king brewer": Ernest Gordon, *The Wrecking of the Eighteenth Amendment*, 279.
69 "The brewers control": Alexander S. McConachie, "The Big Cinch" (Ph.D. diss., Washington University, 1976), 85.
69 "some fanatical": Adolphus Busch to Nagel, Nov. 28, 1910, NP.
69 "like a morning star": Adolphus Busch to August A. Busch, July 22, 1898, CS.
69 "We ought to extract": Adolphus Busch to Zane Cetti, Texas Brewing Co. president, April 25, 1904, Oct. 19, 1905, hearings before the U.S. Congress, Senate Committee on the Judiciary, "Brewing and Liquor Interests and German Propaganda," 1919.
70 "I do not know": Theodore Roosevelt to Adolphus Busch, Nov. 10, 1904, Roosevelt papers, Library of Congress.
70 When Niedringhaus filed: Partial report of Senate Committee Appointed to Investigate Charges Preferred Against Thomas K. Niedringhaus, Jan. 16, 1905, Missouri State Archives.
70 "a personal contribution": Herbert S. Hadley, attorney general, to the Missouri House of Representatives, 44th General Assembly, 1907–08, Herbert Hadley papers, Joint Collection, University of Missouri, Western Historical Manuscript Collection. Columbia, State Historical Society of Missouri Manuscript.
70 If political contributions: HAB, 98.
71 "I never saw him": "Brewing and Liquor Interests."
72 "She is now engaged": Adolphus Busch to Henry Nicolaus, Dec. 25, 1905, Herbert Hadley papers.
72 Tony Faust died: PD, Sept. 30, 1906; SLR, Oct. 11, 1913; records of Bellefontaine Cemetery.
72 Adolphus, according to: Interview, Carola Wagner Wallenstein.
73 Adolphus had his own: PD, Oct. 13, 1913; Deposition, Lilly Busch, June 29, 1918. Justice Department files, National Archives.
73 "the right professor": Adolphus Busch to Nagel, Feb. 11, 1911, NP.
73 Between 1900 and 1910: BW, Sept. 6, 1947; SLR, Dec. 10, 1907, 190.
73 "save the nation": Adolphus Busch to Nagel, Nov. 17, 1909, NP.
74 "Pray that our": Adolphus Busch to Jacob Schmidlapp, June 13, 1906, Taft papers, Library of Congress.
74 "prohibition legislation": Schmidlapp to Taft, June 13, 1906, Taft papers.

74 "I want to assure you": Adolphus Busch to Schmidlapp, July 26, 1908, Taft papers.
74 "And why is": Prohibition: addresses by William Jennings Bryan, 1916.
75 "alcohol enough": Taft to Adolphus Busch, July 8, 1907, Taft papers.
75 "does not": Henry F. Pringle, *The Life and Times of William Howard Taft* (Hamden, Ct.: Anchor Books, 1964), 375.
75 "Didn't I": Adolphus Busch to Taft, Nov. 5, 1908.
75 Adolphus asked Nagel: Adolphus Busch to Nagel, March 19, April 14, 29, 1909, NP.
75 "You cannot imagine": Adolphus Busch to Nagel, Dec. 8, 1909, NP.
75 "The brewer": Nagel to Adolphus Busch, April 14, 1908, NP.
75 Nagel also had: Adolphus Busch to Nagel, July 29, 1911, May 28, 29, 1912; Nagel to Adolphus Busch, May 28, 1912.
76 "Lieutenant Scharrer": Adolphus Busch to Taft, Oct. 12, 1909, NP.
76 In addition to: Walter Gorlitz, *The Kaiser and His Court* (New York: Harcourt, Brace & World, Inc., 1959, xxii).
76 "I never thought": Adolphus Busch to Nagel, Feb. 18, 1911, NP.
77 "Taft Preaches": Taft papers.
77 "You will undoubtedly": Adolphus Busch to Nagel, Feb. 18, 1911, NP.
77 "I often think about it": Ibid.

Chapter 13: The Original Party Animal

Page
78 "No golden wedding": *New York World*, March 7, 1911.
79 Adolphus, quite a judge: LBG, 27.
79 "To our dearest boy": Adolphus Busch to August A. Busch, Dec. 24, 1910, CS.
79 "The ways of beer": PD, March 8, 1911; *New York World*, March 8, 1911.
79 "This is the Garden of Eden": *Sunset Magazine*, Sept. 1911.
80 "You will never see": Phoebe Couzins to Simon Wolf and Myer Cohen, Oct. 14, 1910, Herbert Hadley papers.
80 "will stand firmly": Adolphus Busch to Charles Nagel, April 3, 1911, NP.
80 "They could not": Adolphus Busch to Nagel, July 3, 1912, NP.
81 "know-nothing": Ibid.
81 "My standing with him": Adolphus Busch to Richard Bartholdt, Dec. 29, 1912, NP.
81 "There never was": Adolphus Busch telegram to Nagel, Jan. 14, 1913, NP.
81 "to beg of you": Adolphus Busch telegram to William Howard Taft, Feb. 12, 1913, Taft papers.

Chapter 14: Veni, Vidi, Vici

Page
82 His fragile health: GD, Oct. 12, 1913.
82 "I consider all": Adolphus Busch to August A. Busch, May 17, 1913, CS.

82 "favorite granddaughter": SLR, June 4, 1913.
82 "very ugly thing": Adolphus Busch to Charles Nagel, Aug. 3, 1913, NP.
82 "should entitle me": Adolphus Busch to Nagel, March 27, 1913, NP.
83 "It is not necessary": Adolphus Busch to Nagel, Aug. 3, 1913, NP.
83 "He rallied splendidly" et seq.: PD, Oct. 11, 12, 22, 1913.
84 But there was: *Dictionary of American Biography* (New York: Charles Scribner's Sons, 1943), 143, records of Bellefontaine Cemetery.
84 The passing of Adolphus Busch: SLR, Oct. 14, 1913.
84 One hundred rooms: GD, Oct. 23, 1913.
84 On the morning: GD, Oct. 26, 1913.
85 Services were also held: *Denver Post*, Feb. 27, 1983.
86 "a giant among men": GD, Oct. 25, 1913.
86 "Know ye not": PD, Oct. 25, 1913.
86 "the high priest": Ibid.
86 For days after: SLR, Oct. 11, 1913; FM, Sept. 12, 1988.
87 "There will be no one": Charles Nagel to Mabel T. Boardman, Nov. 1, 1913, NP.
87 "be happy and contented": PD, Oct. 25, 1913.
87 "her intimate acquaintance": PD, Oct. 30, 1913.
88 "a monument": GD, Nov. 12, 1913.
88 "tend to glorify": GD, Oct. 27, 1913, April 2, 3, 1983.
88 a $250,000 mausoleum: FM, July 1935.

Chapter 15: "Here's to the Kaiser!"

Page
90 Like many Germans: Deposition, Lilly Busch, June 29, 1918, Justice Department files, National Archives; GD, Sept. 4, 21, 1914.
90 "Are you alarmed": GD, Oct. 14, 1914.
90 "Here's to the kaiser": GD, April 20, 1916.
91 "My place is": GD, Jan. 26, June 4, 1917.
91 In the meantime: R. A. Huber to Charles Nagel, July 8, 1918, Alien Property Custodian files, National Archives.
91 Anti-German sentiment: HAB, 137–38.
92 "Now whatever money": Baron, *Brewed in America*, 302; PD, Jan. 16, Aug. 26, 1915.
92 "considerably less": GD, Nov. 9, 1915.
93 "I am an American": PD, June 24, 1917.
93 "I wish you had": GD, Nov. 21, 1917.
93 "so that": GD, March 29, 1917.
93 "forget there ever was": Woodrow Wilson, quoted by Frank S. Cobb, in Stanley Coben, *A. Mitchell Palmer, Politician* (New York: DaCapo Press, 1963), 127.
94 Anthony Busch, a cousin: Interview, Anthony Busch.
94 Within one month: Coben, *A. Mitchell Palmer*, 127–38; 149–150.
94 By early November: Nagel to Ralph Stone, director of the Bureau of Trusts, Alien Property Custodian, Dec. 18, 1917, Justice Department files, National Archives; Harry Hawes to Palmer, July 8, 1918; affidavit of Anheuser-Busch treasurer, R. A. Huber, June 29, 1918, Justice Department files, National Archives.

Chapter 16: Behind the Lines

Page
95 "take the short cut": Charles Nagel to August A. Busch, Dec. 26, 1909, NP.

95 "political trickery": Ibid.

95 "squarely responsible": Ibid.

96 "a nest of spies": Harry Hawes to A. Mitchell Palmer, July 18, 1918, Justice Department files, National Archives; PD, June 19, 1918; GD, June 19, 1918.

96 "The consternation": PD, June 19, 1918.

96 "I shall": Ibid.

96 "Good heavens": Ibid.

97 "every pressure": PD, June 19, 1918; GD, June 19, 1918.

97 "My place": Ibid.

98 "The U.S. government": PD, GD, June 4, 1917, Feb. 8, April 9, 17, June 16, May 2, 1918.

98 "Why are": Letter to the editor, PD, April 17, 1918.

98 "I would suggest": Jay Adams letter, March 14, 1918; Lida B. Robertson letter, Sept. 27, 1918, Justice Department files, National Archives; Coben, *A. Mitchell Palmer*, 136.

98 "from the doorway": PD, May 25, June 17, 1918.

99 "Question, search": Navy Secretary Josephus Daniels to Attorney General T.W. Gregory, Aug. 12, 1918, Justice Department files, National Archives.

99 "There's my boy": GD, June 17, 1918.

100 "After the interrogations": Hawes to Gregory, July 2, 1918, Justice Department files, National Archives.

100 "We established the fact" et seq.: SLR, PD, GD, July 12, 1918; GD, Oct. 5, 1918.

100 "This whole" et seq.: SLR, July 12, 1918; PD, July 11, 12, 1918.

101 The owner: Deposition, Lilly Busch, June 14, 1921, Justice Department files, National Archives; PD, July 11, 12, 1918, March 18, 1935; NYT, Dec. 10, 1920.

101 "cruel and unusual": Hawes to Gregory, July 2, 1918.

101 "the Office of Naval Intelligence": Daniels to Gregory, Aug. 12, 1918; Treasury Secretary W. G. McAdoo to Daniels, Oct. 8, 1918; Gregory to Hawes, Nov. 16, 1918; Hawes to Palmer, July 18, 1918, Justice Department files, National Archives.

101 "Her property consists": Palmer to Gregory, Oct. 15, 1918, Justice Department files, National Archives.

102 "We must pay over": Adolphus Busch to Zane Cetti, Oct. 19, 1905, "Brewing and Liquor Interests."

102 "Mr. Busch until his death": LaRue Brown to Gregory, Oct. 18, 1918, Justice Department files, National Archives.

102 "Moreover she came": Palmer to Gregory, Nov. 12, 1918, Justice Department files, National Archives.

103 "release it": Coben, *A. Mitchell Palmer*, 149, 150.

Chapter 17: "What Would Father Have Done?"

Page
104 There was even one: PD, Feb. 19, 1984.
104 "not only willingly": Frederick Lewis Allen, *Only Yesterday* (New York: Harper & Row, 1957), 246.
104 "These miserable hypocrites": CHE, Jan. 16, 1929.
105 "to educate misinformed": HAB, 123.
105 he had joined: Ibid., 131.
105 "touch the spot": GD, Jan. 9, 1916.
105 The construction came: PD, Dec. 4, 1918.
106 "I am a piker": PD, Jan. 9, 1919.
106 indictments in Philadelphia: Sean D. Cashman, *Prohibition: The Lie of the Land* (New York: The Free Press, 1981), 23.
107 An agent of Anheuser-Busch: PD, Nov. 30, 1916.
107 "Personally I know nothing": Ibid.
108 "A man goes": PD, Nov. 22, 1916.
108 "high class": PD, June 4, 1917.
108 There were cries: PD, July 1, 1982.
108 "vote dry": quoted in PD, Dec. 5, 1958.
108 "man's job": PD, date unknown, approximately 1919.
108 Bevo sales fell: Ernest Kirschten, *Catfish and Crystal* (Garden City: Doubleday, 1960), 355.
109 "such a perfect imitation": *Factory and Industrial Management*, May 1929.
109 The situation became: HAB, 163.
109 In 1920 only 583: CR, Jan. 1933, 8.
109 "all his eggs": PD, Feb. 17, 1934.

Chapter 18: A Jumping Frog Named Budweiser

Page
110 The Prince told: LBG, 25.
110 "a very pretentious home": PD, June 13, 1910.
111 "They bear a delicate": PD, June 18, 1916.
112 a monkey named Joko: PD, March 19, 1948.
112 "The children": PD, March 3, 1929.
112 "a nip of a little something" et seq.: PD, Sept. 10, 1916.
112 The derby: LBG, 42.

Chapter 19: The "Completely Forgotten Man"

Page
114 "completely forgotten man": Interview, not for attribution.
115 "one of the most" et seq.: SLS, June 11, 1913.
115 "I am working": PD, May 8, 1912.
115 "I understand": PD, Dec. 4, 1912.
115 "This is all tommyrot": Ibid.
115 And once again: PD, June 11, 1913.

116 "age was definitely stated": SLS, June, date unknown, 1913.
116 "humiliated and insulted": PD, April 20, 1913.
116 "of athletic trend": SLS, June 11, 1913.
116 August A. announced: PD, June 11, 1913.
116 Adolphus, he said: PD, date unknown, 1913.
116 His story now: PD, April 15, 1914.
116 "the poor son": PD, May 23, 1914.
117 jetting off to Hong Kong: Interview, Walter Orthwein.
117 made it clear: Interview, HBC.
117 "Busch a better horse buyer": PD, Jan. 11, 1918.
117 "Adolphus . . . made": Interview, AAB.
118 "Burgling a Busch": PD, Jan. 6, 1915.
118 They had a narrow: PD, May 31, 1917.
118 "very opinionated": Interview, not for attribution.
118 "deep roaring voice": Interview, not for attribution.
118 "They all drank too much": Interview, HBC.
118 "The deputy agreed": PD, Sept. 16, 1919.
118 Florence threw: Interview, HBC.
118 "It was very painful": Interview, not for attribution.
118 "Adolphus Busch Divorced": PD, July 1, 1930.
119 "a close personal": PD, July 1, 1930.
119 "Dallas Woman": PD, Sept. 13, 1930.

Chapter 20: "A Simple Coming Out Ball"

Page
120 "The Baron": *Salt Lake Tribune*, April 11, 1915.
120 "They were always": Interview, Mabel-Ruth Anheuser.
120 "a simple coming out ball": PD, Dec. 5, 1912.
121 "a symphony": PD, Sept. 11, 1913.
121 "There was no tangoing": PD, Dec. 19, 1914.
122 "somewhat slender" et seq.: PD, Oct. 4, 1922.
122 "Believe me": SLS, March 19, 1948.
122 arrested for careless driving: PD, Sept. 16, 1919.

Chapter 21: Peck's Bad Boy

Page
123 "the greatest stud": Interview, Bob Broeg.
123 play "fire": SLS, March 19, 1948.
123 made Alice cook them: LBG, 35–36.
123 One of his earliest: PD, Aug. 25, 1975.
123 Family legend: Interview, Walter Orthwein.
123 "Let's just say": *Time*, July 11, 1955.
123 "Without doubt": Ibid.
124 education stopped: August A. "Gussie" Busch, Jr., v. Gertrude Marie
     Busch, St. Louis County Circuit Court records, Jan. 6, 1978.
124 A classmate recalled: Interview, not for attribution.

124 "The tutors would chase": Interview, HBC.
124 "He was the kind": Interview, not for attribution.
124 "with a tremendous shiner": Interview, HBC.
124 pick fights over women: LBG, 44.
124 "I worked my way": Interview, AAB.
125 He pulled back: Interview, HBC.
125 "I became a union guy": Interview, AAB.
125 "Friends remember": *Time*, July 11, 1955.
125 "He was such a marvelous": Interview, HBC.
125 blond wig and dress: PD, Dec. 17, 1912.
126 "He was very pushy": Interview, not for attribution.
126 "I remember once": PD, May 15, 1977.
126 "We bought a pack": PD, Oct. 30, 1960.
127 bare-backed dress: Interview, HBC.
127 "She was so beautiful": Interview, not for attribution.

Chapter 22: Tom Mix and the Kaiser's Grandson

Page
128 "I understand": August A. Busch to Lilly Busch, Dec. 15, 1919.
128 Anna had put in: PD, Feb. 1, 1914.
129 "simple little entertainment": PD, Jan. 18, 1915.
129 "thoroughly democratic": PD, Sept. 14, 1932.
129 Another visitor: Interview, Adolphus Orthwein.
129 "The dog did wonderful": *Bevo Tattler*, Jan. 24, 1923.
129 Like another famous: Interview, not for attribution.
130 Jacob Sonnen committed suicide: PD, date unknown.

Chapter 23: Scarface Al and the Golden Gates

Page
130 description of Capone gang: Allen, *Only Yesterday*, 264.
131 Gussie meets Capone: HBG, 185.
131 "Daddy took it": Ibid.
131 "I said, no, no": Interview, AAB.
131 "Pleased with Miami's": Polly Redford, *Billion-Dollar Sandbar* (New York: Dutton, 1970), 192.
132 "The extent to which": H.L. Mencken, *A Mencken Chrestomathy* (New York: Knopf, 1948), 414.
132 "August A. Busch realized": HAB, 178.
132 "If you really want": Interview, AAB.
132 "You knew perfectly": Ibid.
133 "I think Mr. Busch": Interview, not for attribution.
133 The worker particularly remembered: Ibid.
133 "Jesus, we spent" et seq.: Interview, AAB.
133 the board reversed itself: HAB, 187.
134 Gussie still bristled: Interview, AAB.
134 "We used to own": Ibid.

134   "So far it has not": *Bevo Tatler*, March 1923.
134   "never was intoxicating": Ibid., Sept. 1921.
135   "Being a friend": Ibid., Feb. 1920.
135   "You'll think that": Interview, AAB.
135   "For decades": HAB, 197.
135   "He comes to my daddy": Interview, AAB.

Chapter 24: A Case of Smuggling

Page
137   "unsuitable for public display": SLS, July 28, 1937.
137   She was a plaintiff: Justice Department files, National Archives.
138   "as settlement": NYT, Nov. 18, 1927.
138   "The rope originally": NYT, Nov. 18, 1927; PD, Nov. 17, 1927; GD, Nov. 18, 1927.
138   Lilly left an estate: GD, Feb. 17, 25, March 3, 1928; PD, Feb. 17, March 2, Oct. 23, 1928, July 6, 1938, May 27, 1942.

Chapter 25: A Kidnapping

Page
139   During the three years: Ludovic Kennedy, *The Air Man and the Carpenter* (New York: Viking, 1984), 91.
139   "delicate features": PD, Jan. 2, 1930.
140   "The parents rushed": Interview, Walter Orthwein.
140   He was armed: PD, Jan. 2, 1931.
140   "no questions asked": Ibid.
141   "who forgot their stations": Ibid.
141   "He didn't talk" et seq.: Ibid.
141   Abernathy's return and quotations: SLC, Jan. 5, 1931.
142   Abernathy and August A. Busch quotations: PD, Jan. 5, 1931.
142   He added: Interview, Adolphus Orthwein.

Chapter 26: The Floating Rum Palace

Page
143   "This makes the United States": PD, date unknown, 1931.
143   "unacquainted with the subject": PD, date unknown, 1931.
143   "It is of course": Ibid.
143   "Respecting your entirely irrelevant": NYT, date unknown, 1931.
144   "A brewer is a person": NYT, date unknown, 1931.
144   "Mr. Busch": NYT, date unknown, 1931.
144   "almost unbelievably": quoted in Allen, *Only Yesterday*, 126.
144   "I am of the opinion": PD, date unknown, 1931.
145   "a great army": Mencken, *A Mencken Chrestomathy*, 411.
145   "has corrupted": August A. Busch to Calvin Coolidge, Joint Collection, University of Missouri, Western Historical Manuscript Collection—Columbia. State Historical Society of Missouri Manuscript.

146 "Grandfather was absolutely livid": Interview, James Orthwein.

146 "After eight years": PD, Aug. 16, 1928.

146 "Beer! Beer!": GD, date unknown.

146 "Prohibition is an awful": quoted in Allen, *Only Yesterday*, 257.

146 The hopeless failure: Kirschten, *Catfish and Crystal*, 355–56.

147 August A. reported: GD, Feb. 14, 1934.

147 "What hit me?": William Reddig, *Tom's Town* (Philadelphia: Lippin-cott, 1947), 51.

147 "our esteemed": August A. Busch to Otto Mathi, Oct. 13, 1932, Joint Collection, University of Missouri, State Historical Society.

147 "to assist": Ibid.

147 When Pendergast . . . died: PD, Jan. 29, 1945.

Chapter 27: August A. Proposes a Beer Cure for the Depression

Page

148 A reorganization occurred: HAB, 199–210.

149 10 percent pay cut: Ibid., 211.

149 The legalization of beer: GD, May 6, 1932.

149 "Mr. Busch's open letter": GD, July 20, 1931.

149 "due to the fact": PD, July 27, 1931.

150 "the undertakers": PD, July 28, 1931.

150 "want and are demanding" et seq.: CD, Jan. 1933.

150 "Happy days": SLS, Dec. 6, 1932.

Chapter 28: A Case of Budweiser for FDR

Page

151 "I deem action": FDR Message to Congress, March 13, 1933.

151 "wisdom and foresight": August A. Busch telegram to FDR, March 23, 1933. FDR Presidential Library.

152 Actually, it was: HAB, 217.

152 "I asked him": Interview, AAB.

153 "April 7th is here" et seq.: PD, April 7, 1933.

Chapter 29: An Elephant Named Tessie

Page

154 "I turned to him" et seq.: Interview, AAB.

155 "Nobody will tinker": Newcomen Society address, 1953.

156 "was depressed": Interview, not for attribution.

156 "Listen, he chased": Interview, not for attribution.

156 "Busch, the story went": Interview, not for attribution.

156 "He felt he was": Interview, Adolphus Orthwein.

157 "In the first place": ST, June 15, 1934.

157 "As to who": Missouri Supreme Court records, Sept. 1937.

158 "They got nasty." et seq.: Interview, Dr. Anthony Busch.

158   "It was very painful" et seq.: Interview, Adolphus Orthwein.
158   "never deceive you": ST, Feb. 14, 1934.

Chapter 30: The Dutch Act

Page
159   The brewer informed: PD, June 19, 1933.
159   He received two: GD, Aug. 17, 1933.
159   Three Filipinos: PD, March 15, 1934.
159   His method of protecting: SLS, Feb. 14, 1934.
160   He purchased sixty: Ibid.
160   "liberal reward": PD, Nov. 16, 1932.
161   "if anything should happen": PD, Feb. 13, 1934.
161   "Can't you do": PD, Feb. 14, 1934.
161   shot of morphine: Ibid.
161   "I can't stand this": Ibid.
161   "almost like an insane person": Ibid.
162   "John, get your": Ibid.
162   "Goodbye precious": PD, Jan. 13, 1934.
162   "You want me": Ibid.
162   shot himself: Ibid.
162   "He lived for": Interview, Adolphus Orthwein.
163   "When my uncle": PD, Feb. 14, 1934.

Chapter 31: "This Is Where I Want to Be Buried"

Page
164   "Suicide due to long": PD, Feb. 14, 1934.
164   "I guess he just": Interview, not for attribution.
164   "The scepter": GD, Feb. 14, 1934.
164   "less solidly": Ibid.
164   "I therefore hope": Will, August A. Busch.
165   "I can see": SLS, Feb. 16, 1934.
165   "sought to give": PD, Feb. 16, 1934.
166   "During my life" et seq.: August A. Busch letter, Oct. 6, 1932, filed with
       will.
166   "sporting pictures" et seq.: Will, August A. Busch.

Chapter 32: Monkey Business

Page
167   "Under Adolphus": Interview, not for attribution.
168   The chimps were dressed: PD, Oct. 30, 1960.
168   "It was so Dutchy": PD, March 20, 1981.
169   "Schwaiger was surpreme": Interview, Robert Weinberg.
169   "See": Interview, Al Fleishman.
169   "He was fantastic" Interview, AAB.
170   As the man in charge: Interview, not for attribution.

170   "not a shard": Interview, not for attribution.
170   Before he left for home: *Forbes*, July 1935.
170   "It was a stormy": Interview, not for attribution.
170   "They were": Interview, not for attribution.
170   "Mrs. Busch opened" et seq.: Interview, not for attribution.
171   "It scared me": Interview, HBC.
171   "They were far" et seq.: Interview, not for attribution.

Chapter 33: Scandals

Page
172   "He rode with elan": PD, Sept. 25, 1989.
172   "It turns out": Interview, not for attribution.
172   "They would have": Interview, not for attribution.
172   By the summer: Elizabeth Overton Dozier v. Lewis D. Dozier, St. Louis County Circuit Court records, Sept. 8, 1933; PD, Sept. 8, 1933.
172   After a brief: Interview, Henry L. Griesedieck; LBG, 50.
173   The marriage between: PD, Jan. 30, 1933.
174   Alice married for the fourth time: PD, June 12, 1936, Nov. 19, 1938, June 13, 1944, Nov. 24, 1961, Jan. 6, 1977.
174   Later that summer: PD, July 17, 1946, Jan. 25, 1948, Dec. 23, 1963.
175   "I don't know": Interview, not for attribution.
175   "You want": Interview, Al Fleishman.
175   "All right, now": Interview, Robert Baskowitz, Jr.
175   "more grown up": Interview, not for attribution.
176   "You're a teetotaler": Ibid.
176   "Nierdieck told": Ibid.
176   "Honey, what's your name?": Interview, not for attribution.
176   "Honey, let's you": Ibid.

Chapter 34: The Man in the Mask

Page
177   "Give me back": PD, April 12, 1931.
178   "philanderer by instinct": PD, May 3, 1944, Dec. 21, 1951.
178   Shortly after Adolf Hitler: PD, March 16, 28, 1933.
178   Lilly Claire, meanwhile: PD, Feb. 8, 9, 10, 1939.
179   The Gontard estate: letter from William D. Bayles, Oct. 3, 1939, *Life*, Jan. 8, 1940.
179   "Rumored here Mrs. Berghaus": Sam Edison Woods telegram no. 247 to Division of World Trade Intelligence, Department of State, Nov. 18, 1942, State Department files, National Archives.
179   "Legation opinion": Sam Edison Woods telegram no. 280 to Secretary of State, Dec. 21, 1942, State Department files, National Archives.
179   "such action": Secretary of State "frozen credit" memorandum to U.S. Department of the Treasury, Nov. 30, 1942, State Department files, National Archives.
179   Meanwhile, a member: PD, Jan. 18, May 3, 6, 11, 13, 1944.

179 Clara Busch von Gontard married again: PD, Feb. 16, 1948, June 26, 1959.
180 On April 16, 1936: SLS, May 8, 1956; PD, April 16, July 6, 1936.
180 Among her later: LBG, 74, 75.

Chapter 35: Budweiser Goes to War

Page
181 The brewers resolved: AAB letter to the board of directors of the U.S. Brewers' Association, Jan. 13, 1942, files of Brewers and Maltsters Union Local 6.
181 "the fanciest major's uniform": Interview, James C. Kirkpatrick.
182 During 1944, Anheuser-Busch: James J. Carroll, Anheuser-Busch sales manager, letter to Attorney General Tom C. Clark, Jan. 26, 1945, Clark papers, Truman Library.
182 he made lieutentant colonel: AAB Military records, U.S. Military Personnel Records Center, Overland, MO, courtesy Joyce Weisner.
182 "in the service": GD, July 10, 1979.
182 "I met him once": Interview, EHV.
182 With so many temptations: Interview, not for attribution.
182 During the war: Affidavits signed by AAB, Aug. 6 and Oct. 16, 1951, August A. Busch, Jr., v. Elizabeth Overton Busch, St. Louis Circuit Court records.

Chapter 36: The Last Queen of Bavaria

Page
183 They called their villa: Walter Wanka, *Bernried and Its Surroundings* (Bernried, Hotel Seeblick, 1987), 75–6.
184 In 1928, when: Walburga Scherbaum, *A 600-Year History of Bernried* (Village of Bernried, 1982), 25, 26.
184 "They had a colossal": Ernst Hanfstaengl, *Unheard Witness* (Philadelphia: Lippincott, 1957), 58.
184 "was more successful": James Pool and Suzanne Pool, *Who Financed Hitler: The Secret Funding of Hitler's Rise to Power* (New York: The Dial Press, 1978), 68.
184 A copy of the house guestbook: Copies of guestbook of Eduard and Wilhelmina Scharrer, Bernried Archives, archivist Walburga Scherbaum, inspected March 1, 1990.
185 "the sort of Jewess" et seq.: *Hitler's Secret Conversations 1941–1944*, trans. Norman Cameron (New York: Farrar, Straus & Young, 1953), 264–65.
185 "Thanks for four days": Scharrers' guestbook, Bernried Archives; William L. Shirer, *Rise and Fall of the Third Reich* (New York: Simon and Schuster, 1960), 907.
185 "She was against": Interview, Walter Eberl.
185 She also had a collection: Interview, Walter Eberl; interview, Erwin Ruckriegel; interview, Dr. Peter Mathes; film clip of Wilhelmina and Eduard Scharrer, 1923, courtesy Erwin Ruckriegel.

186   "He liked food": Interview, Walter Eberl.
186   "Unfortunately for him": *Hitler's Secret Conversations*, 265.
186   In May of 1934: PD, May 4, 1934.
187   Dr. Peter Mathes, Interview, Dr. Peter Mathes; interview, Walter Eberl.
187   With a fortune: Interview, Erwin Ruckriegel; interview, Dr. Peter Mathes.
188   "she claims exemption": Sam E. Woods telegram to Secretary of State Cordell Hull, Dec. 21, 1942, State Department files, National Archives; Herman Simon letter to Truman, Feb. 25, 1947, Truman papers, Truman Library.
188   Wilhelmina was placed: SLS, Jan. 21, 1944.
189   "I knew Ralph": PD, March 29, 1948; Shirer, *The Rise and Fall*, 842, 843; *The Memoirs of Cordell Hull* (New York: Macmillan, 1948), 967.
190   "a loyal American" et seq.: SLS, Jan. 21, 1944; PD, March 29, 1948.
190   On February 22: PD, Feb. 23, 24, 1948; GD, Feb. 16, 29, 1948.
190   "the family was": Interview, not for attribution.
190   Members of the Busch: Interview, Walter Eberl.
190   Gussie longed for: LBG, 91.
190   In 1951, when: American Foreign Service report of the death of an American citizen, May 26, 1953, State Department files, National Archives.
191   Minnie's estate: GD, June 13, 1953, Sept. 1, 1955; PD, Jan. 23, Feb. 28, 1953, Sept. 16, 1954, Sept. 13, Dec. 15, 1955.
191   "Gussie went through": Interview, not for attribution.
191   "She wanted to live": Interview, Dr. Peter Mathes.

Chapter 37: Pigs With Painted Toes

Page
192   After the war: LBG, 68; Death certificate of Adolphus Busch III, Missouri Department of Health records; PD, Feb. 8, 1945.
192   Adolphus III had been ill: Interview, HBC; GD, SLS, Aug. 30, 31, 1946.
192   The truth was otherwise: Records of Brewers and Malsters Union Local 6; LBG, 68.
193   Eighty percent: BW, Sept. 6, 1947.
193   In 1947 his annual salary: GD, June 13, 1949.
193   "Somehow Gussie bought": Interview, not for attribution.
193   The engraved invitations: GD, July 6, 1946; SLS, July 5, 1946; August A. Busch, Jr., v. Elizabeth Overton Busch, St. Louis Circuit Court records, Aug. 7, 1951.
194   The biggest event: PD, Dec. 25, 1949; *Saturday Evening Post*, June 1953.
194   No one threw: PD, SLS, June 22, 1948; GD, Aug. 11, 1948; Interview, Busch family friend, not for attribution.

Chapter 38: Give the Baby Some Budweiser

Page
195   When Carlota was born: LBG, 61.
195   "Five drops of Budweiser": FM, June 1975.

196 "his apparent lack": BW, July 13, 1968.
196 "I expect that": Interview, not for attribution.
196 "a lost childhood": Washington University profile, undated.
196 "You sit around": *BW*, July 13, 1968.
196 "probably before": *American Rifleman*, July 1987.
197 "partly dismantled" et seq.: PD, Nov. 1, 1949.
197 shooting cats: LBG, 73.
197 "The average worker": Interview, not for attribution.
197 "Young August": Interview, Martin Quigley.
197 "We don't hunt": *American Rifleman*, July 1987.
197 In 1954: PD, Nov. 22, 1954.
198 "a bit moody": Interview, David Millstone.
198 "He wasn't one": Interview, not for attribution.
198 "He stood there": Interview, not for attribution.
198 "The next day": Interview, Robert Bassman.
198 "I think we" et seq.: Interview, Eugene Mackey.
199 "The betting": Interview, Richard Stauffer.

Chapter 39: The Swiss Miss

Page
200 At the time: August A. Busch, Jr., v. Elizabeth Overton Busch, St. Louis Circuit Court records. Aug. 7, 1951.
200 More than 8,000: PD, Sept. 17, 1947.
200 In 1946, Pabst: BW, April 3, 1963.
200 Those who knew her: August A. Busch, Jr., v. Gertrude Marie Busch, Jan. 6, 1978; NYT, May 13, 1965.
201 "Who in the hell": PD, Aug. 25, 1975.
201 "He . . . proposed to me": Ibid.
201 She was showered: PD, March 22, 1952.
201 "If and when": Ibid.
202 It alleged general: Affidavits signed by AAB, Aug. 6, Oct. 16, 1951, August A. Busch, Jr., v. Elizabeth Overton Busch, Aug. 7, 1951.
202 "greatly in": GD, Dec. 8, 1951; August A. Busch, Jr., v. Elizabeth Overton Busch, Aug. 7, 1951.
202 "How else could": Ibid.
202 "How much was paid": Ibid.
202 A divorce trial: August A. Busch, Jr., v. Elizabeth Overton Busch, GD, Feb. 21, 1952.
203 "We are very glad": PD, March 22, 23, 1952.
203 "Why? Gussie already thinks": Interview, Monsignor Jerome F. Wilkerson.

Chapter 40: Making Friends

Page
204 "That's when": Interview, Robert L. Lewis.
204 It was common: Harry B. Hawes to Joseph J. Hauser, Sept. 23, 1938,

in the retired files of Brewers and Maltsters Union Local 6, in St. Louis, Mo.

204 "been on the take" et seq.: Interview, Robert L. Lewis.

206 "The battle will never": J. J. Carroll letter, U.S. Brewers' Association, Feb. 26, 1945, Local 6 collection.

207 Buford's feats: PD, Dec. 7, 1959; interview, James C. Kirkpatrick; interview, not for attribution; interview, Ann Buford; Phil Donnelly papers, Joint Collection, University of Missouri, Western Historical Manuscript Collection—Columbia. State Historical Society of Missouri Manuscript; Truman papers, Truman Library.

208 "Personally, I do": Tom C. Clark correspondence, Dec. 5, 1944, July 26, Aug. 11, 1945, Clark papers, Truman Library.

208 Buford also wrote: Buford to Clark, Feb. 10, 1948; Clark to Douglas, first secretary of the embassy, June 10, 1949; Henry E. Stebbins to Clark, June 20, 1949; Clark to AAB, Aug. 15, 1949; Clark papers, Truman Library; Buford to Stuart Symington, March 7, 1958; Busch to Symington, March 10, 1958; Symington to Dr. J. M. Hughes of the U.S. Department of Health, Education and Welfare, March 12, 1958, Symington papers, Joint Collection, University of Missouri, State Historical Society.

208 "Gussie would say": Interview, not for attribution.

208 Gussie began making: GD, Nov. 2, 1934, Oct. 25, 1936; PD, Nov. 26, 1935.

209 Even before: Subcommittee hearings of the Interstate Commerce Committee, U.S. Senate, on S. 517, March 29, 31, 1939.

209 "It may be": *Union Signal*, Aug. 25, 1945.

209 "meant so much": Clark to AAB, Nov. 4, 1948, Clark papers, Truman Library.

209 While Truman was president: Buford to Truman, Aug. 5, Dec. 1, 1948, May 4, 1949; AAB to Truman, Sept. 7, 1949, Truman papers, Truman Library.

210 "Gussie and Truman": Interview, Walter Orthwein.

210 Gussie's friendship: AAB to Truman, Oct. 4, 1955, Truman to AAB, April 16, 1956, Truman papers, Truman Library.

210 "I'll be damned": GD, Dec. 24, 1961.

210 "You will be pleased": Wilson to Eisenhower, June 26, 1953, Eisenhower papers, Eisenhower Library.

210 While Eisenhower was president: Ann C. Whitman, personal secretary to the president, to Salveson, Oct. 4, 1954; Eisenhower to Wilson, Feb. 11, 1956, Eisenhower papers, Eisenhower Library.

210 Attorney General William P. Rogers: United States v. Anheuser-Busch et al., Oct. 30, 1958, Southwest District of Florida, Justice Department files, National Archives.

Chapter 41: "A Personable and Able Huckster"

Page

212 "Man Who Put": SI, Aug. 8, 1988.

212 "is bigger": PD, April 23, 1952.

212 "Baseball without": AF.
212 Gussie told friends: Interview, not for attribution.
212 "I am going": PD, Feb. 20, 1953.
213 "Development of the Cardinals": PD, date unknown, 1953.
213 "Mr. Busch": PD, Feb. 21, 1953.
213 "a personable": PD, Feb. 23, 1954.
213 "lavish and vulgar": PD, March 19, 1954.
213 "goes out the window" et seq.: Ibid.
214 "buying the Cardinals": Ibid.
214 "What the hell": AF.
214 "What caused me": Ibid.
214 "Fleishman orchestrated": Interview, Bob Broeg.
215 "was known as a hellion": Interview, Ted Schafers.
215 "used to tell": Interview, not for attribution.
215 "He arranged": NYT, date unknown.
215 "Suddenly, I became": AF.
215 "Get that crap": Interview, Bob Broeg.
216 "heavy drinking": Ibid.
216 "there was a cheerful": PD, Aug. 2, 1959.
216 "We were debating": Interview, Bing Devine.

Chapter 42: "Fire His Ass!"

Page
218 "Okay, you're appointed": Interview, Bing Devine.
218 "Busch had not": PD, Jan. 24, 1988.
218 "If Frank Lane": Ibid.
218 "Send a telegram": Interview, Al Fleishman.
219 "No, dammit, no": PD, Aug. 28, 1975.
219 "When the Mets": SI, April 23, 1965.
219 "If you were": PD, Sept. 30, 1989.
219 "You were always afraid": Interview, Bing Devine.
219 "Gussie kept trying": Interview, Harry Caray.
220 "Bing didn't": Harry Caray, *Holy Cow* (New York: Villard, 1989), 148.

Chapter 43: "I Was a Bad Son-of-a-Gun"

Page
220 "I couldn't behave": PD, April 18, 1967.
221 "I think he was playing": Interview, not for attribution.
221 "Bob told me": Interview, not for attribution.
221 "At Gussie's request": Interview, not for attribution.
221 "Bob was bleeding" et seq.: Interview, not for attribution.
222 "every little waitress": Ibid.
222 "Young August": Interview, Martin Quigley.
222 "We supposedly had": BW, July 13, 1968, 106.
222 "They were doing jumps.": Interview, Robert Baskowitz, Jr.
223 "When you finished": FM, Jan. 15, 1979, 94.

223 "He must have seen": Interview, not for attribution.
223 "wasn't there": Interview, Robert Lewis.

Chapter 44: Deals With David Beck

Page
224 "All you had to do": O'Neill, quoted by former Sen. Thomas F. Eagleton, PD, Oct. 3, 1989.
224 "abnormal" and "unusual": Testimony of the U.S. Senate Select Committee on Improper Activities in the Labor or Management Field, May 9, 1957, 2071–2104, Robert Kennedy papers, John F. Kennedy Library.
225 "Who is this Bud?" Ibid.
225 "His Majesty": Ibid.
225 Another problem Gussie had: United States of America v. Anheuser-Busch, Inc. and Rahr Malting Co., Civil Action No. 62C45(3), Filed Jan. 31, 1962, Justice Department files, National Archives.
226 "as good a friend": Tony Buford to Senator Stuart Symington, Symington to Buford, Jan. 19, 1954, May 18, 25, 1956; PD, Aug. 2, 1959, May 3, 1961, July 6, Dec. 30, 1962.
226 "You're supposed to have": Stephen Darst, "The Very Last of the Marvelous Beer Barons," *St. Louisan Magazine*, January 1976.
227 "If you pay him": Interview, not for attribution.
227 "Communist threat": AAB to Symington, May 23, 1962; Symington to AAB, June 2, 1962, Symington papers, Joint collection, University of Missouri, Western Historical Manuscript Collection—Columbia, State Historical Society of Missouri manuscript.
227 "We may be accused": AAB to Symington, July 5, 1962, Stan Fike to AAB, Aug. 23, 1962, Ibid.
228 "The Budweiser Memorandum": AAB to Symington, June 1, July 8, 1963, Ibid.

Chapter 45: The Beer Taste Test

Page
228 "He had no morals" et seq.: Interview, EHV.
230 "beer clean glass": Interview, Al Fleishman.
230 "We went there": Interview, Ted Schafers.

Chapter 46: "I Know I'm Curt at Times. But I Just Don't Have Time."

Page
231 paying attention to a cute waitress: Interview, not for attribution.
231 Or it might have: BW, July 13, 1968, 104.
232 "innate, native": Interview, EHV.
232 "He has to measure": FB, Aug. 7, 1978, 36.
232 "If I've told": BW, July 13, 1968.
232 "I said to him": Interview, EHV.

232 "I know I'm curt": BW, July 13, 1968.
232 "If you carry": Ibid.
233 "Ackoff asked August": Interview, EHV.
233 "It's a wonder": PD, Nov. 3, 1975.
234 "I got up" et seq.: Interview, Walter Armbruster.
235 he had the fun idea: LBG, 128.
235 Susan liked to joke: PD, Oct. 8, 1967.
235 "I learned in my 20s": NYT, Oct. 12, 1980.
235 "I had to sit there": Interview, Robert Lewis.
235 "His problem": Interview, EHV.
236 "When August became GM": Ibid.
236 "Eddie had called": Interview, Robert Lewis.
236 "If you leave": Interview, EHV.
236 "absolute indifference": GD, June 25, 1969.
237 "You're either": Interview, Robert Lewis.
237 "I'll give you": Interview, not for attribution.

Chapter 47: Offers in Compromise

Page
238 "Sure enough": PD, Oct. 3, 1989.
238 "You don't ask": AF.
238 "He had the number": Interview, Bob Meyer.
238 Gussie had other reasons: PD, July 14, 15, 21, 1966; Dwight Ingamills, statement, July 14, 1966, and Fleishman telegram to Symington, July 14, 1966, Symington papers, Joint Collection, University of Missouri, Western Manuscript Collection—Columbia. State Historical Society of Missouri manuscript. AF, 25.
239 "striking coincidences" et seq.: Ibid.
239 "All right then": *St Louisan Magazine*, Jan. 1976.
240 "The caterer out there": Interview, Joseph Griesedieck.
240 "shut anybody out": GD, Dec. 28, 1976, Jan. 26, 1977.
240 "Cervantes said": Interview, not for attribution.
240 "They wanted everything": Interview, Sue Ann Wood.
240 "allegiances" "misleading": 1968 Campaign Series, political files, Hubert Humphrey Papers, Minnesota Historical Society.
240 One of the powerful: Flanigan biography, Flanigan papers, White House Central Files, Nixon Presidential Materials, National Archives.
241 "a person who works": GD, Sept. 14, 15, 1972.
242 "Among the recent converts": Flanigan memorandum, Sept. 17, 1972, White House Central Files, Nixon Presidential Materials, National Archives.
242 "an ungrateful millionaire": PD, Oct. 9, 1972.
242 Between 1950 and 1971: PD, July 16, 1971, April 27, Nov. 8, 1972.
242 At the end of 1934: NYT, Dec. 21, 1934.
243 In 1942: Treasury Department, Alcohol, Tobacco and Firearms Division, case No. 73-19(a), June 20, 1973.
243 Later, the numbers: Securities and Exchange Commission v. Anheuser-Busch, Inc., U.S. District Court for the District of Columbia, May 19,

1977; final judgment of permanent injunction, May 20, 1977; report of review person to the auditing committee of the board of directors of Anheuser-Busch, Inc. filed Oct. 27, 1977, Justice Department files, National Archives.

243   "questionable payments": PD, March 31, 1978.
243   "for competitive": Ibid.
243   "sufficient to deter": ATF Abstract and Statement March 30, 1978; Ibid.

Chapter 48: "We Never Talked About Baseball. We Talked About Booze, Broads and Cards."

Page
244   "We never talked": Interview, Harry Caray.
244   One year Caray: Interview, Edward C. Kelley.
245   "amok in taverns": PD, Aug. 14, 1988.
245   Caray was hit by a car: CT, Aug. 18, 1978.
245   "fifty thousand people": Caray, *Holy Cow*, 165–66.
246   "I asked him": Interview, Ted Schafers.
246   "I thought they" et seq.: *Riverfront Times*, May 25–31, 1983.
246   "Gussie Busch is a dear friend": CT, Aug. 18, 1978.
246   "I would have rather": *Riverfront Times*, May 25–31, 1983.
246   "You couldn't say" et seq.: Interview, Harry Caray.
247   "There were rumors": Interview, Susan Busch.
247   "and I don't mean": PD, Sept. 21, 1982.
247   "never extended" et seq.: Curt Flood, *The Way It Is* (New York: Pocketbooks, 1972), 73–74.
248   "I don't like": *St. Petersburg Times*, March 13, 1970.
248   "I sat with": PD, March 14, 1978.
248   "vendetta": *Newsweek*, June 19, 1972.
248   "has the civic pride": *Newsday*, Aug. 23, 1972.
249   "They were a wild": Interview, EHV.
249   "Trudy got": Interview, Harry Chesley.
249   "It was for $50,000": Interview, EHV.
249   Lilly, in fine family tradition: LBG, 139.
249   "I assure you": GD, April 14, 1972.

Chapter 49: Gin and Honors

Page
250   "My happiness is": PD, April 19, 1970.
250   "Even in the can": Interview, Robert Baskowitz, Jr.
250   "Joseph, the butler": Interview, HBC.
250   "Now you know": Interview, Bob Lewis.
250   "Gussie liked gin": Interview, John J. Woulfe.
251   "Gussie was a good": Interview, Robert Baskowitz, Jr.
251   "Gussie would have": Interview, Al Fleishman.
251   "I had to take": PD, August 26, 1975.

251 "Scotch. I only": Interview, Ted Schafers.
251 "Busch-style 'gin and honors' ": PD, Oct. 3, 1989.
251 "Sure, he cheated": Interview, EHV.
251 "There were penalties": Interview, not for attribution.
251 "You had to play": Interview, Butch Portell
252 "Let's play cards" et seq.: Interview, Robert Baskowitz, Jr.
252 "He liked to have": Interview, Bob Meyer.

Chapter 50: Beer Wars I

Page
253 "He's got to resign": Interview, Robert Lewis.
253 Gontard, it was said: Interview, not for attribution; PD, Oct. 1, 1952;
     BW, June 25, 1955.
253 "Gussie was just furious": Interview, not for attribution.
253 "Actually it was": Interview, Fred Saigh.
253 "Gussie used to get": Interview, not for attribution.
254 "Who works": Interview, not for attribution.
254 "Gussie hated Adie": Interview, HBC.
254 "Gussie ran": Interview, Robert Lewis.
254 "I'm so goddamn": Interview, AAB.
255 "I had the goddamnedest": Ibid.
255 The Newark plant: PD, March 12, 1953; FB, March 1, 1968; BW, April
     13, 1963.
255 "He couldn't stand": Interview, Al Fleishman.
255 "Yeah, that famous trip": Interview, AAB.
256 Meyer was at Gussie's side: Interview, Al Fleishman.
256 Following the trip: FB, May 15, 1971; BW, March 24, 1973.
256 "I was standing": Interview, Walter Armbruster.
257 "If you had Busch Jr.": Interview, Robert Weinberg.
257 "They did lots" : Interview, not for attribution.
257 "We'd have a draft": Interview, Bob Griesedieck.

Chapter 51: The Fight at Grant's Farm

Page
258 "I never have cooked": NYT, May 13, 1965; *St. Petersburg Times*, June
     2, 1965.
258 "Sure you like it": Interview, Bob Meyer.
258 "To say that coaching": PD, Aug. 21, 1977.
259 "He said something": Interview, Robert Suits.
259 Although Gussie and his family: GD, June 3, 1958; PD, July 7, 1958.
260 "Because of the deep" et seq.: Will, Alice Busch, St. Louis County
     Probate Court files, Jan. 15, 1958.
260 Gussie and his sister: Interview, not for attribution; interview, not for
     attribution.
260 "Dolph Orthwein . . . tried": Interview, Robert Lewis.
260 "The only thing": Interview, Adolph B. Orthwein.

Chapter 52: The Man Who Could Talk to the Animals

Page
261   "Animals loved Gussie": Interview, EHV.
261   "whoop, whoop, whoop": Interview, HBC.
261   "Go get 'em Ralph": Interview, not for attribution.
261   "He was shouting": Interview, John McGuire.
262   And there was: Interview, not for attribution.
262   His daughter Carlota: LBG, 57.
262   "If overall I could": Interview, not for attribution.
262   "Sounds like": Interview, John J. Woulfe.
262   "I still remember": Interview, Al Fleishman.
262   "For the first time": Interview, not for attribution.
263   The Clydesdales were: PD, Dec. 20, 1964; GD, Sept. 18, 1965.
263   "I told the board": Interview, AAB.

Chapter 53: Gussie and a Different Cardinal

Page
264   "He realized" et seq.: Interview, Father Paul Reinert.
264   "It was a tax": Ibid.
265   "He is tight": Interview, Al Fleishman.
265   "He was not" et seq.: Interview, EHV.
265   Gussie did, however: Memorandum from Richard J. Coyle, Dec. 9, 1969, private papers of Father Paul Reinert.
265   "As you know": AAB to Senator Stuart Symington, Feb. 18, 1963, Symington papers, Joint collection, University of Missouri Western Historical Manuscript Collection—Columbia. State Historical Society of Missouri Manuscript.
266   "Do you know" et seq.: Interview, Father Paul Reinert.
267   "What time do you ring": *St. Louisan Magazine*, January 1976.

Chapter 54: "Dawn Patrol"

Page
268   "The talk was": BW, March 24, 1974.
268   He told them: LBG, 152.
269   "The old man": NYT, Oct. 12, 1980.
269   "They were out": Interview, not for attribution.
269   "They just closed": Ibid.
270   "a snot" et seq.: Interview, Robert S. Weinberg.
270   "In the heat": FM, Jan. 15, 1979.
270   "I don't think": *Washington Post*, date unknown.
270   "They were paying": Interview, Robert S. Weinberg.
271   The cerebral Weinberg: *St. Louis Magazine*, April 1988.
271   "He was pretty clear-cut" et seq.: Interview, not for attribution.
272   "he should have quit": Interview, Al Fleishman.
272   "dawn patrol": Interview, not for attribution.
272   "Denny told me": Ibid.

272   "I was ushered": Interview, not for attribution.
273   "When I asked": Interview, Walter Armbruster.
273   "I doubt if August": Interview, Henry King.
273   "It was like": Interview, not for attribution.
273   "I've never met": Interview, not for attribution.
273   "I explained": Interview, Henry King.

Chapter 55: Heads Roll

Page
274   "Heads Roll": PD, March 10, 1974.
275   "It is hard": FB, June 1, 1974, 27.
275   "If you don't know": Interview, not for attribution.
275   "was going too far": Interview, Al Fleishman.
275   "This is fun": PD, Oct. 20, 1974.

Chapter 56: The Beer Fleet

Page
276   "if they hadn't found": Interview, Fred Saigh.
276   "I'm not unhappy": PD, GD, April 25, May 3, July 17, June 15, 1963.
277   "What about Goat Mountain": GD, April 28, 29, May 17, 1966.
277   The *A & Eagle*: *St. Petersburg Times*, July 18, 1961, Feb. 5, 1967; PD, March 23, 1967.
277   "The letter . . . invited": Interview, Robert Baskowitz, Jr.
277   "There were a lot" et seq.: Interview, Harry Chesley.
278   "Gussie flew back": Interview, John L. Dowling.
279   Fike was a very able: Memo of Stan Fike, administrative assistant to Stuart Symington, June 7, 1974; AAB to Symington, June 12, 1974; Symington to Busch, June 14, 1974; Symington to Commissioner Leonard Chapman, Immigration and Naturalization Service, June 19, 1974; Gertrude Busch to Symington, June 18, 1974; Sen. Thomas F. Eagleton to Gertrude Busch, June 20, 1974; Symington to Dr. Henry G. Schwartz, professor of Neurological Surgery, Washington University, June 13, 1974, Symington papers, Joint Collection, University of Missouri, Western Historical Manuscript Collection—Columbia. State Historical Society of Missouri Manuscript.

Chapter 57: Old Blue Eyes

Page
280   In the 1950s: Interview, Al Fleishman.
280   "The good Lord": PD, Jan. 26, 1957; GD, Jan. 27, 1957.
280   "You've got to remember": Interview, EHV, interview, Harry Chesley.
281   The use of television: GD, May 10, 1951.
281   "That ought to give": BW, March 24, 1973.
281   In many breweries: Interview, Frank J. Sellinger.

282   "You can say": Interview, EHV.
282   "Don't you think": Ibid.

Chapter 58: Honeybee

Page

283   "the last of the Mohicans": GD, April 25, 1966; July 19, 1953; Dec. 8,
       1955; April 28, 1966; August A. Busch, Jr., v Gertrude Marie Busch, St.
       Louis County Circuit Court records, Jan. 6, 1978.
283   "My great-grandfather": Interview, AAB.
283   "Her baptism": Interview, not for attribution.
283   "One day he brought": PD, April 21, 1970; Interview, Yolanda Glog-
       gner.
284   "I was struck by": Interview, not for attribution.
284   "Adolphus is the oldest": Interview, AAB.
285   "a strict loyalty": Interview, John J. Woulfe.
285   Queen of Love and Beauty: PD, Dec. 24, 1972; GD, Dec. 24, 1977.
285   "My parents": GD, Dec. 24, 1977.
285   After she learned: GD, Dec. 6, 1979.
286   The child's death: AAB to Senator Stuart Symington, Jan. 27, 1975,
       Symington papers, Joint Collection, University of Missouri, Western
       Historical Manuscript Collection—Columbia. State Historical Society
       of Missouri Manuscript.
286   "I think it": Interview, Monsignor Jerome F. Wilkerson.
286   "When his daughter": Interview, Al Fleishman.

Chapter 59: "Papa Is Out!"

Page

287   "August has stabbed": Interview, John J. Woulfe.
287   "He reminded me": Interview, not for attribution.
287   "Jimmy Orthwein was pivotal": Interview, not for attribution.
288   "I thought you": Interview, Ted Schafers.
288   "was able to show": Interview, not for attribution.
288   "He saw that": Interview, David Callahan.
288   "They wanted him": Interview, not for attribution.
288   "The old man": Interview, Robert Lewis.
288   "They did threaten": Interview, EHV.
289   "Young August used": Interview, not for attribution.
289   "Robert, papa": Interview, Robert Lewis.
289   Trudy was livid: LBG, 157.
289   "Adolphus and August": Interview, not for attribution.
289   She said their action: LBG, 157.
289   "He had made the mistake": Interview, Robert Baskowitz, Jr.
289   "The yacht": Interview, not for attribution.
290   "Before we cleaned it up": Ibid.
290   "She couldn't use": Interview, EHV.
290   "Since relinquishing": PD, Jan. 11, 1976.

291   "They had an offer": Interview, EHV.
291   "They had every member": Interview, John J. Woulfe.
291   "The kid disliked": Interview, EHV.
291   "Fleishman-Hillard only kept": Interview, Ted Schafers.
291   "The Great Satan": PD, Dec. 5, 1988.
292   "I was always just careful": Interview, David Callahan.
292   "For people who inherit": Interview, Walter Armbruster.

Chapter 60: "Have One for the Ditch!"

Page
293   "Busch ran the ballclub": PD, Sept. 30, 1989.
294   "son of a bitch": Interview, Robert Lewis.
294   "You always hear that": Interview, Ed Vogel.
294   "Luca Brassi" and "Mess with Gussie": *St. Louis Sun*, Oct. 9, 1989.
294   "magical characters": Ibid.
295   "I loved Gussie": Bowie Kuhn, *Hardball: The Education of a Baseball Commissioner* (New York: Timesbooks, 1987), 397.
295   "Gussie Busch loves": PD, Oct. 15, 1975.
295   "kicked in the teeth": GD, June 17, 1976.
296   "getting damn mad": GD, June 24, 1978.
296   "for all his imperious": Kuhn, *Hardball*, 8
296   "I suspect": Ibid., 393.
296   "hard, tough-minded": Ibid., 420.
296   "Listen, Commissioner": PD, March 15, 1978.
296   "Because Anheuser-Busch" et seq: Kuhn, *Hardball*, 377, 420.
297   "rather devastating news": Ibid., 382.
297   "He should clean out": Ibid., 401.
297   "The two would talk baseball": PD, Sept. 30, 1989.
297   "Have one for the ditch": Interview, Bob Broeg.

Chapter 61: ". . . They Can Buy a Life."

Page
298   "almost cursed": Interview, not for attribution.
298   On one occasion: PD, Nov. 11, 1946.
299   "cowboy": Memorandum, St. Louis County prosecuting attorney, undated.
299   "You have to understand": PD, Feb. 10, 1976.
299   "I was always scared": Deposition, Gertrude Busch, Nov. 10, 1979.
299   "an arsenal": interrogatory, quoting police official, A. Elmer and Doris Leeker v. August A. Busch, Jr., et al., St. Louis County Circuit Court, undated. (All depositions cited stem from this case.)
299   "about six handguns": Deposition, Gertrude Busch, Nov. 10, 1979.
299   Peter's guns: Deposition, Peter Busch, Feb. 3, 1979.
299   "All of us": Police report, Feb. 10, 1976.
299   Trudy knew that: Deposition, Gertrude Busch, Nov. 10, 1979.
299   "afraid of Peter": Ibid.
299   "fantasy for guns" et seq.: Deposition, William E. Pike, Sept. 14, 1979.
299   "I was by myself": Deposition, Peter Busch, Feb. 3, 1979.

300 "learned a lesson," father's responsibility: Deposition, Gertrude Busch, Nov. 10, 1979.
300 "I have plenty": Deposition, AAB, Feb. 2, 1979.
300 His collection numbered: Interrogatory, AAB, Dec. 29, 1978.
300 "Well, we have always": Deposition, Peter Busch, Feb. 3, 1979.
300 Gussie often told Trudy: Deposition, Gertrude Busch, Nov. 10, 1979.
300 While in his late teens: Deposition, Peter Busch, Feb. 3, 1979.
301 "What the hell's": Interview, John J. Woulfe.
301 "aggressive" and "passive": Police report, Feb. 19, 1976.
301 "yield to Peter's": Police report, Feb. 10, 1976.
301 "It was Peter": Interview, Leslie Leeker.
301 "You've got to feel sorry": Interview, Elmer and Doris Leeker.
301 "It was as if": Interview, Leslie Leeker.
302 "David was upset": Deposition, Doris Leeker, March 29, 1980.
302 "He was waving it": Deposition, Elmer Leeker, March 29, 1980.
302 What was proven: Deposition, Peter Busch, Feb. 3, 1979.
303 "We weren't doing nothing": Ibid.
303 Shortly after ten; and events at Grant's Farm before the shooting: Ibid.; police report, Feb. 10, 1976.
303 "Thanks for the pillow": Police report, Feb. 10, 1976.
303 "I was going": Deposition, Peter Busch, Feb. 3, 1979.
303 Traveling slightly upward: Deposition, William K. Drake, medical examiner, Nov. 16, 1976.
303 Running to his: Police report, Feb. 10, 1976.
303 "Dad, don't": Ibid.
304 As his panic increased: Ibid.
304 The first squad car: Police report, Feb. 19, 1976.
304 Margaret calls Susman's home, lawyers called: Ibid.
304 Susman calls Fleishman: Deposition, Al Fleishman, Aug. 7, 1981.
305 "I said that": Ibid.
305 "wasn't the right story" et seq.: PD, Jan. 24, 1988.
305 "had already taken care": Deposition, Doris Leeker, March 29, 1980.
305 "We kept wondering" et seq.: Interview, Leslie Leeker.
306 "Forgive me": Deposition, Doris Leeker, March 29, 1980.
306 "David was my": Police report, Feb. 19, 1976.
307 "I remember asking": Interview, Leslie Leeker.
307 "I tried to explain": Deposition, Peter Busch, Feb. 2, 1979.
307 "They said the gun": Interview, Elmer Leeker.
307 "I never wanted": Deposition, August A. Busch, Jr., Feb. 2, 1979.
307 "He explained the difference": Police report, Feb. 10, 1976.
308 "within five feet": PD, March 2, 1976.
308 "the largest single": Ibid.
308 "Peter's final version" et seq.: Memorandum, St. Louis County prosecuting attorney, undated.
308 "unlawfully and feloniously": PD, March 31, 1976.
308 "huge drawing room" et seq.: Interview, Leslie Leeker.
309 "apparently was homosexual": Police report, March 15, 1976.
309 "homosexual affair": Police report, Feb. 19, 1976.
309 "He thought it": Deposition, Elmer Leeker, March 29, 1980.
309 "a sexual experience": Police report, March 15, 1976.

309   "recommend suspended sentence": Records, St. Louis County Circuit
       Court, Jan. 17, 1977.
309   "I am very sorry": PD, Feb. 28, 1977.
310   "not to handle firearms": Ibid.
310   "I do not feel": Letter, Harry J. Stussie, Jan. 31, 1978.
310   "underlying philosophy": *Miami Herald,* Aug. 6, 1985.
310   "He just told him": Interview, John J. Woulfe.
310   "He was very disappointed": Interview, not for attribution.
310   "He told him": Interview, John J. Woulfe.
311   "Gussie was angry": Interview, not for attribution.
311   "A short profile: *Miami Herald,* Aug. 6, 1985.
311   Lawsuit settled: GD, Sept. 15, 1981.
312   "It has a different": Interview, Jason Leeker.
312   "The Busches own": Interview, Leslie Leeker.

Chapter 62: Divorce

Page
312   earrings down toilet: Interview, not for attribution.
312   "got up and put on": Interview, HBC.
313   "What the fuck": Interview, Robert Baskowitz, Jr.
313   "He was pissed": Interview, not for attribution.
313   "Instead of taking it": Interview, HBC.
313   "All those clothes racks": Interview, Bob Meyer; interview, Robert
       Baskowitz, Jr.
313   "He was worried": Interview, not for attribution.
313   "It was a paranoia": Interview, Al Fleishman.
314   "The last two years": Interview, Martina Buholzer.
314   "in the manner": private papers.
314   "It is known": Ibid.
314   "He'd get crocked": Interview, HBC.
315   "harassment, abuse": GD, Jan. 7, 1978; August A. Busch, Jr., v. Ger-
       trude Marie Busch, St. Louis County Court records, Jan. 6, 1978.
315   "We all love you": PD, Jan. 12, 13, 18, 1978; August A. Busch, Jr., v.
       Gertrude Marie Busch, St. Louis County Circuit Court Records Jan. 6,
       1978; GD, Jan. 14, 1978.
315   "I was horrified" et seq.: August A. Busch, Jr., v. Gertrude Marie Busch,
       Jan. 6, 1978, PD, Feb. 28, 1978; GD, March 9, Nov. 18, 1978.
315   "to vacate": August A. Busch, Jr., v. Gertrude Marie Busch, Jan. 6,
       1978.
316   "a few million": PD, Feb. 28, 1978.
316   "That first year": Interview, not for attribution.
316   "Everybody has hard times": GD, Dec. 6, 1979.

Chapter 63: Beer Wars II

Page
317   "After all": FM, Jan. 15, 1979.
317   voodoo doll: FB, Aug. 7, 1978.
317   "There is little": Corporate publication, 1978, 1.

318 "Tell Miller": BW, Nov. 8, 1978.
318 The company counterattacked: PD, Aug. 12, 1979.
318 "It's just a matter": Interview, not for attribution.
318 "was too damn long": FB, Aug. 7, 1978.
318 "dumping chemically treated": PD, Feb. 1, 1979.
318 "Sour grapes": PD, Aug. 12, 1979.
319 "We understand": PD, March 23, 1979.
319 FTC largely agreed: PD, July 23, 1978.
319 "I guess we're": PD, Sept. 28, 1978.
319 "from hunting regions": PD, Aug. 12, 1979.
319 "The irony was": Interview, not for attribution.
320 "The minute": *Industry Week*, July 12, 1982, 54.
320 "August hit the roof": Interview, not for attribution.
320 Even a dentist: WSJ, March 31, 1987.
321 "biologically incapable": PD, Feb. 28, 1974.
321 "But now the union": FB, Aug. 7, 1978, 37.

Chapter 64: Red Neck in the Morning—Executives Take Warning

Page
323 "We brought in" et seq.: Interview, not for attribution.
324 "They would have": Interview, not for attribution.
324 "He looked over": Interview, not for attribution.
324 "Consistency of message": FM, June 22, 1987.
325 "We were simply": FB, Aug. 7, 1978.
325 "They looked at us": SI, Aug. 8, 1988.
325 "Sports figures": PD, March 21, 1980.
325 "That book was": Interview, not for attribution.
327 "the most unique" et seq.: National Catholic Basketball Tournament
     official program, 1990.
327 "And by God": Interview, not for attribution.
327 "He's made his beer": Interview, not for attribution.
327 "When they decide": LAT, Dec. 15, 1985.
328 The command post: WSJ, March 28, 1985.
328 it was estimated: *Sloan Management Review*, Winter 1975.
328 "We want to be here": LAT, Dec. 15, 1985.
328 "In the 1970s": Interview, not for attribution.
329 "were the bible": Congressional testimony, Monty Roberts, July 18,
     1990.
329 "They're tough": LAT, Dec. 15, 1985.
329 "We've seen others": Ibid.
329 "big gorilla": Interview, John Collopy.
329 "And with that kind": SI, Aug. 8, 1988.

Chapter 65: The Missing Heir

Page
330 Adolphus Harvey Gert von Gontard: PD, Oct. 25, 1931.
330 When Paul died: PD, Dec. 21, 1951.

444 *Notes*

330 In 1954, he had married: PD, March 5, 1954.
331 "I don't want to say": PD, March 9, 1986.
332 "Here's a guy": PD, April 11, 29, Aug. 25, Dec. 29, 1982, March 20, 1983, March 9, July 13, Aug. 8, 1986; GD, April 14, 29, 30, May 22, 1982, April 23, July 2, Oct 20, 1983.
332 "knowingly and willingly": GD, July 2, 1983.

Chapter 66: A Beer for Prince Philip

Page
333 "the Busch family prestige": Susan Marie Busch v. August Busch III, St. Louis County Circuit Court records, Dec. 18, 1969.
333 "quarreled . . . nagged": Ibid.
334 "In this family": PD, Dec. 27, 1987.
334 "You can't forget": Interview, not for attribution.
334 "She was sort of embarrassed": Ibid.
334 "August IV is quite adept": *American Rifleman*, July 1987, 22, 23, 78, 79.
335 "It's very hard": Interview, Jerry Clinton.
335 "That got Adolphus": Interview, not for attribution.
335 "Whenever someone": Interview, not for attribution.
335 "You could hear": Interview, not for attribution.
336 "August wanted beer": Interview, not for attribution.
336 "The Democrats did" et seq.: PD, Nov. 10, 1971.
336 "He's a great kid": *Commerce Magazine*, Feb. 1988.

Chapter 67: "Party Animal"

Page
337 Early on the morning, and details of the accident: *Arizona Daily Star*, Nov. 18, 1984: interview, Ronald Benson, Pima County sheriff's deputy; Petition to Obtain Evidence of Physical Characteristics, the State of Arizona in the Matter of August A. Busch IV, Dec. 29, 1983.
339 "a high-profile case": Interview, Thomas J. Zawada.
339 In December 1974: GD, May 10, 1968; PD, May 29, 1942; SLS, June 22, 1950; GD, Nov. 27, 1979; PD, Oct. 28, 1910.
340 "indicated he": Petition to Obtain Evidence.
340 "deadliest street crime": Petition to Obtain Evidence; *Arizona Daily Star*, Nov. 18, 1984.
341 "He was a popular guy": Interview, not for attribution.
342 "All the mother wanted": Interview, Deputy Benson.
343 "was not driving safely": Petition to Obtain Evidence; *Arizona Daily Star*, Nov. 18, 1984.
343 "a user of cocaine": Ibid.
343 "the crime of manslaughter": search warrants filed Nov. 25, 1983, Pima County Superior Court; *Arizona Daily Star*, Nov. 18, 1984; interview, Deputy Benson.
344 Pressing on: Affidavit in Support of Search Warrant, Dec. 8, 1983, Pima County Superior Court.

344 "Zawada and I": Interview, Deputy Benson.

344 Two weeks after: *Arizona Daily Star*, Nov. 18, 1984.

345 "What have": Interview, not for attribution.

345 "This case was": Interview, Deputy Benson.

345 "We (some of us, that is)": Undated letter from Marjorie M. Deutman to the Pima County Sheriff's Department, Tucson, Arizona, Sheriff's Department files.

346 "has been tentatively": Petition to Obtain Evidence.

346 "who stated that": Ibid.

346 His lawyers, Brogna and London: Memorandum in Support of Response and Objection to Petition to Obtain Evidence of Physical Characteristics, Pima County Superior Court, Jan. 11, 1984.

346 But instead: Minute entry of Judge W. E. Druke, Jan. 16, 1984, Motion to Modify, Records of the Superior Court, Pima County, Arizona; August A. Busch v. The Honorable William E. Druke, Supreme Court of Arizona, Feb. 29, 1984.

347 "I felt there was" et seq.: Interview, Deputy Benson.

348 For the Pima County: Interview, Deputy Prosecutor Zawada; *Tucson Citizen*, July 7, 1984; PD, July 7, 1984.

348 "In Arizona": Interview, Deputy Prosecutor Zawada.

348 "In retrospect" et seq.: Interview, Deputy Benson.

349 "Why are you doing": GD, April 16, 1986.

349 "It's going to be": Interview, police source, not for attribution.

350 "Really? No, you should": Ibid; PD, June 1, 9, 1985.

350 "No news. No news": Interview, Father Paul Reinert.

351 "He was so mad": Interview, not for attribution.

351 "You have seen": PD, April 17, 1986.

351 "a party person": PD, April 17, Oct. 7, 1986.

351 "walk a mile": Ibid.

352 "There were no": Interview, not for attribution.

352 "There are so many": Interview, Susan Busch.

352 "He's always with a blonde": Interview, not for attribution.

Chapter 68: "Tell Anheuser-Busch to Leave Our Kids Alone."

Page

353 "That is so" et seq.: NYT, Dec. 24, 1989.

354 "By the time": PD, Oct. 27, 1985.

354 "They essentially create": Interview, not for attribution.

354 "a powerful": *San Francisco Examiner*, Feb. 19, 1989.

354 "very population" et seq.: Marin Institute and AAA Foundation for Traffic Safety study, "Beer and Fast Cars," April 11, 1990.

354 "Kids aren't doing crack." Interview, Pat Taylor.

355 "gateway drug" et seq.: National Commission report, "Toward a Drug-Free Generation: A Nation's Responsibility," 1990, 66.

355 "to increase their market": Ibid.

355 "juiced" workers: Interview, Robert Lewis.

355   St. Louis police would: Interviews, not for attribution.
356   "They stopped providing": Interview, not for attribution.
356   "I think Ackoff": Interview, not for attribution.
356   "The commercials and marketing": PD, Oct. 10, 1987.
356   "youth that alcohol": PD, June 1, 1989.
357   "The message": Ibid.
357   "The whole purpose": Associated Press, 1989, date unknown.
357   "sexy and youthful": AA, Oct. 23, 1989, 115.
357   "Claims against alcohol companies": NYT, July 26, 1988.
358   "The fact is": Interview, Pat Taylor.
359   "The young adult": PD, Aug. 13, 1978.
359   "Spring break": WP, March 28, 1990.
359   "If the alcohol industry": National Commission report, "Toward a Drug-Free Generation": 1990, 67.
359   "We would rather": Ibid, 66.
359   "They tried at first" et seq.: Interview, not for attribution.
360   "I said, well": Interview, Florence M. "Jerri" Beardslee.
360   "outrageous": *Alcohol and Drug Abuse Pulsebeats*, published by Insurance Field Co., Inc., Louisville, Ky., Jan. 1984. (The complete quotation is: "William K. Coors, chairman of Adolph Coors Co., blasted brewing industry's 'outrageous' lack of ethics in promoting beer among college students but admitted to security analysts that Coors also pushes suds on campus. Colorado-based brewer, he said, pays 250 college students throughout nation to promote the beer at campus wet T-shirt contests, and 'chug-a-lug' and 'get drunk' parties. . . . The promotions, he added, are strictly defensive. 'We do this not because we think it is right, but because other brewers do it. They will steal our lunch—they'll eat our lunch—if we don't do it.' ")
360   "College and high school": WP, Feb. 3, 1989.
361   "never proposed": AA, April 17, 1989.
361   "outraged": PD, Aug. 24, 1989.
361   "counteradvertising" et seq.: National Commission on Drug-Free Schools report, 1990, 71.
362   "I was actually": *Newsweek*, quoting *Rolling Stone* interview, Sept. 26, 1988.
363   Little escaped them: Interview, Ed Moses.
363   "stronger, more vocal": *Beverage World*, Aug. 9, 1989.
364   "a bloody six-pack": *Newsweek*, Aug. 17, 1987.

Chapter 69: The "Archetypal Playboy"

Page
366   "I would imagine": PD, Aug. 6, 1982.
366   "known for his": *St. Louis Benefit Polo Magazine*, 1989, 6.
366   "I don't believe": Testimony, William K. Busch, Angela T. Whitson v. William K. Busch, St. Louis County Circuit Court records, April 1989.
367   "It was late" et seq. on ear-biting incident: Ibid.
367   "something vulgar": Ibid.
367   "I reached in on him": GD, Dec. 21, 1982.

367 "I'll buy my way": Ibid.

367 "One gets the sense": PD, April 4, 1989.

368 "Mixed-up soulmates": Testimony, Carmen Rayburn, Angela T. Whitson v. William K. Busch, St. Louis County Circuit Court records, April 1989.

368 "I had a broken": Testimony, Connie Hanna, Angela T. Whitson v. William K. Busch, St. Louis County Circuit Court records, April 1989.

368 "He repulsed me": *Riverfront Times*, Oct. 5–11, 1988.

368 "He charmed the pants": Ibid.

369 "were quite an item": PD, Oct. 16, 1988.

369 "a pooch and monkey": Testimony, William K. Busch, Angela T. Whitson v. William K. Busch, St. Louis County Circuit Court records, April 1989.

369 "three maybe four": Ibid.

370 "approximately six times": Ibid.

370 "promiscuous behavior" et seq.: Ibid.

370 "He hated that": PD, Oct. 16, 1988.

370 "stuck some straw": Testimony, William K. Busch, Angela T. Whitson v. William K. Busch, St. Louis County Circuit Court records, April 1989.

370 "I knew she had": Ibid.

371 "Our daughter Scarlett" et seq.: Court papers filed in custody case, Angela T. Whitson v. William K. Busch, May 26, 1988.

371 "do anything that": Testimony, William K. Busch, Angela T. Whitson v. William K. Busch, St. Louis County Circuit Court records, April 1989.

372 "I'm the type": Ibid.

372 "sociopathic personality" and "drank too much": Master's report, Angela T. Whitson v. William K. Busch, Supreme Court of Missouri, May 5, 1989.

372 "I was bouncing": PD, Oct. 16, 1988.

372 "lunatic psycho": Testimony, William K. Busch, Angela T. Whitson v. William K. Busch, St. Louis County Circuit Court records, April 1989.

372 "Gino told me": Ibid.

373 "Busch wasn't even required": PD, March 26, 1990.

373 "Who else": *Riverfront Times*, Oct. 5–11, 1988.

373 "Being a Busch": PD, Sept. 20, 1989.

373 "except for Billy's": Custody hearing, Arguments, Michael McAvoy, Angela T. Whitson v. William K. Busch, St. Louis County Circuit Court records, April 1989.

374 "This will be": Ibid.

374 "Go ahead, fire away" et seq.: Deposition, William K. Busch, Nov. 3, 1988.

374 "Pregnant six times": Master's report, Angela T. Whitson v. William K. Busch, Supreme Court of Missouri, May 5, 1989.

374 "absolutely unfit": Ibid.

374 "In my heart": PD, May 12, 1989.

375 "I cannot say very much": Ruling, Supreme Court of Missouri, Angela T. Whitson v. William K. Busch, Sept. 8, 1989.

375 "If anyone drinks": PD, Aug. 30, 1989.

Chapter 70: Horses and Horses' Asses

Page
376   "That hip joint": GD, July 10, 1979.
376   "That crazy": Ibid.
376   "Goddammit, get over": Interview, Al Fleishman.
377   "a brother-sister": Interview, not for attribution.
377   "But it was a bust": Ibid.
377   "the sheriff": Interview, Al Fleishman.
377   "Oh my God" et seq.: Ibid.
378   "She was very hurt": Interview, not for attribution.
378   "what can you expect?": Interview, not for attribution.
378   "Gussie and I" et seq.: Interview, Peter Palmer; PD, Sept. 14, 1983,
       April 4, 1985, June 29, Oct. 1, 1989.
378   When Francis Barnes: Interview, Francis M. Barnes.
379   When the market crashed: PD, Sept. 5, 1987; LAT, Oct. 20, 1987, Oct.
       11, 1988; Anheuser-Busch Co. Inc. Notice and Proxy Statement April
       27, 1988; FM, Sept. 12, 1988.
379   "He even went": Interview, not for attribution.

Chapter 71: "Get a Bad Apple at the Top and You've Got Super Trouble."

Page
380   "This is a soft": LAT, April 26, 1987.
381   "inconsistent with corporate policy": WSJ, March 30, 1987.
381   "inquisition atmosphere": WSJ, March 31, 1987.
381   "our Vietnam": WSJ, March 25, 1987.
381   "If you get a bad apple": PD, April 18, 1967.
381   "It was part": WSJ, March 31, 1987.
381   "witnessed incredible greed": Joseph E. Martino, letter to authors.
382   "Polo—you can get" et seq.: PD, Oct. 23, 1988.
382   "Augie does not forgive": WSJ, March 26, 1987.
382   "You get into": LAT, April 26, 1987.
383   "contacts with the PGA": Ibid.
383   "They are buying": Interview, Florence Beardslee.
384   "at bargain prices" et seq.: Interview, Joseph L. Alioto.
384   "Just about every": Interview, not for attribution.
384   "questionable payments": GD, July 19, 1978.
384   "renting, lending" et seq.: Offer in Compromise, of liability incurred
       under Federal Alcohol Administration Act, Dept. of Treasury, June 1,
       1984.
384   "engaged in what": PD, June 1, 1984.
384   "strict compliance": Ibid.
385   "immaterial": Ibid.
385   "It would have given": NYT, Oct. 12, 1980.
386   "Disgusting and disgraceful": PD, Nov. 21, 1979.
386   "A seemingly": Ibid.
386   "As long as" et seq.: PD, Dec. 2, 1979.

386 "When a smart company": *Beverage World*, Sept. 1988.
387 "They think by this": PD, May 7, 1987.
387 "One taste" et seq.: PD, May 26, 1989.
387 "Can you believe": Associated Press, Nov. 19, 1989.
388 "Before I'd give": Interview, not for attribution.

Chapter 72: More Hardball

Page
389 "a private joke": Interview, Robert Weinberg.
389 "The old man": Interview, William F. Smith.
389 "Let's face it": PD, March 14, 1978.
390 "There were the endless": *Sporting News*, Aug. 15, 1983.
390 "The ascendancy": Interview, Fred Saigh.
390 "skillful public relations" et seq.: PD, Aug. 6, 1981.
391 "one of the most": Interview, not for attribution.
392 "I knew they had": Interview, Richard K. Yackey.
393 Pedro Guerrero: PD, Aug. 9, 1989.

Chapter 73: "He Can Hurt You Badly."

Page
393 "You know, it took": Interview, Father Paul Reinert.
394 Another episode: BW, Sept. 25, 1989.
394 "They have a way": Interview, David Callahan.
394 "It would be a horrible": Interview, Ed Vogel.
395 "You never want": *Business Month*, June 1988.
395 "Our firm represents": Interview, Thomas Eagleton.
396 "August is very envious": Interview, EHV.
396 "We look at 50": NYT, Aug. 4, 1985.
396 "one of the most": *St. Louis Business Journal*, Oct. 22–28, 1990.
397 "friends on the tax": *Common Cause*, May-June, 1988.
397 "Working America": Associated Press, March 12, 1990.
398 "We get a feel": NYT, Dec. 24, 1989.
398 "dolphin abusement parks": PD, Oct. 8, 1990.
399 "footprint in Europe": BW, Sept. 25, 1989.
399 "We think this": Anheuser-Busch newsletter, June 1989.
399 "The secret": PD, June 10, 1989.
399 "Budweiser's Sales Slipping" et seq.: AA, Nov. 13, 1989.
400 "The sheer size": Ibid.
400 22,000 cases: PD, March 17, 1991.
400 "Some companies have consistently": PD, March 21, 1990.

Chapter 74: The Last Beer Baron

Page
401 "I don't ever remember": Interview, Al Fleishman.
401 "All right, but" et seq.: Interview, EHV.

402 The day before: Interview, not for attribution.
402 At the time: PD, Oct. 3, Nov. 23, 1989, Aug. 30, 1990; FM, Sept. 11, 1989.
403 In addition to stock: Will, AAB, St. Louis County Probate Court files, July 10, 1987.
403 "Gussie left most": *St. Louis Sun*, Oct. 9, 1989.
404 "There was a lot": Interview, not for attribution.
404 "Dad would just never": Interview, not for attribution.

Chapter 75: "He Might Wind Up Running the Company —If He Can Stay Out of Trouble."

Page
405 "It's an extremely": PD, June 8, 1989.
405 "If they could run": Interview, Adie von Gontard, Jr.
406 "He's a very bright": Interview, not for attribution.

Chapter 76: Bottoms Up

Page
408 "look upon beer": Adolphus Busch, letter, 1905.
409 "beer god": PD, Feb. 24, 1991.
409 "He said that his job" et seq.: Interview, Andrew Brandt.

Acknowledgments

The process of researching, organizing and writing this book took the authors two years, but work began much earlier. As reporters for the *St. Louis Post-Dispatch*, we often encountered stories about Anheuser-Busch and the family who founded it. The sources that were developed over the years for these stories helped provide much of the information for *Under the Influence*.

Anheuser-Busch assisted in producing sources, too. After this book project was launched, the company distributed written memoranda to its employees and distributors recommending they not cooperate with the authors. In some cases, this had the opposite effect. Some people, angered at attempts to be silenced, contacted us with information.

Research for this book took the authors from a seedy bar in St. Petersburg, Florida, to the paneled study of a Catholic university president, from the cab of a beer truck making daily deliveries in northern California to the dusty archives of a tiny village in Germany. Along the way, we met hundreds of people, from brewers to distributors to district managers to vice presidents, who contributed their recollections of life with Anheuser-Busch and members of the Busch family. Some did not want their names used out of fear of repercussions. Others provided information openly.

There is not enough space to thank all of those who helped us. However, special gratitude is owed to the late Ernest Kirschten, Robert L. Lewis, Ronald J. Plavchan, author Martin J. Quigley and Edward H. Vogel. Friends in Germany provided valuable assistance. They included Johannes Westerkamp of

Ginsheim, Carola Wagner Wallenstein of Kastel and Walburga Scherbaum, Walter Eberl, Erwin Ruckriegel and Dr. Peter Mathes of Bernried. Back home, Sandy Schroeder and Meinrad Fishbacher helped with translations.

The authors relied on Kurk Dorsey for researching the papers of Charles Nagel at the Yale University Library. We also are grateful to the archivists, librarians and researchers of the manuscripts division of the Library of Congress, the Missouri Historical Society, the National Archives, the Mercantile Library, the University of Missouri Western Historical Manuscript Collection, the Missouri State Archives, the Harry Truman Presidential Library, the Franklin Roosevelt Presidential Library, the Eisenhower Presidential Library, the John F. Kennedy Library, the Nixon Presidential Materials of the National Archives and the St. Louis Public Library.

To the editors of the *St. Louis Post-Dispatch*, especially William Woo, David Lipman, Richard Weil and Laszlo Domjan, we owe our gratitude for giving us the time and opportunity to complete this project. We likewise owe our thanks to the ever-patient reference department at the newspaper and especially to John Pelly for rounding up so many of the photographs.

We are also grateful to the editors at Simon and Schuster, especially Fred Hills and Burton Beals, who sharpened the original manuscript, and Daphne Bien, who somehow kept it all moving forward. We also wish to thank lawyers Paul Gillow in New York City and Robert Hoemeke in St. Louis.

Finally, there are our spouses and our families—Janice Hernon and daughters Margaret and Clair, and Judy Ganey and David, Tim and Colleen—who put up and persevered with us until this project was completed.

Index

About the authors

PETER HERNON is an award-winning journalist and author of two critically praised books, *A Terrible Thunder* and *Earthly Remains*. A special-projects reporter for the *St. Louis Post-Dispatch*, he lives with his wife and two daughters in St. Louis, Missouri.

TERRY GANEY, the best-selling author of *Innocent Blood*, is also a prize-winning journalist. As state capital bureau chief of the *St. Louis Post-Dispatch*, he has received several journalistic honors, including United Press International's 1985 investigative reporting award. He lives in Jefferson City, Missouri, with his wife and three children.